THE CAMBRIDGE COMPANION TO 1
TWENTIETH-CENTURY ENGLISH NOVEL

The twentieth-century English novel encompasses a vast body of work, and one of the most important and most widely read genres of literature. Balancing close readings of particular novels with a comprehensive survey of the last century of published fiction, this Companion introduces readers to more than a hundred major and minor novelists. It demonstrates continuities in novel-writing that bridge the century's pre- and postwar halves and presents leading critical ideas about English fiction's themes and forms. The essays examine the endurance of modernist style throughout the century, the role of nationality and the contested role of the English language in all its forms, and the relationships between realism and other fictional modes: fantasy, romance, science fiction. Students, scholars and readers will find this Companion an indispensable guide to the history of the English novel.

THE CAMBRIDGE COMPANION TO THE
TWENTIETH-CENTURY ENGLISH NOVEL

EDITED BY
ROBERT L. CASERIO

The Pennsylvania State University, University Park

CAMBRIDGE
UNIVERSITY PRESS

CAMBRIDGE UNIVERSITY PRESS

Cambridge, New York, Melbourne, Madrid, Cape Town, Singapore, São Paulo, Delhi

Cambridge University Press
The Edinburgh Building, Cambridge CB2 8RU, UK

Published in the United States of America by Cambridge University Press, New York

www.cambridge.org
Information on this title: www.cambridge.org/9780521711159

First published 2009

Printed in the United Kingdom at the University Press, Cambridge

A catalogue record for this publication is available from the British Library

Library of Congress Cataloguing in Publication data
The Cambridge companion to the twentieth-century English
novel / edited by Robert L. Caserio.
p.   cm.
Includes bibliographical references and index.
ISBN 978-0-521-88416-7
1. English fiction–20th century–History and criticism.
I. Caserio, Robert L., 1944– II. Title.
PR883.C36 2009
823'.9109–dc22
2008053635

ISBN 978-0-521-88416-7 hardback
ISBN 978-0-521-71115-9 paperback

CONTENTS

CONTENTS

CONTRIBUTORS

JAMES ACHESON is former Senior Lecturer in English at the University of Canterbury in Christchurch, New Zealand. He is the author of *Samuel Beckett's Artistic Theory and Practice* (1997) and *John Fowles* (1998), and has edited volumes on Beckett, and on British and Irish fiction, poetry, and drama. He is working on a book on contemporary British historical fiction.

KRISTIN BLUEMEL is Professor of English at Monmouth University, New Jersey. She is the author of *George Orwell and the Radical Eccentrics: Intermodernism in Literary London* (2004), and *Experimenting on the Borders of Modernism: Dorothy Richardson's Pilgrimage* (1997), and is editing a collection of critical essays, "Intermodernism: Literary Culture in Interwar and Wartime Britain" (forthcoming).

M. KEITH BOOKER is the James E. and Ellen Wadley Roper Professor of English at the University of Arkansas. He has written or edited more than thirty books on literature, literary theory, and popular culture.

ROBERT L. CASERIO, Professor of English at the Pennsylvania State University, University Park, is the author of *Plot, Story, and the Novel* (1979) and *The Novel in England 1900–1950: History and Theory* (1999). He is co-editing, with Clement C. Hawes, *The Cambridge History of the English Novel* (forthcoming).

REED WAY DASENBROCK is the Secretary of Higher Education for the State of New Mexico. He has taught at New Mexico State University, and has been a Dean of Arts and Sciences and a Provost at the University of New Mexico. He is the author or editor of eight books, and of numerous articles on twentieth-century English literature, literary theory, and postcolonial literature.

MARIA DI BATTISTA, Professor of English and Comparative Literature at Princeton University, has published widely on modern narrative and film. Her works include *First Love: The Affections of Modern Fiction* (1991) and

Fast-Talking Dames (2001). Her latest book is *Virginia Woolf: An Experiment in Critical Biography* (forthcoming).

PAUL EDWARDS is Professor of English and History of Art at Bath Spa University. He is the author of *Wyndham Lewis: Painter and Writer* (2000), and has edited several of Lewis's books. He has also published essays on Tom Stoppard and science, Ian McEwan's fictions, and literary memoirs of the First World War.

JED ESTY is Associate Professor of English at the University of Pennsylvania. He is the author of *A Shrinking Island: Modernism and National Culture in England* (2004), and co-editor, with Ania Loomba, Suvir Kaul, Antoinette Burton, and Matti Bunzl, of *Postcolonial Studies and Beyond* (2005). He is completing a book in progress, *Unseasonable Youth: The Bildungsroman and Colonial Modernity*.

ANNE FOGARTY is Professor of James Joyce Studies at University College Dublin and President of the International James Joyce Foundation. She directs the UCD James Joyce Research Center, edits *Irish University Review*, and co-edits, with Luca Crispi, the newly founded *Dublin James Joyce Journal*. She is co-editor with Timothy Martin of *Joyce on the Threshold* (2005). She has published widely on aspects of contemporary Irish fiction.

JOHN FORDHAM is the author of *James Hanley: Modernism and the Working Class* (2002).

ANDRZEJ GASIOREK is Reader in Twentieth-Century Literature at the University of Birmingham. He is the author of *Post-War British Fiction: Realism and After* (1995), *Wyndham Lewis and Modernism* (2004), and *J.G. Ballard* (2005). He has co-edited *T.E. Hulme and the Question of Modernism* (2006), and is a co-editor of the electronic journal *Modernist Cultures*.

DOROTHY J. HALE is Professor of English at the University of California, Berkeley. Her books include *Social Formalism: The Novel in Theory from Henry James to the Present* (1998) and *The Novel: An Anthology of Criticism and Theory, 1900–2000* (2006).

MATTHEW HART, Assistant Professor of English at the University of Illinois-Urbana, is writing a book-in-progress, *Nations of Nothing but Poetry: Modernism, Vernacular Discourse and the State*. He has co-edited, with Jim Hansen, a special issue (2008) of *Contemporary Literature* on the state and contemporary literature.

ALLAN HEPBURN is an Associate Professor of English Literature at McGill University. In addition to many articles on twentieth-century literature, he has published *Intrigue: Espionage and Culture* (2005) and edited *Troubled Legacies: Narrative and Inheritance* (2007). His critical editions of Elizabeth Bowen's uncollected stories and essays will appear under the titles *The Bazaar and Other Stories* and *People, Places, Things: Essays by Elizabeth Bowen* (2008).

MARINA MACKAY is Associate Professor of English at Washington University in St. Louis. She is the author of *Modernism and World War II* (2007), co-editor with Lyndsey Stonebridge of *British Fiction After Modernism* (2007), and editor of *The Cambridge Companion to the Literature of World War II* (2008).

ROD MENGHAM is Reader in Modern English Literature at the University of Cambridge, where he is also Curator of Works of Art at Jesus College. His books include studies of Charles Dickens, Emily Brontë, and Henry Green, and *The Descent of Language* (1993). His most recent book, co-authored with Sophie Gilmartin, is *Thomas Hardy's Shorter Fiction* (2007). He has edited collections of essays on contemporary fiction; violence and avant-garde art; and the fiction of the 1940s. His poems are collected in *Unsung: New and Selected Poems* (2001).

REBECCA L. WALKOWITZ is Associate Professor of English at Rutgers University. She is the author of *Cosmopolitan Style: Modernism Beyond the Nation* (2006) and editor or co-editor of seven books, including *Immigrant Fictions: Contemporary Literature in an Age of Globalization* (2007) and *Bad Modernisms* (with Douglas Mao, 2006). Her essays have appeared in several anthologies and in *PMLA*, *Modern Language Quarterly*, *ELH*, and *Modern Drama*. She is co-editor of *Contemporary Literature*.

TIMOTHY WEISS is Professor of English at the Chinese University of Hong Kong, where he teaches postcolonial, Caribbean, and African literature. He is the author of *Translating Orients: Between Ideology and Utopia* (2004) and *On the Margins: The Art and Exile of V.S. Naipaul* (1992).

CHRONOLOGY

1900	Joseph Conrad, *Lord Jim*
1901	Rudyard Kipling, *Kim*
	Death of Queen Victoria
	Edward VII becomes King
1902	Arthur Conan Doyle, *The Hound of the Baskervilles*
	J. A. Hobson, *Imperialism*
	Boer War ends
1903	Emmeline Pankhurst founds Women's Social and Political Union
1905	H. G. Wells, *A Modern Utopia*
	Henry James begins Prefaces to New York Edition of his works
1906	John Galsworthy, *The Man of Property* (first volume of *The Forsyte Chronicles*)
1907	Joseph Conrad, *The Secret Agent*
	Rudyard Kipling wins Nobel Prize for Literature
	New Zealand becomes a Dominion of the British Empire
1908	Arnold Bennett, *The Old Wives' Tale*
	G. K. Chesterton, *The Man Who Was Thursday*
1909	H. G. Wells, *Tono-Bungay*
	William Beveridge, *Unemployment: A Problem for Industry*
1910	E. M. Forster, *Howards End*
	Post-Impressionist Exhibition in London
	Death of King Edward VII
	George V becomes King
1911	H. G. Wells, *The New Machiavelli*
	National Insurance Act
1912	Conrad, *Chance*
	London dock strike
1913	D. H. Lawrence, *Sons and Lovers*
	Rabindranath Tagore wins Nobel Prize for Literature
	Trade Union Act

1914	Robert Tressell, *The Ragged Trousered Philanthropists*
	Curragh garrison mutiny in Ireland
	Britain declares war on Germany
1915	Ford Madox Ford, *The Good Soldier*
	Dorothy Richardson, *Pointed Roofs* (first volume of *Pilgrimage*)
1916	James Joyce, *A Portrait of the Artist as a Young Man*
1917	Leonard and Virginia Woolf found the Hogarth Press
	Bolshevik Revolution in Russia
1918	Wyndham Lewis, *Tarr*
	Rebecca West, *The Return of the Soldier*
	Armistice signed, November 11
	Representation of the People Act gives universal male suffrage and suffrage to women over thirty
1919	James Tait Black Memorial Prize initiated
	Treaty of Versailles
	Nancy Astor, first female MP, takes seat in Parliament
	Massacre of Indians at Amritsar by British troops
1920	D. H. Lawrence, *Women in Love*
	British mandate over Palestine
	Government of Ireland Act and the creation of Northern Ireland
1921	Irish Free State created by Parliament
1922	James Joyce, *Ulysses*
1924	Ronald Firbank, *The Flower Beneath the Foot*
	Ford Madox Ford, *Joseph Conrad: A Personal Record*
	E. M. Forster, *A Passage to India*
	Death of Joseph Conrad
	Ramsay Macdonald becomes Prime Minister in first Labour government
1925	Virginia Woolf, *Mrs. Dalloway*
1926	Agatha Christie, *The Murder of Roger Ackroyd*
	Sylvia Townsend Warner, *Lolly Willowes*
	BBC chartered
	General Strike, May 3–12
1928	Aldous Huxley, *Point Counter Point*
	D. H. Lawrence, *Lady Chatterley's Lover*
	Virginia Woolf, *Orlando*
	Representation of the People Act gives suffrage to women aged twenty-one
1929	Elizabeth Bowen, *The Last September*
	Virginia Woolf, *A Room of One's Own*
	New York stock market collapse

1930   Death of D. H. Lawrence
       The Great Depression reaches Britain
1931   Ivy Compton-Burnett, *Men and Wives*
1932   Aldous Huxley, *Brave New World*
       John Galsworthy wins Nobel Prize for Literature
1933   John Cowper Powys, *A Glastonbury Romance*
1934   Lewis Grassic Gibbon, *Grey Granite* (final volume of *A Scots Quair*)
       Evelyn Waugh, *A Handful of Dust*
1935   Christopher Isherwood, *Mr. Norris Changes Trains*
       Dorothy Sayers, *Gaudy Night*
       Allen Lane establishes Penguin Books
1936   Mulk Raj Anand, *Coolie*
       James Barke, *Major Operation*
       Winifred Holtby, *South Riding*
       Aldous Huxley, *Eyeless in Gaza*
       C. L. R. James, *Minty Alley*
       Death of Rudyard Kipling
       Left Book Club founded
       Death of George V
       Edward VIII becomes King; Edward VIII abdicates
       George VI becomes King
       Start of Spanish Civil War; Britain signs Nonintervention Agreement and pledges neutrality in Spain
1937   Wyndham Lewis, *The Revenge for Love*
       George Orwell, *The Road to Wigan Pier*
       Olaf Stapledon, *Star Maker*
       Virginia Woolf, *The Years*
1938   Graham Greene, *Brighton Rock*
1939   Joyce Cary, *Mister Johnson*
       Henry Green, *Party Going*
       James Joyce, *Finnegans Wake*
       Flann O'Brien, *At Swim-Two-Birds*
       T. H. White, *The Sword in the Stone*
       Britain declares war on Germany
1940   Graham Greene, *The Power and the Glory*
       W. Somerset Maugham, *The Razor's Edge*
       C. P. Snow, *Strangers and Brothers* (first volume in the *Strangers and Brothers* series)
       Evacuation of Dunkirk
       Battle of Britain begins; London Blitz

1941	Death of James Joyce
	Virginia Woolf commits suicide
1942	John Llewellyn Rhys Prize initiated
	Social Insurance and Allied Services ("The Beveridge Report")
1944	Joyce Cary, *The Horse's Mouth*
1945	R. K. Narayan, *The English Teacher*
	George Orwell, *Animal Farm*
	J. B. Priestley, *Three Men in New Suits*
	Germany surrenders
	Japan surrenders after U.S. atomic bombing of Hiroshima and Nagasaki
	Landslide victory for Labour
1946	Mervyn Peake, *Titus Groan* (first volume of "Gormenghast" trilogy)
	Death of H. G. Wells
	National Health Service Act
	Nationalization of Bank of England, civil aviation, and coal
	BBC Third Programme begins broadcasts
	Burma independence
1947	Somerset Maugham Award initiated
	Nationalization of railways
	Indian independence; India partitioned into India and Pakistan
	Partition of Palestine
1949	Elizabeth Bowen, *The Heat of the Day*
	George Orwell, *Nineteen Eighty-Four*
	Arrival of the *Empire Windrush*
	Britain joins NATO
1951	Samuel Beckett, *Molloy*
	G. V. Desani, *All About H. Hatterr*
	Anthony Powell, *A Question of Upbringing* (first volume of *A Dance to the Music of Time*)
	Henry Williamson, *The Dark Lantern* (first volume of *A Chronicle of Ancient Sunlight*)
1952	Doris Lessing, *Martha Quest* (first volume of *Children of Violence*)
	Barbara Pym, *Excellent Women*
	Angus Wilson, *Hemlock and After*
	Death of George VI
	Elizabeth II becomes Queen
	Britain announces atomic bomb
1953	Ian Fleming, *Casino Royale*

1954	Kingsley Amis, *Lucky Jim*
	William Golding, *Lord of the Flies*
	George Lamming, *The Emigrants*
	J. R. R. Tolkien, *The Fellowship of the Ring* (first volume of *The Lord of the Rings*)
1956	Anthony Burgess, *Time for a Tiger* (first volume of *A Malayan Trilogy*)
	Samuel Selvon, *The Lonely Londoners*
	Angus Wilson, *Anglo-Saxon Attitudes*
	Suez crisis
1957	Lawrence Durrell, *Justine* (first volume of *The Alexandria Quartet*)
1958	V. S. Naipaul, *The Suffrage of Elvira*
	Alan Sillitoe, *Saturday Night and Sunday Morning*
	Campaign for Nuclear Disarmament begins
1960	Wilson Harris, *The Palace of the Peacock* (first volume of *The Guyana Quartet*)
	George Lamming, *The Pleasures of Exile*
	Olivia Manning, *The Great Fortune* (first volume of *The Balkan Trilogy*)
	Edna O'Brien, *The Country Girls*
	Penguin Books acquitted in *Lady Chatterley's Lover* obscenity trial
	Cyprus gains independence
	Nigeria gains independence
1961	Iris Murdoch, *A Severed Head*
	Muriel Spark, *The Prime of Miss Jean Brodie*
	Expulsion of South Africa from Commonwealth
1962	Doris Lessing, *The Golden Notebook*
1963	John Le Carré, *The Spy Who Came in from the Cold*
	Muriel Spark, *The Girls of Slender Means*
1964	B. S. Johnson, *Albert Angelo*
1965	Race Relations Act addresses racial discrimination
1966	Paul Scott, *The Jewel in the Crown* (first volume of *The Raj Quartet*)
1967	Winifred Holtby Award for regional fiction initiated (renamed Ondaatje Prize, 2004)
	Abortion legalized
	Homosexual acts between consenting adults decriminalized
1969	Brigid Brophy, *In Transit*
	John Fowles, *The French Lieutenant's Woman*
	Samuel Beckett wins Nobel Prize for Literature
	Booker Prize initiated (renamed Man Booker Prize, 2002)

1970	J. G. Ballard, *The Atrocity Exhibition*
1971	Iris Murdoch, *The Black Prince*
	Whitbread Book Award initiated (renamed Costa Book Award, 2006)
1972	John Berger, *G*
	John Brunner, *The Sheep Look Up*
1973	Britain joins European Economic Community
1975	Christine Brooke-Rose, *Thru*
	David Lodge, *Changing Places*
1977	Margaret Drabble, *The Ice Age*
1978	Scottish and Welsh Devolution Acts
1979	John Berger, *Pig Earth* (first volume of *Into Their Labours* trilogy)
	Nicholas Mosley, *Catastrophe Practice* (first volume of *Catastrophe Practice* series)
	Conservative victory; Margaret Thatcher becomes Prime Minister
1980	P. D. James, *Innocent Blood*
1981	Alasdair Gray, *Lanark*
1982	Falklands War
1983	William Golding wins Nobel Prize for Literature
1984	Kingsley Amis, *Money*
	Julian Barnes, *Flaubert's Parrot*
	Angela Carter, *Nights at the Circus*
1987	V. S. Naipaul, *The Enigma of Arrival*
	Commonwealth Writers' Prize initiated
1988	Neil Gaiman begins *Sandman* graphic novel series
	Alan Hollinghurst, *The Swimming Pool Library*
	Michael Moorcock, *Mother London*
	Salman Rushdie, *The Satanic Verses*
1989	Kazuo Ishiguro, *The Remains of the Day*
	Islamic decree calls for Salman Rushdie's death for insult to Islam in *The Satanic Verses*
1990	A. S. Byatt, *Possession*
	Hanif Kureishi, *The Buddha of Suburbia*
1991	Angela Carter, *Wise Children*
	Iain Sinclair, *Downriver*
	Pat Barker, *Regeneration* (first volume of *Regeneration* trilogy)
	The Gulf War
	Collapse of the Soviet Union
1992	Ian McEwan, *Black Dogs*

1993   Salman Rushdie's *Midnight's Children* awarded Booker of Bookers Prize (best Booker novel of the prize's first twenty-five years)

Anglo-Irish Peace Declaration in Northern Ireland

1994   James Kelman, *How Late it Was, How Late*

Apartheid ends in South Africa

IRA declares truce in Northern Ireland

1995   Salman Rushdie, *The Moor's Last Sigh*

1996   Orange Prize (for women writers) initiated

1997   Tony Blair's New Labour government elected

1998   China Miéville, *King Rat*

Re-establishment of the Scottish Parliament; creation of the National Assembly for Wales

1999   Use of euro begins; Britain declines participation

2001   V. S. Naipaul wins Nobel Prize for Literature

2007   Doris Lessing wins Nobel Prize for Literature

ROBERT L. CASERIO

Introduction

The following chapters attempt a comprehensive overview of the twentieth-century English novel. Their attempt is unusual, because literary history customarily divides the last century into distinct halves. The first half of the customary division, ending with World War II, focuses on modernist authors and works and their contexts, and thereby consolidates modernism's great achievements in fiction. The second half hypothesizes a postmodern age, and treats fiction in light of hypotheses about what postmodernism is (one of the hypotheses is that postmodernism abandons thinking in terms of great artistic achievements). Sound, subtle and fruitful reasoning, by numerous distinguished commentators, justifies such an apportionment of literary history. But the separation also tends to compartmentalize knowledge, and to insure itself against challenge.

Although compartmentalizing need not refute continuities, it does not always stimulate awareness of them. This volume, bridging pre-1945 and post-1945 fiction, searches out more continuities between modernism and postmodernism than meet the eye. It explores dynamic similarities as well as contrasts among novels that span generational, cultural, and contextual differences. It is common for literary historians to consider post-*Windrush* novelists, who left behind their colonial origins in exchange for life in London, as doubly figures of exile: dislocated from their first home, yet unable to be at ease in their second home, hence perpetually diasporic. What is not common is for literary historians to consider ways in which such an exilic condition is prefigured in the modernist moment, and is attached to it – in terms of repetition and variation – via Henry James, Conrad, Joyce, and Lawrence's self-imposed exiles, or in terms of feminist or "minority" writers who feel internally if not externally exiled from gender roles or social orders that regulate their experience. Differences between modernist and post-*Windrush* phenomenologies of exile certainly are not to be underestimated, above all in regard to race and class differences; but contrasts are not the only story to be told about them. Whatever differentiates dislocations of persons and perspectives across the century, at the very least a common experience of political and economic imperialism, and a continuity of responses to it, binds widely varying novelists together. Equally binding across the century, and not to be underestimated, is novelists' common experience of the aesthetic form they undertake to practice.

To say that diverse novelists share common ground because they have experienced historical and national dislocation strikes a note of paradox or self-contradiction that is the order of things in the previous century. Two compelling paradoxes or self-contradictions loom over the arguments in this book. One is the paradox denominated by the term "English." The national territory signified by the term has become restricted, so as not to denominate and dominate "Scottish," "Irish," or "Welsh," even though the natural language signified by "English" is spoken and written in Scotland, Ireland, and Wales, and is spoken and written globally, thanks to the British Empire's Anglophone legacy. Does the "English" novel's increasingly indeterminate cultural and linguistic identity outrun literary history's comprehensive intentions?

The second problem is the novel's relation to two kinds of history: its own history as a continuous experiment in formal design; and history "proper," the experience and the discourse that historians probe and record, but that novelists do not invent. Essential to the second problem is English modernist fiction's version of what Pierre Bourdieu calls literary art's "conquest of autonomy": i.e., "elaboration of an intrinsically aesthetic mode of perception which situates the principle of 'creation' within the representation and not within the thing represented."[1] What happens to that conquest in the course of a century after modernism (or after a century of modernism), in which reference "to the thing represented" continues to appear in the novel, but then involves itself – paradoxically! – with a firmly established "intrinsically aesthetic mode"?

That there is no way we can now delimit "English" or "English" fiction seems a reasonable conclusion, attested by the tradition these pages survey. We are foredoomed to aim at comprehensiveness, without arriving there. Consider the status in the English novel's history of R. K. Narayan's work. Is the work of an Indian writer living in India yet writing in English and publishing in England to be counted in or out? The wayward identity of English makes a decision impossible, as Narayan clearly knew. Narayan's eponymous Indian narrator in *The English Teacher* (1945) is a poet who teaches English unhappily ("we were strangers to our own culture and camp followers of another . . ., feeding on leavings and garbage"),[2] but he and his wife thrive on English poetry, read it to each other, and attempt to write it. There is a startling address to "English" in a scene where the narrator tricks his wife into thinking he has just improvised his own poem, when in fact he has recited Wordsworth. His wife, discovering the original, wonders if he is not ashamed to copy. He defends himself: "Mine is entirely different. [Wordsworth] had written about someone entirely different from my subject [the Indian narrator's Indian wife]" (p. 464). In this Borgesian moment, a copy of Wordsworth is not Wordsworth; and English is and is not English. "Copying" becomes in *The English Teacher* a thematics of split linguistic and cultural identity, a sign of a fissure and a doubling that, as I will presently note, also puts into question the discrete identities of reality and fantasy, which we might understand as separable modal languages that English novels also speak.

Narayan's challenge to linguistic identity does not mark any turning point; it is an episode in the twentieth century's long perplexing of all things "English." An encounter between another Indian English novelist, Mulk Raj Anand, and Virginia Woolf provides an example from the modernist era. In the 1920s Anand found himself "allied with... inbetween [*sic*] things beyond big words," and found a like spirit in Woolf's "sense of wonder about life, which made her restless and unsure," appealingly in contrast to the men around her. Anand thus finds that Woolf is, like himself, "inbetween" things, especially when she questions him about androgyny in the Hindu pantheon, in pursuit of her "'feeling that we are male-female-male, perhaps more female than male. I am writing a novel, *Orlando*, to suggest this.'"[3] Confirming Woolf's feeling by reference to Shiva and to yoga, Anand suggests that *Orlando* might be an Indian novel that happens to be in English. Meanwhile, so to speak, at the other end of the century, John Berger's trilogy about the disappearance of peasant life, *Into Their Labours* (1979–90) – not incidentally, the work of an expatriate writer – presents French Alpine figures. Inasmuch as Berger's peasantry is a vanishing class, their utterances increasingly belong to a lost language, a "backward" tongue. Berger gives them voice; yet the tongue that must communicate their backwardness and loss is the global cosmopolitan English of Berger's text.

From the start of the twentieth century, then, with the arrival in England of James's American English and Conrad's Polish-French-English, the English novel has spoken a language that is both one and the same, and yet beside itself. The chapters here by Jed Esty, Matthew Hart, Anne Fogarty, John Fordham, Timothy Weiss, Allan Hepburn, and Rebecca Walkowitz have much to say about how local and regional and national languages – of actual persons, of novels, of fictional modes – are ultimately not self-contained, become inextricable from dialogues with translocal, trans-class, transnational contexts. Their chapters suggest a new global tale in process, one that we are tracking in order to shape a new narrative of history, and a new literary historical narrative.

Modernism continues to play a role in such tracking. The new tale might come to look more like *Finnegans Wake*'s entangled events and words than stories we are used to. Does not any representative sentence from Joyce suggest the present condition of "English," of nation, of history, of the history of the English novel? "I'm enormously full of that foreigner, I'll say I am!," says the *Wake*:

> Got by the one goat, suckled by the same nanna, one twitch, one nature makes us oldworld kin. We're as thick and thin now as two tubular jawballs. I hate him about his patent henesy, plasfh it, yet am I amorist. I love him.[4]

That is the language of regional-global experience and interdependence, perhaps of class experience and interdependence too – a language at once secret and open, resistant and amative – to which our novels and histories might yet conform.

Joyce's last book is likely to mean more to the future of novels than *Ulysses* has meant to what now is their past century, especially if the language of *Finnegans Wake* strikes one as a template for a present realism about global life. To make such a claim means submitting Joyce's imaginative fantasy, inasmuch as it transcends documentary occasions, to what is judged to be historically objective and real. Doing so follows a "standard disciplinary pathway," as Richard Todd aptly puts it, whereby English fiction – and contemporary study of it – "can be largely explained by the . . . political tensions that literary criticism uncovers and elaborates with respect to individual works, tensions attendant on the rise of identity politics . . . or on the emergence of poscolonialism."[5]

Whenever such a pathway is exemplified with the probing flexibility of Kristin Bluemel's chapter here on feminist fiction, the standard is eminently self-justifying. Like all standards, however, the disciplinary norm runs risks. It can obscure the novel's role in the "conquest of autonomy." Rod Mengham and Andrjez Gasiorek's chapters suggest that the conquest is repeated, as well as revised or criticized, in English postmodern fiction. Complementing their considerations, another example of a reconquest of autonomy is postmodernist novelist Brigid Brophy's monumental study of modernist Ronald Firbank, *Prancing Novelist* (1973). The study challenges pre-1945, post-1945 and modernist-postmodernist divides. Brophy persuasively assigns Firbank's noncanonical status among modernists to critics' evasion of aesthetic experiment, even when the critics are scholars of modernism. Has the evasion occurred because Firbankian modernism, like much of the modernism of his contemporaries, shows itself as an aggression against naturalism or realism, in favor of an artifice that "isn't a social information service"?[6] Defying assumptions that novelists must respond to political and identity tensions, which is what she means by "social information," Brophy insists that "works of art have and need no justification but themselves" (p. 71).

Brophy's defence of autonomy intends to ward off censorship, above all censorship of daydreams and fantasy, including erotic fantasy. Important as fantasy and daydreams are to the material of fiction, however, Brophy knows that they undergo a transformation at the novelist's hands. "What differentiates a novel from both symptoms and daydreams is its formal organization...the design that organizes the material" (pp. 42, 45). A novel's design is "governed by a more highly evolved function of the Ego than...simple fulfillment of direct Ego wishes." And design is simultaneously an instrument of analytic thought and of pleasure. Analysis and pleasure derive in Firbank, as in all artists, from "set[ting] the author (and the reader) at a distance from his material, without making him emotionally remote from it" (p. 83). One means of achieving distance without remoteness is for the novelist to redirect a reader to the pleasure of design. Because a novel's design is for Brophy an evolved element of its fantasy components, it is not "checked against the real, outside world" (p. 45); the evolved fantasy components are fiction's autonomous core.

No doubt, in defence of fiction and Firbank, Brophy overstates her case. And after all, she goes on to elaborate her defence with a painstaking account of Firbank's life and times, "checked against the real, outside world." In doing so she copies a modernist paradox. The conquest of autonomy did not mean an end of fiction's worldly interests; as with *Ulysses*, it often meant a new capture of reality, because it insured a newly designed distance from, a temporary suspense of, servitude to established ways of seeing. Conrad's elaborate narrative designs, for example in his bestseller *Chance* (1912), with its multiply embedded stories and storytellers and its cultivation of an "inbetween" of realism and romance, seemed even to Henry James to overdo form's potential for independence from content. Yet Conrad's novel, thanks to its autonomy, significantly assaults patriarchy and capitalism; and if Conrad's aesthetic program refuses formulaic responsibility to history or politics, it also insists on evoking "that feeling of unavoidable solidarity...which binds men to each other."[7] Where questions of political responsibility are concerned, it should be noted that Ford Madox Ford's manifestos about the autonomous component in James and Conrad's fiction did not mean that they were not interested in politics. It meant instead, Ford says, that James and Conrad were trying to clear the ground of outworn political "prescription," trying to provide "the very matter upon which we shall build the theory of the new body politic."[8]

The modernist masters' realism was abetted as well as counterbalanced by the autonomy of their fictions. In this *Companion*'s chapters about realism and the novel's attachment to history, Maria Di Battista, Paul Edwards, Marina MacKay, James Acheson and I keep in mind the modernist balancing act that motivates fiction's investments equally in its own designs and in history's designs (at the level of world-historical events and at the level of quotidian reality). Indeed, all the contributors keep that in mind. In regard to history's designs, however, because of limitations of space we have not been able to keep in balance with our other concerns address to the publishing, retailing, reviewing, and prize-giving that have constituted the political economy of art in the twentieth century. That economy has become a new field of distinguished scholarly inquiry.[9] The field raises a concern that the novel's inheritance of any modernist-originated idea of fiction's autonomy is nothing more than illusion, "a perfectly magical guarantor of an imperfectly magical system" (*Economy*, p. 212). Despite the strength of the suggestion, which partly derives from Bourdieu, Bourdieu himself – in an uncanny convergence with Brophy's language about the pleasure of aesthetic design – declares:

> the right we have to salvage, in face of all kinds of objectification [including Bourdieu's own research in the sociology and political economy of art]...
> literary pleasure...In the name of literary pleasure, [of what the French modernist poet Mallarmé calls] "ideal joy," sublime product of sublimation,...one is entitled to save the game of letters, and even...the literary game itself. (pp. 274–5)

In the name of literary pleasure, English fiction in the twentieth century might be seen to save the literary game – in its novelistic form – in several ways. The novel perhaps disseminates modernism's conquest of autonomy into postmodernist fiction's inalienable self-consciousness; and it perhaps especially reconstructs that conquest in – and as – two novelistic modes: satire and fantasy. As Reed Dasenbrock points out in his chapter on satire, satire depends upon a decisively oppositional detachment from the environing world. That towering novelist-satirist among English modernists Wyndham Lewis derided his literary peers because he found their vaunted artistic autonomy not the detached or disinterested thing he himself thought it should be. When Lewis wrote *The Roaring Queen* (1936), a novel hilariously attacking English literary prizes and cultural politics, his publisher suppressed it for its potentially libelous character, suppressing thereby its freedom as fictive design. The incident suggests, as Dasenbrock does with other examples, that satiric autonomy is hard to come by; but the postmodernist version arguably preserves modernist inspiration. The design of

Martin Amis's *Money* (1984) distinctly echoes the design of Lewis's *The Apes of God* (1930).

It is in fantasy fiction, including science fiction, horror, and romance, with their immediate proximity to quotidian daydream and fantasy, that the novel's literary game, rooted in the conquest of autonomy and its accompanying literary pleasure, might especially save itself. Literary historians and critics of fiction have underestimated or underattended the modes surveyed in the concluding chapter here. One presumes that Wells's "scientific romances" have kept him an outsider to the modernist canon, as if fantasy were only incidental to the modernist novel's prevailing character; or as if Wells's ability to write equally in realist-historical and fantasy modes suggested an instability in novelistic form too intense for critical comprehension. Wells himself rejected "the novel" altogether, refusing to believe in its autonomy – even as the autonomy of fantasy gave him his enduring purchase on the form. Despite Wells's self-contradictory gesture, the intermingling of fantasy modes in every moment of the development of the twentieth-century English novel remains an abiding but under-explored fact. The fact is generally looked down on, partly because of the "standard disciplinary pathway" mentioned above. The standard pathway predisposes criticism to a continuing condescension to such things as romance in Conrad and Ford, fantasy in Lawrence, daydream or nightmare in *Finnegans Wake*, inasmuch as those terms name elements – autonomy-related elements – that criticism often believes their writers should be recovered *from*. But the wager of this *Companion*'s concluding segment is that we have the best opportunity to recover a century of the novel's history if we see its realism and its fantasy, its high modernist classics and its low postmodernist science fiction, its early, middle, and late emanations, as all of a piece.

The wholeness, of course, will be no more whole than the split character of "English." The specific handful of fictions I have just traversed exhibit the split character that the literary game of autonomy perennially intrudes into critical notice. Narayan's novel at midpoint becomes a fantasy, inasmuch as the narrator's wife, who has died, returns to him repeatedly, thanks at first to a medium who copies down her words from beyond the grave, and then in her own person. Is the novel thereby a fantasy or a work of historical realism? By making it impossible for us to decide, Narayan asserts his fiction's autonomous resistance to our analytic domination. Berger's trilogy, likewise, moves from realistic to fantastic registers; its third volume takes place in a slum of metropolitan Troy, a mythical city into which the peasants are absorbed. In this "backward" equivalent of reality, which fantasy makes possible, Berger locates his art's political motive: the only point of repair against global capital, which has destroyed Continental peasantry, is an imaginative realm, where history's horrors can be in part redeemed by utopian dimensions of literary design. Significantly, Berger's Troy resembles M. John Harrison's fallen fantasy metropolis, Viriconium, and China Miéville's city of refugees, New Crobuzon.

Critics and literary historians who are skeptical about the novel's continuing conquest of autonomy might receive pleasurable instruction from one last introductory mention of fantasy. Hope Mirrlees's *Lud-in-the-Mist* (1926) tells a story about Dorimare, a middle-class egalitarian land whose revolutionary forebears threw off its former oppressors. They have been banished geographically, as well as temporally; their kingdom, located beyond the Debatable Hills, is Fairyland, a dominion fatal to penetrate. Unfortunately, Fairyland produces a fruit that is a vision-inducing drug, which is smuggled into Dorimare with nefarious effects. They are curiously similar, some citizens realize, to art's effects: "eating... fairy fruit had... always been connected with poetry and visions, which, springing as they do from an ever-present sense of mortality, might easily appear morbid to the sturdy common sense of a burgher-class in the making."[10] The fruit is presumed delusional because it distances eaters from convictions of life and history's solid reality. Despite that solidity, Mirrlees's novel dramatizes, delicately as well as comically, a way to come to terms after all with "fairy fruit," which might be nothing more than fiction's way of remaking reality, so that the historical realm and the imaginative one amount to a condition in which "all our dreams got entangled" (p. 270). Fiction's autonomy makes the entanglement more possible rather than less.

The fairy fruit that is modernism, the lasting effect that it has on the literary game, circulates throughout the chapters that follow. The game itself, one ventures to say, takes place both in history and, as M. Keith Booker's chapter terms it, on history's "other side." That other side is one form of the alterity that Dorothy Hale's fresh view of modernism discloses in Chapter One. While Hale's "other" represents the not-one's self that Joycespeak is "amorist" of, it also might denominate "the other" that is prose fiction, in its independence from history and its service to history, in its submission of design to content and its subordination of content to literary pleasure.

NOTES

1 Pierre Bourdieu, *The Rules of Art: Genesis and Structure of the Literary Field*, trans. Susan Emanuel (Stanford: Stanford University Press, 1995), p. 132.

2 R. K. Narayan, *Swami and Friends, The Bachelor of Arts, The Dark Room, The English Teacher* (New York: Everyman's Library, 2006), p. 602.

3 Mulk Raj Anand, *Conversations in Bloomsbury* (New Delhi: Arnold-Heinemann, 1981), pp. 98, 102.

4 James Joyce, *Finnegans Wake* (Harmondsworth: Penguin Books, 1980), p. 463.
5 Richard Todd, "Literary Fiction and the Book Trade," in James F. English (ed.), *A Concise Companion to Contemporary British Fiction* (Malden: Blackwell Publishing, 2006), pp. 19–20.
6 Brigid Brophy, *Prancing Novelist* (New York: Harper & Row, 1973), p. 48.
7 Joseph Conrad, "Preface" to *The Nigger of the 'Narcissus'* (London: Everyman's Library, 1974), p. xxvi.
8 Ford Madox Ford, *Joseph Conrad: A Personal Remembrance* (Boston: Little, Brown, and Company, 1924), p. 58; Ford Madox Hueffer, *Henry James* (New York: Boni, 1915), p. 48.
9 See James F. English, *The Economy of Prestige* (Cambridge and London: Harvard University Press, 2005); Mark M. Morrisson, *The Public Face of Modernism* (Madison: University of Wisconsin Press, 2001); and Richard Todd, *Consuming Fictions: The Booker Prize and fiction in Britain today* (London: Bloomsbury, 1996).
10 Hope Mirrlees, *Lud-in-the-Mist* (Guernsey: Millennium, 2000), p. 12.

I

DOROTHY J. HALE

The art of English fiction in the twentieth century

"Fascinating and strangely unfamiliar," Virginia Woolf declared Percy Lubbock's new book to be in a 1922 *TLS* review essay.[1] Woolf was referring neither to the literary biographies for which Lubbock was known nor to the novel that he had yet to write but to *The Craft of Fiction*, his recently published study of the novel as a literary art. "To say that it is the best book on the subject is probably true," Woolf judges, "but it is more to the point to say that it is the only one. He has attempted a task which has never been properly attempted, and has tentatively explored a field of inquiry which it is astonishing to find almost untilled" (p. 338). Modernism famously invents itself by imagining the new century as a rupture with the past, and in the first three decades of the twentieth century part of what it meant to fulfill the Poundian imperative to "make it new" was to keep track of the cultural "firsts" as they abounded. The compliment of origination and exceptionalism that Woolf pays Lubbock is one that in *The Craft of Fiction* and elsewhere Lubbock himself pays to Henry James, the "novelist who carried his research into the theory of the art further than any other – the only real *scholar* in the art."[2] Lubbock has in mind the analysis conducted in eighteen prefaces that James wrote for the New York Edition of his best work, selected by (as Lubbock, with an even more extravagant display of indebtedness, proclaimed him) "the master" himself.[3] The prefaces are presented by James as a loving retrospective, an intimate reencounter, with his favorite literary creations. But because for James the creative enterprise was inseparable from his strong sense of the novel as an aesthetic form, Lubbock found in the prefaces a powerful articulation not of one man's "original quiddity" but of the literary properties common to all novels (p. 187).

The authentic newness of *The Craft of Fiction* lies in its belief that the art of the novel might be objectively located in its formal properties and objectively analyzed through empirical critical methods. This distinctively modern method, what Lubbock calls a "theory" of the novel, is influenced as much by contemporary science as classical poetics (pp. 9, 272). Before the twentieth century, the art of the English novel had been measured in terms of its ethical content. The social world created by the novelist was understood as a product of the author's "vision of life," and the depth of insight or quality of wisdom informing that vision was understood as the artistic contribution. By 1921 this kind of evaluation has, on Lubbock's view, taken on a banality that reveals more about the limitations of the English reader's critical vision than the novel's actual aesthetic accomplishment: "That Jane Austen was an acute observer, that Dickens was a great humourist, that George Eliot had a deep knowledge of provincial character, that our living romancers are so full of life that they are neither to hold nor to bind – we know, we have repeated, we have told each other a thousand times" (pp. 272–3). The "strangely unfamiliar" news announced in *The Craft of Fiction* is that novels have techniques of their own – and that good novels can be distinguished from bad novels on aesthetic rather than on biographical, historical, sociological, moral, or any other terms outside of autonomous art. With the formal basis revealed, the novel's future is assured, a "fresh life" opened up. Newly aware of the "immense variety" of technical possibilities "yet untried," the novelist goes forward into the twentieth century, so Lubbock imagines, prepared to perfect the genre through scientific invention, through "unheard-of experiments to be made" (p. 173).

Joyce's *Ulysses* (1922) and Woolf's *Mrs. Dalloway* (1925) and *To the Lighthouse* (1927) must have seemed to Lubbock confirmation of his prediction. But as the century unfolds, writers who attempt to realize the future of the novel by fulfilling the Lubbockian vision of innovation come to feel their unheard-of technical experiments fall upon deaf ears. Christine Brooke-Rose, looking back in 2002 over her forty-year career, laments the English reader's "deep-down . . . preference for content over form, the what over the how, even at a time of technical innovation."[4] The Lubbockian belief that the value of artistic technique is ennobled by the felt and analyzable difficulty of its execution is, for Brooke-Rose, questioned by the reception of her own novels: "Have you ever tried to do something very difficult as well as you can, over a long period, and found that nobody notices?" (p. 1). As late as 1966 David Lodge found the need to repeat Lubbock's plea that the novel be estimated in terms other than the quality of the author's sensibility: "In the last analysis, literary critics can claim special authority not as witnesses to the moral value of works of literature, but as explicators and judges of effective communication, of 'realization.' "[5] The theoretical paradigm has shifted since Lubbock (Lubbock pays almost no attention to the linguistic properties and rhetorical capabilities that for Lodge define the novel as a "realized" form), but, forty years after Lubbock,

Lodge still finds himself arguing that the evaluation of a novel depends upon more than the quality of the author's sensibility, that the "criteria of moral health must be controlled and modified by the aesthetic experience" (p. 68).

Is this enduring resistance to the theory of the novel confirmation, as James and Ford Madox Ford hypothesized, of a critical reticence native to the English character?[6] When we survey the century as a whole and look at what English novelists have to say about their art, we find few following Lubbock into the new field of theory and many re-tilling more subjective critical genres: the pronouncement, the personal statement, the interview, the preface, the lecture, the manifesto, the polemic. There are, of course, English novelists who do publish full-scale works of theory. The most important are written by novelists who are also academics: Iris Murdoch, Raymond Williams, Malcolm Bradbury and David Lodge. But as A. S. Byatt recognizes, the English novelist more typically feels that theory has little or nothing to do with the production of great works of art. This resistance to disciplined criticism is, on Byatt's view, not a national failing but the triumph of the novel as an art form. The flourishing of theory in the academy, the writing of "critical texts [that] are full of quotations . . . not from poems or novels" but from "Freud, Marx, Derrida, Foucault," has brought into being, Byatt suggests, a scholarly mastery different from that which Lubbock admired in James. From her perspective at the turn of the millennium, Byatt sees the professional critic subordinating literature to "fit into the boxes and nets of theoretical quotations." Byatt herself learns more about actual novels from ordinary readers whose love of literature irresistibly overflows into critical conversation: readers are "spending more and more time discussing books – all sorts of books – in the vulgar tongues and frank language of every day, in book clubs. Or writing messages to the Internet and reviews on Internet bookshop pages."[7] Far from being superseded by new media, the novel is freed from the nets of academic masters by the enlargement of public conversation made possible by the web.

Byatt's view of the novel as first and foremost a living art points us to a counter-Lubbockian understanding of the genre that looks back to the nineteenth century and develops alongside academic literary theory in the twentieth century. For the novelist-critic, the novel's aesthetic power lies not in its formal perfection but in the life it represents, creates – and itself possesses. A strong proponent of this view is Woolf herself, whose admiration for Lubbock's new method did not extend to the compliment of imitation. Her own pronouncements about the art of the novel are couched in a far more personal style, explicitly addressed to the common reader. Byatt's description of the irrepressible life of the novel, its refusal to be boxed or netted by theory, reverberates with Woolf's explicit and repeated contention that the novel's only aesthetic imperative is to represent "life." What is life? Woolf is clear that it is not the details of the material world catalogued in *reportage*. In her famous essays "Mr. Bennett and Mrs. Brown" and "Modern Fiction," she lambastes what she terms the "materialist" representation of life pursued by H. G. Wells, Arnold Bennett, and John Galsworthy. But in calling for a view of life that is more "spiritual," Woolf does not mean to return critical conversation to those ethical values that "we have told each other a thousand times" about this or that author.[8] The vision of life conveyed by a novel is, Woolf insists, a "vague, mysterious thing."[9] Every effort of analysis, every attempt to assign positive attributes to "life" or to locate in the novel its objective correlative ends in failure. For Woolf the aesthetic achievement of the novel is to project "life" as a life force, as energy, animation, what she calls the "unknown and uncircumscribed spirit" ("Modern," p. 160). Woolf's mystical pronouncement could not be further from Lubbock's scholarly systems. Yet it is Woolf's formulation that is the one most favored by twentieth-century novelists who have set themselves the public task of talking about the art of the novel.

From the sustained investigations into the novel as an art offered by Vernon Lee, E. M. Forster, Ford Madox Ford, and D. H. Lawrence through Iris Murdoch, Robert Liddell, Brigid Brophy, Laura Riding Jackson, Wilson Harris, Salman Rushdie and A. S. Byatt, there emerges what might usefully be termed an aesthetics of alterity. For these and other English writers, the art of the novel is found in the genre's inherent capacity for otherness, a capacity that comes to life when author and reader participate in a circuit of interanimation, retaining their own subjective particularity even while they are united in their contact with a commonly shared and uncircumscribed spirit (divine or human) that is the basis for their relation. Whether pursuing classic realism or exploring allegory, romance, and symbolic or political modalities, English novelists committed to the aesthetics of alterity aim to present a "vision of life" that is a particular kind of self-reflection: that gives a view of what is outside and beyond self (other to the self) through the lens of subjective perspective. Ford Madox Ford offers the painterly term "impressionism" to describe how a successful literary work paradoxically expresses authorial identity by never directly representing it: on the one hand, the "Impressionist author is sedulous to avoid letting his personality appear in the course of his book. On the other hand, his whole book . . . is merely an expression of his personality."[10] The novelist animates the objective world she projects by successfully imbuing it with her own subjectivity, a subjectivity that, godlike, is invisibly visible, everywhere apparent but nowhere directly manifested as her own image.[11] For Woolf the master of the novelistic art of alterity is Jane Austen, whom we know only through the refracted light of her supreme acts of achieved alterity, who "pervades every word that she wrote," going "in and out of her people's minds like the blood in their veins."[12]

The continuity of the aesthetics of alterity across the twentieth century, and across untrustworthy divides between modernism and postmodernism, can be illustrated if we juxtapose Salman Rushdie's and D. H. Lawrence's thoughts about fiction. Rushdie, like Woolf, attributes to the novel an interanimating aesthetic spirit. The novel's generic capacity for depictions of relationality, its refusal to place any "one set of values above all others," makes the novel for Rushdie the most socially important genre and the most vitally transformative: "Can art be the third principle that mediates between the material and spiritual worlds; might it, by 'swallowing' both worlds, offer us something new – something that might even be called a secular definition of transcendence?" And his answer is yes.[13] D. H. Lawrence would agree. He regards the novel's performance of irreducible relationality as its only generic "law" and believes as well that the fulfillment of this aesthetic law establishes an animating connection between the material and spiritual worlds.[14] "The novel is the highest complex of subtle inter-relatedness that man has discovered," Lawrence declares in 1925. "Everything is true in its own time, place, circumstance . . . If you try to nail anything down, in the novel, either it kills the novel, or the novel gets up and walks away with the nail."[15] The specificity of the novel's depiction of details of everyday life is not important for their referential value but for the irreducibility of their relatedness, to each other and to the subjects for whom they have meaning. In turn, the irreducible relatedness within the material world is, for Lawrence, upheld and animated by that world's irreducible connection with divinity: "In the great novel, the felt but unknown flame stands behind all the characters, and in their words and gestures there is a flicker of the presence . . . The quick is God-flame, in everything. And the dead is dead" ("Novel," pp. 158–9). The unknown flame is invisibly visible, apprehendable as the flickering flame of life animating not just the story world but the novel itself: the novel comes into being as an autonomous art form when it is felt to have irrepressible autonomy, when the form itself seems capable of walking away from any critical attempt to pin it down.

Rushdie's secular transcendence and Lawrence's God-flame are deliberately mysterious energies, like Woolf's notion of "life." What is specified through the aesthetics of alterity is an ethical challenge and opportunity that irreducible relativism holds for modern society. In the English tradition of novel-critics that I am tracing, the novel's world-swallowing life, as Rushdie postulates it, is a means to society's ethical evolution. "The novel," Rushdie writes, "has always been *about* the way in which different languages, values and narratives quarrel, and about the shifting relations between them, which are relations of power" (p. 420). By making cultural difference visible, the novel educates a reader in the irreducible relativity of all value. The novel reader learns that any seemingly objective value is the projection of an interested point of view, a knowledge that in turn leads to self-consciousness about her own standards of evaluation, irreducibly connected with her own subject position.

But the aesthetics of alterity also opens the possibility of seeing through one's point of view to understand the other as other. A novelist's ability to maximize the novel's generic capacity requires not the right set of tools but the right emotion. The right emotion, Rushdie argues, is "love," understood as an emotion of self-restraint. Love enables the self to see the other and honor her difference: to accept "that your tastes, your loves, are your business and not mine" (p. 416). Out of such self-discipline comes novel writing's aesthetic discipline. The aesthetic form of alterity fulfills the novel's relativized perspectivalism. To evaluate this success, a critic must be intuitive and responsive, able to circulate herself "like blood" in and out of the author's projected world. As Lawrence puts it, "Design, in art, is a recognition of the relation between various things, various elements in the creative flux. You can't *invent* a design. You recognise it, in the fourth dimension. That is, with your blood and your bones, even more than with your eyes."[16]

For many twentieth-century novelists the novel's generic capacity for relativized relations centers on an aesthetics of character. "The form of the novel, so clumsy, verbose, and undramatic, so rich, elastic, and alive, has been evolved," Woolf declares, "to express character."[17] Woolf has in mind the novel's ability to provide a prolonged and detailed rendering of an individual, putting into relation inside and outside views, private and public activity, a goal that requires the writer to give herself wholly up to another, "to steep oneself" in another person's "atmosphere" (p. 101). A related understanding of novelistic alterity stresses the genre's capacity for social abundance and variety, its ability to set into relation characters from every walk of life. The novel gives authors and readers alike the opportunity, according to George Eliot, to forge an emotional relation with "those who differ from themselves in everything but the broad fact of being struggling erring human creatures."[18] Joseph Conrad, Iris Murdoch, and A. S. Byatt respectively describe themselves as carrying out the Eliotic project of "enlarging" the spirit of the English citizen by expanding the capacity to respect and honor diversity, to "extend the number and kind of people you are made to take account of."[19] Anticipating Rushdie, Murdoch believes that the multiplicity of social perspectives within the novel is put into a living relation through the quickening power of authorial "love."[20] The novelist is godlike insofar as she feels love not as a will to power but as a will to self-abnegation: the successful novelist is for Murdoch, as for Rushdie and Lawrence, the one who successfully practices the "discipline involved in realizing that something real exists other than oneself" (p. 261). Murdoch stresses that the achievement of discipline is not a god-given capacity but a difficult ethical labor. Explicitly comparing the novelist's achievement of love to the poet's experience of "negative capability" (p. 270), she also suggests a basis of contrast. Whereas for John Keats negative capability describes the feeling of his own effortless absorption in the subjectivity of others, novelistic negative capability – the achievement of an interanimated world of social diversity and multiperspectivalism – is, Murdoch implies, a moral triumph over the ever-present seduction of individual ego. The novelist who successfully practices the self-discipline of love is rewarded as much by the independence of his created characters as he is by his sense of connectedness to them: "the individuals portrayed in the novels are free, independent of their author, and not merely puppets in the exteriorization of some closely locked psychological conflict of his own" (p. 257).

Responding to Lubbock's *The Craft of Fiction* with her own poetics of the novel, *The Handling of Words* (1923), Vernon Lee anticipates Murdoch in her assertion that characters rendered through "love" are those that will seem to the reader independent of their author. In keeping with the aesthetics of characterological alterity I describe, for Lee the art of the novel resides first and foremost in the author's successful subjective projection of autonomous individuals who seem wholly objective. Such characters are not only free from the author but free to be ethically unadmirable: "the Reader may thoroughly detest them," Lee says of aesthetically powerful characters such as Henry James's Olive Chancellor. But through the quickening spirit of authorial alterity, these characters will live for the reader by their own power to "awaken only real feeling" (p. 27). What Woolf calls Lee's poetics of "altruism" thus charts the mutually constitutive circuit of novelistic negative capability, the reciprocating capacity for alterity between author and reader that enables them together to animate and be animated by novelistic characters as autonomous subjects.[21] Lee's discussion of an ethics of novelistic representation leads to an explanation of one of the most enduring and powerful aesthetic effects attributed to fiction: a reader's experience of having an intensely real emotional relationship with imaginary characters whose power lies in their perceived independence from us: "the person who is not ourselves comes to live, somehow, for our consciousness, with the same reality, the same intimate warmth, that we do" (p. 26).

So accomplished is the novel in creating characters who seem alive, real and autonomous that over the century many readers and authors have come to believe that the aesthetics of alterity entails a necessary politics. Robert Liddell, in 1947, draws the connection this way:

> It would be perverse or whimsical to maintain that fictional characters had duties or rights; yet it is hard to find other words for the conviction that a novelist has certain obligations towards them. Perhaps as they are *simulacra* of human beings, we are shocked if they are not treated as we ought to treat other human beings, as ends in themselves, and not as means to ends of our own.[22]

But as Liddell develops this idea, authorial obligation is less a matter of social contract and more a divine "debt" owed by "a God" to "his creatures" (p. 106). The novelist capable of making his characters so real as to seem as if they deserved human rights is the one who possesses not just the godlike power to create, but the godlike power to love social others as others (p. 108) – and to describe this capacity for alterity, Liddell also reaches for the term "negative capability."[23] Doris Lessing keeps to a secular account of the novel's politics, but her view is equally based upon the profound social value of authorial self-abnegation. Through the others she creates, the novelist expresses her ethical "recognition of man, the responsible individual." The author brings these responsible individuals to life by projecting them as autonomous agents, independent of their author. Such subordination of authorial privilege performs what Lessing believes is a political basis for a democratic community of mutually interconnected individuals, who enact their own human rights through self-conscious self-restraint: each individual "voluntarily submitting his will to the collective, but never finally; and insisting on making his own personal and private judgements before every act of submission."[24]

For more visionary political novelists such as Laura Riding Jackson in the 1930s and Wilson Harris in the 1960s, the novel's aesthetics of alterity directs us away from a politics of human rights and the realist idiom of the simulacrum to symbolist and allegorical modes of fiction harnessed for social transformation and revolution. Riding Jackson and Harris both see in "the trembling instability of the [novel's] balance" between materiality and spirituality the opportunity to concretize the difference between what is and what might be (Lawrence, "Morality," p. 150). Especially in her feminist essays, Riding Jackson praises novels that accentuate rather than veil the seam between reality and fiction, between the modalities of verisimilitude and fabrication.[25] The novel best fulfills its generic identity, Riding Jackson argues in 1935, in the open display of irreducible relationality between truth and fiction, between reality as we know it and reality as it might be imagined. In making legible moments "where story-telling changes naturally into truth-telling," the novel includes its reader in the act of re-envisioning the terms of the social contract (p. 170). To invoke the title of an earlier Riding Jackson polemic, "anarchism is not enough." Unlike her contemporary Wyndham Lewis whose *Men without Art* (1934) champions the overthrow of existing conventions (and pretensions) through the outsider perspective of satire, Riding Jackson advocates the cultivation of alterity as a way to know the other, even the oppressive other, from its own point of view. Her belief that imagination can establish a basis of positive relation even between incommensurable subject positions leads her to find such a negotiation at the heart of the novel's narrative structure. Through its very form the novel puts into relation the ethical claims of irreducible variety and the epistemological need for unified understanding: "The key to Story is bountiful sympathy with the immensely varied actualness of life, as the Key to Truth is bountiful knowledge of actualness, in the immense unity of its significances" (p. 170). For Riding Jackson the novel can cast its uncircumscribable spirit over both types of bounty, doing equal justice to "varied actualness" and "immense . . . significances," placing both realms (life and truth) into trembling relation.

From a postcolonial perspective as a Caribbean writer, Wilson Harris provides the most explicit articulation of the novel's contribution to a revolutionary politics of alterity – even as he connects the aesthetics of alterity to his own deeply held religious beliefs. The lack of living spirit that Woolf detected in the "materialists" of her generation is, for Harris, "the supreme casualty" of his own moment in time. The wholly secular world of the realist novel is inseparable, maintains Harris, from the rise of English liberalism and "the death of cosmic love."[26] Any art form that encourages the individual to believe in his or her constitutive freedom simply masks the "ambitions for power" that underlie liberal humanism.[27] To reinvent the novel as an agent of social transformation, Harris's novelist, like Lawrence's, must put matter and spirit into trembling relation. And although Harris feels his belief in spiritual indwelling makes him an outlier to the English liberal tradition, he too uses the term "negative capability" to name the power for alterity that is the defining quality of this cosmic love.[28] Whereas creative vision begins for Woolf with what she calls the imposition of character upon her imagination, Harris is seized by an alterity that to his mind is divinity: "one becomes susceptible to a species of unpredictable arousal, one virtually becomes a species of nature which subsists on both mystery and phenomenon, participating an otherness akin to the terrifying and protean reality of the gods. It is within this instant of arousal that abolishes the 'given' world that one's confession of weakness has really begun" ("Phenomenal," p. 47). The confession of weakness, the recognition that one is not master but mastered, is the precondition for revolutionary politics. The higher power of the gods may be terrifying, but vulnerability brings humility, a shattering of ego that makes possible a transformative imagination of the world.[29]

The novelist's struggle to find the right modality of novelistic expression, to remodel "a form that has already been broken in the past" ("Phenomenal," p. 45) establishes a living relation with the uncircumscribable spirit that becomes for Harris the basis of the novel's aesthetic achievement: "This interaction between sovereign ego and intuitive self is the tormenting reality of changing form, the ecstasy as well of visionary capacity to cleave the prisonhouse of natural bias within a heterogeneous asymmetric context in which the unknowable God – though ceaselessly beyond man-made patterns – infuses art with unfathomable eternity and grace" ("Frontier," p. 135). Because for Harris this visionary spirit is ancient and intuitive, he looks for the future of fiction in his native traditions ("Tradition," p. 30; "Furies," p. 245). This does not mean that the writer is a slave to his own tradition but that he is, if inspirited, able to see his culture as both self and other. On the one hand, the native peoples are "capable *now*," writes Harris in 1967, "of discovering themselves and continuing to discover themselves so that in one sense one relieves and reverses the 'given' conditions of the past, freeing oneself from catastrophic idolatry and blindness to one's own historical and philosophical conceptions and misconceptions" ("Tradition," p. 36, Wilson's emphasis). On the other hand, such discovery accompanies a revelation of the contingency of colonial and postcolonial existence – and of that contingency's resistance to any univocal or unidimensional ways of telling history and of accusing it. Accordingly, the novelist's contingent relation to his own culture, along with the novel's generic capacity for "bewildering variety and surprising complexity of concrete example," will produce the novel as an irreducible multiplicity of cultural perspectives, an achievement that will help combat social "resistance to alterities."[30]

And the political stakes could not be higher. In 2004 Harris links the social atrocities of the century – the "Holocaust, ethnic cleansing, institutional racism, the gross and terrible exploitation of native and aboriginal peoples" – to the resistance to alterity that drives English liberal culture ("Resistances," p. 3). Writers from colonized countries like Wilson's own Guyana can lead the way for transformative social change. The culture that has suffered through colonial domination has an opportunity not to reproduce it. Political promise lies in realization that "the prisonhouse of natural bias" can never be eliminated – but can itself be relativized: "difference rests on diverse cultures, a capacity within diverse cultures to create and re-create windows into the enigma of truth. Each window's susceptibility to rigidity, rigid commandment, breaks, turns . . . into a transitive architecture, a transitive medium into other dimensions within the unfinished genesis of the Imagination."[31]

If Harris's description of the multicultural house of fiction seems a politicized critique of a famous Jamesian figure, it is a revision invited by the figure itself. "The house of fiction," James tells us, "has... not one window, but a million – a number of possible windows not to be reckoned, rather; every one of which has been pierced, or is still pierceable, in its vast front, by the need of the individual vision and by the pressure of the individual will."[32] Although James's depiction of a house filled with a multiplicity of individual watchers all focused on the social scene privileges the liberal subject deplored by Harris, for James as much as for Harris the novel's architecture is a "transitive medium," the form of realized alterity. The Jamesian novelist standing at the window is, to borrow Brigid Brophy's formulation, "genuinely not at home."[33] The view from the house of fiction positions the novelist at "the window" of his character's consciousness, which in turn is realized through its operation as a point of view, the establishment of living relation with something outside and beyond the self. That this point of view then becomes available to a reader is part of the novel's power to establish relativized relations. "One of the symptoms of being in love," Brophy tells us, "is that you want to hear everything the other person can or will tell you, not primarily for the information it may give you about life or even about the person concerned, but the preciousness of seeing the world through his eyes" (p. 97). The escape from the prison house of bias is, for the tradition I have been tracing, through the many-mansioned house of fiction, the dwelling described by E. M. Forster (in his treatise on the novel) as "sogged with humanity."[34]

The English writer's ethico-religious understanding of the novel as the genre of realized alterity means that there can be no real danger of the death of the genre – and no amount of labor that can perfect it as an aesthetic form. As living art, as what Lawrence calls the "bright book of life," the novel is for its twentieth-century creators the genre that keeps its fresh youth because its genesis in irreducible relationality cannot be brought to a halt: it lives its generic life by giving life to the other, a fullness of life that can have no end since that uncircumscribable spirit is, as Lubbock lamented, "neither to hold nor to bind."

NOTES

1 Virginia Woolf, "On Re-reading Novels," *The Essays of Virginia Woolf*, ed. Andrew McNeillie (New York: Harcourt Brace Jovanovich, 1988), vol. III, p. 342.
2 Percy Lubbock, *The Craft of Fiction* (New York: Peter Smith, 1931), pp. 186–7.
3 Percy Lubbock, "Introduction," *The Letters of Henry James* (New York: Scribner's, 1920), pp. xxii, xxviii.

4 Christine Brooke-Rose, *Invisible Author: Last Essays* (Columbus: Ohio State University Press, 2002), p. 13.

5 David Lodge, *The Language of Fiction: Essays in Criticism and Verbal Analysis of the English Novel* (London: Routledge, 1966), p. 68.

6 Henry James, "The Art of Fiction," *Henry James: The Future of the Novel*, ed. Leon Edel (New York: Vintage, 1956), p. 3, and Ford Madox Ford, *The Critical Attitude* (London: Duckworth, 1911), p. 4.

7 A. S. Byatt, *On Histories and Stories: Selected Essays* (Cambridge: Harvard University Press, 2001), p. 6.

8 Virginia Woolf, "Modern Fiction," *The Essays of Virginia Woolf*, ed. Andrew McNeillie (London: The Hogarth Press, 1994), vol. IV, p. 159. The argument for the novel as an art form is routinely positioned against the view of the novel as social document. See for example Iris Murdoch, "The Sublime and the Beautiful Revisited," *The Yale Review* 49 (1959), 264.

9 Virginia Woolf, "The Narrow Bridge of Art," *Granite and Rainbow: Essays* (New York: Harcourt Brace Jovanovich, 1958), p. 13.

10 Ford Madox Ford, "On Impressionism," *Critical Writings of Ford Madox Ford*, ed. Frank MacShane (Lincoln: University of Nebraska Press, 1964), p. 43.

11 The phrase "invisibly visible" comes from Friedrich Schlegel's "Letter About the Novel, 1799–1800," *Dialogue on Poetry and Literary Aphorisms*, trans. Ernst Behler and Roman Struc (University Park: The Pennsylvania State University Press, 1968), p. 99.

12 Virginia Woolf, *A Room of One's Own* (New York: Harcourt Brace, 1929), p. 71, and Woolf, "Phases of Fiction," *Granite and Rainbow*, p. 119.

13 Salman Rushdie, "Is Nothing Sacred?" *Imaginary Homelands: Essays and Criticism, 1981–1991* (New York: Penguin, 1991), p. 420.

14 D. H. Lawrence, "The Novel," *Study of Thomas Hardy and Other Essays*, ed. Bruce Steele (London: Grafton Books, 1986), p. 159.

15 D. H. Lawrence, "Morality and the Novel," *ibid.*, p. 150.

16 D. H. Lawrence, "Art and Morality," *ibid.*, p. 147.

17 Virginia Woolf, "Mr. Bennett and Mrs. Brown," *The Captain's Death Bed* (New York: Harcourt Brace, 1950), p. 102.

18 George Eliot, Letter to Charles Bray, July 5, 1859, *The George Eliot Letters*, ed. Gordon S. Haight (New Haven: Yale University Press, 1954), pp. 110–11.

19 A. S. Byatt in conversation with Ignês Sodré, *Imagining Characters: Six Conversations about Women Writers*, ed. Rebecca Swift (London: Chatto and Windus, 1995), p. 248. See also Joseph Conrad, "Books," *Notes on Life and Letters* (London: J. M. Dent, 1921), p. 11.

20 Iris Murdoch, "The Sublime and the Beautiful Revisited," *The Yale Review* 49 (1959), 257, 261.

21 Virginia Woolf, "Art and Life," *The Essays of Virginia Woolf*, ed. Andrew McNeillie (San Diego: Harcourt Brace Jovanovich, 1986), vol. I, p. 277.

22 Robert Liddell, *A Treatise on the Novel* (London: Jonathan Cape, 1947), p. 106.

23 Robert Liddell, *Some Principles of Fiction* (London: Jonathan Cape, 1953), pp. 65–6.

24 Doris Lessing, "The Small, Personal Voice," *A Small Personal Voice: Essays, Reviews, Interviews*, ed. Paul Schlueter (New York: Knopf, 1974), p. 12.

25 Laura Riding Jackson, "Eve's Side of It," *The Word "Woman" and Other Related Writings*, ed. Elizabeth Friedmann and Alan J. Clark (New York: Persea Books, 1993), p. 170.

26 Wilson Harris, "Apprenticeship to the Furies," *Selected Essays of Wilson Harris: The Unfinished Genesis of Imagination* (London: Routledge, 1999), p. 230.

27 Wilson Harris, "The Frontier on Which *Heart of Darkness* Stands," *Explorations: A Selection of Talks and Articles, 1966–81*, ed. Hera Maes-Jelinek (Mundelstrup: Dangaroo Press, 1981), p. 135.

28 Wilson Harris, "The Phenomenal Legacy," *Explorations: A Selection of Talks and Articles, 1966–81*, p. 46.

29 Wilson Harris, "Tradition and the West Indian Novel," *Selected Essays of Wilson Harris*, p. 144.

30 Wilson Harris, "Books – A Long View," *Tradition, the Writer and Society* (London: New Beacon), p. 21, and Wilson Harris, "Resistances to Alterities," *Resisting Alterities: Wilson Harris and Other Avatars of Otherness*, ed. Marco Fazzini (Amsterdam: Rodolpi, 2004), p. 3.

31 Wilson Harris, "Quetzalcoatl and the Smoking Mirror: Reflections on Originality and Tradition," *Selected Essays of Wilson Harris*, p. 194.

32 Henry James, preface to *The Portrait of a Lady* in *The Art of the Novel*, ed. R. P. Blackmur (New York: Scribner's, 1934), p. 46.

33 Brigid Brophy, "The Novel as a Takeover Bid," *Don't Never Forget: Collected Views and Reviews* (London: Jonathan Cape, 1966), p. 96.

34 E. M. Forster, *Aspects of the Novel* (New York: Harcourt Brace, 1927), p. 24.

2

JED ESTY

The British Empire and the English modernist novel

Many modernist innovators of English fiction during the first half of the twentieth century had personal experience of European colonialism and a significant artistic interest in it. Does their encounter with colonialism, as historical cause, biographical incitement, or literary subject matter, contribute to modernist fiction's unsettling of Victorian values and realist idioms? Does the experimental character of modernist fiction reach its revisionary potential as it assimilates colonial plots and settings, nonwestern cultural objects, and symbols harvested from anthropological research or primitivist myth?

There are two ways to answer these questions. The first way sees in literary modernism an implicit opposition to imperialism. Benita Parry argues that modernist style disrupts the "moral confidence" of western imperialism; Edward Said suggests that modernism's "pervasive irony" undermines the triumphalism of imperialism's agents, the European bourgeoisie.[1] The alternative answer argues that modernism's aesthetic hallmarks, including what Elleke Boehmer calls "multivoicedness," can be understood as stylistic correlates to imperialism.[2] Raymond Williams's concept of "metropolitan perception," representing a key formulation of this second premise, assigns characteristic forms of modernist thought and expression to the cultural privilege of artists working in western imperial centers.[3]

Whether or not one set of answers is more true than the other, perhaps perception or perspective is a formal category that most bears on an investigation of modernist fiction and its imperialist context. Perception or perspective can refer both to local aesthetic experiments with narrative point of view and to global geopolitical and epistemological possibilities associated with life in the Age of Empire. With "perspective" in mind, we can concentrate on formal innovation and colonial content in representatives of at least three generations of novelists: Rudyard Kipling and Rabindranath Tagore, whose fictions of empire and nation helped define the English novel at the outset of the century; Joseph Conrad, H. G. Wells, and Virginia Woolf, whose perspectival experiments newly stretch definitions of what "English" is and what "the novel" is; and Joyce Cary, Lawrence Durrell, and Paul Scott, whose works describe the aftermath of high modernism and British imperialism.

Worlds apart: Kipling and Tagore

If there is a beginning to the story of English fiction and the British Empire in the twentieth century, it is to be found in Kipling's *Kim* (1900). *Kim* centers on a homeless boy who travels down the spine of the Indian continent, escaping the straitjacket of imperial civilization yet shouldering the symbolic burden of a British civilizing mission. The celebrated realism of Kipling's imperial picaresque, unfolding in a sweeping omniscient voice, depends on Kim's ability to stabilize the politics of empire and to negotiate a welter of cultural and ethnic differences. *Kim* figures Kipling's characteristic use of fiction: to depict what can be known and told in British India, even as it comprehends a full array of faiths, landscapes, and dialects held under the British crown. Kipling immerses his reader deeply in a phenomenological world of facts; he is not a novelist of ideas, nor of metaphysical or political doubt, nor even of historical development, but is a master of scenic immediacy and emotional instantaneity. When West meets East in Kipling, the two produce interesting conflicts – raw materials for good fiction – but even in the colonial fray they do not fundamentally unsettle their own cultural essences.

Kipling thus does not write primarily from the standpoint of a cultural go-between seeking to deliver tropical truth values to an English audience. Instead he works as a journalistic observer embedded in the Anglo-Indian scene. His commitment to faithful reproduction of the sprawl and spread of daily life in Raj-era India undercuts political caricatures of him as a hardcore British jingo or white supremacist, caricatures derived more from florid sentiment in his occasional verse than from sharp observation in his best fiction. Salman Rushdie, who adapted much of *Kim*'s plot for his ground breaking national novel *Midnight's Children* (1981), characterizes Kipling as a split personality, "part-bazaar boy, part sahib."[4] Kim the boy-hero is everywhere at home in India, a "Little Friend of all the World"; as Kipling allows Kim's narrative to roam freely over the land, one can attribute the author's realistic command of detail equally to an arrogant colonialist sense of possession and to a naturalized Anglo-Indian sense of belonging.

Kipling stands as one of the last Victorian realists, holding out against the clinical disillusionment of naturalism and the phlegmatic interiority of modernism. His fiction, long and short, takes readers into the mechanical heart of empire. We learn as much about the technical problems of coal mining in a story like "At Twenty-Two" as we do in an entire Zola novel, and without the predictable social determinism and catastrophes of naturalism. Many critics consider Kipling's greatest works to be the stories of the 1880s in *Plain Tales from the Hills* or *In Black and White*; but when Kipling operates on a wider scale, as in *Kim*, he combines his journalistic acuity with impressive sociological comprehensiveness. Noel Annan compares Kipling to the great modern sociologists Max Weber and Emile Durkheim, not only because of Kipling's vivid depictions of empire's social infrastructure (a far cry from the courtship-and-property conventions of the English domestic novel), but also because sociological realism turns on the reproduction of the status quo, not its transformation.[5] Kipling writes fiction that assumes a given political and social equilibrium. Most modernists, in contrast, tend to represent social crisis or potential revolutionary change.

To get a sense of how modernist fiction of the colonial world departs from Kipling's fixedly referential sensibility, we might turn to Rabindranath Tagore. Kipling's realism pares away psychological, metaphysical, and even historical explanation, whereas Tagore's fiction seeks to reveal deeper social forces in crisis and transition. The two great chroniclers of India, Kipling the colonial gazetteer and Tagore the Bengali poet, were among the earliest winners of the Nobel prize in literature (in 1907 and 1913 respectively), and the only two writers from outside continental Europe to win before 1923. In *Gora* (1910) Tagore produced a self-conscious riposte to *Kim*, making his protagonist an Irish orphan adopted by Hindu parents. But we can also take Tagore's best known novel, *The Home and the World* (1915, English translation in 1919), as a foil to *Kim* and as a central text in the field of modernist fiction and empire. *Kim* ranges freely over all India, but *The Home and the World* confines itself to the inner chambers of the estate of its hero, Nikhil, a man as rooted as Kim is rootless. *Kim* rests its realistic presentation of linguistic and cultural diversity on the bedrock assumption of British rule, while *The Home and the World* offers a highly subjective account of a violent devolution to Indian self-government. And where Kipling defers or sidesteps ideological contradictions of modern imperialism, Tagore exposes a deep clash of values produced within and among characters as they come to terms with the nationalist movement known as *swadeshi*.

Tagore's plot unfolds through the voices of three narrators, Nikhil, his wife Bimala, and an Iagoesque interloper Sandip, a nationalist demagogue disrupting the sexual stability of the home and the political stability of the world. In a manner that echoes Conrad's *Lord Jim* (1900) and anticipates Woolf's *The Waves* (1931), Tagore's polyvocal narration provides partly overlapping, partly distorted perspectives, without any final coordination by an omniscient narrator. With this experimental point-of-view model delivered in modernized Bengali prose, and with a candid story of adulterous desire, Tagore flouts novelistic conventions of his day. The humanist land-owner Nikhil represents a rational compromise between tradition and modernity, but his antagonist Sandip endorses a radical stance implied by the novel's fracturing of stable perspective: "He [Nikhil] has such a prejudice in favour of truth – as though there exists such an objective reality! How often have I tried to explain to him that where untruth truly exists, there it is indeed the truth."[6] In theme and technique, in contrast to Kipling, Tagore asks readers to value his work for more than its referential or historical authenticity.

Tagore initially supported anti-colonial and nationalist movements, but later recoiled against the violence and mob mentality that *swadeshi* some-times entailed. Through Nikhil Tagore exposes nationalism ("this making a fetish of one's country") as a western curse: "What a terrible epidemic of sin has been brought into our country from foreign lands" (p. 166). Meanwhile, Sandip uses his credibility as a nationalist revolutionary to seduce Bimala in spirit; driven equally by sincere passions and venal appetites, he seeks to make Bimala into an icon of *swadeshi*, broken free from her fealty to Nikhil. In the end, although Sandip is discredited, and Bimala again embraces Nikhil's modestly progressive values, Nikhil himself discovers the fatal truth that neither enlightened rationality nor an appeal to home ties can match forces or fervor with modern mass movements.

Read against *Kim*, *The Home and the World* appears strikingly modern in both style and theme, not least because it discloses so much psychic and sexual interiority. Where Kipling brushes away dissemblings of desire in order to reveal the social consequences of erotic relationships, Tagore offers a stylized dance of subjectivities that turns a love triangle into a national allegory and vice versa. In Kipling love and sex are morally complex but not politically disruptive; in Tagore they are bound up in the social upheaval of the late-colonial era. On the matter of religion, *Kim* attributes spiritual values to the East and political rationality to the West, but Tagore complicates that contrast by making cosmopolitan Nikhil a spiritual humanist, and anti-western nationalist Sandip a crude oppor-tunist who sacrifices soul for power. *Kim*, which rests its core meaning on an intergenerational love story between Kim and his guardian spirit, the lama, is a worldly novel about otherworldliness that ends in beatific peace; *The Home and the World*, which describes the rupture of both gender and generational relations, is a spiritual drama about worldliness that ends in violent death.

Modernist worlds: Conrad, Wells, and Woolf

Tagore is profoundly skeptical about the value of revolutionary political action. Joseph Conrad, the most important novelist working at the intersection of modernist technique and imperialist themes, shares his skepticism. Conrad's canvas includes Asia and Africa, Latin America, the Caribbean, and eastern and western Europe, yet his work evinces a consistent philosophical and stylistic program over time and across territories. Like Tagore, Conrad uses perspectival narration to reveal doubts and reservations about almost all ideologies and political movements, including both imperialism and anti-imperialist nationalism. He labors to separate pragmatic humanitarian impulses from cynical or corrupt political gestures – a problem that did not plague Kipling, for whom political machination was always a bad subset of the larger colonial enterprise, not its very foundation.

Whereas in Kipling, moreover, action resolves narrative conflict, in Conrad contemplation interrupts and defers action, transferring attention from the basalt of social organization to the quicksand of subjective interpretation. Kipling and Conrad share an interest in the masculine sphere of work and fellowship, but they part ways on the question of whether language can serve as a transparent vehicle for meaning. Where dialects meet and collide, Kipling sees an opportunity for translation or exchange; for Conrad, such collisions produce knots of untranslatability, as in his story of failed English assimilation, "Amy Foster" (1903). In "Youth" (1898), *Heart of Darkness* (1899), and *Lord Jim* (1900), stories, like social power, circulate through an imperfectly filtered relay from man to man, so that both an essential corruptibility of social institutions and a countervailing hope are at once described and enacted by the texts. Later, Conrad transplants the plot of failed relays and intercultural gaps from his exploration of the colonial world to Europe-centered texts such as *The Secret Agent* (1907) and *Under Western Eyes* (1911).

Nostromo (1904) is a *tour de force* that elaborates Conrad's basic model of political instability and perspectival narration. It captures the long trajectory of imperialism itself, from the nineteenth-century model of British colonial rule to the incipient model of US-dominated global capitalism, represented in turn by the English mine owner Gould and the Californian financier-evangelist Holroyd. Conrad's satiric address to both models, as well as to the local forces of church and state in the fictional Central American country of Costaguana, produces a coil of political intrigue from which no ideology, and no man, emerges unsullied. The moral plot concentrates on the titular hero, a rehabilitated Lord Jim who is "absolutely above reproach,"[7] a super-factotum serving multiple European masters and managing the local labor force. Nostromo – literally "our man" – is a skeleton key who fits all social situations, carrying the novel's fantasy of upward mobility and individual autonomy within an economic system that compromises everyone it touches. The arena of empire, which promises clean fortunes but involves rank greed, dramatizes the ebbing of prestige and charismatic power from the modern male quest-romance. And so Nostromo rescues a cargo of silver but comes in the process to recognize that he is merely a pawn of amoral state and business interests; faced with an honorless world, he steals the treasure and loses his soul.

The source of that deadly treasure is the San Tomé mine, a "wealth-producing thing" at the center of *Nostromo*, an "imperium in imperio" whose yield "had been paid for in its own weight of human bones. Whole tribes of Indians had perished in the exploitation" (p. 75). As in other parts of Conrad's colonial world, the wealth of raw materials tempts many to venal actions, but inspires few to genuine industry. The development of Sulaco is a farce, "since all enterprise had been stupidly killed in the land" (p. 124). Gould himself plans to blow up the mine rather than cede it to a Costaguanan military junta. Although the explosion never happens, it is one of many bombs lurking inside Conrad's texts, balancing out the otherwise stultifying sense that plots are bogged down in philosophical speculation, and colonies bogged down in failed modernization. In the pocket-worlds of Conrad's imagination – isolated Sulaco, backwards Patusan, the ship "Narcissus" – there is always the sense of muffled action followed, in the end, by a violent accident or intrusion. Conrad's novels at times emphasize anti-historical stasis even as they address potential for sudden social change in every corner of the globe.

Like his sometime friend H. G. Wells, Conrad rewrites the condition-of-England novel. Conrad's blending of imperial adventure with impressionist narration represents one formal response to dislocations and opportunities that result when social and literary conventions enshrined in national tradition are confronted by a British-administered world empire. In the case of Wells, who was always less deferential to the art-novel tradition of Henry James and Conrad himself, we find formal responses to the same dislocations and opportunities distributed among innovative fictional subgenres, including Wells's "scientific romances" of the 1890s and his "anti-novels" of the Edwardian period.

Wells's romances constitute his most enduring works. Engaging the intellectual and political ferment of the high imperial era, whether in the form of social darwinism or Boer-War-era national anxiety, the romances recurrently exhibit twin specters of degeneration and invasion that threaten the body politic. *The Island of Dr. Moreau* (1896) employs a conceit of forced evolution: the mad vivisectionist Moreau cuts and flays the bodies of large mammals until he has remade them into rough human form, whereupon he reconditions their souls with rudiments of law and social authority. Wells frames this scenario as a gothic horror version of the colonial situation. When Prendick, the narrator, lands on a remote island and encounters Moreau's Beast People, his baffled reactions oscillate between two categories, the nonwhite/native and subhuman/nonhuman. Prendick's delayed decoding of the awful truth reads like a Frankensteinian fever dream organized by an evolutionary thesis. It also anticipates Conrad's *Heart of Darkness*, with Prendick in the role of Conrad's narrator Marlow, the reasonable Englishman who discovers a cruel and corrupted genius of European art and science at the outer reaches of civilization. In these fables of empire, supposedly enlightened but frankly brutal men hold power over physically superior masses whom they control with guns, whips, and laws.

Again like Marlow, Prendick proves to be a self-conscious narrator, drawing our attention back to the filters that limit and color his adventure. The gaps in his tale are not accidental interruptions but the substance of the novel itself. Moreover, Prendick comes to see the irrational, degraded sides of Moreau and his pitiable creatures as intimately, harrowingly reflective of himself. They are not just subhuman others, but secret sharers who release potent Darwinian anxieties provoked by new racial sciences and by late Victorian historiography concerning European decline. Haunted by *doppelgangers* in the manner of R. L. Stevenson's Dr. Jekyll, Bram Stoker's Jonathan Harker, and Oscar Wilde's Dorian Gray, Wells's protagonists confront social and psychic degeneration in fiction that blends gothic sensationalism with realism's objectifying scientific aims.

Thematic preoccupations of Wells's 1890s writings carry over into his Edwardian mid-career novels, where his narrator-protagonists stretch realism's conventions. Thinly veiled doubles of Wells, they chafe against the old-school gentility of Austen and James, and inject copious discursive and polemic materials until the bubble of the reader's suspended disbelief begins to burst. Wells rewrites the condition-of-England novel in terms of two revolutionary pressures on inherited values: the paradigm shift from the Victorian Pax Britannica to the new world order of global capitalism, and the modernization of sexual and gender relations. Although Wells considered his Edwardian novels mainstream fiction, they are notable for their expansive personalities and forms, bulging as if in sympathetic response to the exponential growth of human knowledge and technological power. The modernist ambition to write a book-of-the-world, evident in Joyce's *Ulysses*, Pound's *Cantos* and Stein's *The Making of Americans*, finds a rational and didactic (rather than symbolic or mythic) form in

Wells. Like Leonard Woolf he viewed the coming postcolonial era in terms of an urgent necessity for an enlightened, humane league of nations; indeed it is a hallmark of Wells's outlook that he, unlike other modernists, believed in slow reform of civil institutions, rather than metaphysical doom, as a proper subject for serious fiction.

In Wells's novels the coming globalized world, with its ceaseless economic growth and scientific change, produces rootless heroes eager to throw open the gates to the future, but hampered and hobbled by English traditionalism. In *Tono-Bungay* (1908) Wells reorganizes the coming-of-age novel so that the hero, George Ponderevo, develops along the boom and bust curve of capitalist speculation – his life story as unstable as the business cycle. Ponderevo observes that modern social life is full of "unmanageable realities" forcing him to record "inconsecutive observations" rather than writing a seamless autobiographical account.[8] Tracking "the broad slow decay of the great social organism of England," Ponderevo believes that the problem lies in the "tumorous growth-process" of the London metropolis, center of an imperial system that witnesses an "unassimilable enormity of traffic" (pp. 70, 418). The English novel, like the social system from which it arose, cannot assimilate such global traffic without losing its Jamesian sense of stylistic proportion and its Austenian sense of social composure.

In one episode late in *Tono-Bungay*, Ponderevo extracts a radioactive material, quap, from the African coast, but cannot bring it back to England because it eats away at the ship's hold. In addition to revealing the darker side of colonial resource-extraction, this parodic Conradian episode enacts figuratively the problem of older forms freighted with a new imperial cargo. Wells (ever the didact) makes this clear, noting that the breakup of the quap-loaded ship represents "in matter exactly what the decay of our old culture is in society, a loss of traditions and distinctions and assured reactions" (p. 355).

Wells subsequently links the death of old English ways to a much more hopeful development: the advent of the New Woman, and resulting shifts in sexual mores and gender politics. *The New Machiavelli* (1911), for example, describes a narrator frustrated by the hidebound sexual attitudes of his society, which continues to honor monogamous marriage – patent lunacy to him – as a reasonable way to manage love, sex, reproduction, property rights, and platonic intimacy in one holy social device. This narrator, an ambitious and adulterous politician named Richard Remington, is brought to ruin by his cavalier flouting of middle class propriety. If *Tono-Bungay* rescripts the *Bildungsroman* as the life story of a commodity rather than a soul, *The New Machiavelli* shifts the terrain from commerce to politics, giving us the autobiography of an entirely political animal. The book is, by its own description, one of the first novels ever dedicated to "the white passion of statecraft."[9] The novel fizzes with Remington's mania to rebuild the world along rational lines, his unshakable utilitarian faith in the potency of the modern state, and his grand vision of "harbours and shining navies, great roads engineered marvellously, jungles cleared and conquered" (p. 10).

Wells's interests in the globalizaton of politics and the modernization of sex converge in Remington, who insists that England cannot move forward without a revolution in manners: "A people that will not valiantly face and understand and admit love and passion can understand nothing whatever" (p. 109). The novel sees itself as feminist, though it remains rather strongly focused on the sexual liberation of the hero rather than on his abandoned wife or his compromised mistress. Feminist readers may well be dubious about Remington's deepest legislative wish: to implement a program of eugenicist investment in motherhood for the strengthening of the British Empire, a policy that would transfer sexual control of women from the patriarchal family to the patriarchal state. Like other Wells protagonists, Remington combines thwarted rationalism and sexual persecution, both of which fuel his monomania, and, at the level of the text's form, drive the restless energy that Wells himself exerted against the mortmain of Victorian cultural institutions.

In his pursuit of an unconventional modern novel centered on iconoclastic and sexually restless protagonists, Wells could be said to anticipate Virginia Woolf. Like Wells, Woolf seems to have found plots of colonial travel and themes of imperial adventure highly suggestive devices in her efforts to reinvent English fiction. But Woolf's novels write against the imperial-patriarchal values that Wells sometimes voices. Consider the arch portrait of Victorian life in Woolf's *Orlando* (1928): "The life of the average woman was a succession of childbirths. She married at nineteen and had fifteen or eighteen children by the time she was thirty; for twins abounded. Thus the British Empire came into existence; and thus . . . sentences swelled, adjectives multiplied, lyrics became epics."[10] In a sense Woolf's vocation is to convert epic back into lyric, reworking heroic national or imperial narratives of the British Empire into a splintered set of riffs on the English novel, reconceived as chamber drama, essay-novel of ideas, elegy, ekphrastic prose-poem, and pageant-play. In those formal hybrids Woolf maintains a critical interest in socially influential myths, produced by the English ruling class, that place men at the center of world progress and civilization.

In recent years postcolonial critical approaches to Woolf have concentrated readers' attention on the impassioned suspicion of imperialism and patriarchy that runs through her career. From virile Richard Dalloway in *The Voyage Out* (1915) to graying Peter Walsh in *Mrs. Dalloway* (1925) to retired Colonel Pargiter of *The Years* (1937) to ancient Bart Oliver in *Between the Acts* (1941), Woolf's novels measure the superannuation of the empire man as a fixture of English life. In her most experimental novels, *Orlando* and *The Waves* (1931), Woolf engages Orientalist and imperialist themes obliquely, but they remain crucial predicates to her stylistic innovations. Even in *The Voyage Out*, her most conventionally realist novel, Woolf finds a colonial setting – a South American tourist enclave – useful for developing a dissenting female version of the *Bildungsroman*. Woolf was clearly taken with *Heart of Darkness*: it is no coincidence that *The Voyage Out* begins, like Conrad's, on the banks of the Thames, moves to the edge of a distant continent, then traces a river journey into unknown geographic and psychic territories, ending in death and a thwarted engagement. Both fictions rewrite imperial quest-romance, using physical journeys to stage an exploration of (Western) consciousness. And in both Conradian impressionism and Woolfian stream of consciousness, dissolution of psychic boundaries in a colonial setting serves as a thematic base for the dissolution of realist perspective.

It is precisely at the deepest part of the river journey in *The Voyage Out*, at the farthest geographical remove from English values, that the most semantically ambiguous and sexually iconoclastic writing in the novel occurs. Similarly, in *Orlando* Woolf plunges her reader into a fantasy of gender ambiguity during the most Orientalist portions of the text, set in Constantinople (and inspired by Woolf's vicarious investment in Vita Sackville-West's journeys in Turkey and Persia). Orlando's sudden shift from a male to a female body is Woolf's riposte to the fiction of masculine imperial adventure. It is not hyperbolic to say that a pair of Turkish trousers is the pivotal device that allows Woolf to pull off her gender-shifting plot with a subtle nonchalance. Although Woolf indulges in a stock Western notion of the Orient as a setting for sexual experimentation, the figure of Orlando introduces an unstable layer of irony that indemnifies Woolf to some degree from her fantasy of the sensual, licentious East. The endless play of desire embodied in Orlando, who is always thirsty for experience at the frontiers of known cultural and social space, echoes Conrad's restless narrator Marlow. Neither can quite resolve the contradiction between real and ideal worlds that are thoroughly dramatized in the encounter of East and West.

Ranging over time and space with infinitely flexible narrative devices in *Orlando*, Woolf uses such perspectival freedom in *The Waves* to further destabilize the English novel. A nested account of six lives told through blurred and twining presentations by six voices, *The Waves* enlists imperial adventure – associated with an absent seventh protagonist, Percival – as crucial ground for Woolf's distinctive techniques. Like Joyce's *Ulysses*, *The Waves* bids modernism's farewell to novelistic conventions grown stale and predictable; its surrogate author Bernard expresses Woolf's own feeling that to write complex, innovative fiction means always facing a "devastating sense of grey ashes in a burnt-out grate."[11] Bernard's project falters, but Woolf herself finds a way forward by smashing the base elements of characterization until her protagonists have split into vocal streams, mere tissues of language. Still, her experiment is tethered to Percival, the familiar empire man who serves as a gravitational pole around which the voices swirl and weave. From India, Percival connects Woolf's six linguistic ghosts to the real world of physical action and brute causality, of history and of death. Percival's link to the extramural, extra-English world is a coded story expressing its author's sense of both the fertility and the claustrophobia of the English novel tradition, a vexed inheritance that we might call "the penalty of living in an old civilisation with a notebook" (p. 184).

Afterworlds: Cary, Durrell, and Scott

Many English novels of the late modernist period, including well-known works by George Orwell, Evelyn Waugh, Graham Greene, and Malcolm Lowry, take up dramatic possibilities inherent in the decline of British imperialism. The decline receives sustained treatment in Cary, Durrell, and Scott. Cary's African novels present colonial life with a striking terseness, verging on minimalism. In the preface to his most admired work, *Mister Johnson* (1939), he describes the modest scope of his slice-of-the-end-of-empire novel: it "illuminates only a very narrow scene with a moving ray not much more comprehensive than a handtorch."[12] And *Mister Johnson* is, like Cary's other novels of the period – *Aissa Saved* (1932), *An American Visitor* (1933), and *The African Witch* (1936) – organized by narrative slivers and snapshots, with no great harmonic devices undergirding divisions of time. In effect Cary, who served in the Nigerian Colonial Service during the period 1913–19, uses a dispassionate, almost sardonic tone – what we might call the Administrative Point of View – to ward off the imposition of grand themes on his precise, present-tense depiction of the Anglo-African world. Unlike a modernist author seeking to elevate the colonial encounter into a metaphysical showdown of Self and Other, Cary deflates his own pretensions with a light satirical touch. Here otherness (racial, linguistic, national) operates under the sign of a limited and relativized theory of cultural difference: Africans are not absolutely unlike Europeans as in some primitivist fantasy, but neither are they fully assimilable to European-based social and political life.

For Cary's administrators themselves, such as Rudbeck in *Mister Johnson*, or Gore in *An American Visitor*, the supreme value is "bushcraft," a Kiplingesque capacity to get things done without ideological muddle. As a guide to late-colonial Africa, Cary anticipates the postcolonial era of development motivated by a technocratic rather than a redemptive quest for human betterment. His critique of empire, such as it is, resembles Kipling's: no hard-biting interrogation of imperialism's fundamental values, but frequent and stinging criticisms of colonial failure at the level of practice.

Taken as a whole, Cary's African novels give both an insider's guide to colonial bureaucracy and, at one angle of remove, an antiromantic presentation of native life. The knowing narrators are neither as bloodthirsty as the warriors and soldiers on either side of the colonial line, nor as single-minded as the missionaries and miners chasing God and Mammon in Africa, nor even quite as intellectually naive as the still-green "politicals" who feature as the moral and dramatic center in the novels. In *An American Visitor* the plot centers on Bewsher, an eccentric colonial administrator who has dedicated his career to reorganizing the local Birri villages into a tribal nation, and who is ultimately, and with thick irony, killed in a Birri revolt. Bewsher is a rationalist and an idealist. His comeuppance imparts the lesson that ideal schemes of westernization are as likely to fail in Africa as are idealized schemes of preserving a premodern "African way of life."[13] Bewsher finds a perfect counterpart in the American visitor, Marie Hasluck, an amateur anthropologist who tolerates enlightened British authority while celebrating the putative joy and simplicity of Birri life. Bewsher and Hasluck marry, and we see their naiveté – equal parts starry-eyed modernization and noble-savage preservationism – punished by Bewsher's murder.

The plot of corrected naiveté – which also pertains to other Cary wives such as Celia Rudbeck in *Mister Johnson* – takes center stage, giving the lie to any surviving idealisms, whether pro- or anti colonialist. The administrative point of view undercuts the anthropological one, challenging those who would impute a single moral essence to any ethnic or national collective. Cary's fiction retails racist stereotypes of Africans as childlike and unruly, but it also devotes much energy to skewering the hypocrisy and racism of British colonialism across all of its sectors – military, governmental, religious, and commercial. And if Cary's most memorable depictions of African experience – the Birri in *American Visitor*, Aladai in *The African Witch*, Mister Johnson – represent a stubborn stereotype of the native spiritually mangled by westernization, it is no doubt to expose the colonial mission as a failed or quixotic project of cultural transplantation.

With his laconic and sober sense of British rule in sub-Saharan Africa as a historically limited project, Cary fashions novels that are themselves self-limited and anti-climactic operations. Perspectival shifts in his texts are rapid and dramatically unremarkable. Here colonial life is neither magnificently absurd, as in Conrad, nor morally fraught, as in Greene, nor quite as sour and satirical as in Waugh. Working in the 1930s, Cary offers precisely the kind of bathetic fiction that one might design in order to tell the story of an empire contracting into a commonwealth, a fiction shaped by the tattered idealism of a barely credible social mission, but unwilling to dismantle imperial ideals altogether as long as there is work to be done.

Cary's African novels, bearing the residual responsibility of colonial administration and the residual authority of realism, stand at a striking remove from the work of Lawrence Durrell. Durrell's work eschews both political responsibility and referential authority in the pursuit of a high poetics of prose aimed at recapturing the stylistic brio of the modernist *roman fleuve*. His *The Alexandria Quartet*, comprised of *Justine* (1957), *Balthazar* (1958), *Mountolive* (1958), and *Clea* (1960), stands as the most conceptually intricate of the major fictional projects dedicated to empire's aftermath, with the possible exception of Doris Lessing's *The Golden Notebook* (1962). Like Lessing, Durrell wants to reinvent the novel for the era after modernism, after Freudianism, after imperialism. His is a strenuously experimental prose that expends its gorgeous energy on a floating circle of sexually peripatetic, skittishly introspective characters whose jaded and jangled nerves reflect the heroically anti-heroic stance of the existential 1950s. Like so many others in that era, Durrell uses the novel sequence as a way to reinvigorate the form after modernism's spectacular experiments in megafiction and metafiction. Lessing's *Children of Violence* sequence (1952–69) – set partially in colonial Rhodesia, Anthony Burgess's *A Malayan Trilogy* (1956–59), Paul Scott's *Raj Quartet* (1966–74), and *The Alexandria Quartet* all present late-colonial experience in multi-plot, multi-protagonist, multi-volume form, carrying forward the tradition of Conrad, Joyce, Woolf, and Wells. But they parcel out the narrative in several discrete units, in keeping with a post-World War II market for serious fiction that had begun to devalue the epic grandiosities, symbolic unities, and epistemological privileges associated with high metropolitan modernism.

In *The Alexandria Quartet* Durrell develops an aesthetic of associative logic and aleatory plotting to reflect his characters' sense of social fragmentation. Confronting a world of disintegrating values, Durrell centers his story on an artistic quest, that of the writer Darley, whose frustrated efforts to find a viable form of expression frame the first and last volumes in the Quartet, *Justine* and *Clea*. Durrell's baroque prose incorporates many features of modernist writing: vivid urban patrols in search of sensation, atmospheres of sensual discord and overripe classicism, impairments of sexuality and fertility, occulted versions of high European culture safekept by coteries of seedy intellectuals, pervasive illnesses in bodies glutted on civilized values, fugitive beauties of well-wrought symbols, and, above all, master themes of "deracination and failure."[14] His novels even recycle the names of modernist characters – Donkin from Conrad's *The Nigger of the 'Narcissus,'* Grishkin from Eliot's "Whispers of Immortality," or Scobie from Greene's *The Heart of the Matter* – as if to reassemble the scraps from a disappearing trove of literary meaning.

On the other hand, Durrell rejects a model of the writer as a modernist magus who can contain and explain everything. His authorial surrogate Darley shifts value and meaning away from aesthetic heroism and onto the city itself, Alexandria, that great polyglot beauty. In *Justine* "[o]nly the city is real"; it is also poetry incarnate: "Rue Bab-el-Mandep, Rue Abou-el-Dardar, Minet-el-Barrol (streets slippery with discarded fluff from the cotton marts), Nouzha (the rose-garden, some remembered kisses)" (pp. 9, 63). This kind of writing entails fantasy, but Darley tries his best to forfeit the social power often assumed by alienated Western travelers who suck the juice of the exotic East. Darley is a figure of such deep ennui and inertia that he subsides into the landscape rather than standing astride it. He gives himself and his ego over to the city, experiencing "a death of the self uttered in every repetition of the word Alexandria, Alexandria" (p. 63).

As an Irishman adrift in the postwar, postcolonial world, Darley already understands himself to be a "mental refugee" (p. 39); an existential hero on the margins of Europe, he fashions his story along the lines of the French writer Albert Camus, cut with the sexual threnodies and literary tricks of another great expatriate of the 1950s, Vladimir Nabokov. Darley finds himself alone, yet immersed in a tangle of emotional and sexual relations; isolated from Europe, yet at the very crossroads of ancient and modern Mediterranean empires. For Darley as for the other principle characters, there is no need to challenge prevailing sexual, aesthetic, or social conventions, because in old Alexandria everything is already historically contingent. Here corroded or abandoned, there revived or rediscovered, human values are subject only to the test of immediate existence rather than to any transcendental standard.

The jaded worldview at the core of Durrell's project clashes throughout with the earnestness and beauty of his prose. As a self-styled "investigation of modern love," *The Alexandria Quartet* has its own kind of serious business, which is to drill down to the core of "the whole portentous scrimmage of sex itself" (p. 185). Both that project and Durrell's open presentation of shifting sexual appetites and practices are attached to the Orientalist fantasy of escape from the sexual puritanism of bourgeois

Europe. Alert to the clichés that hover around his libidinal experimentation in Alexandria, Durrell tries to mitigate them with a relentlessly self-conscious and elegiac tone. How, his writing seems to ask, can one truly reinvent the language of sex in the mannerly English novel, when one finds oneself so hopelessly belated, and outflanked by the long human history of love in the Mediterranean? Durrell's singular contribution to the English novel at mid-century emerges from this predicament. He represents both the intimacy and the alienation of East and West as a long bout of postimperial, postcoital tristesse. In *Clea*, at the end of the sequence, a wounded Darley, bleached of mere human passion, writes from an insular retreat away from the hothouse of Alexandria, a fitting etiolation and miniaturization of the arena for English fiction in the era after empire. But Durrell does not indulge in melancholic farewells to, nor anxious disavowals of, the old burden of British world hegemony. Although he was, like Joyce Cary, an Irishman and was, like Kipling, born and bred in India, his fiction finds a roost in a semicolonial, classical city-state that quite defies the predictable Manichean dualisms of Ireland, India, and the rest of the English-speaking colonial world.

By contrast, Paul Scott's *The Raj Quartet* offers a *summa* of the agonized, intimate relations of colonizer and colonized as a subject for English fiction in the twentieth century. His novel sequence – *The Jewel in the Crown* (1966), *The Day of the Scorpion* (1968), *The Towers of Silence* (1971), and *A Division of the Spoils* (1974) – constitutes perhaps the most ambitious treatment of the life and death of the British Empire in the contemporary era. It presents a number of familiar characters from earlier works like Forster's *A Passage to India* (1924): the dutiful military man, the overzealous junior officer, the grizzled liberal, the naive white woman, the wise crone, the earnest, Anglicized native intellectual. In fact *The Raj Quartet* reads like *A Passage to India* rewritten so that Forster's Ronny Heaslop and Dr. Aziz's wife and all the Burtons and the Turtons have their say in embedded first-person narratives. In this perspectival mode, Scott himself functions as a master editor, sifting through the recollections of several characters in a scrupulous attempt to approach the truth by parallax, to remove bias from his chronicle of the end of the Anglo-Indian colonial experiment.

The very scale of *The Raj Quartet*, whose first and last volumes are especially hefty, is a formal feature suggestive of the efforts undergone by Scott to do justice to his theme: every point of view must get its due until the accounts have been rendered. In the first volume, for example, the voluble sophisticate Lady Chatterjee follows the prim professional Miss Crane, just as the progressive bureaucrat White redresses the old soldier Brigadier Reid. But these are not black-and-white cartoon voices: Scott never fails to offer moral nuance and sympathetic shade, relativizing and ironizing the expected views associated with class, gender, race, and national stereotypes. Looking back on events during the Mayapore uprising in the early 1940s, the administrator White gives voice to the underlying thrust of Scott's method, noting that even when one combines "civil and military" views, "there are of course some inaccuracies, or anyway gaps in the narrative or alternative interpretations, that would need attention if a more general and impersonal picture were required to emerge."[15] The more general picture offered by the *Quartet* builds out of Scott's infinite attention to detail, his wariness of symbolic condensation, and his bravura reinvention of an expansive Victorian social realism that oversees characters and scenes, "like toys set out by kneeling children intent on pursuing their grim but necessary games" (p. 114).

Such jovial narratorial confidence sets Scott's work apart from the modernists whose fictions were dedicated to exploring limits of human knowledge, whether philosophical and cultural for Conrad, practical and political for Wells, or psychic and historical for Woolf. Piling up facts and scenes, sights and smells of late colonial India, Scott instead seeks – at times anxiously – to remove aesthetic distortion and thereby to mitigate political misunderstanding between East and West. *The Jewel in the Crown* opens the narrative sequence by recounting "two dastardly attacks on Englishwomen" and proceeds almost as a series of testimonies given at trial (p. 282). In this juridical plot, Scott poses sadistic English policeman Ronald Merrick against elegant repatriated Indian Hari Kumar: the first is a born outsider moved to the inside of the colonial apparatus of white supremacy, the other a bred insider (and public school boy) thrust to the margins of Mayapore society and revealed to himself as a "lickspittle of the Raj" (p. 257). For Merrick and Kumar, as for so many others, ethical contours of the self are shaped and warped by a system of structural injustice, a situation that Scott confronts with full faith in historical fiction as an instrument for cross-cultural understanding.

Moving between the intimacy of rape and the grand historical scale of nation-formation, Scott's work painstakingly reproduces Anglo-Indian life in all of its everyday particularity, echoing the fiction of Kipling with its deep verisimilitude of detail and dialect. Scott's commitment to clear, forensic explanation and to concrete sensual commemoration can have two perhaps unwelcome effects. First, his didactic narrators are given to pat allegorical gestures: "You understand what I am telling you? That MacGregor and Bibighar are the place of the white and the place of the black?" (p. 141). Second, the rich, evocative realism can, perhaps inadvertently, produce a sepia-tinted nostalgia for empire that mutes any criticism of British rule in the first place. Indeed Scott's writing does revive some familiar colonial clichés: here the air is warm and voluptuous; there we find "great inky pools of darkness" (p. 133). In this sense Scott's fiction sometimes reinforces rather than unsettles established cultural values, with the odd result that his novels of the 1960s can appear to twenty-first-century readers as emanations from the old colonial era, while the restless, self-divided modernist fiction of Tagore, Conrad, Wells, and Woolf continues to offer shocking anticipatory glimpses of our present world, a world never quite postcolonial and therefore not yet postmodern.

NOTES

1 Benita Parry, "Problems in Current Theories of Colonial Discourse," *Oxford Literary Review* 9 (1987), 55; Edward Said, *Culture and Imperialism* (New York: Vintage, 1994), p. 188.

2 Elleke Boehmer, *Empire, The National, and the Postcolonial 1890–1920* (New York: Oxford University Press, 2005), p. 175.

3 Raymond Williams, *The Politics of Modernism* (London: Verso, 1989), p. 44.

4 Salman Rushdie, Introduction to Kipling's *Soldiers Three* and *In Black and White* (London: Penguin, 1993), p. ix.

5 Noel Annan, "Kipling's Place in the History of Ideas," *Victorian Studies* 3 (1959–60), 323–44.

6 Rabindranath Tagore, *The Home and the World*, trans. Surendranath Tagore (London: Penguin, 2005), p. 121.

7 Joseph Conrad, *Nostromo* (Harmondsworth: Penguin, 1983), p. 46.

8 H. G. Wells, *Tono–Bungay* (Oxford: Oxford University Press, 1997), pp. 13, 11.

9 H. G. Wells, *The New Machiavelli* (London: Penguin, 2005), p. 10.

10 Virginia Woolf, *Orlando* (San Diego: Harcourt, 1956), p. 229.

11 Virginia Woolf, *The Waves* (San Diego: Harcourt, 1956), p. 80.

12 Joyce Cary, *Mister Johnson* (New York: New Directions, 1989), p. vi.

13 Joyce Cary, *An American Visitor* (London: Everyman, 1995), p. 209.

14 Lawrence Durrell, *Justine* (New York: Penguin, 1985), p. 180.

15 Paul Scott, *The Jewel in the Crown* (New York: Avon, 1966), p. 324.

3

MARIA DI BATTISTA

Realism and rebellion in Edwardian and Georgian fiction

The objective and impartial account of the world that realist fiction purports to give its readers is not calculated to foment rebellion, or rally public will to rectify economic injustice, or press for legislative remedies for social wrongs. The Edwardians and the Georgians (people living during Edward VII and George V's successive reigns) wrote about socially inflammatory issues such as marriage and labor laws, property rights, women's suffrage, Home Rule for Ireland, and colonialist rule over an unsettled empire. Yet even when most inflamed, Edwardian and Georgian fiction appealed less to emotional outrage than to the educated heart. Rebel authors, those "dangerous clever fellows with all their atheism, sex and socialism," as J. B. Priestley drolly characterized them, wrote in "an atmosphere of hopeful debate," persuaded "that men might be converted to a cause, that society might be rationally transformed, if they could win the debate."[1]

They carried that debate into novels, through richly detailed representations of the sorry but changeable state of things. Inheriting and refining conventions developed by Victorian and French realism and naturalism, Edwardian realism's documentary machinery was so efficient at presenting social data that Arnold Bennett could envision for fiction the possibility of an "absolute realism." The possibility had occurred to Bennett in reviewing Chekhov's stories, in which "no part of the truth is left out, no part is exaggerated."[2] A Chekhovian ideal, translated into the empirical language of British realism, is reflected in meticulous representations of where and how people lived (including building materials, layout, the décor of their houses, apartments or, as the case may be, hovels); inventories of the things they bought and sold, and at what price; detailed accounts of routines that regulated their lives and the wages they earned, or had garnished; candid reports of how they courted, and under what constraints; what class they belonged to; how they made their money and how they held onto – or lost – it. The narrator of *Kipps* (1905), H. G. Wells's comic *Bildungsroman* of a lower-class hero daunted by obstacles to his social betterment, sums up the realist credo when he proclaims, "The business of a novelist is not ethical principle, but facts."[3]

In realist fiction's draconian separation of fact and value facts had a way of assuming the accusatory form of Dreadful Statistics[4] that exposed whatever was false and deplorable in the existing order. "We are going to write about it all," Wells, in a burst of reformist energy, wrote in "The Contemporary Novel" (1914): "We are going to write about business and finance and politics and precedence and pretentiousness and decorum and indecorum, until a thousand pretences and ten thousand impostures shrivel in the cold, clear air of our elucidations."[5]

Wells thus articulates a common assumption that a cool-headed realist rather than a hot-blooded agitator was more likely to advance a progressive agenda of social reform, especially in a country that, haunted by memories of its own Civil War and of the French Terror of 1789, recoiled from any use of the word *Revolution* that did not have the word *Glorious* preceding it. Perhaps playing on this endemic fear of violent revolution, Ford Madox Ford, writing an editorial manifesto to inaugurate his journal *The English Review* (1908), proposed that "Only from the arts can any safety for the future of the State be found."[6] Ford went on to sound a rallying cry that was to unite two generations of realists in a shared belief:

> What we so very much need today is a picture of the life we live. It is only the imaginative writer who can supply this, since no collection of facts, and no tabulation of figures, can give us any sense of proportion. In England, the country of Accepted Ideas, the novelist who is intent merely to register . . . is almost unknown. Yet it is England probably that most needs him, for England, less than any of the nations, knows where it stands, or to what it tends. (p. 31)

However willing and able to contest the reality claims of Accepted Ideas, the Edwardian and Georgian realists were generally more concerned with presenting the evidentiary case for social and moral reform than in suggesting concrete strategies for achieving it. Novelists rather than policy-makers, they shared the general outlook of the Schlegel sisters as Forster describes them in *Howards End* (1910):

> In their own fashion they cared deeply about politics, though not as politicians would have us care; they desired that public life should mirror whatever is good in the life within. Temperance, tolerance and sexual equality were intelligible cries to them; whereas they did not follow our Forward Policy in Tibet with the keen attention that it merits, and would at times dismiss the whole British Empire with a puzzled, if reverent sigh. Not out of them are the

shows of history erected: the world would be a gray, bloodless place were it composed of Miss Schlegels. But the world being what it is, perhaps they shine out in it like stars.[7]

Forster was entitled to be proud of his morally radiant heroines, for there are, in fact, very few stellar beings in the realist fiction of the time. They were overshadowed and outnumbered by characters representative of ordinary rather than exceptional humanity. The more typical the character, the more credible the novelist's claims that temperance, tolerance, and sexual equality are public and not just private goods. Bennett, for example, records how a public laughingstock who inspired *The Old Wives' Tale* (1908) – "a fat, shapeless, ugly, and grotesque" woman whose life, unknown to those enjoying a laugh at her expense, was a tragedy – was too odd to serve as a novelistic heroine. "It is an absolute rule," Bennett explained: "I knew that I must choose the sort of woman who would pass unnoticed in a crowd."[8] In forswearing oddity and championing the inconspicuous, Edwardian and Georgian realists created characters that often were morally undistinguished and sometimes barely likeable. Wells's Kipps is singularly without any laudable traits except the ability to survive a spirit-killing job and a soul-killing engagement long enough to inherit a fortune that makes him a free and happy man. Galsworthy often finds himself repelled by the unremitting stolidity of his most original creation, Soames Forsyte, and seems surprised at the thorough unlovability of the man. Even when characters possess a certain charm, they are meant to "interest" – an important word in the realist lexicon – but never dazzle us. Constance and Sophia, "heroines" of *The Old Wives' Tale*, appeal to our sympathy during the course of the long narrative of their lives, as do "The Daughters of the Late Colonel" in the briefer space Katherine Mansfield devotes to them; yet none can transfix us like Hardy's passionate beings or pique our moral curiosity like any one of Joyce's Dubliners. D. H. Lawrence in *Sons and Lovers* (1913) is so fierce a realist in depicting the human debacle of industrial capitalism that he hardly cares whether we cheer for Paul Morel, his mother, or Miriam and Clara, the women who love him – only Paul's coal miner father shines out, in the physical dignity of his baffled and corroded nature.

This dethronement of character from the elevated place it had attained in much Victorian fiction was part of a larger realist revolt against idealism as a moral and social creed. Idealistic conceptions of a humanity ruled by a higher, selfless and sexless nature paled in the unflattering light cast by Darwin's theory of evolution, Herbert Spencer's evolutionary sociology,[9] Schopenhauer's all-consuming Will to Live, and Nietzsche's iconoclastic vitalism exalting the Will to Power. After these soul- and tradition-shattering ideas were naturalized in Ibsen's disconcerting realism, which revealed degradation and incoherence just beneath the well-appointed surfaces of bourgeois life, no realist deserving of the name could idealize patriarchal regimes or look sympathetically on their attempts to sublimate sexuality. When a male family friend willing to support Wells's feminist heroine Ann Veronica in her bid for independence confesses that "when I hear you talk of earning a living it's as if I heard of an archangel going on the Stock Exchange – or Christ selling doves," she risks offending her male ally by objecting that

> all this sort of thing is very well as sentiment, but does it correspond with the realities? Are women truly such angelic things and men so chivalrous? You men have, I know, meant to make us queens and goddesses, but in practice – well, look...at the stream of girls one meets going to work of a morning, round-shouldered, cheap and underfed! They aren't queens, and no one is treating them as queens. (p. 103)

The world being what it was and human nature being what it is, any sentimental appeal to exalted character as a moral beacon seemed a futile gesture. Realists depended instead on an array of incriminating facts to bring dark and disgraceful conditions of modern life into public view and so expose the baleful human costs of class, empire, and male domination. In thus challenging the most obdurate and venerated institutions of the British social system – Family, Property, Religion, Class, Sexual Idealism – whose laws often made it hard, if not impossible to cultivate the good "life within," Edwardian and Georgian realists were as subversive of tradition as the most militant avant-gardist.

That we seldom think of them this way, that we might be surprised to see Edwardian luminaries (Wells, Bennett, Galsworthy) coupled with less conventional Georgians (the modernists Lawrence, Woolf, Joyce), is largely due to an historic myth about the advent of modernist literature that was crafted, with less ambivalence than the facts required, by Virginia Woolf. Identifying herself by birth and imaginative disposition with the Georgians, Woolf pronounced a surprisingly harsh historical verdict on "the failure of the Edwardians – comparative but disastrous . . . how the reign of Edward the Seventh was barren of poet, novelist, or critic; how it followed that the Georgians read Russian novelists in translations . . . how different a story we might have told today had there been living heroes to worship and destroy."[10] In Woolf's estimation, the Edwardians lacked creative power and authority, hence inspired no murderous Oedipal revolt in their artistically ambitious heirs. Their sterility, Woolf implies, had tremendous consequences for literary if not social history. While the

Edwardians, however critical of the social order, remained bound, in name and in spirit, to the reign of their king, the Georgians soon shed the label that affiliated them with a king, a class, a nation, an empire – any association that compromised their ambition to be, in every way, modern. Compared to brash Georgian-modernist experimentations with styles and forms, the conventional storytelling of Edwardian novelists seemed complacent. The Edwardians, as novelist May Sinclair (herself one of them) said of the Humanism, Pragmatism and Vitalism that many of them espoused philosophically, "did little but revolt; they were incapable of accomplishing a revolution."[11]

Sinclair's crucial distinction helps explain an artistic divide that eventually separated Edwardian "materialists," scrupulously chronicling moral, economic, social and environmental conditions of their age, from the "spiritual" Georgians, as Woolf characterizes them. Woolf in particular objected that the Edwardians' "enormous stress upon the fabric of things"[12] had impeded our understanding of "what Life is." Richard Ellmann, responding to Woolf's charge, argued that the Edwardians were secularists convinced "that the transcendent is immanent in the earthy, that to go down far enough is to go up."[13] Whereas traditional novelists capitalized God, the secular Edwardians, Ellmann observes, capitalized Life, endowing it with all the mystery of an allegorical presence, only to be known through its material signs. But Ellmann does not dispute that Woolf and the Georgians, in giving us their vision of "what Life is," did not confine themselves to the external fabric of things, but plunged into an inner world of wayward emotions and unsolicited memories, penetrating unvisited recesses of the mind. Neither cohort, in truth, remained untouched and uninfluenced by the example of the other: Galsworthy concludes *The Man of Property* (1906) with a quasi-mystical interlude, Jolyon Forsyte's inner meditations on time, beauty, and joy as he slips into death; and the Georgians claimed the Edwardian Joseph Conrad for themselves, albeit Conrad's *The Secret Agent* (1907), among the most disjunctively structured and morally opaque of his narratives, owes much of its caricature of British lower-class life and English officialdom to Wells, to whom Conrad dedicated the novel.

Still, the myth of generational and artistic schism has persisted pretty much intact. Like all myths, it has probative value. The Edwardians suffer from low repute for adhering to a thorough but formally sedate realism that pales before the "scrupulous meanness"[14] of Joyce's *Dubliners* (1914). Not that the Edwardians were uninterested in the nature and appalling variety of human meanness – Henry Earlforward, the protagonist of Bennett's *Riceyman Steps* (1923), is a harrowing portrait of a miserly, anorexic soul – but they never seemed willing to risk appearing mean themselves. Certainly not as mean as D. H. Lawrence in excoriating a society that ignored the geological and human slag heaps created by its fuel-hungry industrial and social machinery; or as mean as Katherine Mansfield, who begins one of her first stories, "The Tiredness of Rosabel," by noting "the sickening smell of warm humanity,"[15] and concludes one of her last by recounting how a "boss," seized anew by grief for a son six years dead, methodically blots out the life of a fly by dousing its wings with dollops of ink. The Edwardians were more considerate of their readers' sensibilities. They could deliver harsh truths but never in such harsh terms. Little wonder, then, that Rebecca West, normally caustic in her opinions, was genial in assessing H. G. Wells, George Bernard Shaw, John Galsworthy, and Arnold Bennett – "the Big Four" she calls them – to whom she attributed "the generosity, the charm, the loquacity of visiting uncles."[16]

That they are considered visiting uncles rather than resident patriarchs suggests how little the Edwardians impressed their Georgian successors as authority figures. Where Woolf saw a generational divide, West saw less a chronological than a moral difference between those who "have the courage to recognize change, who dare to remold the status quo" and those who stand by it. West hails the artist of the status quo for his "panache," which, West insists, "is never, no matter what the mob says, insolence. For the insolent artist displays himself in his craftsmanship" (p. 201). The distinction between panache and insolence helps rescue Edwardian realists from the ranks of affable Establishment entertainers to which they are often consigned. Moreover, the Edwardian uncles might reasonably point out to their upstart nephews and nieces that the insolence generally associated with the new modernist style, however artistically dazzling, might not be the most effective way of advancing social reform. Galsworthy's extra-literary career provides an exemplary case in point. He defected from his own class in denouncing the Boer War, supported reform of the House of Lords, and refused a knighthood. He later became first President of PEN, an organization that, according to its charter statement, championed "the principle of unhampered transmission of thought within each nation and between all nations," and asserted its belief that "the necessary advance of the world towards a more highly organized political and economic order renders a free criticism of governments, administrations and institutions imperative."[17] Galsworthy presents an instance of Edwardian revolt that might exceed Sinclair's description.

Wells certainly aimed to exceed it. In Wells one sees the insolence of the writer-activist disparaging the achievements of the too fastidious artist, Henry James, with whom he quarreled over the question of who was the true and not just the finer realist. The quarrel began in earnest when Wells lampooned James in *Boon* (1915) as "the culmination of the Superficial type" for his obsessive attention to form, his all-too-ready acceptance of the very "etiquettes, precedences, associations, claims"[18] that Wells hoped to shrivel with his elucidations. Wells declared his completely different intentions and hopes for the novel: "It is to be the social mediator, . . . the instrument of self-examination, . . . the factory of customs, the criticism of laws and institutions and of social dogmas and ideals" ("The Contemporary Novel," p. 168).

There is more wishful than realistic thinking behind Wells's boast of the novel's potential to manufacture socially enlightened, sexually liberal customs that will forge civil and moral accord. Wells's pursuit of this utopian possibility often takes him to the brink of romantic fantasy – and leaves him there. Kipps and Ann Veronica owe the happy conclusion of their love stories to Wells's tendency to implant fantasy where the facts of the case plausibly dictate a grim outcome. *Tono-Bungay*, his most ambitious "Condition of England" novel, is a bleak exception that proves the rule. The novel's love story concludes when Beatrice, a spoiled heiress whom the narrator has desired since childhood, rejects his offer of marriage, citing an emotional realism supposedly available only to ruined, if still resplendent, women like herself: "You don't understand, because you're a man. A woman, when she's spoilt, is *spoilt*. She's dirty in grain. She's done."[19] This conclusion serves notice that even the most "enlightened" modern fiction – Wells's, for one – is not immune, is alarmingly susceptible, to retrograde sexual politics, with their emotional falsity and invidious distinctions between experienced men of the world and sexually soiled women. Wells's sexual realism turns out to be limited by his own complicated personal history. Even *Ann Veronica*, which does not make an unhappy first love a crucial episode in the emotional life of its heroine, is haunted by the erotic misery of Ramage, a dark double of Wells. In Ramage's towering rage at Ann Veronica's rejection of his advances, Wells approaches the incendiary core of those blind sexual desires that destroy the "good people" of Ford's *The Good Soldier* (1915) and that fuel the ruinous passion of Gerald Crich, a doomed industrial magnate in Lawrence's *Women in Love* (1920), for Gudrun Brangwen, Lawrence's despairing figure of the mad modern artist who favors mechanism over Life.

Wells never confronts the dark gods that in Lawrence preside over the union of Eros with Death. But Wells does brave the malignant idols of mercantile capitalism, whose sinister power is at work in the success and collapse of Tono-Bungay, a magical elixir for a disconsolate humanity. The narrator of *Kipps* had warned, "We're in the beginning of the Sickness of the World" (p. 231). *Love and Mr Lewisham* (1900), *Kipps*, and *Ann Veronica* keep a calibrated fever chart of an ailing social order, but in *Tono-Bungay* disease is a permanent feature of civilization, and of the universe itself. The sickness of the world is symbolized in "quap," the excremental name Wells invents for a commercially valuable radioactive substance. In the narrator's view, radioactivity "is in matter exactly what the decay of our old culture is in society, a loss of traditions and distinctions and assured reactions." Wells sounds here like a Jamesian upholder of distinctions and reactions in elaborating this "grotesque fancy of the ultimate eating away and dry-rotting and dispersal" (p. 314) of material and cultural matter. As a coda to this nightmare-vision of slow annihilation eating away at the world, Wells describes how his narrator-protagonist sails a destroyer, the latest invention of modern engineering genius, down the Thames and out to sea. The author who touted the novel as a factory of customs also insinuates its uses as an engine of destruction.

Whereas Wells embraces methods of "comparative social anatomy" (p. 91) to diagnose the ills of the British social system, Galsworthy is the historian, ethnographer, "house" satirist of the British middle classes, chiding their moral faults while reassuring them about their social future. For Rebecca West, for whom this was a suspect if necessary occupation, he was "really Uncle Phagocyte." She explained:

> For it is the phagocytes who, when the blood is attacked by hostile bacteria, rush to the seat of infection and eat up the invading hosts, and this is the function that Uncle Galsworthy has performed for the middle class. That class had enjoyed a degree of peace and prosperity which was positively unwholesome in the long fat period between the Crimean and the South African Wars, and it had, therefore, fallen a party to the infections of materialism and self-righteousness and narrowness and all the more detestable, decorous, unpalatable forms of hoggishness. Uncle Galsworthy repelled these infections. *(Strange, pp. 202, 203)*

That heroic battle with infection is chronicled in *The Forsyte Saga*, a trilogy spanning three generations of a family whose social importance, property and clannish feeling epitomize the class and the epoch they dominated and whose end they were to oversee. Galsworthy was especially adept at assimilating history into his narrative, so that it seems less like a backdrop against which his drama unfolds than an active force within it. Historic events – the death of Queen Victoria and the Boer War; and legal reforms – the Married Women's Property Act, which recognized the right of women to own property, and the Matrimonial Clauses Act, which granted abused wives the right to seek legal separation – directly affect the trilogy's characters and either limit or extend their freedom.

Given the historical sweep of his tale, Galsworthy feels justified in calling his trilogy a saga, a word he thought communicated the tribal character and heroic endurance of a family whose acquisitive traits embody a national genotype, "the Forsytean tenacity which is in all of us" (p. 5). *Saga* epitomizes Galsworthy's purpose: to give epic gravity to his declared theme – the invasion and subsequent "dissolution" of the rich and well-fortified Forsyte preserve by those "wild raiders, Beauty and Passion" (p. 59). An accomplished and decidedly Liberal storyteller, Galsworthy doesn't pretend to be an impartial observer in depicting hostility between the forces of commerce (and its regard for "real" property) and the powers of art (with its beautiful forms and spiritual goods). He clearly means for Beauty and Passion, incarnated in the quiet, ravishing presence of Irene, Soames's abused wife, to win the final battle, no matter how many brutal defeats, including a marital rape of Irene, and the suicide of Irene's lover, occur along the way.

But the triumph of Galsworthy's realism is his moral portrait of Soames as a man who is so perfectly socialized that he is incapable of individual relationships with other human beings: "Out of his other property, out of all things he had collected, his silver, his pictures, his houses, his investments, he got a secret and intimate feeling; out of her he got none" (p. 70). If it be true that Galsworthy and other Edwardian realists fell short in representing the inner life of their characters, they remain unsurpassed in making us feel how deep "a secret and intimate feeling" for things can go in men, and in societies, where property is bought and valued as an ultimate good. In displacing intimate feelings away from persons and towards things, Soames is the most repellent, obdurate, and pathetic, but also the most *genuine* Forsyte in the saga.

Lawrence, always a shrewd reader, remarked how the Forsytes "seem to us to have lost caste as human beings, and to have sunk to the level of the social being, that peculiar creature that takes the place in our civilization of the slave in the old civilizations."[20] Lawrence, who dismissed Galsworthy's "rebels" as "merely social beings behaving in an anti-social manner" (p. 547), did wonder if Galsworthy had something "more serious" in him that would propel him into an unpropertied world where rebels can actually pursue their revolution and not merely dream of change. Was Galsworthy ultimately paralyzed by "a fear that the world contained nothing but Forsytes"? (p. 544).

If Galsworthy failed to see what a non-Forsytean Briton might be like, Bennett could envision him with dispassionate clarity. Unlike Wells he could imagine characters sufficiently different from his sexual and moral nature to avoid rationalizing and idealizing his own sexual restlessness; and unlike Galsworthy he didn't confine himself to satirizing self-satisfied Island Pharisees. Although the Five Towns, the locale of his most famous fiction, are in their "excessive provincialism" a modern-day wonder of "sublime stupidity,"[21] this only proves to Bennett how necessary the realist is for a culture so ignorant of itself. What its inhabitants dismiss as an arid desert Bennett extols as a microcosm teeming with Life: "It is England in little, lost in the midst of England, unsung by searchers after the extreme; perhaps occasionally somewhat sore at this neglect, but how proud in the instinctive cognizance of its representative features and traits!" (p. 37).

Something resembling Wordsworth's counsel of wise passiveness infuses Bennett's attitude toward the limited prospects and daily repressions he chronicles. Mrs. Baines, the mother in *The Old Wives' Tale* distraught by her daughter's desire to leave home and forge an independent life, is prompted by "a good angel" to glance out her drawing room window "upon the empty, shuttered Square." In that outward glance she momentarily shares her daughter's rebellion. "She too, majestic matron, had strange, brief yearnings for an existence more romantic than this; shootings across her spirit's firmament of tailed comets; soft, inexplicable melancholies" (p. 97). One sees here that Bennett's realism also is infused with a Wordworthian sense of romance lurking in the unsung life of provincial England, disregarded by "searchers after the extreme." But the good angel also returns the mother to the muted but vital drama of daily life. The *Clayhanger* trilogy, *The Old Wives' Tale* and *Riceyman Steps* are written under the protection of this good angel of realism. Bennett trusts its power to divert the melancholy of unromantic existences by turning their inward gazes outward, upon the "interesting details" of their quotidian surroundings.

Some of Bennett's readers believed that Bennett should have wrestled with this good angel rather than submitted to its commands. Henry James, for one, faulted Bennett for failing to exercise the full authority of art in making Life answer questions put to it. Bennett's "dense unconfined array" of "every fact required . . . to make the life of the Five Towns press upon us," James asserts, might captivate readers; but it also would stimulate them to exclaim "'Yes, yes – but is this *all?*'"[22] James's question is later taken up by Woolf in her essay, "Modern Fiction," in which she offers, in answer, her famous definition of life as a luminous halo rather than a series of gig lamps symmetrically arranged.[23]

The gig lamps that guided readers through the well-appointed thoroughfares of Edwardian fiction were smashed to pieces in Ford's *The Good Soldier* (1915), a *"Tale of Passion,"* as the subtitle tells us, that memorializes the materialist culture whose values it so thoroughly indicts. Realist objectivity is demolished in the non-consecutive, partial but apparently candid reminiscences of John Dowell, a Forsytean man of property without Forsytean tenacity of will, who genially dispenses with any pretense of understanding, much less coherently narrating, the events leading to the "break up" of the "four square coterie" of which he formed a particularly obtuse angle. Dowell pleads incapacity to illuminate the moral darkness in which his rapacious, status-seeking and adulterous wife Florence moved and died. He betrays an almost culpable ignorance of the implacable Eros that claims Edward Ashburnham, the good soldier of the title, first as its woefully anachronistic knight of courtly love, finally as its martyr to the "morals of sex" (as Dowell primly calls them). Bennett's vision of an absolute realism, objective and unemphatic, fades before Ford's *ultimate* realism, which, as Ford himself described and practiced it, was programmatically impressionistic and exclamatory to the point of hysteria. Given how Ford and his fellow Impressionists (Joseph Conrad, for one) subverted literary and moral conventions, Ford would later recall that Impressionist novelists were often "considered to be bad people: Atheists, Reds, wearing red ties with which to frighten households. But we accepted the name because . . . we saw that Life did not narrate, but made impressions on our brains. We in turn, if we wished to produce on you an effect of life, must not narrate but render. . . impressions."[24]

In rejecting narration, Impressionists gained an effect of Life, but at the expense of readily communicable knowledge. Dowell's repeated protestations, "I don't know," or "It is all a darkness," represent his perplexity as a storyteller obliged to render phenomena whose significance continually eludes him. Impressions also serve as a psychological subterfuge to avoid confronting erotic demons lurking just beyond the threshold of the public spaces Dowell prefers to inhabit. By novel's end Dowell's ideological alibis for "good society" become, even to himself, almost comically encrusted by irony: "Society can only exist if the normal, if the virtuous, and the slightly deceitful flourish, and if the passionate, the headstrong, and the too-truthful are condemned to suicide and madness."[25] In rendering the moral antagonism between convention and passion, and exposing an epistemological gap between reality and social forms, Impressionism threatens to dissolve realism altogether.

Ford, the most ironic of realists, has Dowell pronounce a cynical verdict that society must go on, simply because it must breed, like rabbits. Lawrence, although enraged by the debacle of modern life, never stopped dreaming of a future populated by "wonderful distinct individuals, like angels . . . each one being himself, perfect as a complete melody or a pure colour."[26] His novels aspire to create and justify these angelic beings; but like Alvina Houghton, the restless heroine of *The Lost Girl* (1920), he must first confront, and contend with, "the inferno of the human animal, the human organism in its convulsions, the human social beast in its abjection and its degradation."[27]

Such remarks make clear why Lawrence's radicalism continues to affront. Intensely romantic in an age that looked with suspicion on ungovernable individualism, Lawrence faults the social world, not the natural man, for transforming angels into demons and turning distinct individuals into anonymous slaves. Rejecting both reactionary and progressivist ideologies, Lawrence prophesied gods he knew no one would want to acknowledge, much less honor: "The puerile world went on crying out for a new Jesus, another Saviour from the sky, another heavenly superman. When what was wanted was a Dark Master from the underworld" (p. 52). *Women in Love* and *Kangaroo* (1923) grimly recount a modern search for Saviours amidst the "collapse of the love-ideal"[28] into sexual disorder, social hatred, and all-out war. Yet Lawrence's own Dark Master was no Satanic demiurge. He preached the gospel of "the God-mystery within us" which sends forth "promptings of desire and aspiration,"[29] urging us to renounce false gods of mechanism and money and to invent modes of being befitting our angelic nature. Such promptings provoke Alvina "to take some part in the wild dislocation of life" (p. 278), and urge Ursula Brangwen in *The Rainbow* (1915) to seek Life beyond the spirit-deadening traditions of home and family; they inspire Birkin's vision of mystic marriage and his longing for a transfiguring *Blutbrüderschaft* with Gerald in *Women in Love;* they flower in the tender, erotic pastoralism of *Lady Chatterley's Lover* (1928). Lawrence's rebel imagination, despairing of realism's bondage to what is rather than to what might be, drifts toward fable and myth.

Resisting the allure of myth, to which so many Georgian realists responded, Katherine Mansfield remained the "purest" realist in the sheer, nonideological pleasure she took in "beautiful, external life to watch and ponder."[30] But her fiction was equally attentive to what was invisible, internal, even non-existent or patently unrealizable. The "wonder... like longing" her stories express offers a greater criticism of the world than any Edwardian's fact-laden indictment. Wonder unaccountably seizes Constantia, one of the daughters of the late colonel, "at her own past and the feelings it calls up in her." Her everyday life of selfless service – "running out, bringing things home in bags, getting things on approval ... and taking them back to get more things on approval, and arranging father's trays and trying not to annoy father" seems "to have happened in a kind of tunnel. It wasn't real. It was only when she came out of the tunnel into the moonlight or by the sea or into a thunderstorm that she really felt herself. What did it mean? What was it she was always wanting? What did it all lead to?" (p. 229).

One thing it leads to is Mansfield's stories, which explore this felt discrepancy between actual and real life. Mansfield's descriptive intensity is myopic – she scrutinizes life so closely that we begin to see stress fractures undermining realism. In "Prelude" the narrator describes how a luncheon party "melted away, leaving the charming table, leaving the rissoles and the poached eggs to the ants and to an old snail who pushed his quivering horns over the edge of the garden seat and began to nibble a geranium plate" (p. 102). Not until that old snail pushes itself over the edges of the garden seat and into the story with which it has nothing to do, do we realize how odd it is that the narrator lingers over a scene from which all human life has departed. This is a moment, the richest *kind* of moment in Mansfield's fiction, when things that have no utilitarian value to any human creature "come alive." Such a moment is poetically realized in "Prelude" when Linda, a dreamy and distracted mother, feels a poppy on the wallpaper, and her furniture, start into life, and "the tassel fringe of her quilt change into a funny procession of dancers with priests attending" (p. 91).

Linda's feeling for things is different from the intimacy with possessions that Soames takes comfort in, because for Linda things "swell out with some mysterious important content" (p. 91) and become the doorway whereby metamorphosis and new meaning, eating away at realism, enter her otherwise static world. Linda's most exalted experience of this miraculous transformation of reality occurs when, lying in bed, "everything had come alive down to the minutest, tiniest particle, and she did not feel her bed, she floated, held up in the air. Only she seemed to be listening with her wide open watchful eyes, waiting for someone to come who just did not come, watching for something to happen that just did not happen" (p. 92). Linda's disappointed watchfulness reflects a growing breach between life and reality that is expressed more impersonally, yet more sadly in *Sons and Lovers*: "Sometimes life takes hold of one, carries the body along, accomplishes one's history, and yet is not real, but leaves oneself as it were slurred over."[31]

Forster also foresaw an impending break between matter and spirit; and measured a growing distance between what happens and what does not, perhaps cannot, happen. Yet while Mansfield believed the truth (not fact) of life was to be found in tension between material actuality and spiritual reality, between minutely observed things and the large questions that such observation raises in the mind, Forster did not. Nullity for him did not surface in sequestered places during private moments of reverie, but paraded the world. Helen Schlegel, the endearing, reckless but never dangerous rebel sister of *Howards End*, is struck and appalled by a "panic and emptiness" she glimpses lurking behind the "wall of newspapers and motor-cars and golf-clubs" that shields and represents prosperous and powerful families, like the Wilcoxes (and the Forsytes), who administer the order of things.

Helen earns the right to judge the Wilcox clan adversely, because she once thought of marrying into it. Her sister, Margaret, who does marry into it, is more generous, arguing that "Without their spirit life might never have moved out of protoplasm." Margaret certainly entertains a complex moral and political vision of her position in the world in refusing "to sneer at those who guarantee" her income (p. 159). Realism doesn't get more fair-minded than Margaret's appreciation of Mr Wilcox (another man of property) for his entrepreneurial virility that "banished morbidity"; and for his eyes that had "an agreeable menace in them whether they were turned towards the slums or towards the stars." At this point Forster's narrator intervenes with a less personal perspective: "Some day – in the millennium – there may be no need for his type. At present, homage is due to it from those who think themselves superior, and who possibly are" (p. 148). The word "possibly" absorbs the passive aggressiveness and resentment that the artist, exponent of beauty and passion, feels toward the tenacity of the Wilcoxian-Forsytean man of property. Some day we might do without men who make things and money; but, Forster advises, not here, not now (if ever).

Clearly, then, when the good angel of realism spoke to Forster it offered hope, but also pragmatic counsel: Only connect. Forster, sounding almost sacerdotal, glosses this angelic, supremely novelistic injunction "to build the rainbow bridge that connects the prose in us with the passion": "without it," he extols us, "we are meaningless fragments, half monks, half beasts, unconnected arches that have never joined into a man... Happy the man who sees from either aspect the glory of those outspread wings. The roads of his soul lie clear, and he and his friends shall find easy going" (p. 167). Forster was wrong, however. The way was not easy, as he was to discover in *A Passage to India*, at once his most realistic, prophetic, and reluctantly Georgian-modernist novel. Impasse rather than connection is the modernist reality. Such is the message, sympathetic with Lawrence and Ford's pessimism, that Forster gleans from the earth and sky of India, land of contradictions and of impossible bridges between East and West.

Yet because the route was not easy did not mean that successors to Edwardian and Georgian realists abandoned the way. Margaret Drabble, Bennett's biographer, remains an eloquent devotee of his art. Scrupulous historical realism grounds Pat Barker's World War I *Regeneration* trilogy. Zadie Smith's *On Beauty* (2004) resurrects the name and spirit of Wells's indomitable Kipps, transplants him to the environs of a contemporary academic novel, entangles him in a property-based inheritance plot derived from *Howards End*, and transfuses an ideology of connection into *On Beauty*'s emotional veins. Postmodernists might see Smith's homage as a retrogressive fall into Forster's conciliatory Liberalism; Smith regards it as a movement beyond the impasse of cultural isolation. A young boy rebels against his family, his heritage, and his culture by falling in love, not just with a girl, but with her entire family, the Kippses. This love, however temporary or ill-fated, is indispensable for initiating the Forsterian passage to another way of Being: "How could he explain how pleasurable it had truly been to give himself up to the Kippses? It was a kind of blissful un-selfing . . .; he had allowed the Kippses' world and their way to take him over entirely."[32]

Such works attest to a robust interest in Edwardian and Georgian realism as models of that "unselfing" with which our connection to the world, the reality, and the plight of others begins. After the pathbreaking literary revolution spearheaded by the Georgians' experimental modernism, and after the dazzling wizardry of postmodernism, contemporary novelists seem anxious that the roads of narrative be made clear for impoverished and overburdened, frantic and stultified, bewildered and brutalized Life. Many look to the good angel of realism to attend them on their way.

NOTES

1 J. B. Priestley, *The Edwardians* (New York: Harper and Row, 1970), p. 89; Robert L. Caserio, "Edwardians to Georgians," *The Cambridge History of Twentieth Century Literature* (Cambridge: Cambridge University Press, 2004), p. 83.

2 Arnold Bennett, *Books and Persons* (London: Chatto & Windus, 1917), p. 118.

3 H. G. Wells, *Kipps* (London and New York: Penguin, 2005), p. 283.

4 H. G. Wells, *Ann Veronica* (London: Virago, 1980), p. 103.

5 "The Contemporary Novel," in H. G. Wells, *An Englishman Looks at the World* (London: Cassells and Co., 1914), p. 169.

6 Ford Madox Hueffer [Ford Madox Ford], "On the Functions of the Arts in the Republic," *The Critical Attitude* (London: Duckworth, 1911), p. 29.

7 E. M. Forster, *Howards End* (New York: Vintage, 1921), p. 28.

8 Arnold Bennett, *The Old Wives' Tale* (London and New York: Penguin Books, 1990), pp. 31–2.

9 Bennett is the most open about the influence of Spencer: "You can see *First Principles* in nearly every line I write." Arnold Bennett, *The Journals* (London: Penguin, 1971) p. 335.

10 Virginia Woolf, "On Re-reading Novels," *The Essays of Virginia Woolf*, vol. III, ed. Andrew McNeillie (New York: Harcourt Brace Jovanovich, 1988), p. 336.

11 May Sinclair, *A Defense of Idealism* (NewYork: Macmillan, 1917), p. 32.

12 Virginia Woolf, "Mr. Bennett and Mrs. Brown," *The Captain's Death Bed* (London: Hogarth Press, 1981), p. 106.

13 Richard Ellmann, *The Golden Codgers* (New York: Oxford University Press, 1973), pp. 120–1.

14 *Letters of James Joyce*, Vol. II, ed. Richard Ellmann (New York: Viking, 1966), p. 135.

15 Katherine Mansfield, *Selected Stories*, ed. Vincent O'Sullivan (New York: Norton, 2006), p. 3.

16 Rebecca West, *The Strange Necessity* (London: Virago, 1987), p. 199.
17 The International P.E.N. Charter, www.international-pen.org.uk/index.php? pid=11
18 H. G. Wells, *Boon* (New York: George H. Doran Co, 1915), pp. 104–5.
19 H. G. Wells, *Tono-Bungay* (New York: Modern Library, 2003), p. 362.
20 D. H. Lawrence, "John Galsworthy," *Phoenix*, (New York: Viking, 1936), p. 540.
21 Arnold Bennett, *Clayhanger* (London: Penguin, 1989) p. 31.
22 Henry James, *The Future of the Novel* (New York: Vintage Books, 1956), ed. Leon Edel, p. 267.
23 Virginia Woolf, "Modern Fiction," *The Common Reader* (New York: Harcourt Brace, 2002), p. 154.
24 Ford Madox Ford, *Joseph Conrad: A Personal Remembrance* (London: Gerald Duckworth, 1924), p. 200.
25 Ford Madox Ford, *The Good Soldier* (New York: Penguin, 2007), p. 197.
26 D. H. Lawrence, "Study of Thomas Hardy," *Phoenix*, p. 432.
27 D. H. Lawrence, *The Lost Girl* (New York: Modern Library, 2003), p. 35.
28 D. H. Lawrence, *Kangaroo* (New York Penguin, 1980) p. 361.
29 D. H. Lawrence, "Foreword," *Women in Love* (New York: Penguin, 2004), p. 484.
30 Katherine Mansfield, *Journal of Katherine Mansfield* (London: Persephone, 2006), p. 120.
31 D. H. Lawrence, *Sons and Lovers* (New York: Penguin, 1988), p. 6.
32 Zadie Smith, *On Beauty* (New York: Harcourt Brace Jovanovich, 2005), p. 44.

4

PAUL EDWARDS

The Great War in English fiction

It is the response of the Great War's poets that has dominated literary and popular representations of the 1914–1918 conflict. According to the resulting myth, British soldiers were needlessly and profligately sent over the top to face barbed wire, shelling, and machine-gun fire in futile attacks by incompetent and complacent generals who lacked imagination for any other strategy. The war achieved nothing, the myth continues, thanks to the Versailles settlement that virtually ensured it would be repeated twenty years later. Revisionist historians, notably John Terraine and Gary Sheffield, have protested against the dominance of this popular myth.[1] Sheffield complains that indeed "it is teachers of English, not history, who have had the greatest impact on the shaping of views on World War I through the teaching of war poetry" (p. 15).

In place of this myth, Sheffield argues that an autocratic and militaristic Germany was largely responsible for the war and needed to be defeated. As far as the prosecution of the war is concerned, Sheffield (along with Terraine) points out that it culminated in military victory, achieved largely by the British Army, and that British generals were in fact far from inflexible or incompetent. There were failures and mistakes, but the overall pattern was one of learning from them to develop weapons systems and tactics that brought victory. Britain and France fought for a common democratic heritage, if not for the more radical democratic values promulgated by Woodrow Wilson. Viewed from the perspective of 2001, World War I was the first step in a process of establishing a world hegemony of liberal democracy: "By the last decade of the bloodiest century in history," Sheffield writes, "Wilson's creed emerged victorious" (p. 56).

This might be too whiggish an interpretation to accept after 9/11, but I cite it as a kind of synoptic view that was simply not available to those in the fighting. To be a member of Britain's citizen army was equivalent to being a citizen of a mass-society without the freedoms that go with citizenship; and larger perspectives necessarily lacked any coherence in the face of the sheer extremity of individual experience. It is this lack that made lyric poetry (and its alienated mirror-image, anti-lyric poetry) the most penetrating literary mode of expression during the war. The novel, as a genre, aspires to bridge the gap between individual experience and a larger perspective in which it acquires meaning; hence novelistic representations of the war are faced from the outset with a problematic contradiction between a locally truthful account and the larger truth that fiction hopes to achieve.

The gap is bridged in one of the earliest novels of the war, John Buchan's spy thriller, *Greenmantle* (1916), but in ways that provide very limited explanatory power. Here the active initiative of Richard Hannay foils a dastardly plot by Germany to foment *jihad* in the Middle East. Were such an uprising to occur, the war effort in Europe might well founder. Hannay makes his way across Europe, at first in the guise of a disgruntled Boer helping Germany, later simply as an agent whose cover has been blown. The climax is the taking of Erzerum in Turkey by the Russians, aided by Hannay, who has secured a map of the town's defenses. "Greenmantle," the expected prophet of *jihad*, turns out to be Hannay's comrade Sandy, last seen at the head of charging Cossacks: "He was turbaned and rode like one possessed, and against the snow I caught the dark sheen of emerald."[2] Individual heroism turns the tide of the war; more generally, the romantic model of military prowess, the charging cavalryman, is reinstated. Significantly, Greenmantle is partly modeled on T. E. Lawrence ("Lawrence of Arabia"), a romantic but peripheral figure in the war. Buchan's plot devices are even more significant. Hannay secures plans of Erzerum only because he has been captured by his enemy, Colonel von Stumm; success depends on a prior defeat, and this plot mechanism, in which setbacks prove to be launching points, has a wider resonance in view of the setbacks faced by the British Army at the Battles of Loos and the Somme.

For realist novelists Buchan's derring-do optimism was irrelevant. Arnold Bennett in *The Pretty Lady* (1918) concentrates on civilian experience, stressing its continuity – in a London subject to Zeppelin raids – with that of the forces in France. Bennett strikes a note that becomes familiar in later novels set at the front when his male protagonist G. J. (who heads a committee supervising charitably funded hospitals for the wounded) is caught in a raid and concussed by a bomb blast. G. J. switches on his torch to look for his lost walking stick: "The sole object of interest which the torch revealed was a child's severed arm, with a fragment of brown frock on it and a tinsel ring on one of the fingers of the dirty little hand. The blood from the other end had stained the ground."[3]

The main structural function of G. J. is to link the three women who carry the story's meaning. Through the fashionable young aristocrat, Queenie Paull, Bennett articulates an attack on English modernism that would reach its fullest force immediately after the war. Queenie is a "flapper" who has commissioned a quasi-Vorticist décor for her apartment. "The place resembled a gigantic and glittering kaleidoscope deranged and arrested." This violent decoration is simply a "war phenomenon due to the war, begotten by the war" (p. 172). In keeping with the instability the décor indicates, Queenie's "war work" is self-indulgent and frivolous. With her plans for an artists' ball at which she will perform as Salome, and her idea for a first aid post for "distressed beauties" to be designed by Roger Fry, Queenie is a leftover from the irresponsible prewar period. Modernism is presented here as at best a self-destructive symptom of war hysteria, and accordingly Queenie's insistence on regarding a zeppelin raid as an exciting spectacle for rooftop viewing leads to her death.

Queenie's friend Concepcion, whose husband has been killed fighting, is presented far more appealingly. Through her Bennett brings trauma into the heart of civilian experience. Exhausted from organizing canteens at war factories in Glasgow, she describes an accident that happened to a girl new to work at a machine: "The machine behind her must have caught some hair that wasn't under the cap. All her hair was dragged from under the cap, and in no time all her hair was torn out and the whole of her scalp ripped clean off" (p. 182). Concepcion suffers a nervous breakdown, and even after a Weir-Mitchell cure she remains suicidal. Crucially, she has also been masculinized by her experience, until G. J.'s friendship works a miracle that restores her to femininity and "reality" (pp. 306–7). Wartime gender roles are unsustainable.

There is never any doubt about the femininity of Bennett's third and principal female, the French *cocotte*, Christine, "the pretty lady" of the novel's title – and the cause of Bennett's novel being considered scandalous. G. J. sets her up as his mistress in a flat; but Christine takes pity on a neurasthenic and alcoholic soldier on leave, cares for him, and ensures he returns to the front. Her actions hint at a religious (Roman Catholic) self-sacrifice that is beyond the other characters in the book. She fits the Virgin–whore archetype absolutely, but finally transcends the whore aspect. G. J. gives up on her when he spots her in the darkened streets, walking purposefully where soldiers gather, apparently on the lookout for clients. But the reader knows that she is now more Florence Nightingale than streetwalker, and is searching for the neurasthenic soldier because she is "a self-convinced mystic envoy passionately repentant after apostasy... seeking – though in vain this second time – the protégé of the Virgin so that she might once more succour and assuage his affliction" (p. 306). Christine represents a restoration of Charity and the old France: the conservative lessons provided by the examples of these three women are clear.

At first sight Rebecca West's *The Return of the Soldier* (1918) is a more complete rejection of contemporary modernity, including the war itself, than Bennett's. It is also reputed to be the first novel in which shellshock plays an important part. Like Bennett's novel it is concerned with women, but is formally more sophisticated, in that its narrator, Jenny, is both participant and witness – and possibly unreliable. Jenny is an unmarried relative who shares an apparently idyllic mansion at Harrowweald with the soldier of the title, Chris Baldry, and his wife. She imagines the soldier returning from the front as a ghost: "I heard, amazed, his step ring strong upon the stone, for I had felt his absence as a kind of death from which he would emerge ghostlike, impalpable."[4] In fact he is lively and palpable enough, but he surfaces as an outlier of the past, existing now only anomalously in the present. His shellshock breaks through the illusory and snobbish idyll of the household at Harrowweald and functions as a mechanism whereby West can explore an alternative idyll of true love and soulfulness, in order to show up the materialistic snobbery of his marriage and career. The "return" of the title is not just a return to England, but a "return" to his life as it was fifteen years before the present moment – because the form his shellshock takes is partial amnesia.

Thanks to amnesia, then, Baldry thinks he is still a young man head over heels in love with Margaret, daughter of an innkeeper who lives on an island in the Thames. Baldry's snobbish, selfish wife Kitty has been completely erased from his memory. And, as the narrator puts it,

> it became plain that if madness means a liability to wild error about the world Chris was not mad...he had attained to something saner than sanity. His very loss of memory was a triumph over the limitations of language which prevent the mass of men from making explicit statements about their spiritual relationships.
>
> (pp. 128–9)

West's version of shellshock is a narrative device that might be felt to have little connection with the war as such. But what it implies is a total rejection of war, for war is of a piece with the "madness" and "wild error" that prevents true spiritual self-realization. That realization is found in Baldry's "saner" return to Margaret. In the real world of wartime England, his long-lost beloved is a shabby, impoverished, and worn-out working-class woman who is regarded with disgust and disdain by the wealthy. Yet even in this world, or in the portion of it that Baldry Court seals off from suburban squalor, she represents deeper values. Jenny sees her cradling Chris's head on her lap:

> It was not until now, when it happened to my friends, when it was my dear Chris and my dear Margaret who sat thus englobed in peace as in a crystal sphere, that I knew it was the most significant, as it was the loveliest, attitude

in the world. It means that the woman has gathered the soul of the man into her soul and is keeping it warm in love and peace so that his body can rest quiet for a little time. That is a great thing for a woman to do. I know there are things at least as great for those women whose independent spirits can ride fearlessly and with interest outside the home park of their personal relationships, but independence is not the occupation of most of us.   (pp. 139–40)

An element of continuing wish-fulfillment in the narrator is signaled by her choice of words, however, for her vision of Margaret and Chris continues her earlier fantasy of Baldry Court as fit for photo-spreads in the illustrated papers: "I tried to build about me such a little globe of ease as always ensphered [Kitty], and thought of all that remained good in our lives"(p. 10).

What brings Chris back to normal is his recognition of death, which negates all Edens. It is not the death of anyone in the trenches that effects this, but that of his own child, who died before the war, another fact that his amnesia blots out. Once "cured," he returns to a reality in which he appears "every inch a soldier" (p. 185), a state that is really an automaton's. The real world is intolerable, unjust and cruel, and quite at variance with our true desires: war is simply an extreme example of this general rule. West uses shellshock as a catalyst enabling a depiction of what a world actually fitted to those desires might be like. Might be, but can't be, since that desirable world is without death, and perhaps is only a product of conventional English nostalgia for a bit of lovely countryside. There is no way out of this impasse, at least in wartime; and West simply leaves unspoken what "those women whose independent spirits can ride fearlessly and with interest outside the home park of their personal relationships" might actually do.

The experience of the ordinary soldier at the front began to be the subject of serious fiction from the 1920s on, when the promise of a "land fit for heroes" looked increasingly hollow. Henry Williamson's *The Patriot's Progress* (1930) is an example of the best kind of work of this time. Williamson was commissioned to supply text to linocuts of stark expressionist simplicity by the Australian artist William Kermode. Williamson's style is correspondingly plain, and the narrative has an archetypal simplicity that achieves for this "progress" of a young city clerk, from enlistment and training to shipment to France and the trenches, the representative status claimed by the title. The patriot's name, John Bullock, reinforces this, but also implies a particular view of military service in this war: not the bombastic and overwhelming brute strength of John Bull, but the youthful uncertainty of the bull's offspring, destined for the shambles. Bullock remains largely passive throughout. At moments of extreme stress, during attacks and bombardments, Williamson's prose changes and reaches an expressionist intensity that matches the starkness of Kermode's most violently distorted designs. Bullock climbs out of the trench and advances:

> Cushy! Nothing in going over the top! Then his heart instead of finishing its beat again swelled out its beat into an ear-bursting agony and great lurid light that leapt out of his broken-apart body
>> with a spinning shriek
>> and the earth was in his eyes and up his nostrils and going away smaller and smaller
>> into blackness
>> and tiny far away
> Rough and smooth. Rough was wide and large and tilting with sickness.[5]

There is no depiction of the war as nightmare more effective than *The Patriot's Progress*, partly because Bullock remains a tentative uniformed civilian throughout. The conclusion on Armistice Day, when the now one-legged Bullock is approached by an "old toff" during the celebrations, epitomizes the myth of the war as a futile sacrifice of a generation. The toff explains to his small son,

> "This good man is a hero. Yes," he went on, "we'll see that England doesn't forget you fellows."
> "We are England," said John Bullock with a slow smile. The old gentleman could not look him in the eyes; and the boy ceased to wave his flag, and stared sorrowfully at the poor man.
> (p. 194)

Williamson was dissatisfied with the book, feeling it was narrowly rooted in the mood of its time. He wanted to write more "balanced" novels. In fact he harbored a Tolstoyan ambition to encompass and explain the whole sweep of history as it affected civilians and soldiers during and beyond World War I. He went on to produce a sequence of fifteen novels, *A Chronicle of Ancient Sunlight*, begun in 1951 in the wake of the Second World War, and completed in 1969.

The narrow focus of *A Patriot's Progress* may be considered a strength when the book is compared with the far more ambitious *Death of a Hero* (1929) by Richard Aldington. Like Arnold Bennett before him, Aldington provides an indictment of "modernism" – particularly of modernist bohemian lives of the period leading up to, and persisting through, the war. The "hero," George Winterbourne, is scarcely less passive than John Bullock, though his civilian life is considerably more complicated. He is sucked into bohemianism and a confusingly "open" marriage in reaction to the hypocrisies of his parents' generation. The novel contains recognizable caricatures of T. S. Eliot and Wyndham Lewis, treating them as examples of the empty pretensions of bohemian society. But the chief target is the bad faith of the sexual "freedom" that leaves Winterbourne confused and resentful. The confusion and resentment are Aldington's own, at least as an artist: *Death of a Hero*, despite vivid evocations of the soldier's experience in France, is an uncontrolled tirade by a narrator who is indistinguishable from the omniscient author of the novel though he supposedly writes about Winterbourne with the limited knowledge of recent military acquaintanceship. The war takes on significance as a symptom of the impasse civilization has reached in working out its values, and George's own death repeats this in miniature: he deliberately exposes himself to enemy gunfire. No positive way out is adumbrated, only an impossible return to elemental, pagan values and nature worship:

> These are the gods, the gods who must endure for ever, as long as man endures, the gods whom the perverse, blood-lustful, torturing Oriental myths cannot kill...In ever-increasing numbers the motor-cars clattered and hammered along the dusty roads; the devils of golf leaped on the acres and made them desolate; sport and gentility made barren men's lives. The gods shrank away...Hamadryads, fauns, do not fly from me! I am not one of "them," one of the perverse life-torturers![6]

Aldington's novel caused controversy on account of the censorship imposed on it for its sexual frankness and the freedom with which it reproduced the then taboo words common in soldiers' speech. Another novel, *Her Privates We*, by "Private 19022" (1930), like *Death of a Hero* a huge commercial success, had its "obscenities" bowdlerized by the author himself, revealed in 1943 as Frederic Manning, an Australian man of letters based in England. The novel first appeared in an uncensored limited edition in 1929 as *The Middle Parts of Fortune*. It is set entirely in France, and depicts the life of infantrymen during several weeks in 1916. The central figure is the semi-autobiographical Bourne, a private who has formed a friendship with two others, Shem and Martlow. The novel's insight into such friendships (disrupted and replaced by others in the vicissitudes of war) and into everyday "politics" of military life at the front gives it enduring value as a record of the war. Civilian life is not present except in the form of letters and parcels. Unlike Aldington's or Williamson's, this is not an anti-war novel; instead, it is a novel about war whose Shakespearian title and epigraphs indicate an ambition to find a perspective from which this particular war may be seen as part of a longer history, rather than as a violent incursion of destructive modernity into a traditional culture. Not that this renders war unproblematic. The author's prefatory note explains:

> War is waged by men; not by beasts, or by gods. It is a peculiarly human activity. To call it a crime against mankind is to miss at least half its

significance; it is also the punishment of a crime. That raises a moral question, the kind of problem with which the present age is disinclined to deal.[7]

The novel engages this uncertain moral terrain, somewhere between crime and punishment, just as the location of "humanity" between beast and god is also uncertain and ambiguous, as is shown by the range of types, moods, and actions of the men whom Manning depicts. Whatever the extremity of this range, the novel never abdicates the responsibility of making human and moral sense of its figures. The human and the moral are present in language itself, which is precisely adjusted to Manning's characterization of social class and the temper of the moment. Survivors return from an attack, fall in for a brief inspection by an officer:

> and then the will which bound them together dissolved, the enervated muscles relaxed, and they lurched off to their tents as silent and as dispirited as beaten men. One of the tailors took his pipe out of his mouth and spat on the ground.
> "They can say what they bloody well like," he said appreciatively, "but we're a fuckin' fine mob."　　　　　　　　　　　　　　　　　　(pp. 5–6)

This kind of "coarse" utterance – and there are many examples throughout the novel – now simply seems realistic; it alternates with passages of high-flown reflective analysis in free indirect discourse that, without their grounding in realism, would appear inflated and tendentious. World War I, after all, is supposed to have drained the meaning out of abstractions – patriotism, duty, sacrifice – that were invoked in order to justify it. Bourne's or the narrator's analysis is abstract, but honors the fact that the people it addresses remain moral beings even though they have no power, and even though their moral problem has no solution:

> The problem which confronted them all equally . . . did not concern death so much as the affirmation of their own will in the face of death; and . . . they realized that its solution was continuous, and could never be final. Death set a limit to a continuance of one factor in the problem, and peace to that of the other; but neither really affected the nature of the problem itself.　　(p. 184)

It is the "middle part" of dualities of this kind that the soldiers of this novel have to inhabit, always under the aegis of fortune (which finally turns against Bourne when he is killed on a raid). The military and political meaning of the war remains in abeyance, but the abeyance, Manning persuades us, is simply a special instance of a general fact about life; and this enables him to carry conviction when he refers to the condition of his common soldiers as a tragic one.

Attempts to address larger meanings of the war in terms of a disruption of British culture have usually resulted in larger fictional structures. The earliest and most celebrated of these is Ford Madox Ford's tetralogy, *Parade's End* (1924–8).[8] Ford called himself a Tory anarchist, and his Toryism consists largely in a fantasized version of a Roman Catholic England, still benevolently governed by a paternalistic landed gentry.[9] The sequence of novels tells the story of the last representative of those feudal values, Christopher Tietjens, the only gentleman still living scrupulously by the moral code they prescribe. Beginning in the apparent social stability of Edwardian England, the sequence follows Tietjens's experience as a civil servant in the department of statistics, through wartime service at the front, to a postwar livelihood as a dealer in antiques in a rural village. His experience is largely one of being slandered, taken advantage of, and persecuted by those who cannot believe he is not, like them, a hypocrite. His unfaithful wife Sylvia tortures and humiliates him precisely because of his all-forbearing secular sainthood. Tietjens's enemies represent the modern world, especially the Whig and Liberal dispensation that has dominated England since the expulsion of the last Tory king, James II, in favor of "Dutch William" in the Glorious Revolution of 1688. Social climbers like Tietjens's eminently respectable (but in truth adulterous) colleague Macmaster achieve eminence largely through Tietjens's selfless financial and intellectual assistance.

In a remarkable early scene, towards dawn Tietjens and a young suffragette, Valentine Wannop, drive along a country lane in a dog-cart (a small horse-drawn vehicle) attempting to find their way through a sea of silver mist. The slim young girl, with her "advanced" opinions, and the older, physically clumsy Tory almost unconsciously initiate a friendship based on common standards of time-honored decency, when suddenly their horse is struck and fatally injured by a car. The reckless driver is General Campion (a persistent bugbear for Tietjens throughout the sequence), who will later be in command of Tietjens in France. Like scenes in *The Return of the Soldier*, this represents the brutal intervention of modernity into a romantic idyll; the First World War General will be no more fit to command a modern army than he is to drive a car. But Ford has the benefit of more hindsight than West. Tietjens and Valentine will eventually see off all their enemies and construct something resembling the idyll foreshadowed by their drive, though it will be a precarious one quite dissociated from the public sphere (in which Tietjens and his brother previously had a secure place).

The scene is recalled by Tietjens at the front, when one of his soldiers is killed by shellfire: "it was as if a whole pail of scarlet paint had been dashed across the man's face on the left and his chest . . . He felt as he did when you patch up a horse that has been badly hurt" (p. 307). Tietjens had refused home-leave to the victim ("O Nine Morgan") to protect him from his wife's lover; for Ford the war and domestic troubles are inextricably entangled. Tietjens too, while in France, cannot escape his vindictive wife Sylvia. Against all rules she pursues him and installs herself in the luxury hotel used by the Staff, bringing more humiliation upon him. A good officer, respected by his men (one pays him the ultimate compliment of believing he must have risen from the ranks), Tietjens is withdrawn from the front by General Campion thanks to Sylvia's malign influence.

On one level *Parade's End* is an overblown fantasy of an impossibly perfect man surviving comprehensive victimization. In this fantasy World War I is simply another stage for him to demonstrate outstanding virtues that the world resents. Tietjens, on this reading, is a version of Ford's paranoid self-image. Yet Ford is a powerful novelist, and there is a reality-principle in him that offers resistance to fantasy. It takes its revenge on the political fantasy of perfect feudalism, too. The Tietjens family (ideal feudal landlords) took over their estate of Groby when they arrived with "Dutch William." Their wealth does not derive from agriculture but from coalmines on their land, hence from the basis of the industrialism that put an end to the life Tietjens idealizes. The heritage that he defends is something of a fake antique, and it is fitting that his infallible instinct for genuine antique furniture should finally be turned to the trade of cobbling together plausible fakes for the American market (p. 705). In the conflict between fantasy and realism, Ford's novel allows a reader to treat its interpretation of history with skepticism, and its marginalizing relocation of the main characters into the private sphere may be taken as an admission that the historical interpretation has nowhere to go.

In 1928 Wyndham Lewis issued the first part of his projected trilogy, *The Childermass*. It eschews realism, transposing World War I and its effects into a fantasy of life after death, the two principal ghost protagonists both having been killed in the conflict. They are herded with others, all male, in an encampment in a landscape reminiscent of the Western front, awaiting admission, they hope, to Heaven. The dead are encouraged to form small groups of the kind depicted in Manning's novel. The war, thus transposed, remains only obliquely present, and the fantasy is predominantly focused on aspects of culture and society in the 1920s that Lewis identified as the war's aftershocks. Pullman and Satters form two halves of a dissociated integer; Pullman is a prissy, conformist intellectual, while the childish Satters, traumatized by shellshock, has been reduced to a quivering mass of affect. Gender roles have been remodeled in this society; an infantilized and "effeminate" mass have abandoned the demands of masculinity, while a smaller hypermasculine warrior caste, in Greek or Viking costume, follows a charismatic "last Aryan hero," the self-styled Hyperides.

The comprehensive social analysis that Lewis accomplished in his political treatise *The Art of Being Ruled* (1926) is not fully deployed in *The Childermass*, which is both a symptom and a prediction of emergent Fascist movements (such as Nazism) that looked to ancient European myths as a "remedy" for the war's social effects. *The Childermass* appears to favor Hyperides' "masculine" group over the controlling ideology of the afterworld. This is the cynical ideology of what Lewis called the "democratic educationalist state" (crucial for mass-mobilization) promulgated by a Mussolini-like demagogue, "the Bailiff." As originally planned, the narrative would have culminated in mass-slaughter and chaos. Through fantasy Lewis was able to evoke aspects of the war's social and political effects that realism could not achieve, but fantasy was no more satisfactory than realism in adumbrating a historical future that remained unwritten. Only after World War II could Lewis resume his unfinished work (as *The Human Age*), and when he did so he decisively rejected Hyperides and his Fascist ideology.

W. Somerset Maugham's *Ashenden: The British Agent* (1927) fictionalizes Maugham's wartime intelligence service in a way that, in decided contrast with Buchan, projects espionage as a sickening and isolating business. Ashenden, Maugham's surrogate, is assigned to work alongside a Mexican who is to intercept secret information passing between Germany and Turkey. When the Mexican mistakenly murders a man whom he thinks is the Turkish courier, his blithe indifference to his mistake sickens Ashenden. Ashenden himself captures an English traitor, sees him executed, and then must cope with the dead man's wife. Some of Ashenden's informers invent what they report, dizzyingly confusing wartime fact and fiction; they themselves can no longer distinguish the two. During the next global war Maugham imagined in *The Razor's Edge* (1944) a Great War flying ace whom Vedantic study in India inspires to adopt anti-imperialist pacifism. In Maugham's novel the withdrawn, disenchanted vision of the poets of the earlier conflict are brought to bear on the fascist era.

If Wyndham Lewis rejected the "Aryan" myths of the Sun and repudiated his early view of Hitler as a "man of peace," Henry Williamson never lost faith. *A Chronicle of Ancient Sunlight* attempts to justify a lasting allegiance to such myths. It does so through what is, in terms of the resources that modernism had developed, a formally unambitious realist mode. In any other terms, however, the ambition is huge, since the intention is to make sense of the history of the twentieth century through the experience of one man, Phillip Maddison, particularly his First World War experience. Nearly every major action of the war is described, often in detail, and the descriptions encompass both the General Staff's plans and the local chances that determine their success or failure. Phillip's intervals of family life in a

London suburb are also recorded; the war is a twofold process of education, leading to a hoped-for maturity. What must remain controversial about this realism, however, is that it serves a mythological structure that, in Williamson's inflection of it, leads directly to Fascism.

Phillip is initially blighted by his thinly-rooted suburban existence, but by recognizing the remnants of a "feudal" land-based way of life governed by benevolent aristocrats (Ford's fantasy) he begins to acquire stability. In his military experience, too, he starts off as an unstable, uncontrolled outsider, but with the patronage of soldier heroes like "Spectre" West, who show faith in him, he reaches a maturity that enables him to provide moral support to others at the front and, at the climax of his military career (which is not officially a success), he has the opportunity of describing personally to Field-Marshall Sir Douglas Haig the terrible conditions in the morass of mud faced by soldiers attempting to secure Passchendaele in late 1917. Williamson was writing when Haig's reputation was low and declining, but Phillip's reaction to him is that he is a good father figure:

> He felt exhilarated, he was free, he had crossed over the shadowline, left forever the old life. For him, Phillip Maddison, a Field-Marshall had opened a door. He thought of Father, who had always tapped on his bedroom door... but why was he crying?[10]

Earlier, Phillip reached an accommodation with an equivalent mother principle. The most telling and symbolic moment is the Christmas truce of 1914, when Phillip fraternizes with German troops and discovers that they too are fighting for "freedom," they too called out for their mothers when scared or wounded; the German dead rest in God, as the English rest in peace: "Both German and Englishman shared the same deep deep sleep, side by side."[11] This essential fellowship, while not undermining his military commitment, remains the foundation for an understanding Phillip must achieve to transcend the cheap chauvinism of the popular press. In *The Golden Virgin* (1957), he learns this by the example of a not-so-virginal (but unsullied) young woman's selfless love. Lily (another version of Bennett's Christine) is the Golden Virgin of the title, which also refers to a statue of the Virgin precariously hanging from the church tower at Albert near the front in France. Through talking with a padre, Father Aloysius, Phillip learns that "the spiritual relation between the boy and the image of the mother was of the same relation between the Son and Mary, the Mother of God, but lifted beyond the struggling human spirit into the realm of the soul... over the Abyss."[12]

Few would dispute the values that Maddison learns from the war: "the secret was tenderness or kindness, as all the great poets knew. That was the secret of the world, to which the world would not trust itself, through fear" (*Love*, p. 54). But the novels' conviction that it is through a fascist revival of the "natural" hierarchies of feudal leadership that these values could be reestablished was based on gross misinterpretations of fascism, whose "heroic" leaders were altogether more Bailiff-like and "modern" in their manipulation of myth than Williamson could understand. His *Chronicle* has fallen into neglect, probably because of the myth that it gradually shapes; but it deserves better, for its realism is that of a compulsive recorder of detail with a remarkable power of description, if not of characterization; as with Manning, the writing transmits a conviction that this is what the war was like.

The most ambitious attempt by someone from a later generation to newly address the meaning of the war has been that of Pat Barker, whose 1991–5 *Regeneration* trilogy starts from the familiar myth of the war (fostered by the poetry of Wilfred Owen and Siegfried Sassoon) as a uniquely horrific and futile sacrifice. But if Owen and Sassoon at Craiglockhart hospital are where the series opens, Barker is really concerned with tracing social and cultural transformations now taken for granted back to their birth in a period when they were felt as traumatic shocks to a settled order. Like Wyndham Lewis, Barker sees issues of masculinity, ideological control, and traumatic dissociation as central, but she can treat them with far more equanimity, in a realist mode that does not disguise its dependence on documentary record and that occasionally foregrounds its own intertextuality. The hinge on which the narrative structure turns is the historically real anthropologist and neurologist W. H. R. Rivers, the doctor treating both Sassoon (whose protest against the war brings him to Craiglockhart as a supposed shellshock victim) and shellshocked Billy Prior, a fictional character raised from the ranks to officer status yet retaining characteristics of a working-class upbringing. Class is indeed a central topic. As a doctor Rivers functions as a reflector of his patients' experiences; as a man he is able to do so because his own experiences mark him in minor ways with some of the same forms of trauma and repression; as the narrative hinge he reflects for the reader the transition to modernity that the sequence enacts. He is both a repressed Victorian and an emancipated psychotherapist (the novels are entirely committed to the "talking cure"). As an anthropologist, Rivers begins as a tolerant relativist. In *Regeneration* he recounts to a colleague an experience in the Solomon Islands when his ethnographic questions were suddenly turned back on him by the islanders. His answers simply caused laughter:

> "I suddenly saw that their reactions to my society were neither more nor less valid than mine to theirs. And do you know that was a moment of the most

amazing freedom. I lay back and I closed my eyes and I felt as if a ton of weight had been lifted."

"*Sexual* freedom?"

"That too. But it was more than that. It was...the Great White God dethroned, I suppose... suddenly I saw not only that we weren't the measure of all things, *but that there was no measure.*"[13]

Rivers may conceptualize this consequence, but he does not, except vicariously, enact or suffer it (he remains sexually inert). It is above all Billy Prior who enacts it, and his personality undergoes violent disruption as a consequence. Apparently cured in the first volume, in the second (*The Eye in the Door*) his allegiance to working-class political activists who oppose the war and organize strikes in munitions factories is in clear conflict with his commitment to the troops at the front who depend upon the munitions. He undergoes fugue states when this tension becomes unbearable, apparently betraying a childhood friend to the authorities in either the Jekyll or the Hyde mode of his dissociation. The self-division is an aggravated version of what all combatants must undergo to tolerate action. Sexually, Prior also enacts the freedom that Rivers only theorizes; he is prophetic of a period of shifting gender identities and sexual orientations, falling in love with and courting a girl from a munitions factory yet happy to satisfy his undirected sexual appetite with any randomly encountered male or female partner. His working-class identity is particularly rough; Barker's working class is nasty, brutish and (through undernourishment) short. There is no "respectability" here, even in a middle-aged character of whom the narrator contemptuously remarks, "Respectability was Ada's God"; two pages later Prior notices a smell of urine on her skirt: "when taken short in the street [Ada] straddled her legs like a mare and pissed in the gutter" (pp. 466, 468). Barker's working class is not Manning's.

An emergent working class, new identities for women, the breakdown of sexual and cultural rigidities are painful processes brought about by this war; and although Barker's novels at times seem too pat an illustration of modern theories (in the trilogy's second volume, pacifist prisoners presciently paraphrase Foucault), they are not complacently progressive narratives. In *The Ghost Road* Rivers's relativism finally has to submit to a more searching test, as he remembers from his research that the missionaries' elimination of head hunting from the islanders' culture robbed their lives of meaning and purpose; the practice sustained them and they are dying out. The rebounding echoes and ironies that connect this to the war being fought in the "civilized" West (and to subsequent conflicts) are left to the reader to explore. If "there is no measure" by which homicide may be judged, what can replace the "big white god"? New identities emerge, the novel suggests, and they will simply be followed; the humanism that we might expect as a ground of value for the novel is scarcely asserted, though some readers might feel it emerge in Billy Prior's journal, which recounts his final return to France in the same company as Wilfred Owen. Both characters are billeted among wrecked but beautiful ruins of gardens overgrown with roses. Less troubled than at any time previously, Prior advances to the final action, to futile sacrifice. Dying, Prior witnesses Owen's body in filmic slow-mo "lifted off the ground by bullets, describing a slow arc in the air as it fell" (p. 588). Meanwhile in a London hospital, another doomed youth, his head half shot away, tells Rivers "*Shotvarfet.*" Rivers intuits the intended utterance: "It's not worth it" (p. 588). The myth of World War I endures almost unchanged through a century of literary configurations and the historical circumstances in which it has been repeated.

NOTES

1 John Terraine, "British Military Leadership In The First World War" (1999), www.westernfrontassociation.com/thegreatwar/articles/research/britishmilitar-yleadership.htm#top (accessed February 1, 2008); Gary Sheffield, *Forgotten Victory: The First World War, Myths and Realities* (London: Headline, 2001).

2 John Buchan, *Greenmantle*, ed. Kate Macdonald (Oxford: Oxford University Press, 1999), p. 272.

3 Arnold Bennett, *The Pretty Lady* (London: Cassell, 1932), p. 208.

4 Rebecca West, *The Return of the Soldier* (New York: The Century Company, 1918), p. 42.

5 Henry Williamson, *The Patriot's Progress: Being the Vicissitudes of Pte. John Bullock* (London: Geoffrey Bles, 1930), p. 171.

6 Richard Aldington, *Death of a Hero* (London: Penguin, 1936), p. 81.

7 Frederic Manning, *The Middle Parts of Fortune* (London: Granada, 1977), p. viii.

8 Ford Madox Ford, *Some do Not...* (1924), *No More Parades* (1925), *A Man Could Stand Up –* (1926) and *The Last Post* (1928). Ford later regretted including *The Last Post*. References will be to *Parade's End* (New York: Vintage, 1979), first assembled after Ford's death.

9 See Andrzej Gasiorek, "The Politics of Cultural Nostalgia: History and Tradition in Ford Madox Ford's *Parade's End*," *Literature and History*, 11: 2 (Autumn 2002), 52–77 for an argument that locates Ford's views in a political tradition of conservative radicalism that the novel sequence itself undercuts.

10 Henry Williamson, *Love and the Loveless* (London: Macdonald, 1957), pp. 314, 316.

11 Henry Williamson, *A Fox under My Cloak* (Bath: Chivers Press, 1983), p. 51.

12 Henry Williamson, *The Golden Virgin* (London: Macdonald, 1957), p. 258.

13 Pat Barker, *The Regeneration Trilogy* (London: Penguin, 1998), p. 212; italics in original.

5

ROD MENGHAM

Postwar modernism in the 1920s and 1930s: The mammoth in the basement

The experimental novelists of the 1920s and 1930s had to cope with the divided legacy of the first generation of modernist writers who had pursued parallel but mutually contradictory paths. The revitalizing of tradition, and the realigning of values with an impersonal standard, were motive forces behind the cultural programming of T. S. Eliot, Ezra Pound, and Wyndham Lewis, while an antithetical investment in the fleeting moment and multi-faceted solipsism were fundamental to the narrative routines of Dorothy Richardson and Virginia Woolf. The Joycean literary apparatus was virtu-ally unique in comprehending the different strains of this Janus-faced modernism. This essay will consider the work of nine writers for whom the demands of a national cultural politics, or the issues of sexuality, gender and class, required an adaptation of the self-conscious internationalism of the earlier modernists, with their attempted transfusions of cultural experience from one historical epoch to another. One of the busiest pivots around which the debate over different philosophies of writing generated a constant heat was the critical activity of Wyndham Lewis.

For Lewis, immersion in the medium of time that was guaranteed by the use of interior monologue, or by versions of the "stream of consciousness" model derived from Bergson, was totally abhorrent. Fidelity to the spon-taneous movements, the changes in direction, of thought and feeling in the experience of the individual subject, reduced the intensely psychologized versions of modernist fiction to examples of a souped-up form of realism. From early on in his career, Lewis's hope for modernist experimentation was that it would lead to the abandonment of all representational modes of writing, thus helping to abolish what he regarded as a universally supine attitude towards the world as given, in favour of a form of abstraction that would reinvent the world from the wholly independent point of view of the truly creative individual. Mere simulation of the constantly changing impulses of thought and feeling in real time would encourage a desire for empathy in the reader, a blurring of boundaries between separate selves that Lewis recoiled from as inimical to the realization of the individual will:

> We all to-day (possibly with a coldness reminiscent of the insect-world) are in each other's vitals – overlap, intersect, and are Siamese to any extent...
>
> All clean, clear cut emotions depend on the element of strangeness, and surprise and primitive detachment.
>
> Dehumanization is the chief diagnostic of the Modern World.[1]

Lewis's opposition between empathy and detachment in the context of arguing for the confrontation of the modern with the primitive is clearly indebted to Wilhelm Worringer's art-historical categories of "empathy" and "abstraction." For Worringer, the cultural dominance of empathy occurs in historical conditions where there is a "relationship of confidence between man and the phenomena of the external world," while abstraction takes precedence with "a great inner unrest inspired in man by the phenomena of the outside world."[2] The urge to abstraction is characterized as the urge to

> wrest the object of the external world out of its natural context, out of the unending flux of being, to purify it of all its dependence upon life, i.e. of everything about it that was arbitrary, to render it necessary and irrefragable, to approximate it to its absolute value.[3]

This supplies Lewis with a pretext for rejecting the practice of the Bergsonian artist absorbed precisely in ways of apprehending the "flux of being" by reproducing the arbitrariness of the mind's operations. Because empathetic art is predicated on a commitment to organic existence, abstract art defines itself by attraction towards the inorganic, towards an "absolute" with both formal and spiritual implications that must be approached through a process of what Lewis terms "dehumanization." This dehumanizing project is seen to best effect in Lewis's own fiction in the strategic unmanageability of the human body:

> The intense uneasiness that all these people aroused in her was as it were perfectly expressed by the sort of place in which they were at present con-gregated. As she listened to their voices – big, baying, upper-class voices, with top-dog notes, both high and low – shouting out boldly in haughty brazen privileged tones what they thought, as only the Freeman is allowed to – the subject of their discourse invariably the commonplaces of open conspiracy and unabashed sedition – *coups d'état* and gunpowder plots – she felt a sinking of the heart. It seemed to spell, for her private existence, that of Victor and her, nothing but a sort of lunatic menace, or arrogant futility. They were not so much "human persons," as she described it to herself, as big portentous

wax-dolls, mysteriously doped with some impenetrable nonsense, out of a Caligari's drug-cabinet, and wound up with wicked fingers to jerk about in a threatening way – their mouths backfiring every other second, to spit out a manufactured hatred, as their eyeballs moved.[4]

The character Margot's unease derives from a recognition of the "strangeness" that Lewis welcomes in "The New Egos" as a precondition for authentic selfhood. The puppet-like status of the body, seemingly under the control of external forces, its behavior both mechanical and unpredictable, is inhabited by a personality that is no less subject to manipulation. Lewis dismisses the political creeds of the day as virtually indistinguishable from each other in their ability to produce stereotypes of attitude and behavior. While he is accurate enough in his understanding of the workings of ideology, this particular novel's setting during the Spanish Civil War raises questions about Lewis's cynicism in obliterating the differences between Fascist, Communist, and Anarchist motivations. If the ultimate goal of writing is to transcend the limitations of group identity in order to establish the basis for a truly independent creativity, much of Lewis's very considerable energy is expended in a lifelong harrassing of the commonplace and the mediocre, incurring discomfort for his readers as well as characters in a systematic assault upon the security they take most for granted, that of their relationship to their own bodies.

Lewis's impulsive and vehement inscriptions of the body as an alien contraption are equalled nowhere else in English language writing of the period. However, a more embellished appreciation of modernist subjectivity in terms of encrusted habits of mind and ritualized forms of behavior can be found in the ornate fictions of Ronald Firbank. *Concerning the Eccentricities of Cardinal Pirelli* (1926) exhibits better than any of his other works Firbank's qualifications as a master of modernist supererogation. Set in a Spanish cathedral city (clearly modelled on Seville) the negligible action takes place in the social milieu of the eponymous cardinal whose eccentricities include the baptising of pet dogs. The repercussions of this act might justify any amount of sensationalism in the development of an extravagant story line, and yet the fallout is captured almost entirely by an arrangement of tableaux that evoke the life-styles of Cardinal Pirelli's patrons, associates and acolytes. The various satellites of the central figure are very clearly moved much more by the theatrical than the spiritual aspects of their religion, and so is he.

The plot is exiguous, the characters diaphanous; Firbank waives any substantial investment in either through his preference for the novella over the novel; his writing simulates narrative as the merest pretext for a series of caressing descriptions, for the accumulation of surplus textures and ensemble effects. These can read like extended captions in an auction catalogue. Although there is little dialogue, there is plenty of direct speech, uttered by characters in moments of self-communion, of self-performance, using verbal propositions to feed the same sort of pleasure they would derive from striking poses before a mirror. Virtually nothing in this brocaded prose gives any hint of what lies below the surface: speech, gesture, and physical appearance all point toward the choreographing of identity; the characters are attuned to their positions within the hierarchies of reputation and privilege; their behavior is toiled in protocols, even when it subverts and contradicts what is expected of them; their costumes of language and visible aspect have become second nature. But the narrator is even less interested than the characters in getting behind this charade to uncover individual psychological motivation, or the idiosyncrasies of memory and desire. Indeed, the narrator often looks past the characters, or sees them as part of a composite setting for the articulation of certain cravings, appetites, compulsions. In this respect, the prehensile character of the writing, reaching out to catch hold of the world, resembles an extension of the body rather than a projection of the mind; though this is not a Joycean body, completely porous to every kind of experience, engrossing and purging the materials of existence without bias or preference, but the body of an epicure, highly selective in its tastes and addictions. Firbank's sensibility is that of the connoisseur, whose world shrinks to the compass of his own fixations, and these are pursued with the avidity of a collector whose only versatility lies in the sourcing of more variations on the same theme. If this turns his writing into the work of a displaced aesthete, an uprooted twentieth-century orphan of the Decadence, his general textual cupidity is nonetheless modernist in its systematic deflections. Although there are small revelations of perverted sexuality among the characters, these are flimsy and weightless compared to the constant transferability of desire in the point of view of the narrator, whose ogling style of perception diffuses sexuality like a sticky coating over the world of objects.

Equal to Firbank in its relentless formality, but opposite to his stylistic humidity is the scrupulously abstinent prose of Ivy Compton-Burnett. Her work is notorious, or celebrated, depending on the point of view, for its agonistic dialogue. The greater part of each novel resolves itself into what the characters can debate, in a series of minor skirmishes designed to test the strengths and weaknesses of opponents precisely in order to secure advantage piecemeal, without a degree of open confrontation that would be regarded as vulgar. Compton-Burnett's characters are positively animated by a reverence for convention that seems peculiarly foreign to the modernist spirit. Reading her novels, it is as if *Blast* had never happened, and yet her writing is governed by a phobia for sentiment equal to that of Wyndham Lewis himself. The reader may sense the remote agitation of currents of attraction and repulsion swirling around all the characters, and yet their emotional lives are kept firmly submerged beneath narration and dialogue in equal degrees. And this suppression is amplified when its effects are seen within the context of the typically closed communities of Compton-Burnett's novels, where characters are moved into and out of each other's company like chess pieces in an especially elaborate game.

Closed in and quarantined in another sense, these texts are composed in a language derived almost entirely from conventions of speech developed in English fiction and drama between the late eighteenth and late nineteenth centuries; between the orderly, adjudicating language of Jane Austen, rendering every variety of human behavior it encounters both identifiable and comprehensible on its own terms, and the ostentatious repartee of Oscar Wilde, capable of adjusting any subject matter to the purposes of amusement. The opening pages of the 1933 novel, *More Women Than Men*, illustrate the limits within which a typical Compton-Burnett work will range itself:

> "Did you have a pleasant journey, my dear?"
>
> "Yes, very pleasant, thank you. The train was rather crowded. But I see no reason myself for objecting to the presence of my fellow creature." Miss Luke looked full at Josephine as she set forth her individual view. "It is extraordinary how seldom we meet unpleasant people, or see an unpleasant face. Have you ever met a repulsive person, Mrs Napier? I think I have not."
>
> "No, I think all faces I have met have had their human dignity and charm. But then I have spent my life amongst educated and intelligent people. I would not say that some faces might not show signs of – shall we say a different history? I hope" – Josephine bent towards her companion with a humorously guilty smile – "that you had none of those in your carriage?"
>
> Miss Luke yielded for a moment to laughter.
>
> "Well, what I always feel, Mrs Napier, in meeting such people, is simply respect for their harder experience. I pay the rightful homage of the highly civilized – yes, that is what I choose to call myself – to those whose lives are spent at the base of the civilization Surely no other view should be admissible?"[5]

The subject matter of this exchange was political dynamite during the decade in which *More Women Than Men* was first published. Class differences and the opportunities for encountering and perceiving the strangeness of other people's lives were placed at the center of literary attention in the work of proletarian and left-wing avant-garde novelists, and yet for Compton-Burnett's characters, these experiences have little meaning beyond the occasion they provide for "civilized" interlocution, with the asymmetries of privilege in material existence being amended only by the symmetries of deductive prose.

The forensic chill in the atmosphere of Compton-Burnett's patrician analyses of a culture under threat is well below the environmental temperature of fiction during the 1930s that responded with genuine warmth to the challenge of imagining unfamiliar lives, especially those that lay on the other side of the class barrier. Of all the upper- and middle-class writers who attempted to render the grain of working-class life in their fiction, none was more dynamic in the attempt than Henry Green. His second novel, *Living*, was identified early on as an inaugural text in the 1930s school of proletarian writing, and yet its most obvious form of homage to working-class culture, its almost delirious adaptation of demotic speech, was not reflected in subsequent imitations, perhaps because the livingness of its chosen idiom was most vividly conveyed through an effect of breathlessness that was not attributed to characters alone but shared by the narration itself:

> And Dale asked him why he went round with Tupe then and Mr Gates said me never and Dale said he seen him and Joe Gates answered it might have been once.[6]

> Once she had said to Mrs Eames she had said it made you ridiculous she had said walking with him, yes she had said that to Mrs Eames.

> (pp. 41–2)

The rapid pace of inordinate talk is given an even greater impetus through the shedding of punctuation and the frequent omission of definite articles: "Sparrows flew by belts that ran from lathes on floor up to shafting above by skylights" (p. 3). The streamlining of the narrative idiom infuses the representation of proletarian work and leisure with a sense of velocity, like a film speeded up to underline the dramatic changeability of material existence. If the body is an inconvenient machine in the work of Wyndham Lewis, in this early novel by Green, it becomes the medium for demonstrating the organic mutability of life in every class of society; the equality of illness, while it always takes the individual by surprise, is one of the most inevitable refrains in a text that accelerates through the life-cycles of numerous characters: "Ah, so it goes on, every day, and then one day it breaks, the blood comes running out of your nose as you might be a fish has got a knock on the snout" (p. 17). But the writing is organized around a variety of kinds of repetition. Exact repetition of verbal formulae, such as the attributions of speech – "she had said" – is reminiscent of the techniques employed by Gertrude Stein and serves a similar purpose. Stein's habit of circling back time and time again to variations on the same phrasing is intended to create the effect of a "continuous present." This method of converting narration into a medium for experiencing the passage of time does not represent a fictional mind in the process of self-reflexion but draws the reader directly into a performance of this process. Green deploys the method to suggest the extent to which his characters inhabit the reality of historical time, taking each moment as a fresh beginning, an opportunity to revise their previous thought and readjust to the next one: "But he was sincere in his thinking the old place wanted a rouser and in his thinking he was always building, always building in his thinking" (p. 57).

But the text employs another kind of repetition that works in quite different ways. If reiterative phrasing disturbs the linearity of the reading experience with its effect of looping and splicing, recurrent images are strung together with an emphasis that seems to offer access to the hermeneutic code of the narrative. The most spectacular examples are the obsessive evocations of the behaviour of birds:

> He saw these and as the sun comes out from behind clouds then birds whistle for the sun, so love came out in his eyes (at the victory, at making her cry) and he whispered things senseless as whistling birds.
>
> (p. 163)

> Then, as after rain so the sky shines and again birds rise up into the sky and turn there with still movements so her sorrow folded wings, so gently crying she sank deeper into the bed and was quieted.
>
> (p. 239)

These quotations both take the form of epic similes, but there are many instances of both metaphorical and literal uses of the same imagery. Some appear to have symbolic or allegorical status, as does the example given earlier: "Sparrows flew by belts that ran from lathes on floor up to shafting above by skylights." This is one of several glimpses of airborne birds that seem to echo Bede's comparison of the life of Man with the flight of a sparrow into a lighted hall and out again into the night. But there are many more occasions when the use of bird imagery seems gratuitous, so that the interpretative value of this authorial obsession remains unclear, quite literally volatile. *Living* combines both realist and modernist techniques in its accurate rendition of vernacular culture and in its flaunting and flouting of subtextual meanings. Very few of Green's contemporaries repeated the experiment, especially those whose left-wing politics required some negotiation with the Communist Party's endorsement of socialist realism.

One of the most intriguing attempts to renegotiate the official contract between socialism and realism was James Barke's immense novel about

Glasgow, *Major Operation*, one of the most ambitious fictional projects of the 1930s. Dividing his text into four parts and ninety separate sections, Barke tried to set Glasgow alongside Dublin, Berlin, and St. Petersburg, by emulating Joyce, Doblin, and Bely in their comprehensive portraits of a single city. There are key characters, especially the businessman George Anderson, whose medical operation is paralleled by the strikes and demonstrations intended to cure the political ills of the city; but there is a large number of minor characters, and a high proportion of scenes devoted to the general conditions of life in the workplaces and on the streets. The individual section headings recall Joyce's pastiche of newspaper headlines in the "Aeolus" section of *Ulysses*, while the systematic cutting between unrelated scenes recalls the montage effects of Dziga Vertov and Walter Ruttmann, in their filmed portraits of the cities of Moscow and Berlin. But Barke's style of writing is at its most modernist in the second part of the novel, the "Complexes of Sensations" section, which adopts a free-floating, constantly migrating point of view, and a versatile narrative idiom that camouflages itself with an assortment of accents, registers and conventions of speech:

Politics, thy name is acrimony. Let's have – music!

Sit, Jessica! Let the sound of music creep in our ears. Your name isn't Jessica by any chance?

Getting fresh, are you? My name's Sarah. Sarah Cannan. Call a flute band music?

Sorry, can't give you henry hall and His band. But don't despise the flute, dear lady. Orpheus and his lute – which, as you doubtless were told at school, is just the polite name for flute. It is the little rift within the flute . . . Afraid it's the flutes that are causing the rift, however. Suppose you'd rather hear a Mae West story? Ah, Mae West! Sex! Taboo! Wonder what Mrs. Bloom would have thought about Mae West? Or Mae West about Marion Bloom? Mummmh! Bulged right out in his face! Seven miles! Guess I've nothing on you, dearie.

Labour on the bench and a smutty story round the corner: under the trees. Music down the street. Hold the mirror up to nature and you get – sex and politics (moonlight is extra, but always in request) . . .

Well, we don't mind a little sex, sir, providing it's treated in a light, aphrodisiacal manner and provided there's a high moral tone prevailing throughout. Nothing the public likes better in fact. But – no politics! No, siree. Keep politics out of literature.

A little bit of bread and no chee-e-e-ese? Well, them flutes don't seem to be coming any nearer . . .

But the Mirror and Nature, you know. I must bow to your superior knowledge of what the public wants. The syndicate that runs your library in there . . .

Hold the Mirror up to Nature by all means. But hold it up to her *face*.

Ain't nature grand! (How'ma doin' boys?) You mean: put the blind eye to the telescope?

Unless you're a Peeping Tom.

Sorry you've been troubled. Rather afraid there's a spot of trouble coming to you all the same...[7]

Both this passage and the novel as a whole challenge the view that politics and aesthetics should be mutually exclusive, that they represent a choice between the acrimonious and the harmonious. The play on homonyms, the variations on lines of Shakespeare, the deployment of different voices, all give a strong musical aspect to the way the writing is structured. And the range of allusions to Shakespeare, to James Joyce, to popular music, and to a Hollywood celebrity, emphasize the cultural dimension of politics. The comparison between Molly Bloom and Mae West is between a fictional character in an avant-garde literary text and a performer in a modern mass medium, but what they have in common is a transgressive attitude toward conventional gender roles, suggesting the need to expand the concept of politics to include sexual politics, a connexion already made in the adaptation of the quotation from *Hamlet* ("Frailty, thy name is woman") to present the idea of politics as a field of contested meanings. It is just as difficult to unravel sex from politics as it is to prise politics apart from music. The second half of the passage as given questions the value of mimesis in the representation of politics, since the definition of what constitutes the political is variable, and because mimesis is subject to issues of selection and omission as much as any other mode of inscription. Barke is clearly arguing for inclusiveness, both in the range of topics that contemporary literature should represent, and in the range of techniques it should make use of, but his relationship to modernism is not an easy one. His emulation of Joyce is partly an act of homage, partly an attempt at disengagement. He revels in the opportunity to complicate the texture of his writing through citation, parody, rapid transition from one idea to another, and deft maneuvering between different voices and different fictional minds, but he is also self-conscious about over-indulging himself, on guard against the charge of showing off – "(How'ma doin' boys?)" – that would identify him as an irresponsible avant-gardist rather than a serious political novelist.

Underneath the fluctuations of style and cadenza-like passages of experiment, trial runs for a projected socialist modernism, Barke keeps his sights trained on home: the imported language of revolutionary struggle is translated into the pressures of a local cultural and social politics. Almost the opposite is true of the writings of Christopher Isherwood during this period.

His cultivation of an unwavering, unpremeditated gaze of inspection ("I am a camera") as the model for a steadily maintained documentary style of notation is carried like luggage to as many exotic destinations as possible. His many narrators share their histories with the known trajectory of their author during the late 1920s and 1930s, including extended periods of residence in Berlin, and brief forays to other parts of Europe. Isherwood's surrogates base their fictional accounts of the constant novelties of experience available to the Englishman abroad on the generic template of the travel writer, with the added intellectual backing of the contemporary vogue for anthropology. The investigative privilege of the anthropological stranger is borrowed imaginatively by a wide range of texts and discourses during the 1930s, ranging from the poetry of Auden to the films of Humphrey Jennings and including a very diverse array of novels, novellas, and short stories by Julia Strachey, Edward Upward, Rex Warner, and George Orwell, amongst others.[8] In all these cases, as in the founding document of Mass Observation, "Anthropology at Home,"[9] the object of scrutiny is not the unfamiliar culture of a society remote from western civilization, but the present-day condition of England itself, seen as if by an anthropologist in a first encounter. The imaginative movement is towards what is over-familiar, rather than away from it; Isherwood had followed this direction in the company of Edward Upward during the composition of the "Mortmere" stories and in his earliest novels, *All the Conspirators* (1928) and *The Memorial* (1932), but then simply reversed it. From around 1934 onward, his cultural-political stance became increasingly reminiscent of an earlier generation of emigré modernists whose work was the medium of their assimilation to an adopted habitat and a means of accreditation within an alternative tradition. The danger of this stance was the temptation to travel light and assemble an arbitrary set of keepsakes in a purely subjective representation of the culture in question. Isherwood was to admit as much over twenty years later, with reference to the narrator figure in *Mr Norris Changes Trains* (1935):

> I arrived in Berlin on the lookout for civil monsters. And, since my imagination had very little contact with reality, I soon persuaded myself that I had found several.
>
> What repels me now about *Mr Norris* is its heartlessness. It is a heartless fairy-story about a real city in which human beings were suffering the miseries of political violence and near-starvation . . . The only genuine monster was the young foreigner who passed gaily through these scenes of desolation, misinterpreting them to suit his childish fantasy.[10]

This honesty became unavoidable when Isherwood agreed to clarify the relationship between his narrator and his former friend of Berlin days,

Gerald Hamilton. He had not felt the need to be so forthright for twenty years beforehand. Nevertheless, there is a remarkable story, published in the same year as the first Berlin novel, that exposes Isherwood's fundamental discomfort with his chosen role as cultural tourist. Set on the Canary Islands, the text divides its attention between two pairs of characters: the narrator and his friend Heinz, and two eccentric and slightly mysterious travellers who share the same means of earning a living, although the figures they present could not be more different from one another; the elder, more disreputable-looking, is Spanish; the younger, more suave and dapper, is Hungarian. They are both confidence-tricksters who solicit financial sponsorship for their journeys around the world. They do in fact travel the world, but only in order to access new sources of easy money. The more successful, because more plausible, of these two figures, is the chameleon-like Hungarian, whose calling card has been printed in seven languages, and who dresses well in order to pass himself off as more prosperous than he is:

> "You must always be smartly dressed," he told us, "especially if the village is very poor. No peasant gives much to a shabbily dressed man. They think he's a swindler – that's quite natural. Why, you yourself: who do you pay to see at the cinema – Greta Garbo or some down-and-out actress nobody has heard of? You don't think to yourself: Garbo's rolling in money and this girl hasn't got enough for a meal? Of course you don't."[11]

The evasion of one's background and upbringing, and the simulation of a different class position, are the stock-in-trade of many middle-class writers anxious to identify with the political interests of the working class; Isherwood's confidence-trickster is pretending to be a toff, but his itinerant narrator feels no less fraudulent in his attempt – and failure – to overcome his bourgeois fastidiousness:

> Both of us were dirty and sleepy after a night on deck. I had been looking forward to a wash and bed at once. The Hungarian must have guessed this, for he jumped out of bed in his underclothes and said kindly: "You get in. You look tired."
> "There's no hurry," I answered crossly, unwilling, in my stupid British way, either to lie in his sheets or to tell him I wanted the bedclothes changed. The Hungarian smiled and sat down on a chair.
>
> (p. 213)

Both the Hungarian and the narrator are embarked on a succession of departures from their own histories and the reality of their economic and social positions – there is very little to choose between them, as the narrator's final reference to "our fellow-parasite" makes clear.

The systematic dislocation of identity in Isherwood's writing across genres is an outcome of modernity itself; the constant migration of point of view is related ultimately to the increased mobility of labour, to the multiplication and acceleration of modern forms of transport and communication, to the shifting of borders and the movement of ethnic groups and language communities.

The modernism of Mary Butts is in full-scale retreat from this version of modernity. "Speed the Plough" (1921), one of the most remarkable of all stories to emerge from the experience of the Great War, features a protagonist whose absorption in the scenarios of high fashion is equal to Firbank's relish for luxury and spectacle. And yet in Butts's analysis, this emphasis on the attributes of conspicuous leisure and prosperity is not the subject matter of a sustained authorial reverie, but the sign of an almost pathological resourcefulness on the part of a lamed ex-soldier, recovering from traumatic injury:

> Coquetterie, mannequin, lingerie, and all one could say in English was underwear. He flicked over the pages of the battered *Sketch*, and then looked at the little nurse touching her lips with carmine.
>
> "Georgette," he murmured sleepily, "crepe georgette."
>
> He would always be lame. For years his nerves would rise and quiver and knot themselves, and project loathsome images. But he had a fine body, and his soldiering had set his shoulders and hardened his hands and arms.
>
> "Get him back on to the land," the doctors said.
>
> The smells in the ward began to assail him, interlacing spirals of odour, subtle but distinct. Disinfectant and distemper, the homely smell of blankets, the faint tang of blood, and then a sour draught from the third bed where a man had been sick.
>
> He crept down under the clothes. Their associations rather than their textures were abhorrent to him, they reminded him of evil noises . . . the crackle of starched aprons, clashing plates, unmodulated sounds. Georgette would never wear harsh things like that. She would wear . . . beautiful things with names . . . velours and organdie, and that faint windy stuff aerophane.
>
> He drowsed back to France, and saw in the sky great aeroplanes dipping and swerving, or holding on their line of steady flight like a travelling eye of God. The wisps of cloud that trailed a moment behind them were not more delicate than her dress . . .[12]

The facile transition from "aerophane" to "aeroplanes," and the rapid imaginative conversion of wisps of cloud into wispy dress material indicate something of the pressure behind this particular casualty's readiness to displace the evidence of the senses with the repertoire of the fetishist. Even more radical is the substitution of hearing for touch, and of words for things, in the subject's complete reorganization of his sensory and visual environment. Sent back to the countryside in order to stabilize and normalize his reactions to his surroundings, the protagonist retreats even further into his obsession, translating the sights and sounds of the English landscape into the remembered lyrics of a music-hall song. He exchanges one form of alienation for another, the anonymized subjectivity of industrial warfare for the stereotypes of desire and desirability made available by a burgeoning consumer culture.

The prescribed return to the land is equally stereotypical, a one-size-fits-all gesture that is crudely inadequate. However, "getting back to the land" as to a source of cultural health is an idea that Mary Butts takes very seriously in the context of imagining forms of continuity that will earth the individual, quite literally, in certain kinds of shared experience. If the social spaces of modernity, with their massing of isolated individuals, obliterate the traditional means of establishing a community, then alternative modes of connection must be sought in the collective experience of time, in the shared memories that are attached to individual places. If this sounds like an Eliotic concept, it is not quite that, since the defining memories are not supposed to be embodied in art, however broadly conceived, but somehow, mysteriously, in the land itself:

> They followed one another through the copse. Each willow trunk was a separate man and woman. They came down the farther side to where, when it had been sea, the plain had worn a little bay under the hill. There was long wet grass where the tide-mark had been. They came to a dyke and an old house. There were willows along the glass water, very tall; along it and over it, one flung across and an elm tree drowned in it, its root out of the ground in a flat earth-cake. The house was a deserted farm. An orchard reached it, down a small valley between the rising of another hill. There was no path. They went up through the apple-trees, through a place wholly sheltered, where no wind came but only sun; where, when there was no sun, there was always light; so that in mid-winter, in the stripped world, the seasons did not exist there. They called it the Apple Land, remembering there something which they could not recall, that seemed to have the importance of a just-escaped dream. The orchard ended sharply in an overhanging quickset, and a sharp climb to the top of the hill. To follow the valley to its head there was glen on the left, sickly with flies and thin shoots and a scummed choked stream up to a short fall, almost in the dark, which was not quite wholesome, whose pool was without stir or light. The way out of that was also sharp and steep but quite different – to a shut cottage on top and a garden with tansy in it, and herbs used in magic.[13]

The journey through the landscape involves an imaginative movement through time, as far back as prehistory, spanning the history of settlement and its abandonment. In "remembering" what they cannot "recall," the characters are intimating a form of inherited knowledge that underlies their individual conscious awareness. And yet their exploration of the contours of this landscape, and the reader's attempt to penetrate its obscurity, is not guided by an individual or a collective point of view, but focused through the experience of a pair, a primal couple, who are seen not turning away from their "Apple Land" in order to populate the world, but turning toward it. Butts's writing is partly an attempt to regain a paradise lost, a territory instinct with the history of both innocence and experience. If it has not actually been made by humanity, it has nonetheless been remade by it time and time over, in ways that are magically imprinted on successive generations through their interaction with the landscape itself.

In Sylvia Townsend Warner's novel, *Lolly Willowes* (1926), the connection with the underlying meaning of the land is willed back, further and further, to a primeval condition that remains infinitely more potent than any subsequent interference by humanity. There is a family resemblance between the preoccupations of Butts and Warner, but a crucial difference in the way they organize the relations between the various points of view at stake: those of author, narrator, character, and reader. In Butts's text, there is a collapsing together of points of view, a suspension of differences between them at precisely those moments when the imagination is put to work on the intersections of history and geography. But in Warner's novel, the belief in the existence of a "deep" England, underlying the surface appearances of modernity, is identified with a character who believes herself to be a witch but whose visions may be the product of her psychological history. The authorial attitude is scrupulously withheld, leaving the reader to choose between alternative frameworks within which to place the writing's enthusiasm for conjuring up the subliminal presences within the landscape:

> Once a wood, always a wood. The words rang true, and she sat silent, considering them. Pious Asa might hew down the groves, but as far as the Devil was concerned he hewed in vain. Once a wood, always a wood: trees where he sat would crowd into a shade. And people going by in broad sunlight would be aware of slow voices overhead, and a sudden chill would fall upon their flesh. Then, if like her they had a natural leaning towards the Devil, they would linger, listening about them with half-closed eyes and averted senses; but if they were respectable people like Henry and Caroline they would talk rather louder and hurry on. There remaineth a rest for the people of God (somehow the thought of the Devil always propelled her mind to the Holy Scriptures), and for the other people, the people of Satan, there remained a rest also. Held fast in that strong memory no wild thing could be shaken, no secret covert destroyed, no haunt of shadow and silence laid open. The goods

yard at Paddington, for instance – a savage place! as holy and enchanted as ever it had been. Not one of the monuments and tinkerings of man could impose on the satanic mind. The Vatican and the Crystal Palace, and all the neat human nest-boxes in rows, Balham and Fulham and the Cromwell Road – he saw through them, they went flop like card-houses, the bricks were earth again, and the steel girders burrowed shrieking into the veins of earth, and the dead timber was restored to the ghostly groves. Wolves howled through the streets of Paris, the foxes played in the throne-room of Schönbrunn, and in the basement at Apsley Terrace the mammoth slowly revolved, trampling out its lair.[14]

Whether this trance-like response to the land is prompted by intimations of the supernatural or by compulsions that have their origin in the unconscious, Warner's imaginative wager allows her to strip away the accretions of modernity as so much trash, giving a fictional pretext for one of the defining paradoxes of modernist poetry that builds its meanings around the juxtaposition and contrast between past and present, between authentic and specious, between what is whole and what is fragmentary. The evocation of the spirit world as the means of access to a buried original parallels the fascination with haunting that breaks the surface of many of the key texts of high modernism concerned with their obligations toward tradition. However, the magisterial and patronising attitude that keeps these revenants under authorial control is unavailable to the reader of Warner's novel, where the forces unleashed are more liable to overthrow than to contribute to the systems of order, taste and decency seemingly embodied in the outward lives of middle-class spinsters like Lolly Willowes. The symptoms of social malaise in this novel are very close to those that lead to the mental disintegration of Dorothy Hare in George Orwell's early novel *A Clergyman's Daughter* (1935), coincidentally the text that includes his most experimental writing.

If Warner's modernism drags the novel some distance from realism toward supernaturalism, it does not go as far as Laura Riding's parabolic fictions in *Progress of Stories* (1935). Although some of the texts in this volume refer to facets of the contemporary social world, seen from a disturbingly alien viewpoint, others are metaphysical fables that observe life on earth through a prism of time–space distortions. The final text, "In the End," although particularly bizarre, is also the most expository in its reimagining of the meaning, not just of the concept of "land," but of the entire terrestrial globe:

For indeed the earth had been never any more than a surface. When the surface was called an earth it was as a lining turned outward to seem the very thing it is meant to line. Thus the earth seemed a world. And since it was not truly a world – since it was only the lining of the true world turned outward against its destined use – instead of the true world there was only an inner surface without an inside. Instead of an inside there was only an outside; instead of a house there was only an emptiness; instead of a place to live in there was only a surface to cling to, against the fear of falling into the emptiness which began with the sky . . . And so for a time it seemed that men lived on the earth, though this could not be. They were permitted to seem to live there, as if the earth were a place, because of their fear of falling into the emptiness which began with the sky. For this fear was their confession that by itself the earth was only the lining of an emptiness. By clinging to the earth they told the truth: that they knew that the world which they tried in themselves to be, as a world in itself, was only a lining and an emptiness.[15]

The text anticipates a future referred to in the past tense, employing a rhetorical sleight of hand to make its imaginings seem incontrovertible, a matter of future historical record. Riding's hypothetical reversal of inside and outside, of the recto and verso of available systems of meaning, has to be understood in the context of her renunciation of poetry three years later, in 1938. Her view of the history of poetic writing in terms of an aggregation of truth culminating in her own work must be seen in conjunction with her impatience of what she calls "period-modernism" with its literary products that encourage the general acceptance of semantic "confusion."[16] Riding contends that language divided into various discourses maintained by professional custodians is language separated from the truth. She supposes that her own work offers only a "fore-sense" of "Something After" (p. 13). This "Something After" is a "single terminology of truth to supersede our terminological diversity" – a desideratum, it might be argued, whose credibility would entirely depend on its *being* after; so that, to carry us with her, Riding would have to have ceased to write. Her absolute silence as a poet after 1938 might be tested as the only adequate correspondent to the manner of speaking the truth that she has in mind: a species of utterance so unprecedented that it is unrecognizable: "I expect you only to know that there has been a change when there has been a change."[17]

Riding's bulletins since 1938 have been remarkable for their religiosity; poems are distinguished from the poetic motive in terms of the "ritualistic" and the "religious"; "craft" as opposed to "creed." Poetry is credited with a potential spirituality – it could be the perfect induction to a "state of grace" – but it also courts the "unholy" danger of pride in artistry. At the same time, the "Something After" is not beyond human scope, and it is most emphatically not extra-linguistic, so that Riding's attempt to confer a spiritual status on what poetry is an obstacle to, has to struggle with the religious conception of the doubleness of language; of the coexistence of human and divine orders of meaning in the figure of the Incarnation; of a truth whose completeness is assured by its being able to cope with the "sensuosity" that Riding rejects. Her insistence that religion always involves "a break between past and present; the stories do not reach into the present, and reach over it only into futures that grow instantly old at touch"(p. 39), effectively gives warning of the limit of her own schema of truth as being "Something After"; something that must either remain after, or grow instantly old at touch.

Whatever else it does, Riding's future comes after modernism. By contrast, the fictions of Butts and Warner retrieve a spiritual dimension in their arching backward, rather than forward, in time; and in this they share a general modernist investment in the past, whether as the matrix of values that now seem remote; as the starting-point for the emulation of forerunners; as a triangulation point for the dialectic; or finally as an anchor that creates cultural inertia, a reverse traction that the contemporary artist must survive through immersion in the fluidity and unpredictability of consciousness in time. To reject all of that as a series of mistakes is to break with modernism altogether, in one of the first, and still one of the most authoritative, formulations of what constitutes the postmodern.

NOTES

1 Wyndham Lewis, "The New Egos," *Blast*, 1 (June 20, 1914) p. 141.
2 Wilhelm Worringer, *Abstraction and Empathy: A Contribution to the Psychology of Style*, trans. Michael Bullock (London: Routledge and Kegan Paul, 1953) p. 15.
3 Ibid., p17
4 Wyndham Lewis, *The Revenge for Love* (1937; London: Secker & Warburg, 1982) p. 161.
5 Ivy Compton-Burnett, *More Women Than Men* (1933; London: Gollancz, 1972) pp. 5–6.
6 Henry Green, *Living* (London: Hogarth Press, 1929) p. 29.
7 James Barke, *Major Operation* (London: Collins, 1936) pp. 122–3.
8 See Rod Mengham, "The thirties: politics, authority, perspective," *The Cambridge History of Twentieth Century English Literature*, ed. Laura Marcus and Peter Nicholls (Cambridge: Cambridge University Press, 2004) pp. 359–78; and "Anthropology at Home: domestic interiors in British film and fiction of the 1930s and 1940s," *Imagined Interiors: representing the domestic interior since the Renaissance*, ed. Jeremy Aynsley and Charlotte Grant (London: V&A Publications, 2006) pp. 244–55.
9 "Anthropology at Home," *New Statesman and Nation* (January 30, 1937).
10 Christopher Isherwood, "Prologue," in Gerald Hamilton, *Mr Norris and I* (London: Allan Wingate, 1956); reprinted in *Exhumations: Stories, Articles, Verses* (London: Methuen, 1966) pp. 86–7.
11 Christopher Isherwood, "The Turn Round the World," *Exhumations*, p. 214.

12 Mary Butts, "Speed the Plough," *With and Without Buttons and other stories*, ed. Nathalie Blondel (Manchester: Carcanet, 1991) pp. 9–10.

13 Mary Butts, "Green," *With and Without Buttons and other stories*, pp. 74–5.

14 Sylvia Townsend Warner, *Lolly Willowes* (London: Chatto Windus, 1926) pp. 230–1.

15 Laura Riding, "In the End," *Progress of Stories* (London: Constable, 1935) pp. 334–5.

16 Laura Riding, "Preface," *Selected Poems: in Five Sets* (London: Faber and Faber, 1970) p. 11.

17 Laura (Riding) Jackson, *The Telling* (London: The Athlone Press, 1972) p. 52.

6

MATTHEW HART

Regionalism in English fiction between the wars

Writing about romanticism in 1924, A. O. Lovejoy lamented that the word "romantic" had "come to mean so many things that, by itself, it means nothing. It has ceased to perform the function of a verbal sign."[1] While I will not suggest that a similar lament applies to terms like *regionalism*, an essay on the interwar English regional novel cannot afford to bracket similar worries. In a 1941 PEN pamphlet, *The English Regional Novel*, Phyllis Bentley identifies the 1920s and 1930s as a period of resurgence in regional fiction, a time during which novelists like Winifred Holtby added "the last touch of consciousness to the regional *genre*."[2] But what, after all, is "the regional"? A region can be as large as the European peninsula. Within the political enterprise that is the European Union, however, regions subdivide a continent already sliced up into nation-states – and even then what counts as a region is far from certain. According to the latest *Map of European Regions*, a region might be an abstract geographical area like "Mid East Ireland"; a subnational cultural and political unit like Bavaria; or a national but substate territory like Scotland or Wales. England appears to present a different problem altogether: the Assembly of European Regions divides it into some eighty-seven portions, including counties, parts of counties, and metropolitan authorities.[3] Things are hardly more clear at the level of literary history, where "region" is used to describe something as diverse as multilingual and multi-national literatures of the Caribbean archipelago and as specific as 1960s "Liverpool Scene" poetry. If we are fully to grasp the implications of regionalism as a thematic and generic trend in English fiction of the interwar years, then we must first be clear about the protean nature of this thing called a region.

***

The Winifred Holtby Memorial Prize for best regional novel of the year was awarded annually by the Royal Society of Literature (RSL) from 1967 until 2003. The list of winners includes texts as regionally distinct as Anita Desai's novel set in the India hill station of Kasauli (*Fire on the Mountain* [1977]), Adam Thorpe's historical novel about a Wessex village (*Ulverton* [1992]), and Giles Foden's account of a Scottish doctor's residence in Uganda (*The Last King of Scotland* [1998]). This diversity of geographical settings suggests that the Holtby Prize list can tell us little about insular English regionalism other than that "the regional" is an elastic concept with transnational applicability. Nevertheless, a brief reading of one of the prizewinners – Graham Swift's *Waterland* (1983) – helps illuminate relative and permeable aspects of regions as fiction represents them.

Waterland moves between Tom Crick's history classroom in London and his childhood home in the Fens of East Anglia. Though framed by Crick's 1980s, Swift ranges historically from the ice age that severed Britain from Europe, through the epoch of Empire and industry that saw rivers and bogs transformed into navigable waterways and workable farmland, to the days when the presence of American airbases testifies to the waning of British power. Described thus, *Waterland* could be an allegory about the transience of an empire built on water (more unstable even than sand); but it is less a narrative of historical decline than one about the permeability of categories that structure devolutionary stories. Everything in *Waterland* – landscape, memory, desire, guilt – oozes and shifts like the River Ouse itself, which "flows on, unconcerned with ambition, whether local or national."[4] The waters that shape the topography of the Fens guarantee their distinctiveness. But water is also a medium that connects East Anglia to England and the world. Addressing the coming of World War I, Crick explains how "for centuries" his ancestors had "remained untouched by the wide world" (p. 16). In 1916, however, conscription had shorn the Fens of men needed to complete a never-ending job of drainage. The floodwaters return and the Cricks are packed off to Flanders where, in a "familiar-but-foreign" landscape ridden by flooding, they learn that their region and others are hopelessly intermeshed. "Who will not feel in this twentieth century of ours," Crick lectures, "the mud of Flanders sucking at his feet?" (p. 17).

Waterland foregrounds a truth that will be useful in reading earlier twentieth-century regional fictions: that while we might think of a richly imagined locale like the Fens as a little world unto itself, regions cannot be defined in self-sufficient terms. Indeed, if we are to follow the RSL's thinking, "the regional" is now a hopelessly old-fashioned term for the more diffuse concept of "place," a word less contaminated by a sense of parochial apartness. "Place" defines the RSL's successor to the Holtby award since 2004: the Ondaatje Prize, given for a "work of fiction, non-fiction or poetry, evoking the spirit of a place."[5] But whatever the present status of "region" among members of the RSL and in the world of literary prizes, the term is commensurate with "place" in that it is most meaningful in relation to a "constitutive outside" – to the metropolis, for instance, or to the nation-state or the global marketplace.[6] In the modern world, moreover, with its rapid advances in transportation and telecommunications, the "outside" of the city, exchange, or foreign battlefield more and more interpenetrates the space of a region. Indeed, in the first half of the twentieth century and after, interpenetration of the local and its alternatives often becomes the very theme or structuring principle of regional writing. J. B. Priestley's tour through English regions *English Journey* (1934) therefore begins not with a meditation on an ineradicable otherness between Priestley's Yorkshire birthplace and his London domicile but with a hymn to the comfort, speed, and omnipresence of mass transportation – "there seems to be a motor coach going anywhere in this island" – and with reflections on how the Great West Road confounds the landscape of Hampshire with the streetscape of California.[7]

Mobility afforded by modern communications also helps explain how, in the context of the four nations that constitute Britain, "English" regionalisms rarely are merely regional. In Dorothy L. Sayers's *The Five Red Herrings* (1931), for example, representation of the Scottish region of Galloway and of crime and crime detection there depends upon transnational (but intrastate) transportation. For in this mystery about the death of a local artist in the area around Kirkcudbright, it is only through skillful employment and interpretation of the railway timetable that Sayers's sleuth Lord Peter Wimsey identifies and captures the murderer, who has made similarly canny use of the trains to escape discovery. It is the very accessibility of Galloway – a picturesque stop off the main route from Glasgow to London – that turns an erstwhile mill town (Gatehouse of Fleet) into an artists' colony that is home not only to local types and English nobles but also to Scots from all regions and provincial Englishmen too. As a place of cross-border mixing, Sayers's Galloway becomes both more Scottish and less, a literary region rather than a space of national difference.

Priestley's travelogue and Sayers's mystery, although very different kinds of writing, together reveal metropolitan meanings in regional narratives, where writer and reader think in terms of identities, differences, and inequalities that make a region a constitutive part of larger political and economic spaces. While one sense of "region" refers to an autonomous district, this usage, as Raymond Williams put it, has been steadily overtaken by a scalar language implying a relation of power, as in the discourse of political regionalism, which suggests "passing power *down*: an act within the terms of domination and subordination."[8] This language of subordination implies a complementary regional *ressentiment*, as in an assertion like Angel Clare's in Hardy's *Tess of the D'Urbervilles* (1891) that Wessex milk is too rich for London "centurions."[9] Yet while it is important to recognize oppositional aspects in regionalist assertions of independence, it is equally important to resist uncritical notions of regional differentiation, which help construct "essentialist definitions of the [geographical] subject" and thereby depoliticize the very injustices that motivate Angel's contempt for the imperial shocktroops of the metropolis.[10]

What Cheryl Herr calls "critical regionalism" demystifies any image of unique and autochthonous space that we might fantasize to be the truth of regional geography and identity. For whereas a region might *feel* like a redoubt from national governments or global markets, states have long known the benefits of devolving certain powers to their margins, while the marketing departments of transnational corporations "actually benefit from people's absorption in regional diversity."[11] A reminder that regional fictions have long been written and published – and avidly read – by metropolitan women and men highlights the literary dimensions of this problem. For a reluctant city dweller like Conservative Prime Minister Stanley Baldwin, Mary Webb's *Precious Bane* (1924), a bestseller about rural life during the Napoleonic Wars, features such a profound "blending of human passion with the fields and skies" that "one who reads some passages in Whitehall," as Baldwin writes in his introduction to the novel, "has almost the physical sense of being in Shropshire cornfields."[12] Baldwin's comment suggests that "regional writing's popularity was sustained by its ability to fill an imagined need in its urban readers"[13] – a need to assuage urban life's dislocations with soothing ideas about the magic of the countryside; and to project onto "regions" a definable and manageable character, in order to compensate for unmanageable formations of class, culture, and identity that increasingly define readers' lives. It is in this latter context that Webb's novels, which Phyllis Bentley describes as shining "a rich strange light...which was never shone on the real sea or land," become more than romantic compendia of Shropshire dialect and folklore (*English*, p. 34). They are legible instead as allegories about historical change and mutable identities in all regions, and in metropolitan or cosmopolitan places as well. *Precious Bane* exhibits such allegorical character when Prudence Sarn, watching a dragonfly struggle to escape its chrysalis, notes the difficulty of creating what is new from within the skin of what is old: " 'Well,' I says, with a bit of a laugh and summat near a bit of a sob, 'well, you've done it! It's cost you summat, but you've won free.' "[14] Webb's novel is an exemplary illustration of what David Harvey argues in *Spaces of Capital*: "regions are 'made' or 'constructed' as much in imagination as in material form" (p. 225). This mix of imaginative and material elements appears throughout interwar regional fictions.

***

What these fictions might share most, however, is their sense of regions as points of difference that are linked, if not continuous, with the space of the nation-state and with international and transnational movements.

The point of difference is often expressed most immediately, and in condensed form, as a response to a specific landscape. Katherine, an immigrant heroine in Philip Larkin's *A Girl in Winter* (1947), delights in the sight of Oxfordshire's "extraordinary soft greenness."[15] By contrast, George Orwell on his way to Wigan through the Potteries revolts against the "pot-banks like monstrous burgundy bottles half buried in the soil, belching forth smoke."[16] In both responses a regional topography becomes a motive for unfolding more "extraordinary" differences than are signified by the place when it first elicits an impression. For Katherine Oxfordshire's greenness reveals a foreign but characteristically English pastoral that survives only in memory, an ironic contrast to the drabness and moral dullness of a provincial city in wartime. For Orwell the ugliness of England's depressed industrial regions discloses how the country is "notoriously two nations, the rich and the poor."[17]

Orwell's analysis of England's economic divide in *The Road to Wigan Pier* (1937) is complicated by his decision to go to Lancashire "partly because I wanted to see what mass unemployment is like at its worst, partly in order to see the most typical section of the English working class at close quarters."[18] Orwell's decision to treat the region as simultaneously typical and exceptional places a strain on the veracity of his judgments – a strain, characteristic of regional narratives, that shows itself in Orwell's indulging his Cockney roommate's description of Northerners as backwards in their squalor ("The filthy bloody bastards!") while simultaneously accusing Left Book Club readers of believing the "four frightful words" that their politics otherwise forbid: "The lower classes smell" (pp. 28, 112).

Tension between exceptionality and typicality is frequently found in literary regionalism. Writers like Orwell often try to ease this tension through appeals to underdevelopment, whereby the association of regions with "backwardness" mixes spatial and temporal forms to become what Mikhail Bakhtin called *chronotopes*, narrative structures in which "time...takes on flesh, becomes artistically visible" and "space becomes charged and responsive to...movements of time, plot, and history."[19] The popularity of regional chronotopes in British fiction after the Romantic period can be explained as a reaction to the state's enclosure of common land and mapping of it, subjecting it to "the political demography of the age." A creation of "invented" regions like Webb's Shropshire is thus a "natural and understandable" compensatory device for the depredations of modernity, with backwardness losing its pejorative connotations and gaining an oppositional charge (Wade, p. 17). However, the regional chronotope does not simply *mingle* time and place so as to assert or isolate regional difference; instead the spatial axis disrupts the nation-state's assumption that all its components share a progressive and uniform historical time. Far from representing a unitary temporal space, regions within the imagined community of the nation reveal a non-contemporaneous political space, "a collection of communities," Leigh Ann Duck argues, "moving at different rates in trajectories characterized by different customs."[20] Regionalism therefore gives the lie to unifying and universal narratives of economic or technological progress. At the same time, the apparently oppositional force of regionalism can be undercut by the way it also works to make geographically organized inequalities appear normal and natural within ostensibly unified states.

In the English or British context strongly regional trends in the years between the wars can be attributed to two major historical processes, both of which attest to the ideologically charged character of regional chronotopes. The first is the decline of Britain's global empire; the second, of particular interest to interwar reporters like Orwell and Priestley, is the fact of the Great Depression.

Although Britain's overseas territories were never more extensive than in the 1920s, having been newly enlarged by Mandate protectorates in the Middle East and Tanganyika, in retrospect it is clear that imperial decline began with the Second Boer War of 1899–1901, and was made inevitable by effects of the 1914–18 conflagration. Ireland rebelled in 1916 and the twenty-six counties of the Free State left the UK in 1922. In the same year Egypt won rights of limited self-government. The temporary end of Gandhi's campaign of civil disobedience in India signaled less a downturn in his fortunes than the fact that, in an "intermittently ungovernable" India, "British rule . . . depended on his moderation – far more than on [the] police and army."[21] One consequence of the decline in imperial confidence can be felt in writers' search for ideals and spaces that, in their ostensibly local and self-sufficient qualities, aggrandize national experience without reference to the messy and increasingly unsatisfactory realities of Empire. Indeed England's regional riches increasingly come to substitute for dangerous and decolonizing differences "abroad."

The pattern is already observable in a pre-war novel like H. G. Wells's *The History of Mr. Polly* (1909). Though better described as a romance about

England's "nation of shopkeepers" than as a regional text, *Mr. Polly* has much to say about the relation of country life to foreign parts. As a youth in the fictional town of Port Burdock, Polly joins his fellow apprentice salesmen in rambles through "an old-fashioned, scarcely disturbed English country-side."[22] This invocation of primordial England soon gives occasion for the following digression:

> There is no country-side like the English country-side for those who have learnt to love it...Other country-sides have their pleasant aspects, but none such variety, none that shine so steadfastly throughout the year. Picardy is pink and white and pleasant in the blossom time...the Ardennes has its woods and gorges – Touraine and the Rhineland, the wide Campagna with its distant Apennines, and the neat prosperities and mountain backgrounds of South Germany, all clamour their attention at one's memory...But none of these change scene and character in three miles of walking, nor have so mellow a sunlight nor so diversified a cloudland, nor confess the perpetual refreshment of the strong soft winds that blow from off the sea as our Mother England does. (pp. 25, 26)

What begins here in simple contingency ("for those who have learnt to love it") soon becomes more complex in origin. For whereas Wells's points of comparison – Picardy, the Rhineland, and so on – are regions unto themselves, England is both essentially diverse *and* entire to itself, an essence of regional heterogeneity and of heterogeneity's immanent negation. The nation has become the region or, better, *regionalism*. A related paradox comes up later for Polly when, fleeing his failed marriage and business, he sees a beautiful Kentish sunset. Spellbound by twilight's effect on the hills, he feels as if he has been "transported to some strange country" in which it would be "no surprise if the old labourer he came upon leaning silently over a gate had addressed him in an unfamiliar tongue" (p. 267). In the first quotation England's regional characteristics guarantee her motherly wholeness. But the second quotation separates Kent from the whole, making it foreign to itself, a functional equivalent for alien places that Polly never sees but that long supplied the textiles sold in his shop.

Mr. Polly's references to empire are restricted to commodity culture and an allusion to a picture that might have represented "Empire teaching her Sons" (p. 9). Its ending bears comparison, however, to Wells's *The Time Machine* (1895), where time travel is based on a structural reversal of the way that Victorian imperial romances figure journeys to distant lands as voyages to sites in the savage past – a chronotope that requires civilizing government by "advanced" people. For Wells travel into the future is already predicted by a temporal principle that undergirded Britain's exploitation of far-off lands: to travel in the Empire's space is to travel in time, because whether the imperialist goes backwards or forwards, he measures distance from the metropolis in years as well as miles.[23] But whereas *The Time Machine* transports us to a world in which Eloi and Morlocks exist in a dreadful parody of nineteenth-century class exploitation, *Mr. Polly* ends with its hero's unlikely triumph as the lover of the buxom proprietress of the Potwell Inn, freed from a modern world he could never live up to, content to mark time amid rural poplars. As a representative of England's hopeless lower middle class, condemned to perpetuate the slow, chronic failure of Britain's petty capitalists, Polly makes the right decision: he retreats to the country, gives up on futurity, and finds his empire at home.

Wells's prewar novel predicts developments in the 1920s and 1930s. In that context one can build on Jed Esty's work about later modernism in interpreting regionalism as part of an era when "British intellectuals translated the end of empire into a resurgent concept of national culture" – when an insular specificity (rather than imperial universality) of English spaces and customs becomes a promise of redemptive political or social agency.[24] Seen in this light, regional novels are linked to Graham Swift's "wide world" not only by virtue of their mingling with "a constitutive outside," but because their attempt to develop answers to a *general* crisis of modernity on the basis of *local* mores embeds them in a cultural logic of imperial devolution.

John Cowper Powys's *Wolf Solent* (1929) illustrates this logic. The title character begins in full retreat from metropolitan modernity, which he describes as "tyrannous machinery" opposed to man's "individual magnetic strength."[25] Returning to his childhood home in Dorset, Wolf spends much of the novel philosophizing upon things like the unity between his "primitive life-feeling" and pollarded elms. Powys's dramatization of primitive drives is a classic example of counter-modern modernism, wherein excrescences like the empire and the city are only present in their radical absence. Trading London for Dorset, Powys pits Wolf's imaginative spiritual biography against the instrumental rationality of modernity, whereby a victory of science over myth has been won at the cost of an expansive sensuality – an eroticized relation to mind and matter that alone can account for the way a region whispers an "inexplicable prophetic greeting to its returned native-born" (I, pp. 85, 44).

Wolf's struggle ends ambivalently. He is left chastened and cuckolded, his personal mythology reduced to a binary imperative: "*Endure or escape*" (II, p. 966). The effect of Wolf's narrative on the reader is equally uncertain. The reader is either carried away by Powys's mythopoetic imagination or forced to wonder, as Leonard Woolf suggests, whether his regional fantasia amounts to more than "sentimentalism, mysticism, and honest quackery."²⁶ But beyond such responses, *Wolf Solent* reveals a more fundamental ambivalence between its picture of almost complete regional autochthony and its intimations of an ethno-geographic outside. For all its cosmic implications, the world of *Wolf Solent* is only a few square miles wide: Wolf's corner of Dorset and sliver of Somerset, where a Northerner's dialect forever distinguishes him from West Country speakers. And yet this miniature world never escapes an image that haunts Wolf from the start of the novel. At Waterloo Station he sees the face of a beggar whose English visage is a palimpsest of foreign faces: "It was an English face; and it was also a Chinese face, a Russian face, an Indian face . . . And the woe upon the face was of such a character that Wolf knew at once that no conceivable social readjustments or ameliorative revolutions could ever atone for it" (I, pp. 4, 5).

While an undoing of regional retreats by ethnonational globalism is rarely more than implicit in *Wolf Solent*, it is the overt theme of *Sunset Song*, the first volume of *A Scots Quair* (1932–34) by Lewis Grassic Gibbon. Though written in Welwyn Garden City, *Sunset Song* is not only Scottish in language and subject matter but demands to be read within the context of the period's renaissance of cultural and political nationalism. Gibbon's regionalism reminds us, however, that for Scottish writers in Britain the foreign presence in one's beloved region originates close to home, and is legible as contamination *by* Englishness. In *Sunset Song*'s Aberdeenshire village of Kinraddie, therefore, empire is present not only in Chae Strachan's tall tales of life in South Africa or the cultural and economic violence wrought by the 1916 Conscription Act, which sent Scottish farmers to fight in Europe; it is at hand throughout in the way Chris Guthrie is torn between her "English" and "Scottish" selves, between "the sweetness of the Scottish land and skies" and a south that promises liberty and education, "the English words so sharp and clean and true."²⁷ The symbolic geography of *Sunset Song* is similarly torn between Scottish region and Scottish nation, whose capital is identified on its first page as "the foreign south parts." Clearly, in imagining Kinraddie, Grassic Gibbon does not merely set Scottish regional difference against English hegemony. He demonstrates how the small places of the world are caught up in a state of emergency that is global and permanent, where civilization is both blessing and curse and where a novelist's duty to imagine the past and places we have lost does not stop him from passing judgment on their insularity.

Grassic Gibbon's ambivalence about "English" modernity is linked to the material benefits it can bring to an impoverished laboring class – and to the hope that socialism might redistribute those goods for emancipatory ends. It is in this sense that the question of the late empire links up with the

Depression of the 1930s. For Phyllis Bentley the expanded "number" and local "consciousness" of regional novelists after 1929 was due to the "great sociological cause" of the slump, the key fact being that "a trade in England is often coterminous with a region." As the economic crisis "hit the trades of the English one by one" so did it move through the regions, exposing "the common occupation on which we all depended, which linked us to our native soil" (pp. 38–9). Common economic pain bred communal feeling, which then found expression among writers and artists in terms and texts of regional difference. Their feeling of distinctness was not, however, merely a product of "native soil"; rather it was a result of a contingent process that geographers call "sectoral spatial specialization" – a local form of the international division of labor.[28]

The Depression was most marked in industries that followed an old imperial logic of importing raw materials for manufacture and resale to Britain's captive markets in Africa, Asia, and the Caribbean. This is something we see in Walter Greenwood's popular novel *Love on the Dole* (1933), which narrates the scourges of unemployment and poverty as they affect the Hardcastle family of "Hanky Park" in Salford. The characters of *Love on the Dole* speak with what one recent critic celebrates as "local peculiarities of pronunciation and slang [that validate] the truth of what [Greenwood] portrays."[29] As a documentary fiction about a collapse of Lancashire's export industries during the 1930s, *Love on the Dole* testifies to the problem that Orwell described in regard to neighboring Wigan – that "the high standard of life we enjoy in England depends on keeping a tight hold on the Empire" (p. 191) – and thus also testifies to the economic reality that drove a resurgence of regional fictions in the 1930s: "When overseas markets did not want our cloth," Bentley writes, "all of us...suffered" (p. 39). Not for nothing did Priestley explain how the Hindi word "*dhootie*" for cotton loincloth became a "tragic word" in Blackburn which, with the coincidence of the slump and Gandhi's homespun movement, saw a local economy "based on the gigantic output of cheap stuff for the East" all but decimated (p. 277).

Priestley laments that only local charities appear to be battling effects of poverty. "Since when," he asks, "did Lancashire cease to be a part of England?" (p. 286). This question about a region's structural relation to the state is the centerpiece of Winifred Holtby's *South Riding* (1936), which from its prefatory letter to Holtby's mother, who was an Alderman, to the imaginary council documents that introduce each of the novel's parts, is deeply interested in the politics of regional government. Holtby's prologue foregrounds the embedding of the local in the national and international as if they were a set of Russian nesting dolls: "Local government was an epitome of national government. Here was World Tragedy in embryo."[30]

The author of that credo is an inexperienced journalist, Lovell Brown, whose breathless language about "gallant Labour" fighting "armoured Capital" is only partly endorsed by the novel's events (p. 21). *South Riding* has room among its vast cast for the saintly socialist Alderman Astell and for tragic Councilor Robert Carne, who reads like a cross between Jane Austen's Darcy and Christopher Tietjens, the "last English Tory" of Ford Madox Ford's *Parade's End* tetralogy (1924–28). Though Holtby gives space to arguments about the relative values of radical political militancy and reform, she suggests that conflict between workers and gentry ought to be mitigated, first, by an ethical distinction between self-interest and civic duty and, second, by an awareness of the profound limits to what one can achieve politically in either a regional or a national context. In light of the latter awareness, Holtby deploys indefatigable female characters like the local headmistress, Sarah Burton, and Alderman Mrs. Beddows in order to show how a revolutionary like Astell has more in common with an honorable reactionary like Carne than either man would believe or avow. For as Mrs. Beddows insists to Sarah, "all this local government, it's just working together," and as Sarah realizes at the novel's close: "We all pay, she thought; we all take; we are members of one another" (pp. 495, 509).

Holtby's women are not mere bearers of clichés about human fraternity. As players in political battles who are animated by more than chauvinism or factional interest, they are most attuned to the limitations of the communities to which they passionately belong. The final chapter of *South Riding* attests to why local government (or national government) cannot equal self-government. Sarah is on board an aircraft, flying above the South Riding as the people below celebrate George V's silver jubilee. Seeing the cliffs that mark Yorkshire's maritime border, Sarah thinks: "This is the edge of England . . . The bulwark that no longer fortifies." And turning back towards land from her vision of an island vulnerable to invasion from without – whether by aircraft, infection, or global slump – she sees "a huge Union Jack" that flaps "grandly, but to the passengers in the plane it showed no more than a solitary dot of colour" (p. 501). Committed to local government yet internationalist in outlook, *South Riding* oscillates between a view from the air and a view from the ground, now insisting that local politics is the world in miniature, now mourning how the Carnes of Maythorpe are destroyed by "the wind and the rain and the storms from west to east, taxes and tariffs and subsidies and quotas, beef from the Argentine, wool from Australia" (p. 444). Designated until 2003 by the Royal Society of Literature as a signal example of the regional novel, *South Riding* shows as well as any contemporary text how under conditions of global capital that have long shaped the English landscape and the English novel, the dream of regional difference gives way – as the Holtby Prize gave way to the Ondaatje Prize. It gives way to a language of place that designates regions, and their borders, as bulwarks that no longer fortify.

NOTES

1 A. O. Lovejoy, "On the Discrimination of Romanticisms," *PMLA* 39 (1924), 232.
2 Phyllis Bentley, *The English Regional Novel* (London: George Allen and Unwin/ PEN Books, 1948), p. 38; italics in original.
3 See the website of the Assembly of European Regions. www.a-e-r.org/filead-min/user_upload/PressComm/Publications/Tabula/Tabula2005/Tabula2005. jpg. Accessed November 11, 2007.
4 Graham Swift, *Waterland* (London: Heinemann, 1983), p. 127.
5 www.rslit.org/ondaatje.htm. Accessed November 15, 2007.
6 Chantal Mouffe, in *On the Political* (London: Routledge, 2004), p. 15, glosses "constitutive outside" as naming "the fact that the creation of an identity implies the establishment of a difference . . . on the basis of a hierarchy."
7 J. B. Priestley, *English Journey* (London: Heinemann, 1934), pp. 3–4.
8 Raymond Williams, *Keywords: A Vocabulary of Culture and Society*, rev. edn. (New York: Oxford University Press, 1983), p. 265. Italics in original.
9 Thomas Hardy, *Tess of the D'Urbervilles* (London: Penguin, 1985), p. 251.
10 David Harvey, *Spaces of Capital: Towards a Critical Geography* (New York: Routledge, 2001), p. 224.
11 Cheryl Herr, *Critical Regionalism and Cultural Studies: From Ireland to the American Midwest* (Gainesville: University of Florida Press, 1996), p. 4.
12 Stanley Baldwin, "Introduction" (1928) to Mary Webb, *Precious Bane* (South Bend: University of Notre Dame Press, 2003), p. 12.
13 Stephanie Foote, *Regional Fictions: Culture and Identity in Nineteenth-Century American Literature* (Madison: University of Wisconsin Press, 2001), p. 5.
14 Mary Webb, *Precious Bane*, p. 217.
15 Philip Larkin, *A Girl in Winter* (London: Faber, 1982), p. 157.
16 George Orwell, "The *Road to Wigan Pier* Diary," *Collected Essays, Journalism and Letters of George Orwell, Vol. 1: An Age Like This: 1920–40*, eds. Sonia Orwell and Ian Angus (London: Penguin, 1987), p. 196.
17 George Orwell, "The Lion and the Unicorn," *Collected Essays, Journalism and Letters of George Orwell, Vol. 2: My Country Right or Left: 1940–43*, eds. Sonia Orwell and Ian Angus (Boston: Nonpareil Books, 2000), p. 64.
18 George Orwell, *The Road to Wigan Pier* (London: Victor Gollancz, 1937), p. 153.
19 Mikhail Bakhtin, *The Dialogic Imagination*, ed. Michael Holquist; trans. Holquist and Caryll Emerson (Houston: University of Texas Press, 1981), p. 84. Quoted in Stephen Wade, *In My Own Shire: Region and Belonging in British Writing, 1840–1970* (Westport and London: Praeger, 2002), p. 17.
20 Leigh Anne Duck, *The Nation's Region: Southern Modernism, Segregation, and U.S. Nationalism* (Athens: University of Georgia Press, 2006), p. 5.
21 Eric Hobsbawm, *Age of Extremes: A History of the World, 1914–91* (New York: Vintage, 1994), p. 211.

22 H. G. Wells, *The History of Mr. Polly* (New York: Press of the Readers Club, 1941), p. 24.
23 Paul A. Cantor and Peter Hufnagel, "The Empire of the Future: Imperialism and Modernism in H. G. Wells," *Studies in the Novel* 38 (2006), 36–8.
24 Jed Esty, *A Shrinking Island: Modernism and National Culture in England* (Princeton: Princeton University Press, 2004), p. 3.
25 John Cowper Powys, *Wolf Solent*, 2 vols. (New York: Simon and Schuster, 1929), vol. 1, p. 6.
26 Leonard Woolf, "Much Ado About Nothing," *The Nation and Athenaeum* (January 3, 1931), p. 461.
27 Lewis Grassic Gibbon, *Sunset Song* (Edinburgh: Canongate, 1994), p. 32.
28 Doreen Massey, *Space, Place, and Gender* (Minneapolis: University of Minnesota Press, 1994), p. 52
29 Stephen Ross, "Authenticity Betrayed: the 'idiotic folk' of *Love on the Dole*," *Cultural Critique* 56 (2004), 191.
30 Winifred Holtby, *South Riding: An English Landscape* (Glasgow: William Collins, 1981), p. 21.

7

ANNE FOGARTY

Ireland and English fiction

Aesthetic and political struggles shaped fiction writing in Ireland in the twentieth century. Twin but warring needs impelled the contestation. Writers sought to institute a discrete and purpose-built tradition that could mirror and mediate divisions and ideological conflicts endemic in a colonial society and that could treat the traumatic effects of a postcolonial legacy. Yet writers also chafed against such imperatives and resolutely endeavored to escape them. Whereas the English novel was seen as determined by an unbroken lineage rooted in seventeenth- and eighteenth-century antecedents and nurtured by a stable and flourishing bourgeois society, the Irish novel in lacking such accouterments was found wanting. In particular, Irish political ruptures with England in the nineteenth century meant that the conventions of realism did not readily establish themselves. They seemed ill-suited to novelists' aims to render dissension and social upheaval. Instead, absurdist fables, political allegories, Gothic romances, metafictions, peasant tales, and versions of what R. F. Foster has dubbed "the Irish story" took the place of realism.[1]

Sean O'Faolain provocatively claims in his autobiography that "there is no such genre as the Irish Novel."[2] In making this polemical assertion, he does not dispute the achievement of individual Irish authors but laments the absence of a continuous, overarching literary tradition. Colm Tóibín launches a similarly devastating broadside in his account of the vicissitudes of the novel in Ireland.[3] Tóibín holds that fiction is preempted by the already fabulous nature of Irish history, with its dependence on tragic denouements and heroic narratives; and that conflict-laden political realities in the country have loaned themselves more readily to fragmented stories than to the cohesive vision demanded of the novelist. Moreover, Tóibín points out that the swingeing censorship regime exercised in Ireland from the 1930s onwards had the effect of turning writers like Flann O'Brien and John McGahern inwards, compelling them to have recourse to techniques of fracture and evasion rather than to well-turned, linear fictions.

O'Faolain and Tóibín's comments are symptomatic. They indicate that Irish novelists themselves persistently call into question the essence and purchase of the novel in Ireland. Moreover, Irish novelists view narrative form not as a free aesthetic choice but as an inherently politicized imposition or calculation. They hence find themselves in the peculiar position of being forced to invent things afresh and yet of always being subsumed into an inescapable literary inheritance that is itself fundamentally unstable. However, as many critics have contended, precisely this sense of discontinuity and embattlement has given Irish fiction its distinctive contours and dynamism.[4] The Irish novel is always at odds with itself, constantly pitted against the deficits and limitations of the formal structures with which it makes an uneasy compromise.

James Joyce and Irish modernist fiction

The Irish Literary Revival under the aegis of such writers as W. B. Yeats and George Russell (AE) sought to foster a spirit of national independence and political opposition by creating a distinctive and separate cultural sphere. Even though the Revival numbered several novelists in its midst, it concentrated its attentions largely on drama and poetry. James Joyce's choice to produce novelistic fiction explicitly endorsed a literary form that his contemporaries had sidelined. His aim was to harness the novel's political and ethical power and to subvert its apparently fixed conventions in order to capture the essence and slumbering potential of the demoralized Dublin that he had left behind. *A Portrait of the Artist as a Young Man* (1916) adopts the mode of the European *Bildungsroman* but radically alters its tenor, plot lines, and symbolic capacity. The novel provides a succession of conflicting and ironized views of its putative hero, Stephen Dedalus, and culminates in moments of crisis or transformation. The development of the protagonist is depicted not as a smooth progression but as a series of jolting discoveries and insights. Stephen's discomfiture at the fact that the very language he uses is a borrowed one – it is a product of English colonial rule – fuels his final decision to pursue rebellion through art, thereby creating "the uncreated conscience" of his race.[5] Vocational aspiration and utopian social transformation are thus linked at the end of *A Portrait of the Artist as a Young Man*, even though the destiny of the hero remains poised between success and failure, between the resourceful creativity of Daedalus on the one hand and the tragic fall of Icarus on the other.

In *Ulysses* (1922) Joyce invents a capacious form in order to construct what he termed an epic of everyday life. Modern fiction in this new guise becomes an archive for the minutiae of material reality; and captures, in the represented space of a single day, the textures and rhythms of urban experience and the distracted, alienated nature of twentieth-century subjectivity. The wanderings of Homer's *Odyssey* are reconfigured in the travails and intersecting fates of Joyce's protagonists, Leopold Bloom, Stephen Dedalus, and Molly Bloom. Even though a homecoming of sorts is effected when Bloom and Stephen repair to No. 7 Eccles Street for late-night conversation and Epps cocoa, *Ulysses* underscores a sense of dispossession that is a characteristic of a colonial society such as Ireland's. The characters meet in makeshift locales and public spaces such as city streets, pubs, a library, a graveyard, a brothel, and a maternity hospital. Even the characters' seemingly privatized reflections (captured by the stream of consciousness device that Joyce deploys amidst a panoply of other novelistic techniques) are shown to be porous and infiltrated by political and social memory. The Boer War, World War I, the Phoenix Park murders, and a divorce scandal triggering the deposition and death of Irish nationalist leader Charles Stewart Parnell surface in characters' thoughts and exchanges throughout the day. A climactic encounter in *Ulysses'* "Cyclops" episode hinges on a heated dispute about definitions of national and ethnic identity.

Ulysses foregrounds the determining role of language in aesthetic practice. In the novel's pages the transparency of words that is often a given of mimetic fiction no longer obtains. Rather, in a manner characteristic of modernist aesthetics, style predominates and assumes control; and the resulting obtrusive mechanics of narration frequently appear to impede instead of facilitate our comprehension of things. But thanks to this proliferation of seemingly self-propelling styles, *Ulysses* ultimately urges its readers actively to reflect on how meanings and social and political values are created, and to be wary of the ideological power that accepted linguistic codes and conventions can wield over us. "Penelope," the final episode of the text, fulfills such a function in prompting us to rethink unassailable features of the novel such as the life-likeness of character and the causality posited by fictional plots. For "Penelope" counters much of what we had gleaned about Molly Bloom as a figure while insisting that the perspectives that the episode affords are equally error-prone and grounded in illusion. Yet despite the autocritique of the novel that "Penelope" enacts, the episode concludes on a promising note. Molly's mingled memories of the sensual delights of Gibraltar and of the erotic pleasures of an outing with Bloom to Howth convert recollection into a mode of desire that is open to an unforeclosed future. Desire's prospects of unfettered freedom are abetted by the novel's multiple modalities, evading closure and conclusiveness.

If *Ulysses* in part succeeds in decoupling the novel from representation, Joyce's *Finnegans Wake* (1939) even more radically fractures the decorum of mimetic form. Even though narrative and character are not abandoned in Joyce's final fictional experiment, it is the polysemic nature of language that generates the text's symbolic patterns and that acts as the dynamo of its febrile palimpsest of meanings. Individual words here become hypercharged with signification, while phrases and paragraphs suggest coinciding micro-narratives that have to be deciphered and unraveled. In fusing at least sixty-five natural languages in *Finnegans Wake*, Joyce prosecutes his quest to invent a form of expression that frees him from tutelage to English. Although the *Wake* retains aspects of English syntax and semantics, it also systematically displaces them and deconstructs them.

Joyce's "book about the night" projects opaque, phantom narratives, many of which revolve around a protean, archetypal family that he places at its core.[6] HCE, a paterfamilias, whose mysterious sexual transgressions in Phoenix Park have led to his downfall; Issy, a wayward and alluring daughter who is the object of erotic attention from her erring father; Anna Livia Plurabelle, a maternal river of language with a troubled past; and warring fraternal twins Shem and Shaun are all in the family. But the familial components ramify, like everything else in the *Wake*, into a myriad roles and stories. Mythic tales of patricide, of guilt and reparation, and of death and rebirth also give contour to the text: HCE reawakens in the course of the narrative just as a final lyrical threnody by Anna Livia presages a return to its beginnings. The *Wake* telescopes and interfuses all literature and world history. It reflects particularly on betrayals and reversals in the Irish past through the figures of Roderick O'Connor, Tristram and Isolde, the four Masters of the Gospels, and St. Kevin and St. Patrick, in order to locate elemental patterns. However, this compendious, endlessly enigmatic text ultimately resists reduction to pat universals or conveniently streamlined narratives.[7] *Finnegans Wake* invites readerly engagement while forcing us always to recognize the provisionality of the cognitive frames that we adduce in order to make sense of Joyce's anarchic excess.

Whereas Joyce's writing is qualified by its encyclopaedism and expansiveness, Samuel Beckett's is characterized by attenuation and contraction. Although Beckett consciously struggled against the influence of his literary forebear, he may also be seen as redefining the contours of the Irish novel in a manner that continues aspects of modernism's Joycean legacy. Like Joyce, Beckett confounds our expectations about language and narrative. He does so by subjecting the hermeneutic power of fiction to relentless scrutiny. Storytelling is an inveterate habit for Beckett's characters; it is revealed to be at once a necessary prop of Being and also one of its chief illusions. In an early novel, *Murphy* (1938), the eponymous hero tries to sidestep the messy contingencies of physical existence and to retreat into an unalloyed state of abstraction while tied naked to a rocking chair. His attempt to retreat completely into the mind is, however, doomed to failure. His death, whether by misadventure or design, seems precipitated by his encounter with the manic Mr. Endon, who shares his solipsism and desire to obliterate the world outside himself. The characters of the Beckett trilogy, *Molloy, Malone Dies, The Unnamable* (1950–52), are driven to acts of narration that are instantly countermanded or subsequently canceled out. Yet this very process of negation is the means by which Beckett's characters grapple with reality and strive for ontological insight.[8] The Unnamable sheds all of the fictional identities that he has projected or that have been foisted on him, only to be drawn back into an attempt to track down the essence of a subjectivity that remains insecure and unfathomable: "I say I, knowing it's not I."[9] His ruminations reveal the falsity of fiction – and its unabating necessity. The Unnamable ends in the frail expectation that he has at last arrived at the threshold of his own story, even while realizing that this new narrative will lead only to further desolate confrontations with the nullity that constitutes the self: "where I am, I don't know, I'll never know, in the silence you don't know, you must go on, I can't go, I'll go on" (p. 382).

From 1960 onwards Beckett's late short fiction, which he composed in French and later translated into English, sketches imaginative scenes that are even more curtailed and opaque than those envisaged in the trilogy. His final prose works are couched in a style of a stark lyrical plangency. Yet, narratologically and philosophically, they address the fundamental complexities that form the kernel of all his writing. The haunting *Ill Seen Ill Said* (1981), for example, records the movements of a white-haired old woman, declared to be both dying and dead, in an abandoned cabin that resembles the inside of the skull. The fumbling, impersonal narrator desperately tries to capture the scene and to recover aspects of memory in the face of encroaching annihilation: "Absence supreme good and yet."[10] The quest of all of Beckett's work is to find a means of narrating the "first last moment" (p. 59) and of restaging the dilemma of human identity, despite suffused awareness of its own finiteness. Beckett's metatextual experiments deconstruct the premises of a metaphysics that they can never quite abandon.

Self-conscious narration is the mainstay of the fiction of Flann O'Brien, one of the pseudonyms of Brian O'Nolan. Whereas Joyce and Beckett left Ireland and chose a self-preserving exile as a prerequisite for their pursuit of writing, O'Brien remained in the country and, despite his combativeness, perhaps became a casualty of its provincialism. His brilliantly inventive, absurdist metafictions may be said to provide a commentary on the inhibiting conservatism of Irish Catholicism and on the anxieties of an author who never securely established his persona or located a viable audience. *At-Swim-Two-Birds* (1939) concerns a student who is writing a novel about an author who also is composing a novel. This secondary novelist, Dermot Trellis, embarking on a book that is an unlikely composite of smut and moral tract, has forced all of his characters to reside with him. The characters, including a son he has fathered by raping one of his fictional creations, rebel against his tyranny, hold him hostage, rework bits of his text, and bring him to trial for his abusive treatment and denial of their freedom. Their insurrection allows O'Brien to interleave numerous authorial texts and to mimic the intertextual design, with multiple sources and voices, of modernist works. A struggle between autonomy and subordination thus underlies the comic pastiche that O'Brien assembles. In also producing parodies of early Irish texts such as the epics of Finn McCool, O'Brien is at once satirizing the translations of members of the Irish Literary Revival as well as techniques of literary modernism. Yet O'Brien never relinquishes the controlling and shaping power of the author, despite his seeming endorsement of a radical empowerment of readers and texts, and his pointed attack on conflicting artistic traditions to which he was heir. The final fragmentary installment of *At-Swim-Two-Birds* notes that death is a full stop. The text ends in a melancholic albeit ironic quietus with a disquisition on mental illness and the description of the death of an obsessive compulsive. O'Brien's rebellious remodeling of the Irish novel is at once flamboyant and muted. A specter of defeat underlies and dogs his satirical bravado and aesthetic subversiveness.

"Exquisite sadness": rewriting domesticity in the "Big House" novel

The "Big House" novel, which has as its chosen locale the country houses and estates of the Anglo-Irish Protestant landowning class, is a peculiarly female preserve. Maria Edgeworth's *Castle Rackrent* (1800) is the earliest manifestation of a genre that has been successfully adapted by women writers in the twentieth century, including Elizabeth Bowen, Molly Keane, and Jennifer Johnston. This mode flourishes when the class that it describes is in decline and forced to cede the status and privilege that it had once enjoyed. Consequently, romantic and familial themes explored in such fictions do not lend themselves to harmonious endings. The dissonances that form its substance also permit an inspection of the travails of femininity and of gender roles. Marriage and domesticity in these novels are shown to be intertwined with usurpation and disempowerment. The Big House also is a Gothic space haunted by violent traces of past traumas, by repressed subaltern histories that it harbors, and by the psychic aftermath of human struggle.

Elizabeth Bowen represents Danielstown, the Big House setting of *The Last September* (1929), as an uncanny domain, a place of "toppling immanence."[11] The seemingly inconsequential activities of Danielstown's owners, the Naylors, and their guests, mask unsettling connections among all the disparate social groups in the North Cork countryside during the Irish War of Independence: the local Irish middle class, the IRA gunmen, the British Army troops, and the beleaguered and hapless Anglo-Irish. Bowen's distinctive prose style – featuring syntactical inversions, contortions, and double negatives – and her endowment of objects and spaces with a sentience that her characters often lack, facilitate her creation of a narrative mode that renders the disjointedness and strained relations of the Irish social world during the era of anti-colonialist unrest. In making Lois Farquar, a motherless and brooding adolescent, the key protagonist, moreover, Bowen creates a further medium through which to channel the uncanny forces of the novel. Lois, desiring adult identity and romance, brings disturbing memories, such as the abortive love affair of her mother, back to the surface of life; and challenges proprieties in fantasizing equally about the IRA gunman she encounters and about the British soldier, Gerald Lesworth, who is her fiancé. Gerald's death constitutes a further trailing non-event in this novel, which Bowen insistently structures around lacunae rather than in terms of clarifying highlights or dramatic moments of action. Jarring with our expectations of a *Bildungsroman*, Lois's progress as romantic heroine or as a presiding alienated presence is summarily cut short when, banished to France, she disappears from the narrative. An abrupt fast-forwarding in the novel's final paragraph to the burning of Danielstown shockingly crystallizes hidden but palpable hostilities that define Irish colonial relations. Yet the novel, while courting an apocalyptic ending, refuses a sense of elegy. It instead produces an exacting philosophical meditation on the violence and losses of Irish history.[12]

Molly Keane also exploits the Big House novel, infusing it with biting comedy and flamboyantly grotesque satire. *Two Days in Aragon* (1941) recounts events in 1920 that lead to the burning of Aragon, the home of the Anglo-Irish Fox family.[13] The narrative notes the "exquisite sadness" of such domains, which it avers is caused by "an acceptance of violence and desertion" (p. 139). The plot uncovers cruelty caused by the sexual philandering of male landlords with their Irish servants. Nan O'Neill the housekeeper and former family nurse is driven by an irrational loyalty to the house because she is the illegitimate child of a previous master. The affair between her son Foley, who has IRA sympathies, and Grania Fox, a daughter of the house, precipitates the crises of the novel. Keane is especially interested in tracking the transgenerational impact of abuse within the Big

House, and the way in which miscegenation, undermining the family, issues in sadistic pathologies. But she also plots how the exchange of power might be effected in a riven community; and, unlike Bowen, she considers what happens after the demise of the Big House. Grania survives in *Two Days in Aragon* because of her ability to love across ethnic divides; and in *Loving and Giving* (1988) ultimately the house is inherited by Willie, the ostracized Irish servant.

Embattled realisms: identity and critique in Southern Irish fiction (1941–1999)

Modernist experimentalism and the fixed genre of the Big House novel represent only two facets of the twentieth-century Irish novel. Key writers have adapted other modes in order to create narratives that permit critical engagement with Irish society. In particular the *Bildungsroman* and realist novels concentrating on intergenerational conflict are reworked and utilized to examine vexed relations between self and society and degrees to which the family, an ideological bulwark of modern Ireland, stifles personal development.[14] In *The Land of Spices* (1941) Kate O'Brien depicts the interwoven fates of a Belgian nun, Mère Marie Hélène, and her pupil, Anna Murphy, at an Irish boarding school. Both are marked by family tribulations: the Reverend Mother is haunted by her inadvertent discovery of her father's homosexuality while the Irish schoolgirl's domestic life is marred by her father's alcoholism. The bounded feminocentric world of the convent school is shown to be a partial counterweight to the power structures of patriarchal society. O'Brien's heroines succeed in co-ordinating their vocation and need for freedom, but are forced to sacrifice commonplace happiness as a consequence. Edna O'Brien in *The Country Girls Trilogy* (1960–1964) also posits the pursuit of desire as the key problem of her twinned heroines, romantic Kate Brady and pragmatic Baba Brennan. While their sexual transgressiveness flouts nationalist pieties and Catholic morality, neither of the protagonists can free herself from the debilitating legacy of her family. Each becomes caught in a self-defeating cycle of suffering and self-abasement. In particular, identificatory attachment with their mothers scars O'Brien's heroines, making it difficult for them to escape the fate of abjection with which the maternal role is associated.[15]

John McGahern has consistently composed naturalistic family fables that probe faultlines in Irish society and challenge the readiness of newly prosperous Ireland to edit aspects of the past – particularly its ideological conflicts – that seem unsavory and outmoded. Moran in *Amongst Women* (1990) constantly relives his erstwhile existence as a guerrilla fighter in the

War of Independence and imposes a domestic despotism that saps the spirit of his family, especially that of his young wife and daughters. History for McGahern is never neatly linear and the past can rarely be securely ousted. Moran's death at the end of the novel reinforces the links of his daughters to their rural home instead of being a moment of their liberation. Irish social existence, it is intimated, will continue to be torn between opposing possibilities of the quest for utopian values and the danger of capitulation to pettiness and false authorities. Colm Tóibín's *The Blackwater Lightship* (1999) also explores the destructive but defining impact of the family in the way it hampers individualism and deviations from heterosexual norms. Declan Breen who is dying of AIDS returns to his grandmother's house in Wexford and forces the generations of his family to assemble. Over the course of a weekend they arrive at a deeper understanding of one another and breach taboos about death and sexuality that are usually held at abeyance. While Tóibín succeeds in reorienting the Irish novel by introducing gay identity and desire into it, his vision is bleak and unappeasing. His fiction lays bare the psychic struggles of his characters, but eschews a consolatory philosophy.

From Troubles to post-Troubles Fiction: Representing conflict in the Northern Irish novel (1983–2008)

The search for a form appropriate to the representation of atrocity and the effects of political conflict within a closed community divided by ethnic affiliations and religious beliefs is the challenge faced by Northern Irish novelists who set out to portray the Troubles. Even though cross-ethnic liaisons, betrayal, and the trauma of violence are recurrently depicted in Troubles fiction, a wide variety of genres and forms has been co-opted to delineate this shared nucleus of plots. The insufficiency of narrative whatever its shape is, moreover, another unifying emphasis in Troubles writing. Bernard MacLaverty's *Cal* (1983) tracks the story of an entanglement of a young man who has been drawn into IRA militancy and the widow of an RUC reserve policeman who has been assassinated by his IRA organization. The progress of the love affair is counterpointed by Cal's increasing sense of guilt and disconnection from reality. His abrupt arrest at the end of the novel destroys the illusion of harmony created by the romance that has dominated the plot, and fractures the text that we have been reading. The submerged narrative that has detailed the burning of his family home by the UVF and his attempts to evade his associates in the IRA overwhelms the overt story of romance and reconciliation. Glenn Patterson adopts a Joycean format in *The International* (1999) by unfolding the history of the eponymous Belfast hotel during the course of a weekend in January 1967 that marked the beginning of the Civil Rights movement and the escalation of hostilities in Northern Ireland. Patterson endeavors to capture history as immanence, and to get back to a point of innocence before violence and embittered division had become defining features of descriptions of Belfast. His narrator, Danny, has secured his job in the hotel because a previous barman has been killed. He tells us about his struggle with his homosexuality, and describes guests and functions at the hotel in the course of what seems like a routine evening. The fact that the Northern Ireland Civil Rights Association is formed on the premises on that January weekend and that the deceased barman Peter Ward had been shot on the Shankill Road by the UVF for supposed IRA involvement, however, cast shadows over Danny's narration and endow its details with a retrospective portentousness. The murder of the barman happens outside the frame of the action and is depicted by Patterson as a trauma that cannot be incorporated into the text except as an unspeakable lacuna.

Robert McLiam Wilson's *Ripley Bogle* (1998) also plays with fictional form in telling the story of his vagrant hero, a down-and-out from Belfast who is living rough on the streets of London. Bogle, who acts as the narrator, self-consciously toys with literary allusion as he details aspects of his daily existence. His jaunty, picaresque self-portrait and postmodern mockery of notions of Irishness and belonging are gradually revealed to be a feint masking traumatic events in his past, especially his betrayal of his friend Maurice Kelly, a Republican, who is assassinated by IRA paramilitaries for defection from the group. Bogle's supposed escape into the anonymity of London and the freedom of the literary inheritance with which he associates it, such as the novels of Dickens, are shown to be spurious. The disturbing Northern Irish counter-narratives that he brings with him are increasingly stripped of their irony and divulged in their full horror.

Edward Said has argued that the novel may be viewed as a battle between invention and restraint or between authority and molestation.[16] His thesis that innovative, beginning fictions must constantly negotiate the critical boundaries of form particularly holds good for the twentieth-century Irish novel, which endeavored to find indigenous and distinctive narrative modes, to avoid the lure of fixity, and to maintain a dialog with the British and European novel with which it has oblique affinities. Joyce and Beckett's experimentation with narrative proved impossible for subsequent authors, but their spirit of contestation may be seen in the restless questioning of mimetic possibility even by those novelists who, like McGahern and Edna O'Brien, have embraced the conventions of naturalism. This process of formal inquiry continues to be an aspect of the Irish novel at the turn of the century. John Banville who has persistently associated his skeptical, epistemological narratives with a European tradition has, under the pseudonym Benjamin Black, newly begun to compose detective novels set in Ireland. David Park's *Swallowing the Sun* (2004) and *The Truth Commissioner* (2008) have initiated a mode of post-Troubles fiction that probes questions of truth and justice. Joseph O'Connor, in *Star of the Sea* (2002) and *Redemption Falls* (2007), produced historical novels that grapple with forgotten aspects of the Irish past by enlisting postmodernist techniques. And Anne Enright's *The Gathering* (2007) finds fresh ways of broaching narratives of buried traumas underlying dysfunctional families. The novel continues to be a "form of discovery and also a way of accommodating discovery" (Said, p. 82). Perpetual reengagement with the symbolic function and limitations of fictional form is the enduring legacy of the disparate and variegated achievements of twentieth-century Irish novelists.

NOTES

1 R. F. Foster, *The Irish Story: Telling Tales and Making it Up in Ireland* (London: Allen Lane, 2001). Foster contends that an invariable nationalist plot about the story of Ireland is repeated compulsively in Irish narratives in the nineteenth and twentieth centuries.

2 Sean O'Faolain, *Vive Moi!* (London: Sinclair-Stevenson, 1993), p. 300.

3 Colm Tóibín, "Martyrs and Metaphors," *Letters from The New Island*, ed. Dermot Bolger (Dublin: Raven Arts Press, 1991), pp. 44–55. For a discussion of Tóibín's arguments and of recent changes in Irish society facilitating production of more conventional novels, see R. F. Foster, "How the Short Stories Became Novels," *Luck and the Irish: A Brief History of Change: c.1970–2000* (London: Allen Lane, 2007), pp. 147–83.

4 See Terry Eagleton, *Heathcliff and the Great Hunger: Studies in Irish Culture* (London: Verso, 1995) and Declan Kiberd, *Inventing Ireland: The Literature of the Modern Nation* (London: Jonathan Cape, 1995) for analyses of the political underpinnings and the revolutionary force of Irish fiction.

5 James Joyce, *A Portrait of the Artist as a Young Man*, ed. Seamus Deane (London: Penguin, 1992), p. 276.

6 For Joyce's comments on nocturnal dimensions of the *Wake* see Richard Ellmann, *James Joyce* (Oxford: Oxford University Press, 1983), p. 695; and John Bishop, *Joyce's Book of the Dark: Finnegans Wake* (Madison: University of Wisconsin Press, 1986).

7 See Finn Fordham, *Lots of Fun at Finnegans Wake: Unravelling Universals* (Oxford: Oxford University Press, 2007).

8 On the function of negation in Beckett, see Wolfgang Iser, "The Pattern of Negativity in Beckett's Prose," *Prospecting: From Reader Response to Literary Anthropology* (Baltimore: Johns Hopkins University Press, 1989), pp. 140–51. For the Irish dimensions of the Trilogy, see Declan Kiberd, "*Molloy, Malone Dies*, and *The Unnamable*," *The Novel Volume 2: Forms and Themes*, ed. Franco Moretti (Princeton: Princeton University Press, 2006), pp. 912–18.

9 Samuel Beckett, *The Beckett Trilogy: Molloy, Malone Dies, The Unnamable* (1950–2; London: Picador, 1979), p. 372.

10 Samuel Beckett, *Ill Seen Ill Said* (London: Calder, 1981), p. 58.

11 Elizabeth Bowen, *The Last September* (London: Penguin, 1942), p. 30.

12 For accounts of Bowen's modernism and her historical and political themes see Maud Ellmann, *Elizabeth Bowen: The Shadow Across the Page* (Edinburgh: Edinburgh University Press, 2003) and Neil Corcoran, *Elizabeth Bowen: The Enforced Return* (Oxford: Clarendon Press, 2004).

13 Molly Keane, *Two Days in Aragon* (London: Virago, 1985). For a comparison of Keane and Bowen, see Derek Hand, "The Anglo-Irish Big House under Pressure: Bowen's *The Last September* and Keane's *Two Days in Aragon*," in Eibhear Walshe and Gwenda Young (eds.), *Molly Keane: Essays in Contemporary Criticism* (Dublin: Four Courts Press, 2006).

14 For a persuasive account of how family structures preclude open engagement with alternative sexualities, see Kathryn A. Conrad, *Locked in the Family Cell: Gender, Sexuality and Political Agency in Irish National Discourse* (Madison: University of Wisconsin Press, 2004).

15 For accounts of the conflicted feminism of O'Brien's work, see Kathryn Laing, Sinéad Mooney, and Maureen O'Connor (eds.), *Edna O'Brien: New Critical Perspectives* (Dublin: Carysfort Press, 2006).

16 Edward W. Said, *Beginnings: Intention and Method* (New York: Columbia University Press, 1985), pp. 83–5.

8

KRISTIN BLUEMEL

Feminist fiction

Miriam Henderson, heroine of Dorothy Richardson's 1931 novel *Dawn's Left Hand*, rails against her literary mentor, lover, and antagonist Hypo Wilson, "The torment of *all* novels is what is left out. The moment you are aware of it, there is torment in them. Bang, bang, bang, on they go, these men's books, like an L.C.C. tram, yet unable to make you forget them, the authors, for a moment."[1] Miriam, a fiercely independent New Woman who works as a secretary in a Harley Street dental surgery and spends her nights writing book reviews and translations, is resisting Hypo's efforts to turn her into *his* kind of female novelist. Hypo, a character based on H. G. Wells, envisions Miriam swept out of the bustle of London, nesting in "green solitude" with an infant – her infant – at her side. Miriam rejects Hypo's image of her in the role of mother as part of her effort to discover in London a freedom from others' demands and values. Along with Richardson, Miriam also rejects the known pleasures of plot, character, and narration. Like many feminist writers of the twentieth century, Richardson believed that only a radically new imagining of the novel's forms could enrich literature with the truth of modern female experience, an experience left out of "*all* novels" and especially "these men's books."

Richardson's desire to invent a new woman's novel led to her epic 13-volume *Pilgrimage*, of which *Dawn's Left Hand* is the tenth part. Unfinished at Richardson's death in 1957, *Pilgrimage* is one of the most innovative and important English fictions, but it is also one of the most neglected, rarely earning in-depth critical attention or even a reprinting. The difficulty of gaining access to *Pilgrimage* (and other texts discussed in this chapter) points to an unfinished quest by feminist literary critics, who are just now able to look back at a century of novels with some sense of surveying a contained field. As they continue their efforts, they have only to look around or ahead at a new era of postfeminist interrogation to be reminded of how tenuous is the hold on literary history of what Miriam might wonderingly call "these women's books."

This chapter surveys the effort to write "these women's books" even as their political projects are being called into question.[2] Postfeminists criticize the theories of language and subjectivity underlying twentieth-century feminist novels and their constructions of sex and gender difference. Yet debate about the origins and meaning of sexual difference has always been at the center of feminist thought. Virginia Woolf, writing *A Room of One's Own* (1929) and *Three Guineas* (1938) at the height of first-wave feminism, anticipates poststructuralist critiques of second-wave feminism of the 1960s and 1970s. Woolf effectively contests the underlying epistemologies of writers such as Margaret Drabble and Fay Weldon, whose fictions represent the limited concerns of white, middle-class women who dominated second wave feminism. Valuing debate between the century's Woolfs and Weldons, this chapter analyzes currents and cross-currents of feminist thought as it emerges in women's novels whose history traverses an alleged "Great Divide" separating first-wave feminism from second wave feminism, modernism from postmodernism, elite from mass culture, masculine from feminine.[3] *Pilgrimage*, a representative text, certainly invites reading that spans any "divide": begun in 1915 with publication of *Pointed Roofs*, continued through two world wars, and ended with posthumous publication of *March Moonlight* (1967), Richardson's feminist "modernist" masterpiece emerged in its final form in the midst of the publication of Doris Lessing's *Children of Violence* series (1952–1969), and in the same year as Angela Carter's *The Magic Toyshop* (1967).

Both *Children of Violence* and *The Magic Toyshop* figure in this chapter, but not at its end where they might be expected to instance "postmodern" novels of feminist import. Rather, my critical storytelling, revising Virginia Woolf's recommendation that we "think back through our mothers," intends instead to think back and forth between metaphorical sisters.[4] Resisting a vocabulary of tradition, with its implied genealogical, chronological "line," I employ geographical metaphors, mapping a winding route through extended textual territory.

I have written with the assumption that feminist novels examine the experience and construction of sexual difference and gendered identities in order either to celebrate them as a source of feminine aesthetics and politics or to bemoan them as a source of sex discrimination and oppression. Writers need not identify as feminists in order to write feminist novels (though Rebecca West, Woolf, and Richardson did). Nor need they be women. West and Richardson's ideological and personal relations with H. G. Wells speak to his influence on the century's feminist fiction. I have not elected to examine novels by Wells or other male writers for my own ideological (and practical) reasons, but readers should keep in mind my exclusions.

The women's novels that I have included direct us to imagine freedom for their protagonists from rigid gender codes as they seek to define the meaning of their bodies, minds, families, communities, work, and spiritual lives. It is a search in the grandest sense, one that is attested to in Richardson's title, *Pilgrimage*, in the same way as in the title of Lessing's *Martha Quest*, and one that continues to provoke deceptively simple questions that early twentieth-century theorists of the feminist novel asked themselves: What is a free woman? How can women become free? Free to do what? Free to be what?

Building feminist foundations for the twentieth century

West, Richardson, and Woolf were prepared to work through those questions in their fiction, having engaged in debate with each other and with nonfeminist adversaries in the nonfiction press. Although West and Woolf did most to shape popular controversy about women and fiction, all three writers participated in conversations about feminine identity and its relation to sexuality, society, and history; about feminine aesthetics, including a possibility that there might be uniquely feminine sentences or discourses; and about conditions that had made female genius invisible and how it might find expression in contemporary literature.

We see such concerns in West's earliest work in the feminist weekly *The Freewoman*, where her book reviews take to task anti-suffragettes and closed-minded socialists for their shoddy logic, low expectations, stupidity, and cruelty in regard to women. West's articles foreground the meaning for feminist ideology of poverty and class, concerns that are equally central to Richardson's 1917 essay, "The Reality of Feminism."[5] Richardson describes two camps of feminists, those who like West "stand for the sexual and economic independence of all women, irrespective of class, and working towards the complete socialization of industry" (p. 402), and those who stand for the "preservation of the traditional insulated home; seeking to improve the status of women by giving them votes, solving woman's economic problem by training her in youth to earn her living, 'if need be'" (p. 403). The latter type she dismissively labels "a class feminism – feminism for ladies" (p. 401), demonstrating that like West, she considers work, class, and poverty to be integral to female emancipation.

Richardson, continuing her discussion of gender identity in "Women in the Arts" (1925), focuses on psychological demands on women that hamper their creation of art bearing marks of genius. Having already worked for ten years on the novel that she hoped would prove her own genius, Richardson seems to anticipate a cause of failure that most critics would eventually assign to *Pilgrimage*: the demand, more disruptive than housework, for "an inclusive awareness" (*Gender of Modernism*, p. 423). Seeking escape from "human demand" for inclusiveness, from what anti-feminist critics might regard as woman's natural maternal calling to care for the world, Richardson – unmarried and childless – sought total isolation in order to begin *Pilgrimage*. Her art exists because she found a room of her own in a Cornish village, remote from friends, family, and work.

Pilgrimage remained unfinished at Richardson's death, due in part to her later capitulation to house- and husband-keeping. Even unfinished, however, *Pilgrimage* is a success, to judge by a criterion that Richardson established in her 1938 Foreword to her novel: it provides readers with "a feminine equivalent of the current masculine realism" (*Gender of Modernism*, p. 430). It achieved its aim to invent a specifically feminine – and oppositional – aesthetic. Richardson's emphasis on the origins of a feminine aesthetic in sexual difference is somewhat at odds with Woolf's interpretation of *Pilgrimage*. Reviewing its seventh installment *Revolving Lights* (1923), Woolf praises Richardson for having "invented, or...developed and applied to her own uses, a sentence which we might call the psychological sentence of the feminine gender...It is a woman's sentence...in the sense that it is used to describe a woman's mind by a writer who is neither proud nor afraid of anything that she may discover in the psychology of her sex."[6] These terms of praise measure Richardson against other women novelists of "genius" whom Woolf examines in *A Room of One's Own* and in her 1929 essay, "Women and Fiction." There, looking back at women's writing for examples of novels free of feminist bitterness and protest, Woolf affirms the genius of Jane Austen and Emily Brontë because they "resist the temptation to anger" (*Women and Writing*, p. 47), despite their awareness of gender inequality. While many second-wave feminists would argue that Woolf's affirmation is misguided, Woolf's terms, fearlessly accepting "a feminine sentence," bring Richardson into the circle of female genius, if in somewhat grudging tones.

West's first intervention in the debate about female genius came in the form of a 1912 review essay, "So Simple," that asks why women "will not be geniuses." She says that anticipating books by Wells and Conrad or Bennett – Richardson's masculine realists – "is like planning a journey to the Isles of Greece," while the names of two women, Violet Hunt and May Sinclair, evoke "excitement but no certainty": "In spite of their first rate intelligences and sense of character they escape genius. It would be hard to say why women have refused to become great writers. Undoubtedly marriage eats like a cancer into the artistic development of women."[7] It is not surprising to learn that this same May Sinclair, an unmarried feminist novelist named by West as one of the age's few women writers even approaching the stature of genius, reviewed the first three book-chapters of *Pilgrimage* in Ezra Pound's *Egoist*, which had in a previous, more political incarnation been the feminist *Freewoman*. In this 1918 review Sinclair famously exclaimed that Richardson's novels "show an art and method and form carried to punctilious perfection.... In this series there is no drama, no situation, no set scene. Nothing happens. It is just life going on and on. It is Miriam Henderson's stream of consciousness going on and on" (*Gender of Modernism*, p. 444).

An irony of literary history is that Woolf, not Richardson, is associated with feminist stream of consciousness novels. Similarly, Woolf, not Richardson, has emerged as the most effective theorist of historical causes for women's failure to write a literature of genius. Woolf famously concludes in the Judith Shakespeare section of *A Room of One's Own* that "it needs little skill in psychology to be sure that a highly gifted girl [in the sixteenth century] who had tried to use her gift for poetry would have been so thwarted and hindered by other people, so tortured and pulled asunder by her own contrary instincts, that she must have lost her health and sanity to a certainty" (p. 49). Surveying contemporary England, Woolf conjures up a character named Mary Carmichael to imagine another ending for a woman artist. In this character, a novelist, Woolf finds more hope though less brains than in her fictive Judith Shakespeare. Mary Carmichael might be a woman of "no 'genius,'" but she proves a figure of possibility and resilience. "[S]he had – I began to think – mastered the first great lesson; she wrote as a woman, but as a woman who has forgotten that she is a woman, so that her pages were full of that curious sexual quality which comes only when sex is unconscious of itself" (p. 93). It would seem that fictional Mary Carmichael writes in 1929 like the real Dorothy Richardson of 1923, who is "neither proud nor afraid of anything that she may discover in the psychology of her sex."

Beginnings

Many of the best loved feminist novels of the twentieth century are *Bildungsromane*, novels of individual development in which each fictional life imagines a new start: a feminist future wherein heroines move beyond the endings of marriage or romantic death. All begin with young, naïve heroines who are thrust out into the world to discover meanings of gender in relation to English ideologies of class, empire, sex, race, religion, and colonialism.

Jean Rhys exhibits in negative form why a new start is necessary. The daughter of a Creole mother and Welsh father, Rhys drew upon her own life in order to bring the world outside of London and England to

English readers. Her *Voyage in the Dark* (1934) tells the story of an eighteen-year-old West Indian planter's daughter who emigrates to London, where she drifts from the role of chorus line dancer, to mistress, manicurist, and finally, "tart." Her pilgrimage to a new life cannot escape gender exploitations that accompany empire and capitalism; her identification with her father's black servants, offspring of slavery's middle passage, only reinforces her sense of gendered exile and abandonment in the city's cold streets and bed sitters. Rhys's *Wide Sargasso Sea* (1966) begins in Jamaica shortly after the passage of the Emancipation Act, at a time when land-owners hope for compensation from England for the loss of their slaves. Antoinette, biracial daughter of a dead and dissolute Englishman and his much younger Martinician wife, awaits a future that can only take the form of a man. The man who chooses Antoinette is Charlotte Brontë's Rochester (the male protagonist in Brontë's *Jane Eyre*). The rest of Rhys's novel is a tragic imagining of how Rochester's first wife becomes Brontë's confined madwoman in the attic. Rhys's narrative exhibits Antoinette's marriage as a state of internal and external exile, a betrayal by the gendered plot of the traditional English novel, conventionally ending in happy marriage, and by the racialized plot of British imperialism, conventionally asserting English white superiority.

It is worth comparing doomed Antoinette Mason to another insecure, young heroine in a very different kind of feminist novel, Rosamond Lehmann's *Invitation to the Waltz* (1932). Lehmann's tender account of seventeen-year-old Olivia Curtis's first dance at the home of local aristocrats is a picture of adolescent female interiority. Unlike Rhys's *Wide Sargasso Sea*, Lehmann's narrative features no violent, mad protest, let alone a painful exile. Nevertheless, its project is arguably feminist. It introduces a happy "square house" called "The Lodge" that nourishes Olivia and her sister Kate even as Lehmann emphasizes that it belongs to their father, and will belong to their young brother. Beginning her novel with the line of inheritance from Victorian patriarch to his male heirs, Lehmann encourages us to see this place both as "safe," complete in itself, "a world," and as "something alarming, oppressive, not altogether to be trusted: nefarious perhaps."[8] The alarming shadow that falls across the young women's start in life does not manifest itself in anything other than a hint, here and there, that Mr. James Curtis will be able to offer "nothing" to either of his two pretty daughters upon their marriages.

The threat becomes explicit in *The Weather in the Streets* (1936), the sequel to *Invitation to the Waltz*. Olivia, now a twenty-seven-year-old divorced woman living in a tiny London house with her cousin, is getting by on that "nothing" her father had promised her. She falls in love again, this time with married Rollo Spencer, the very aristocrat who, with a few minutes' conversation, salvaged her first dance at his family's home in the previous novel. They begin an affair, and this love leads not to marriage or death, but to an abortion that Lehmann's American publishers desperately tried to expunge from the novel. Lehmann did not alter her novel, but earned criticism for daring to treat such a controversial subject. This alone does not make her a feminist novelist, but it led her to see herself as a woman's novelist. According to Lehmann, male critics of *The Weather in the Streets* tended to assume that she didn't like men, that the novel sprang out of bitterness and negativity; women readers, on the other hand, identified strongly with Olivia, seeing the novel as an affirmation of their invisible, supposedly irrelevant emotional and sexual lives.

Second wave feminist critics were not sure what to make of Lehmann. Elaine Showalter groups Lehmann with Jean Rhys, arguing that both novelists of the 1930s create heroines who are disappointingly "passive and self-destructive," even as they inhabit narratives that boast "a new frankness about the body and about such topics as adultery, abortion, lesbianism, and sexual oppression."[9] More recent critics have been just as likely to marginalize Lehmann, perhaps even more so than they marginalize Richardson. Lehmann seems to have been too popular, too prolific, and too happy being a woman's novelist to earn sustained feminist attention. Her interest in the common spaces of women's lives and speech (and are not the spaces of love – the bedroom, hotel room – common indeed?), limited her usefulness for theorists of either equality feminism or a female aesthetic. While mainstream critics of the 1930s might have damned her for trespassing the threshold of decent silence about women's bodies, feminist critics of the 1970s and 1980s were suspicious of her audience and impressive sales. Prior to a cultural theory of feminist production that could account for women writers who symbolically left their own rooms of privilege (Lehmann was a scholar at Girton College) to contribute to, and be consumed by, a feminized vernacular of the country house, tea shop, kitchen, or parlor, figures like Lehmann were not considered feminist novelists. Nevertheless, Lehmann's near invisibility in the classic texts of second wave feminist literary criticism is a test of the meaning of middle-class identities, social formations, and emotions for a feminism that supposedly doesn't see outside of its own middle-class interests. In fact Lehmann's solidly middle-class heroines are embedded in narratives that veer too close to middlebrow ones, transforming middle-class origins and alliances from a near-necessary foundation for feminist literary production into a near guarantee of its failure in the eyes of second wave feminist critics. A feminism that understands itself as a radical movement based in sexual revolution finds it difficult, not surprisingly, to reconcile "free" revolutionary sexual representation (e.g., adultery, abortion) with mainstream appeal.

One solution to the problems "vernacular" women's novels such as *Invitation to the Dance* or *The Weather in the Streets* raise for feminist criticism is to argue that Lehmann's work in the 1930s reinvents the vocabulary of feminism through invocations of shared interior spaces. Just as feminist novelists had to struggle in 1915 to teach readers to see feminist values in a particular aesthetic – the values of a room of one's own – so too, we can see, feminist novelists of the century's middle decades asked readers to consider another set of feminist values in a very different aesthetic: the aesthetic of a room shared with others. Lehmann, like other women novelists of the 1930s and 1940s, including Stevie Smith, Betty Miller, Rose Macaulay, E. H. Young, and Phyllis Bottome, typically replaced a familiar feminist script of exile with one about home, opening the way for a new kind of feminist realist novel and a new generation of middle-class English women novelists, women who had the vote, were gaining access to quality education, and were newly able to enter the professions or serve in government. Little did they know they were also opening up the way for working-class and colonial women novelists.

One of the most accomplished working-class novels to come out of the twentieth century is Maureen Duffy's *Bildungsroman*, *That's How It Was* (1962). It is based like *Pilgrimage* on the author's life, but like Richardson's novel claims to be fiction rather than autobiography. Duffy's heroine Paddy introduces a vital, Irish-English working-class vernacular into English feminism, taking us far beyond the language and assumptions of Richardson or Lehmann's middle-class heroines. Acutely aware of the grand narratives of war, disease, and national policy that dictate contours of poverty in England, Duffy defines politicized spaces of female experience as much by negative impacts of class discrimination as by an intense love binding Paddy to her mother. Relations of mothers and daughters, central to feminist fiction, are cherished in Duffy's novel all the more for the tenuousness of their hold. The novel begins "Lucky for me I was born at all really, I mean she could have decided not to bother. Like she told me, she was tempted, head in the gas oven, in front of a bus, oh a thousand ways."[10] Paddy's ferocious thin mother, despite tuberculosis that will prove fatal, fosters her daughter's aspirations beyond home, toward education and London. This too is exile, but it protects Paddy, who loves poetry and women, from her stepfamily's ceaseless pressure to accept boys, pregnancy, and a job in the mill as the end of her story. Breathing the thick London air, "expelling the past," Paddy's exile is at last a new beginning – and also a homecoming. When Paddy approaches the door of her Aunt Lyddy's house where she'd visited when she was four, she thinks, "I was coming home. In a way [mother] was coming home too" (p. 217). Like Richardson's Miriam, who also loses her mother, Duffy's Paddy seeks a solution to aching questions that maternal absence leaves in its wake by reinventing her self in fiction.

Tsitsi Dangarembga's *Nervous Conditions* (1988) shares with other *Bildungsromane* the subject of feminine self-awakening, but it is set in colonial Rhodesia during the last years of British rule. Political repression structuring all levels of Rhodesian social relations, and the poverty that oppresses history's underprivileged, complicate Dangarembga's tale of female education and self-development. The story's narrator Tambu begins with the words, "I was not sorry when my brother died."[11] Eschewing apology, Tambu describes how the death of her older brother at her uncle's mission school facilitated her escape from the dusty homestead where her mother struggled to keep her children from starving and her father perfected a beggar's art of ingratiation.

Dangarembga has written an "English" novel to the extent that she draws from an English narrative tradition, represents Zimbabwe as a British colony, and places at the center of a feminist exploration of postcolonial Africa the effects of an idealized Englishness upon Tambu and her extended family. One family member is Nyasha, Tambu's rebellious, fashionably "English" cousin who becomes her best friend, her alter ego, and ultimately her cautionary other. Nyasha, born in Rhodesia, educated in London, and returned to Rhodesia, describes herself as a hybrid who is torn by conflicting ideologies about what it means to be a good woman and good African. She ends up like the woman artist Woolf imagines in *A Room of One's Own* who was "so thwarted and hindered by other people, so tortured and pulled asunder by her own contrary instincts, that she must have lost her health and sanity": Nyasha suffers a mental breakdown after suffering for months as an untreated anorexic. Tambu wonders, "If Nyasha who had everything could not make it, where could I expect to go?" (p. 202). Compounding her worries, Tambu's mother predicts that Tambu is in danger of "succumb [ing]" like her brother and Nyasha to the deadly forces of identification with an idealized Englishness (p. 203). Tambu represses her mother's prophecy, choosing to live as an exile from her African family and roots by embracing life at an elite colonial English boarding school. We do not learn what happens to Nyasha, but we do learn that Tambu survives. She alludes to a "long and painful . . . process of expansion" that brings her to a point where she can "question things and refuse to be brainwashed" (p. 204). She thereby is ready to begin her own story in English about the dangerous fantasy of

"Englishness." Like Miriam and Paddy, Tambu is poised to become a feminist novelist. The real work is just beginning.

Middles

Novels that begin and end in a protagonist's middle years are driven by a unique set of narrative problems. Bypassing life's beginnings, with their fantasy of self-invention or social transformation, and not claiming satisfactions from life's final moments of meaning that retroactively illuminate all previous action, middles must appeal to readers on terms of their own. The extended middle of Richardson's novel-sequence is taken up with questions about art and consciousness that to many readers seem evidence of a stalled imagination rather than a narrative corollary of Richardson's philosophy of being. Woolf's *To the Lighthouse* (1927) and *Between the Acts* (1941) are, in the eyes of those same readers, more successful examples of feminist novels that begin in the middle. They are driven more by questions about artists who are in the midst of creative processes than about the *Bildungsroman's* questions of character development or plot resolution. How will Lily Briscoe go on with her painting? How will Miss La Trobe manage the messy amateur pageant at Pointz Hall? Will the female artist's vision of experimental form endure amidst the pressures of social convention?

Second wave feminist critics embraced *To The Lighthouse* and *Between the Acts* as works that uphold for feminist consumption and emulation images of individual, eccentric, psychologically exiled female artists triumphing, in their middle years, against the odds of an antagonistic history. Other troubled or troubling middle-aged protagonists at the center of feminist novels include West's bedraggled Margaret Grey and her cousin Jenny in *The Return of the Soldier* (1918), Rhys's Marya Zelli in *Quartet* (1928) and Julia Marin in *After Leaving Mr. Mackenzie* (1930), Rosamund Stacey in Margaret Drabble's *The Millstone* (1965), Duffy's lesbian heroine Matt in *The Microcosm* (1966), and Ruth Patchett in Fay Weldon's *The Life and Loves of a She-Devil* (1983). Whether triumphant or defeated, however, those characters encourage readers to consider alternate kinds of feminist confrontation with history, including narrative representations of political affiliation and collective action. An example of such an alternative is Sylvia Townsend Warner's historical novel *Summer Will Show* (1936), which begins in the middle of the nineteenth century in the middle years of its protagonist's life. Sophia Willoughby is a young, married aristocrat who manages her English estate until her two children die from smallpox. Then, in her grief and simultaneous freedom from maternal cares, Sophia sets off to

Paris in the spring of 1848, hoping to retrieve her errant husband from the arms of an unlikely rival, a middle-aged artist, "half actress, half strumpet," a revolutionary and Jew named Minna Lemuel.[12] To the surprise of herself and her husband, Sophia falls in love with her husband's lover, and the two women embark on a journey of political and sexual discovery that brings them to the barricades. It is not clear whether Minna survives the fighting. Separated from Minna, Sophia finds herself back in "this empty room where she had felt such impassioned happiness, such freedom, such release," alone again but with "changed ideas" (p. 405). The novel does not end with the certain death of Sophia's lesbian lover, as convention would dictate, but with an uncertain intellectual middle, and a certain political beginning: the narrative's last page pictures Sophia in the midst of reading a pamphlet left in Minna's room by a fellow revolutionary. It is the *Communist Manifesto*.

Doris Lessing's *A Ripple from the Storm* (1958), the middle book of her *Children of Violence* series, and her *The Golden Notebook* (1962) continue Warner's feminist interest in collective movements' supersession of individual dilemmas. Lessing, more than any writer since Richardson, self-consciously playing with uncertainties associated with narrative middles, daringly suspends the process of meaning-making that attends closure. Her experiments with middle-effects (so to speak) result in different narrative forms for *A Ripple from the Storm* and *The Golden Notebook*, but the novels share important qualities. Written in the middle years of the century, both feature heroines entering middle age, both link individual psychological breakdown to instances of collective social breakdown (manifesting themselves as the sickness of racism or sexism), and both use realist frameworks to explore possibilities of revolutionary social change through a medium of women's social alliances in work, politics, and love.

A Ripple from the Storm is interesting to analyze as an "English" novel because it is set in Zambesia, a fictional colony modeled on Lessing and Dangarembga's colonial Rhodesia. Martha Quest (legally Martha Knowell) at first does not question her national identity: she is "British." Yet the uncertain English identity of Zambesia gives *A Ripple* much of its narrative shape. As one of Martha's antagonists reminds her, "[W]hile you are running around shouting about socialism and all the rest, this isn't Britain, which makes allowances for social adolescents. This country's a powder-keg and you know it."[13] Those words, spoken by a member of Zambesia's British legal and social establishment, symbolize his commitment to the notion that strict apartheid is the socially mature way to organize life in the British colony. For Martha, membership in the Communist Party, what she calls with reverence "the group," is the most recent manifestation of her lifelong rebellion against the class and race privilege that underlie British colonial rule in Africa. As a child she escaped the poverty, repression, and racism that are the necessary effects of imperialism by constructing an elaborate fantasy of a "fabulous and ancient city," a "noble city, set four-square and colonnaded along its falling, flower-bordered terraces...Its citizens moved, grave and beautiful, black and white and brown together."[14] In adulthood her need for escape endures although the terms of her fantasy shift. Until the breakup of "the group" in the last pages of *A Ripple*, her fantasy is sustained by a sense of "pledged faith" in her fellow socialists and "all humanity" (p. 74). A German war refugee (whom she later marries) points out to Martha the path imagination must take to collective action:

> Marxism is a key to the understanding of phenomena; we, in our epoch, see an end to that terrible process, shown...in the French Revolution, when men went to their deaths in thousands for noble ends – in their case, liberty, fraternity and equality, when what they were actually doing was to destroy one class and give another the power to rob and destroy.　　(*Ripple*, p. 74)

Like Sophia Willoughby, Martha throws herself into Communist politics, after attempting and abandoning the "happy ending" of marriage and motherhood offered to respectable British women. But unlike Sophia, Martha's political quest expresses naïve arrogance born of hindsight. She and her fellow socialists, believing that all Europe will be Communist after the war, imagine this political future "as a release into freedom, a sudden flowering into goodness and justice" that they are already a part of (*Ripple*, p. 200). Yet these fantasies of participation cannot entirely replace Martha's childhood feelings of exile. Her dream of the four-gated city is also redirected to " 'that country'," a "pale, misted, flat" place with gulls crying and the smell of sea salt in its air. Realizing that the new dreamland is England, Martha wonders, "[H]ow can I be an exile from England when it has nothing to do with me?" (*Ripple*, p. 113). This question eventually provokes Martha's post-war emigration to England in *The Four-Gated City*, but more immediately, it recreates the years of war when even respectable citizens of Zambesia seemed potential recruits to leftism. But these years pass like a ripple from a storm. Martha finds herself stuck, as before, in the middle of colonial Africa, in the middle of her life, in the middle of a marriage of political convenience. Worse yet is the grimly humorous realization on the part of women in "the group" that "when we get socialism we'll have to fight another revolution against men" (p. 317). And that second revolution – the "sex war" that takes place in streets and courtrooms and bedrooms of England – is what many readers have understood to be the theme of *The Golden Notebook*.

Such an understanding might give us pause. It is time for critics, after years of comparing *The Golden Notebook*'s Anna Wulf with Virginia Woolf, to explore new relations among feminist novels by restructuring narratives about twentieth-century literary history. The first step in this process would dislodge a dominant logic of chronology, reminding ourselves that the ends imposed by critical tales, like those imposed by fictional tales, are artificial and temporary. Any narrative about the century's feminist fiction, like the narratives that are its subject, can aspire to be a text that leads readers into production, rather than consumption, of meaning. Readers will continue to produce feminist meanings of feminist novels differently, depending on how they retrospectively create middle meanings as they approach the endings of individual novels – and as they approach what they take to be the beginning, middle, and end points of feminist writing's history. Such a dynamic critical reading emerges from readers' encounters with multiple endings created by intermediary installments of series novels like *Pilgrimage* or *The Children of Violence*, but also structural discontinuities between sections in experimental novels like *The Golden Notebook*. It emerges as well from literary histories that map alternate routes to and away from particular novels. *The Golden Notebook* will produce different feminist meanings depending on how readers approach it, from acquaintance with Richardson's *Pilgrimage*, or Warner's *Summer Will Show*, or Dangarembga's *Nervous Conditions*. Its feminist meanings also depend on what textual encounters readers experience upon leaving it.

Ends

Endings have tremendous power to shape narrative meaning, which may be one reason feminist novels such as Warner's *Lolly Willowes* (1926), Lehmann's *The Ballad and the Source* (1944), Margaret Drabble's *The Witch of Exmoor* (1996), and Angela Carter's *Wise Children* (1991) adopt as their protagonists old women looking back on their lives. Certainly one of the many sources of appeal of Woolf's *Mrs. Dalloway* (1925) is a sense of ultimate meaning that informs the heroine's memories and experiences of an ordinary London day. The overdetermined parallels between the lives of Clarissa Dalloway and Septimus Warren Smith are established in part through our awareness that Clarissa, like Septimus, has reached the end of her life. Though the vital center of her party, Clarissa "with her horror of death" is failing.[15] The narrator quietly announces in the beginning of the novel, "It was all over for her. The sheet was stretched and the bed narrow. She had gone up into the tower alone and left them blackberrying in the sun" (p. 70). With this intimation of an end so early in the novel, *Mrs. Dalloway* "means" differently than novels featuring middle-aged protagonists. The narrative of Clarissa's life, as virginal after marriage and childbirth as before, is one of desire contained, of life partially lived. Read against the impact of illness and withdrawal, however, Clarissa's memories of youthful denial and loss add up to small victories won for a deeply felt integrity – a Richardsonian freedom in isolation – extracted from the social demand that women like Mrs. Dalloway live at the behest of others, as objects for others' consumption.

In Warner's *Lolly Willowes* (1926) the same threats to self that motivate Clarissa's internal exile lead to an external exile for another aging, virginal female. Laura Willowes, nicknamed Lolly by her infant niece, withdraws in middle age from her brother Henry's comfortable house on Apsley Terrace, London, to take up life as a spinster in the remote village of Great Mop in the Chilterns. Lolly, like Martha Quest and Anna Wulf (or Septimus Warren Smith, for that matter), "breaks down," but not into madness. Rather she "breaks down" into magic, a fate predicted by her youthful habit of reading Glanvil on witches.[16] When Laura announces that she will "live alone in the country" (p. 103), Henry accuses her of being mad. But Laura's madness leads to sane lodgings in the home of Mrs. Leak, an excellent cook who provides exactly the sanctuary Laura needs. Yet half-way through the novel we, like Laura, find ourselves passing almost imperceptibly from familiar domestic realism into the worlds of fairy tale. Lolly observes odd goings on in the village – strange music, curious gath-erings, terrifying night noises that Mrs. Leak's explanations do not account for. Warner's novel ends with Lolly accepting an ancient magical role reserved for literature's old and odd women: she becomes a witch who "in England, in the year 1922, had entered into a compact with the devil" (p. 172). Upon this announcement, readers retrospectively reevaluate the meaning of the first half of the novel (Was it a fairy tale all along? Is Lolly mad?), just as Lolly too looks back over the course of her life and sees for the first time her secret vocation – to be a happy feminist disciple of Satan – organizing the whole. Warner's parable about feminism's strongest ally emerges in Lolly's affirmation of her new mentor: "she felt no shame at all. It had pleased Satan to come to her aid. Considering carefully, she did not see who else would have done so. Custom, public opinion, law, church, and state – all would have shaken their massive heads against her plea, and sent her back to bondage [of family life]" (p. 223).

Sixty-five years later Angela Carter published a rollicking novel, *Wise Children*, about twins Dora and Nora Chance, a retired song and dance team, who at seventy-five prepare to celebrate the hundredth birthday of their father, Sir Melchior Hazard, a Shakespearean actor. Dora, the narra-tor, is not a witch exactly, but a spellbinding storyteller who seems a direct descendant of Lolly Willowes. Her tale radiates a carnevalesque humor, but this comedy, like the laughter it generates, has its limits. As she says, "Comedy is tragedy that happens to *other* people."[17] For readers, Dora and Nora play the role of female "other" – "*other* people" – to perfection. They are old, illegitimate, promiscuous, grotesque, and born in Brixton (on what Dora calls "the *bastard* side of Old Father Thames" [p. 1]). The comedy we find in Dora's narrative about their lives is for them at best "a farce, at worst, a tragedy, and a chronic inconvenience the rest of the time" (p. 11). Abandoned by their famous father, they find a substitute in Melchior's twin brother Peregrine, but spend their lives trying to win their way into the bosom of their father's legitimately sired family. They manage to achieve this goal, but only through outrageous, scandalous twists of plot that include incest between 75-year-old Dora and 100-year-old Uncle Perry.

Like other feminist novelists, Carter foregrounds a self-serving logic of patriarchy, in this case the very notion that the House of Hazard can be defined by its fathers rather than its mothers. She does so by insisting on the regenerative capacity, the productivity, of what is implausible – of what has no legitimacy as "reality." Dora and Nora become at seventy-five the adoptive parents (mother and father both) of three-month-old twins who are the progeny of an unknown mother and Melchior's son Gareth, a priest and thereby another "illegitimate father" (p. 7) in the Hazard "line" (a deliberately ill-fitting metaphor, given the splits within and among the family's theatrical generations). Perry, an illusionist who arrives at the birthday party in a halo of butterflies, "had not only upstaged his brother but also plausibility" (p. 207). So does Carter. Though not as consistently devoted to the strategies that undermine realism in Carter's *Nights at the Circus* or *The Passion of New Eve*, *Wise Children* tests our suspension of disbelief with a feminist desire to affirm the antipatriarchal fantasy of the Chance sisters' fatherless, motherless genealogy.

Wise Children develops in semirealist form another instance of free self-invention that motivates the century's many examples of realist feminist *Bildungsroman*. Late in the novel Uncle Perry suggests that the twins' "real" mother, a 17-year-old maid, seduced and abandoned by Melchior toward the end of World War I, is a fiction. Dora praises her adoptive Grandma for "invent[ing] this family...She created it by sheer force of personality" (p. 35). Grandma's (pro)creation is possible only because of Dora and Nora's freedom from sure claims by both father *and* mother; while it may indeed be a wise child who knows its own father, in this narrative it is an equally wise child who knows its own mother. Surprisingly, critics tend to read the feminism of the novel through an adage about paternity, which Carter cites as one of her three epigraphs, while neglecting to consider the last epigraph, attributed to actress Ellen Terry: "How many times

Shakespeare draws fathers and daughters, never mothers and daughters."
Attending to mother–daughter relations, Carter attempts to make up
Shakespeare's lack. And while Woolf, Richardson, Lessing, and Duffy have
earnestly made mother–daughter relations central to their narratives, Carter
assumes that those relations, in all their goodness, badness, and ambivalence, are so important to English literature that they can be played with.
Her novel ostentatiously points to its own parody of the centuries' long quest
of male writers to know the father when Dora quotes a Brighton Pier performer to great effect; "'Don't worry, darlin', 'e's not your father!'" She
then wonders "What if Horatio had whispered that to Hamlet in Act 1,
Scene i?" (p. 213). *Wise Children* shows us what kinds of energies might be
liberated when someone backstage whispers to the actors, to counteract
their tragic agony, "Don't worry, darlin', *she*'s not your mother."

To suggest that the "mood" of Carter's experiment anticipates the
"revisionary energies of post-feminism"[18] overlooks her novel's continuity
with earlier experimental feminist fables such as *Lolly Willowes*, Woolf's
Orlando (1928), or Stevie Smith's *Over the Frontier* (1938). To assume,
from a perspective of postfeminist wisdom, that we can summarily map
and know a winding course of nearly 100 years of feminist fictions would,
indeed, be folly. If the child is parent to the mother or father, Carter and
other late-twentieth-century feminist novelists have much to teach us about
their feminist parents, both female and male. I have chosen to make *Wise
Children* a happy ending of my critical narrative, but it is an ending that
pretends to no permanence and no final authority over structure or design
of narratives about the century's feminist fiction. Rather, it is one that
admits its provisional hold on selective materials of an arbitrarily designated period in English literary history. It recognizes that its treatment of
women novelists falls exclusively on the "other" side of Carter's genealogical error, fetishizing the metaphorical mother's (zig-zag) line in fiction,
instead of the father's. It ends with an invitation to new students of feminist
fiction to construct alternately legitimate and bastard genealogies that
admit both women and men to their critical narratives, and to search for
contents and structuring paradigms within and without the framework of
this chapter and this book.

NOTES

1 Dorothy Richardson, *Pilgrimage* (London: Virago, 1979), vol. IV, p. 239.
2 The category "women's books" can overlap with that of "feminist novels," but
  not necessarily. This chapter's survey adopts Richardson's bias toward "women's
  books," but it does so with regard for complex relations between "women" and
  "feminist."

3 "The Great Divide" alludes to Andreas Huyssen, *After the Great Divide: Modernism, Mass Culture, Postmodernism* (Bloomington: Indiana University Press, 1986).

4 Virginia Woolf, *A Room of One's Own* (New York: Harcourt, 1957), p. 27.

5 Dorothy Richardson, "The Reality of Feminism," *The Gender of Modernism*, ed. Bonnie Kime Scott (Bloomington: Indiana University Press, 1990), pp. 402–417.

6 Virginia Woolf, "Dorothy Richardson," *Virginia Woolf: Women and Writing*, ed. Michele Barrett (New York: Harcourt, 1978), p. 191.

7 Rebecca West, *The Young Rebecca*, ed. Jane Marcus (Bloomington: Indiana University Press, 1982), pp. 70–1.

8 Rosamond Lehmann, *Invitation to the Waltz* (London: Virago, 1981), p. 4.

9 Elaine Showalter, *A Literature of Their Own* (Princeton: Princeton University Press, 1977), p. 299.

10 Maureen Duffy, *That's How It Was* (London: Virago, 1983), p. 217.

11 Tsitsi Dangarembga, *Nervous Conditions* (Seattle: Seal Press, 1988), p. 1.

12 Sylvia Townsend Warner, *Summer Will Show* (London: Virago, 1987), p. 31.

13 Doris Lessing, *A Ripple from the Storm* (New York: Harper Perennial, 1995), p. 11.

14 Doris Lessing, *Martha Quest* (New York: Harper Perennial, 1995), p. 64.

15 Virginia Woolf, *Mrs. Dalloway* (New York: Harcourt, 1953), p. 231.

16 Sylvia Townsend Warner, *Lolly Willowes* (Chicago: Academy, 1979), p. 24.

17 Angela Carter, *Wise Children* (New York: Penguin, 1993), p. 213.

18 Dominic Head, *The Cambridge Introduction to Modern British Fiction, 1950–2000* (Cambridge: Cambridge University Press, 2002), p. 103.

9

JOHN FORDHAM

Working-class fiction across the century

Toward a theory of working-class fiction

Since Ian Watt's groundbreaking work on the development of the novel, there is overwhelming evidence that the form has been from its inception the preserve of the middle class, despite its being extended or qualified to include subgenres. However, this chapter argues that working-class fiction can be distinguished from a dominant tradition in the history of the novel. Working-class fiction will be defined here by the way that it responds, in a peculiarly local and vital way, to a *lived* experience that middle-class novels have only been able to *observe*. Working-class fiction thus sees beyond the limited horizon of bourgeois knowledge to articulate the actual experience and the felt consequences of industrialization. Shaped and determined by the processes of production itself, working-class writing is a product of a distinct form of consciousness.

As the Marxist philosopher Georg Lukács has argued, such consciousness is able to perceive and hence disclose the true nature of a society which reduces all relations and values to those of the commodity, and insists that "the principle of rational mechanisation and calculability must embrace every aspect of life." [1] Commodification integrates social being and commodities into a "specialized process...in which [the worker] is no more than a cipher reduced to an abstract quantity, a mechanised and rationalised tool." Working-class life-experience and consciousness embodies a dialectic – a consciousness of itself, the *subject*, as *object* – that comprehends the condition of "society as a whole" because the working class typically "reveals in all its starkness the dehumanised and dehumanising function of the commodity relation" (p. 92).

In Marx's original formulation of commodification, however, reification (the turning of a human subject into a thing) does not locate the worker within an indissoluble *system*, but discloses capitalism as a *process*, in which objects are "constituted out of flows, processes and relations." [2] If the worker appears to him- or herself to be an "abstract quantity," this is only an initial stage in a developing consciousness, through which change becomes possible and eventually is realized. Nevertheless, in the articulation of working-class consciousness in written forms, such as in the novel, what is often of primary value is a sense of embeddedness in place and community, in those values of the lived experience which bind and sustain people through hardship and struggle. In this sense, it is the relative permanence or stability of the common life that becomes the source of working-class resistance to a capitalist world in which "all that is solid melts into air."[3]

A dialectical interplay of permanence and change is central to the nature of working-class writing, since its narratives are constituted not only by an internal relationship of worker to community, but by individual and communal relationships to the outside world. The lived experience is represented not by means of fixed, once-and-for-all, categories of social relations, but through exchanges in which an affection for, and active affiliation with, a particular place are in conflict with a countervailing desire to break the bonds of otherwise restrictive customs and practices. Working-class writing, therefore, embodies a consciousness of process in which, to extend Lukács, and to borrow a phrase from E. P. Thompson, the working-class is "present at its own making," and at its continual remaking.[4]

Furthermore, because production and process have been fundamental to the making and development of working-class consciousness, its cultural forms are similarly constituted: that is, actively made in response to, rather than passively received from, the culture of the middle class and the dominant realist mode of its fiction. In working-class writing, the bourgeois novel's convention of internal focalization will be displaced by a figural representation of consciousness – the worker transformed into automaton or machine part – or realist conventions will shift into modes of romance or of music-hall performance. This is why the category of "realism" is not always an adequate means of analyzing the working-class novel: its formal properties often derive from models or traditions outside the literary mainstream. Such considerations will constitute the following analysis of representative works, organized into discrete historical periods, in order to demonstrate how, from its original formation, working-class fiction continues to be produced and re-envisioned.

Early twentieth-century political awakenings: MacGill and Tressell

It is no coincidence that the two most significant working-class literary voices of the early century were Irish – Patrick MacGill, born into the Donegal peasantry in 1890; Robert Tressell (Robert Noonan) into "middle-class" Dublin in 1869 – because it is their combination of class and diasporic consciousness that enables their texts to adopt a unique narrative position: one that observes the changing nature of labor from both within and beyond the laboring class. The formal implication for such writing is that, as distinct from classic English realism, it has no affirming tendency toward "settlement and stability," but, as Terry Eagleton suggests, is characterized by strategies of irresolution that "cut against the grain of the fiction itself."[5] MacGill's first novel *Children of the Dead End* (1914) purports to be an autobiography, a form that was, until the first decade of the century, the most accessible and readily available for worker-writers.[6] However, a reader's expectations of autobiographical form are disrupted in MacGill's text by a dialectical relation between two parallel formations: that of worker and that of writer. The opening pages disclose an "I" who is both peasant and poet: the subject as a child hearing the voice of a mountain stream "crying out at night . . . lamenting over something it had lost."[7] The suggestion here of a Celtic twilight idealization of lost innocence is quickly dispelled. Such romanticism, MacGill indicates, has been nurtured in a quasi-feudal society of chronic poverty, cruelly parasitical priests, and intractable landowners. When his protagonist Dermod Flynn embarks on an itinerant life – from the ancient agricultural valleys of Donegal, through the new construction works of Kinlochleven, to the streets of modern London and the slums of Glasgow – "autobiography" shifts into chronicle, and a subjective narrative of geographical movement is objectified as historical process. Subject–object commodification is first realized in the text when Dermod observes that he is "not a human being" but "a ware purchased in the market-place . . . only an article of exchange" (p. 37). His reified condition is further confirmed when he eventually crosses the water to Scotland: first to dig potatoes and then, as a "navvy," to become gripped by "the great industrial machine . . . a mere spoke in the car of progress" (p. 144).

Despite the navvy's consciousness of his own commodification, there is also in MacGill's work a sense of the worker's modernist collusion in the transformative power of modernity: lamenting the latter's destructive capabilities and at the same time rejoicing in the sheer scale of industrial projects. Although navvies are outsiders "treated like swine in a sty all the years of our life" (p. 244), the narrative voice expresses, albeit with irony, a laborer's pride in the skills of construction. Nature's largest edifices, the mountains, are imbued with a "sinister strength, undefied and unconquered . . . until man, with puny hands and little tools of labour, came to break the spirit of their ancient mightiness" (p. 226). (Such a willingness to adapt to the "moods and tempers of my environment" is also evident in MacGill's novel of World War I, in which relentless "destruction, decay, degradation" is matched by moments when the "I" of the text is "at home in [the] thunder" of the artillery, "accommodat[ing him]self to the Olympian roar."[8]) Arriving in the modern city, Dermod, learning now a writer's trade, hovers on the threshold of social advancement, but realizes that he is in danger, as he says, of "betraying my own class" (*Children*, p. 285). In order to reestablish old allegiances, he goes in quest of his childhood love, Nora, at which moment the dialectic of textual form and class crystallizes. Dermod discovers that his "poetic ideal" (p. 268) has become a prostitute, and is now dying in a Glasgow garret: reduced to the ultimate human commodity, but at the same time sublimated as the icon of a class that should be "judged accordin' to our sufferin's."[9] The novel here visits the domain of romance, in a final vignette of sentimental solidarity; but MacGill's working-class dialectic inheres in his text's formal irresolution, divided as it is between the subject-narrative's appeal to an Irish sublime and the object-narrative's consciousness of "social ugliness."[10]

Questions of form are paramount in considering Tressell's *The Ragged-Trousered Philanthropists* (1914), which, since its first publication, when it was closely compared with MacGill's work, has achieved scriptural status among working-class readers. Its inspirational function is attributable to no straightforward prescriptions in it; rather, its impact emerges, as Raymond Williams argues, from a structural complexity that is indebted to Tressell's unusual class status: as a journeyman craftsman and political activist, he came to his work in the painting and decorating trades of the southern coastal town of Hastings by way of Irish emigration to South Africa (*Writing*, p. 248). The itinerant's oblique relationship to colonial Britain, as with MacGill's, determines the critical position of the narrative.

Tressell's form has been described as "proletarian socialist realism," "collective *Bildungsroman*," and "proletarian modernism."[11] Although the third description appropriately represents Tressell's formal experiments, the second one more aptly encapsulates the novel's project "to explain . . . [in a "readable story"] how Socialists propose to abolish poverty."[12] Accordingly, the reader of Tressell's book experiences the maturation not of an individual, as in classic bourgeois novelistic form, but of a whole class. This is achieved on two simultaneous levels: on the level of discursive engagement with "philanthropists" of the working class – so named because of their unwitting benevolence towards their oppressors – and on the level of form. Formally, the text explores Socratic method, a tradition traceable from Plato, through Thomas More, to the revolutionary utopianism of William Morris's *News from Nowhere* (1890). In Morris's novel the reader comes to political consciousness by means of a time-traveller's dialogue, in question-and-answer form, between an advanced society of the future and a declining one in the present. The dialogue enables Morris's traveller to *discover* the process whereby nineteenth-century capitalist society was materially and ideologically transformed. Tressell's novel also works by means of temporal comparisons, except that here a reader's perspective is from within a process, and not a result of mere hindsight. Tressell's utopianism thus is not "systematic," but functions to "form desire": working through "imaginative encouragement" rather than explicit didacticism.[13]

So Tressell's "socialist-realism," describing the degraded conditions of the "Mugsborough" working class, gives way at key moments to Socratic dialogue, in which Frank Owen, the socialist, explains to his fellow workers the origins of poverty. The responses of his fellow workers to his serial discourses on the political state of the nation, on "landlordism" and monopoly capitalism, and on the Marxist theory of surplus value are antagonistic and hostile; however, what mitigates Owen's hatred for workers who "deserve to suffer because they have supported and defended the system that robbed them" (p. 89) is the text's engagement with working-class popular culture. Owen's earnestness and frustration is offset – made engaging and palatable – by Tressell's framing of the political instruction within a carnivalesque admixture of comic heckling, slapstick humor, songs, mock debates, sermons, and protest marches. Dinner time in the workplace is by turns transformed into music hall, revivalist meeting, or lecture, Owen being "oot [ed]" into action by "howls, groans and catcalls...mingled with cries of 'Fraud!' 'Impostor!' 'Give us our money back!' 'Let's wreck the 'all!'" (p. 225) or his being invited to mount an improvised pulpit, when the "Professor's" discourse is interrupted by Easton's making "a pint of order" and Philpot's rising to "order a pint" (p. 284). The result for a reader is no overall "social-realist" conversion – no ideology of what Theodor Adorno derisively calls "affirmation" (p. 49) – but an *ironic* glimpse, by means of the philanthropists' mockery of democratic processes and their parodies of political clichés, into what would become, with the raising of political consciousness, an achieved emancipation.

Aesthetics and politics in the interwar years: Harold Heslop, Ellen Wilkinson, Ethel Mannin, Lewis Grassic Gibbon

Itinerary or social discontinuity is a dominant theme in fiction of the interwar decades – in novels of the seagoing working class by James Hanley, George Garret, Jim Phelan; in novels of social mobility by Gibbon, Mannin, Wilkinson – but this is also a period when worker-writers from Britain's industrial heartlands produce fictional "documents rooted in the continuity of class and *place*," primarily in the locations of *heavy* industry, such as mining and shipbuilding.[14] The proliferation of such writing gave rise to the term "proletarian literature"[15] and to a publishing vogue in which every major house would have its token working-class writer. In the documentary novels community strength forms a bedrock of resilience in the face of continual threats to any *stable* working life, above all to the chronic economic decline of the 1920s and the Depression of the 1930s. The result is a diverse yet collective response to economic and political crisis, in which the traditional virtues of living *within* a class are modified, challenged or reaffirmed by influences and pressures from "*beyond.*" In the interests of accurate documentation of conditions, this writing, although relying on established codes of realism, discloses the influences of European modernism, in which narrative movement is toward isolation, disintegration and crisis, rather than towards affirmative resolution. The former movement defines the novel of the mining industry, whose workers were chronically subject to "the hazards of unemployment, short-time working and low wages." Walter Brierley's *Means Test Man* (1935) is characteristic in that its "naturalistic surface" describing the daily life of an unemployed miner "is constantly fracturing to disclose...a strange otherworld of dark anxiety and existential terror." '[16] This is already the case in the earliest work of Harold Heslop. While means-test man's fears threaten to shatter the precarious "equilibrium" of the household, Heslop's miners are haunted by the dark symbol of the mine's dangers: the *goaf*. The "dreaded" space left "when all the coal has been extracted" is "the home of a tremendous darkness... soundless as the uttermost depths of the sea";[17] yet also underground the miner experiences pleasure in the "gleaming seam of silver coal," the love of a "darkness [that] is so intimate, so much part of their lives"(*Goaf*, p. 113). The simultaneous aesthetic of labor and the expressionist horror of miners' "engoafment" is echoed in sailors' ambivalence towards the sea, in what the merchant-seaman James Hanley calls in his 1930s writing its "fury and magnificence"; a medium at once "terrible" and "beautiful."[18]

In parallel with formal complexity is the inherent dialectic of class relations. In Heslop's novels the dialectic is revealed in an ambivalent attitude to region and place: a struggle between the virtues of *local* tradition and practice – the "steel frigidity" of the mine tempered by pride in a "warm and gentle" comradeship – and "the desire of a freer and better existence," whether the latter be achieved by the "conservative effect" of trade unionism and parliamentary Labour, or by "the sanction of [Soviet] revolution"(*Goaf*, pp. 17, 20, 78; *Last Cage*, p. 44). Similarly, in the work of the Manchester writer Helen Wilkinson, who was to become the first female Labour MP, there is ambivalence in its descriptions of the effects of social mobility on working-class women. Wilkinson's *Clash* (1929), like Heslop's *Gate of a*

Strange Field (1929), focuses on the General Strike of 1926, and the ways in which, after its failure, class allegiances are actively remade. Besides concern with details of agitation and struggle, both writers represent subtle processes of workers' *embourgeoisement*: anxieties about "becoming sophisticated," "all the edges get[ting] blunted" by contact with the "fleshpots."[19] Tensions are symbolically acted out in romantic relationships, through which the protagonists' sexual and class interests are eventually reconciled. Heslop's union official, Joe Tarrant, disdainful of Emily's longing for "industrial peace," relinquishes her intellectual companionship in favor of Molly, an idealized figure of class and sexuality (*Gate*, pp. 243, 285). Wilkinson's union organizer, Joan Craig, finally rejects the too easy "detachment" of sexually desirable Tony in favor of damaged war veteran Gerry, for whom always "the work comes first" (*Clash*, pp. 156, 310).

Ways in which the formal paradigm of romance can be deployed to express both personal longing and political aspiration are more extensively articulated in the novels of Ethel Mannin who, in conscious emulation of D. H. Lawrence, at first ranges far beyond the working-class domain of her South-East-London upbringing. From 1932, however, she returns from excursions into Lawrentian subjectivist modernism (culminating in *Ragged Banners*, 1931) to produce novels of "social consciousness," such as *Linda Shawn* (1932) and *Venetian Blinds* (1933), and thus to "identify [her]self" with her working-class roots.[20] She modifies the romance mode of her earlier works to create a form grounded in the *known* community, but which nevertheless stays focused on the *imagined* beyond: a possibility of a parochial and imperialist Britain being transformed by the formation of unofficial, international networks of affinity and solidarity. *Venetian Blinds* divides streets and families into subclasses – the "respectable" and the "common" – and the reader follows, in a process of discovery, the protagonist Stephen's struggle with the two kinds of identity. For the socially aspiring "labour aristocracy" "respectability" signifies the "domestic ideal,"[21] but for those others defined as "common" what counts is the defiant domain of "the street,"or the "secret life of alleyways, waste-ground and river."[22] Yet also discoverable at the "common end" are marginalized families like the Leiders, German émigrés through whom Stephen develops a political and social consciousness and begins "to think about the whole business of being common" (p. 113). Subsequently, Stephen's bourgeois progress is measured against the secretly "cherished" longings of his adolescence, when creative spirit and political aspiration were harmonized. It is only after revisiting his former home that he finally rediscovers "where he had dreamed, and groped for the ends of being, and where, innately, he belonged" (p. 450).

The dialectical process in Mannin is more systematically evident in Gibbon's trilogy, *A Scots Quair*, which structurally emulates MacGill's geographical/historical progressions. In *Sunset Song* (1931) Chris Guthrie's rural life of struggle is ended by World War I when her husband Ewan succumbs to "that madness beyond the hills."[23] Despite, however, an ostensible elegiac mode, lamenting the "last of the farming folk that wrung their living from the land with their bare hands" (p. 67), the narrative embarks on a quest for other forms of social existence: subsequently tracing Chris's progress to the "borough" in *Cloud Howe* (1932) – she marries a radical minister during the events of the General Strike – and finally, in *Grey Granite* (1934), to the city, as a widow, during the new industrial struggles and hunger marches of the 1930s.

What sets Gibbon's fiction apart from its contemporaries is its embeddedness in the language of a particular location and culture, through which it realizes the immense expressive potential of Scots, conveying with an arresting poignancy the struggle of a community in "words to tell to *your* heart, how they wrung it and held it, the toil of their days and unendingly their fight" (p. 37, emphasis added). The direct second-person form of address shifts between two modes of working-class consciousness, the personal and the communal, where the "you" merges with the impersonal "folk" of local anecdote and gossip.

It is the latter that constantly registers and critically evaluates effects on the rural community of national and international events, creating a modernist tension between immutability and perpetual change. The developing historical-materialist discourse is constantly undercut by frequent recursions to a mythic mode: visionary episodes in which figures of the ancient past suddenly appear and vanish in formerly sacred places (p. 158). For Chris's second husband, Robert, some human or nationalistic ideal is evoked by the spatial and temporal remoteness of the Howe's stone circles, and beyond them by the mythic Golden Age of a "simple" humanity "living high in the race of the wind and the race of life, mating as simple as beasts or birds, dying with a like keen simpleness" (p. 300).

Any tendency here toward an edenic nostalgia is countered in the trilogy's second novel by its metaphorical construction: its sections named after different cloud formations suggest that any political aspiration grounded in the past will not be fulfilled, even when founded on the hope of a materialist redemption; i.e., that the coming general strike would mean "man splendid again" (p. 301). Chris's reservation is that the Howe's "stratus mists and pillars of spume" represent the ephemera of human ideals – including "christianity, socialism and nationalism" – which, after all, are "with men that took them for gods: just clouds, they passed and finished. Nothing endured but the Seeker himself, him and the everlasting Hills" (p. 300).

In *Grey Granite* Chris's son, Ewan the younger, devotes his early youth to an archaeological quest for meaning in the past, observing "how alike ourselves [were the ancients] in the things they believed, unessentials different – blood, bone, thought the same"(p. 386). Yet the coming of Ewan and Chris to a fictional "Dundairn" develops the dialectic of the deeply ancient and the radically modern in new directions. In a narrative structured on the taxonomy of granite, we discover that there are in modernity different glints and lustres, mineral streaks or facets which, just like Gibbon's own Aberdeen, constitute "the *essential*...something lighted and shining with a fine flame, cold and amber and gold, the flinty cliffs of Union Street, the flinty cheekbones of the disharmonic faces that press about you in an Aberdeen tram."[24]

The implication is that the "geological stratum" has undermined – or broken through as an outcrop – Chris's deep reverence for "the land" as the only enduring quality in existence: besides of course the central and perpetual human subject. Ewan's eventual radicalization and his becoming a political organizer constitute a conscious refusal of any recourse to idealism and individualism. But the dialectics prevail. Granite is both the oldest known rock and the most durable material for building new foundations and thus is an exemplary metaphor for what new qualities are to be discovered in human beings. However, a final question remains about the function of destruction in Chris's new vision of the perpetuity of "Change" as "Deliverer, Destroyer and Friend in one" (p. 496). The suggestion is that destruction rather than production is, like granite, perpetual and ineradicable.

Post-war prosperity? Jack Common, Alan Sillitoe, Jessie Kesson, Raymond Williams

A resolution of the privations and struggles of the 1930s in the election of the Labour government of 1945, and the establishment of the "welfare state," suggest that "prosperity" is the signified of a new political dawn. But what is remarkable about the novels emerging in the postwar period is the sense of continuity between a pre- and postwar structure of feeling. If a perceived "renaissance" of working-class fiction sat uneasily with the claim that during the 1950s workers were growing more "middle-class,"[25] then it was because this misconceived claim failed to understand the long memory – individual or collective – of writers such as Jack Common from Tyneside, Alan Sillitoe from Nottingham, Jessie Kesson from Moray, and Raymond

Williams from the Welsh borderlands. The writers' struggle continues to be waged in ways that are effectively countercultural. Jack Common, who began writing in the 1930s, and his successor, Sid Chaplin, adapt the occasionally sardonic tone of their predecessor, Heslop, and sharpen it into a sustained vaudevillean routine, a comic self-consciousness which both acknowledges and denies its own literariness. For instance, Common in 1951 disrupts the expectations of the bourgeois *Bildungsroman* by imagining an ante-natal incident that "spoilt my autobiography in advance," a genetic blunder when "me and my genes . . . hanging about on the other side of Time . . . made a mess of things": that is, eschewed the places "where the wealthy, talented and beautiful lay coupled" and undertook a "working-class" life of obscurity and "no novelty."[26]

Despite the mocking irony of such novels, a critical orthodoxy emerged, fueled by the British "New Wave" cinema's adaptations during the 1960s, inextricably equating working-class novels and "realism."[27] Any such simple equation, however, is denied by the writers' continuing commitment to narrative innovation. Sillitoe, for instance, often deploys the symbolic vocabulary of his *local* predecessor, D. H. Lawrence, but there is a studied departure from the Lawrentian legacy in his first novel, *Saturday Night and Sunday Morning* (1958), which, although constructed through a subjectively focalized narrative, evokes a consciousness that is always collective and inclusive. Nevertheless, there is also a movement from within the working class to a more distanced or critical outside, achieved through a dialectic of narrative perspective: that is, in shifts from a third-person position that tells of how "Arthur worked on his lathe like a model of industry" to Arthur's own second-person narrative advising that "if you had any brains at all," you would work neither fast nor slow but "do everything deliberately yet with a crafty show of speed."[28] The rehearsed cunning of the factory worker is mirrored in the lad's everyday practice of deception, proclaimed in Arthur's reiterated claim that he "allus was a liar . . . a good 'un an' all" (p. 18). Yet such boasting is also revealed to be self-deceptive, since what confers on Arthur the legitimacy of the liar and the braggart is the authority of "popular reading." He is as insidiously persuasive as the popular newspapers that he consistently claims to be the verifiable source of his storytelling: his narrative must be true because he "read it in the *Post* last week" or "in the Sunday papers" (pp. 23, 78). It is the authority of the popular press, to which everybody pays admiring attention but never gives credence, that bolsters the self-delusion of the working-class hero. Sillitoe's text self-referentially discloses the myth of the "lad": the lad's reading is what constructs him and, at the same time, reveals the precariousness of the construct.

Self-conscious critique of working-class masculinity has its complement in writing by women, notable among whom is Jessie Kesson. What distinguishes her contribution in *The White Bird Passes* (1958) is a narrative method that, like Gibbon's, displays no hierarchy of verbal register. Her writing takes characteristic pleasure in the sounds of words: pleasure equally in discovering the poetic strangeness of the exotic "Muskoday" and in uttering the native Scots "ootlins" or outsiders.[29] At the same time, Kesson's narrative expresses, as does Mannin's, a preference for the "common" in the face of an ideology of "respectability." In contrast with Gibbon, however, the progression in her two loosely autobiographical novels is from urban to rural poverty. In *The White Bird Passes* the child Janie's movement from "Lady's Lane" to a rural orphanage is entirely circumscribed by the community of women, conspiratorially "in league against the man" (p. 31). The women's constant struggle against poverty, although sometimes alleviated by part-time prostitution, is aggravated by their everyday fears of masculine authority: of being arrested or "inspected" by the Cruelty Man (childcare), the School Board Man (education) or the Sanitary Man (health). Yet there is no voice of moral sanction or condemnation, since as with Kesson's contemporary Catherine Cookson – whose formal domain in *Kate Hannigan* (1950) is a fantasy of idealized class relations – personal movement outwards towards educational or marital achievement does not diminish the sense of class solidarity and belonging: for Kesson, to the protective "world of song and colour, and whirling petticoats and warm, dark women..." (p. 12); for Cookson, to "her people...good, bad and indifferent, they were her kindred."[30]

The idea of belonging also preoccupies the Marxist intellectual Raymond Williams in *Border Country* (1960), in which he discovers a means, through a redefined realism, of representing both "the internally seen working-class community" (particularly in the remembered events of the National Strike) and the "movement of people still feeling their family and political connections out of it."[31] Williams's protagonist crosses and recrosses the borderlands between two emblematic territories: metropolitan London, where as a lecturer he has adopted his father's preferred name, Matthew, and the Welsh rural/industrial borderlands, where he is still known by his birth name, Will. The border becomes an exploratory metaphor, in which Matthew/Will constructs a new form of social consciousness, recognizing the value of rootedness in labor and place and at the same time realizing that "settlement" can lead to complacency: "satisfaction is all very well but change comes from dissatisfaction, we can settle and lose."[32]

Post-industrial: Pat Barker, James Kelman

While Kesson's poetical regionalism, Cookson's working-class romances, and Williams's new realism rely on class as a secure or unified marker of social identity, their successors in the later decades begin to register its disintegration. The clearly drawn lines of conflict of a firmly established modernist culture – whether of class, gender, or political conviction – were now becoming blurred, or atomized, into multiple nodes of "difference," "plurality," "fragmentation"[33]: characteristics that define post-modern or "post-industrial society."[34] Such atomization is evident in the irony of Pat Barker's title for *Union Street* (1982), a novel which, by its division into separate, semi-autonomous stories, signifies the breakdown of working-class social cohesion in Barker's native Teesside. Here the dependable chorus of gossips or community of women or extended family is displaced by women in isolation, the female subject captured in images of disintegration: a broken mirror reflecting "[l]ines and cracks radiat[ing] out, trapping at the centre of the web, her shattered face"; or a mother's "hard exterior [which] had cracked to reveal an inner corruption."[35] The only common factor is reification: women as tools of household work, vessels of progeny, or objects of sexual gratification. Yet there are also signs of resistance: as when Jo works against the "impersonal machine-like passion" of Ken by "imposing upon him the rhythm of the train" passing overhead, making the act "abruptly ridiculous" and causing the loss of "his erection" (p. 101). More vivid still are other accumulating incidents: unexpected "moments of vision," when a symbolic light – of the moon or a transfigured tree – produces an epiphany, a sudden revelation of an alternative consciousness, a differently gendered world (pp. 176, 264–5). In such ways Barker endorses a refusal to lament the passing of the traditional male-dominated communities, revealing instead how women are actively "changing themselves and changing the character of their class."[36]

The stories of *Union Street* form the basis upon which Barker establishes her reputation, maintaining her working-class allegiance, but developing her incisive analyses of class and gender, masculinity, and violence in *The Regeneration Trilogy* (1991–5), and *Another World* (1998). However, it is again from Scotland that the more innovative writing of the final decades emerges, extending the range of linguistic experiment by taking the reader not only to hitherto unvisited locations of working-class life, but to the borderlands of new kinds of class encounter. Notable are Irvine Welsh's narratives of a drug-taking underclass, written mostly in a Leith dialect, but slipping effortlessly into other registers that include parodies of courtroom legal speech, or of educated, literary modes of expression. The uneasy relationship between a working-class consciousness or culture and the one that supposedly must be adopted in order to write characterizes the work of both Alan Warner from Oban (*Morvern Callar*, 1995) and James Kelman of Glasgow; but it is the latter who most consistently surprises the reader with an expressive range of Glaswegian working-class thought and speech. Kelman's novels work by means of negative apprehension, stripping away the barriers of bourgeois abstraction to express the tangible reality of working-class existence. This entails relinquishing the habit of being "off with the concepts,"[37] and getting down instead to "the primaries," a process of what his protagonist in *The Busconductor Hines* (1984) calls "the substractives," a feat of thinking that combines the creative energies of the artist and the footballer:

> The magenta the yellow the cyan. The black. It has to be the black. To fuck with the white it's no good. The items to be being produced
>   Take it calmly. Send over a cross. Up go the heads. Bang.[38]

Undeterred by the voice in his head of communal censure – " 'Naw son, naw; fucking rubbish. I'm sorry" ' – Hines persists, and eventually arrives at the goal of transparency:

> the world has become distinct, the black transforming into the most clear, the pure, it is purity...spewing out in terms of whatever the fuck it doesnt matter, it doesnt matter; it does not matter, fuck them all, just straight in, straight in to clear it all out.   (p. 104).

That final paring away to an ultimately concrete yet transparent clarity is achieved in *How Late It Was, How Late* (1994) in Kelman's ex-con, Sammy, suddenly made blind by a beating from "the sodjers": the generic name for all uniformed authority. The narrative strategy of reducing all experience to a brutalized sensory bewilderment and disorientation enables paradoxically a sharpened focus on the processes of consciousness. Here the subtle modulations of "fuck" and its derivatives become the medium of a clarity that only a working-class consciousness is able to achieve:

> Folk take a battering but, they do; they get born and they get brought up and they get fuckt. That's the story; the cot to the fucking funeral pyre.[39]

The words of the solitary but "bold Sammy" echo Beckett's modernist reductionism, but he is no figure of a reduced human condition, since his concrete utterances have no universal validity: the folk are not all folk, but his folk. The blinded Sammy is a *working-class* survivor engaged in strategies of resistance, struggling against the determining forces of a society in which "most of the time ye get fuckt." Yet it is that same chronic state that also enables the "small victories": "the wee times you don't, and it's the wee times ye look for. This was one of them. It made ye feel good...when ye fucking know it man when ye know it...the sodjers thought they had him figured man but they didnay" (p. 323).

The figure of Kelman is an appropriate one for concluding a survey of twentieth-century working-class writing. In the face of the steady erosion of class as a valid political and cultural category he points to the ways that a working-class consciousness and a distinctively working-class writing can be actively remade.

NOTES

1 Georg Lukács, *History and Class Consciousness*, trans. Rodney Livingstone (London: Merlin Press, 1971), p. 91.
2 David Harvey, *Justice, Nature and the Geography of Difference* (Oxford: Blackwell, 1996), p. 50.
3 Karl Marx and Friedrich Engels, *The Communist Manifesto* (Harmondsworth: Penguin, 1968), p. 83.
4 E. P. Thompson, *The Making of the English Working Class* (Harmondsworth: Penguin, 1975), p. 8.
5 Terry Eagleton, *Heathcliff and the Great Hunger: Studies in Irish Culture* (London: Verso, 1995), p. 147.
6 Raymond Williams, *Writing in Society* (London: Verso, 1979), p. 241.
7 Patrick MacGill, *Children of the Dead End. The autobiography of a navvy* (London: Herbert Jenkins, 1914), p. 2.
8 Patrick MacGill, *The Great Push. An episode of the Great War* (London: Herbert Jenkins, 1916), pp. 251, 161.
9 Uttered in MacGill's companion volume, *The Rat-Pit* (London: Herbert Jenkins, 1915), p. 296.
10 Theodor Adorno, *Aesthetic Theory*, trans. Robert Hulot-Kentor (Minneapolis: University of Minnesota Press, 1997), p. 49.
11 Jack Mitchell, *The Socialist Novel in Britain: Towards the Recovery of a Tradition* (Brighton: Harvester Press, 1984), p. 69; Ian Haywood, *Working-Class Fiction: from Chartism to 'Trainspotting'* (Plymouth: Northcote House, 1997) p. 23; Ian Birchall, "Proletarian Modernism? Form and Content in *The Ragged Trousered Philanthropists*," *Notebooks* 1 (1994), 48.
12 Robert Tressell, *The Ragged Trousered Philanthropists* (London: Lawrence and Wishart, 1955), pp. 11–12.
13 Raymond Williams, *Towards 2000* (London: Chatto and Windus, 1983), p. 13.
14 Ken Worpole, *Dockers and Detectives: Popular Reading, Popular Writing* (London: Verso, 1983), p. 78.
15 See George Orwell "The Proletarian Writer" (1940) in *The Collected Essays, Journalism and Letters of George Orwell, Vol II, My Country Right or Left*, eds. Sonia Orwell and Ian Angus (London: Secker & Warburg, 1968), pp. 38–46; William Empson, *Some Versions of Pastoral* (Harmondsworth: Penguin, 1966), pp. 11–25.

16 Graham Holderness, "Miners and the Novel," *The British Working-Class Novel in the Twentieth Century*, ed. Jeremy Hawthorn (London: Edward Arnold, 1984), p. 27.

17 Harold Heslop, *Last Cage Down* (London: Lawrence and Wishart, 1983), p. 8; *Goaf* (London: The Fortune Press, 1934), p. 124.

18 James Hanley, *Boy* (London: André Deutsch, 1990), p. 74; *Men in Darkness* (London: The Bodley Head, 1931), p. 213.

19 Harold Heslop, *The Gate of a Strange Field* (New York: D. Appleton, 1929), p. 189; Helen Wilkinson, *Clash* (London: Virago, 1983), p. 232.

20 Ethel Mannin, *Privileged Spectator* (London: Jarrolds, 1939), pp. 23, 319.

21 Beverly Skeggs, *Formations of Class and Gender: Becoming Respectable* (London: Sage, 1997), p. 46.

22 Ethel Mannin, *Venetian Blinds* (London: Hutchinson, 1972), p. 93.

23 Lewis Grassic Gibbon, *A Scots Quair* (Harmondsworth: Penguin, 1986), p. 176

24 Lewis Grassic Gibbon, *A Scots Hairst* (London: Hutchinson, 1978), p. 107, emphasis added.

25 The *Times Literary Supplement*, quoted in Stuart Laing, *Representations of Working-Class Life, 1957–1964* (London: Macmillan, 1986), p. 1.

26 Jack Common, *Kiddar's Luck* (London: Turnstile Press, 1951), p. 7.

27 Tony Davies, "Realism and Working-Class Writing," *Working-Class Novel*, ed. Hawthorn, pp. 125–6.

28 Alan Sillitoe, *Saturday Night and Sunday Morning* (London: W. H. Allen, 1978), p. 30.

29 Jessie Kesson, *The White Bird Passes* (London: Virago, 1993), pp. 21, 118.

30 Catherine Cookson, *Kate Hannigan* (London: Corgi, 1972), p. 218.

31 Raymond Williams, *Politics and Letters* (London: Verso, 1979), p. 272.

32 Raymond Williams, *Border Country* (London, Chatto & Windus, 1960), p. 288.

33 See Craig Owens, "The Discourse of Others," *Postmodern Culture*, ed. Hal Foster (London: Pluto Press, 1984), p. 58; Harvey, p. 59

34 Daniel Bell, "The Coming of the Post-Industrial Society," *The Postmodern Reader*, ed. Charles Jencks (New York: St Martin's Press, 1973), p. 262.

35 Pat Barker, *Union Street* (London: Virago Press, 1982), pp. 54, 59.

36 See Bea Campbell, *Wigan Pier Re-visited* (London: Virago Press, 1984), p. 230.

37 James Kelman, *A Disaffection* (London: Secker & Warburg, 1989), p. 10.

38 James Kelman, *The Busconductor Hines* (London: Secker & Warburg, 1995), p. 104.

39 James Kelman, *How Late it Was, How Late* (London: Secker & Warburg, 1994), p. 16.

IO

MARINA MACKAY

World War II, the welfare state, and postwar "humanism"

"Children is all little 'Itlers these days," proclaims a character in Henry Green's *Loving* (1945), one of the best English novels of World War II.[1] Set in an Anglo-Irish mansion in the neutral Republic of Ireland, *Loving* is about the daily lives of the servants during their mistress's absence. The "little 'Itler" here is the hilariously precocious Albert, an urban evacuee from England who has strangled one of the estate's peacocks with his bare hands. "Oh I screamed out," recounts his aunt, "but 'e'ad it about finished the little storm trooper."[2] All the novel's main characters are obsessed by invasions, as well they might be in wartime Ireland, but there is an important sense in which the enemy has already landed. In part, it is this insight – that "'Itler" and the storm troopers aren't out there but right here – that makes *Loving* so typical of the novels of World War II. If this seems a bleak conclusion to draw from a novel that is otherwise as exuberant as its title suggests, I hope to explain in this chapter why the grimly comic clear-sightedness one encounters in a novel like *Loving* might itself be seen as characteristic of English fiction in the middle of the twentieth century.

Allies and enemies

In an essay written a few months before her suicide in 1941, Virginia Woolf spoke of "a subconscious Hitlerism in the hearts of men": "It is the desire for aggression; the desire to dominate and enslave."[3] The unconscious impulses that found political expression in Nazism were not a German problem but everyone's problem, and although Woolf would ultimately support World War II (she and her Jewish husband knew well what was at stake), patriotism never came naturally to her. This is why her final novel, *Between the Acts* (1941), is as much concerned with the Nazi within as the Nazi without. Set in an English village in the summer of 1939, the novel insists that acts of brutality abroad have domestic counterparts: while Giles Oliver reads in the newspaper of totalitarian enormities on the continent, his wife Isa reads of a girl gang-raped by English soldiers. That no nation has a monopoly on militarism had always been central to Woolf's long-held pacifism, but *Between the Acts* goes further than this: violence is primordial and ineradicable. During the interval of the pageant play that takes up most of the novel, Giles is startled by a symbolic atrocity right in the English heartland, literally a snake in the grass: "Dead? No, choked with a toad in its mouth. The snake was unable to swallow; the toad was unable to die. A spasm made the ribs contract; blood oozed. It was birth the wrong way round – a monstrous inversion."[4] Haunted by the possibility of a return to the barbaric primeval swamp, *Between the Acts* is filled with terror. And yet it is also – a crucial qualification – an unexpectedly comic novel. After all, only the dotty Anglican Lucy Swithin spends much time pondering the "elephant-bodied, seal-necked, heaving, surging, slowly writhing... monsters" of the prehistoric landscape (p. 8).

The need to "save civilization" was a conventional call to arms in the propaganda of both world wars, and Woolf seems to be asking what, pre-cisely, would qualify the British to save it. Her reading of Freud during the first winter of the war helps to account for the pessimism of *Between the Acts*: "Freud is upsetting," she wrote in her diary: "If we're all instinct, the unconscious, what's all this about civilisation, the whole man, freedom &c?"[5] In Freud's *Civilization and Its Discontents* (1930), republished by the Woolfs' Hogarth Press in 1939,[6] civilization is the fragile collective effort to save us from our own destructive compulsions. Human beings are inherently aggressive, Freud argued:

> their neighbour is for them not only a potential helper or sexual object, but also someone who tempts them to satisfy their aggressiveness on him, to exploit his capacity for work without compensation, to use him sexually without his consent, to seize his possessions, to humiliate him, to cause him pain, to torture and to kill him. *Homo homini lupus*. ["Man is a wolf to man."] Who, in the face of all his experience of life and of history, will have the courage to dispute this assertion?[7]

Like many English intellectuals of her class and generation, Woolf was a liberal humanist, believing in the coherence and rationality of the individual, the integrity of personal relationships, and the dignity of human accom-plishments. These prewar articles of faith are already in crisis in her late work and had she lived a few years longer she would have seen Freud's un-consoling apprehensions about human possibility realized in the deadliest war ever fought. A war that killed an unprecedented sixty million people saw other truly catastrophic human "firsts": the industrial-scale murder of Jews and other political undesirables; the deliberate destruction by fire of civilians and their cities; the first use of the atomic bomb. Homo homini lupus.

Although it comes as no surprise, then, that there are crucial discontinuities between prewar and postwar culture, many novelists of World War II borrowed the vocabulary formulated by the experimental writers of Woolf's generation as a way of communicating the shattering psychological effects of wartime conditions. As if history itself had turned literary modernism into realism, London becomes the ghost-walked city of 1920s modernism, its living citizens burdened by the civilian dead, who, in Elizabeth Bowen's account of the Blitz, "made their anonymous presence...felt through London. Uncounted, they continued to move through the city day, pervading everything to be seen or heard or felt with their torn-off senses."[8] Bowen literalizes the metaphor in her chilling story "The Demon Lover" (1945), in which a soldier killed in World War I returns in World War II to reclaim his lover. The walking dead are a powerful presence, too, in Robert Liddell's *Unreal City* (1952), which, from the title onwards, uses T. S. Eliot's *The Waste Land* (1922), written in the aftermath of the Great War, to articulate the hallucinatory experience of a bereaved English civilian in the Mediterranean city of Caesarea during World War II. Liddell and Bowen both underscore the continuities of traumatic experience that stretch across the first half of the century but with the important difference that Liddell closes with a degree of humanist optimism about rebuilding a life after war. In contrast, an ominous air of unfinished business lingers around Bowen's wartime fiction.

The specifically formal extension of modernism comes in Henry Green's novels. Set in the first year of the war and based on Green's wartime work as an auxiliary fireman, his experimental *Caught* (1943) tells the story of two firemen: the volunteer Richard Roe, an upper-middle-class widower, and the working-class Albert Pye, whose insane sister is confined to an asylum for abducting Roe's son. Like *Loving* this novel is interested in the enemy within: Roe's son, for instance, is another little Hitler, harassing the birds in his garden because "They're Polish people...and I'm a German policeman, rootling them about."[9] Like *Loving*, too, this novel is preoccupied with rumor and misconception: people are in the dark not only about each other – the wartime blackout is as much figurative as literal – but about themselves. Initially, for instance, Pye thinks nostalgically about a girl he had sex with one pitch-black night of his rural adolescence, but eventually it comes to him, "clear, false, that it might have been his own sister he was with that night... And he had always known, and never realized" (p. 119).

This ambiguity about whether the memory is fake ("clear, false") or real ("he had always known") is never resolved, and, incapable of laying claim even to his own past, Pye commits suicide by the end of the novel. Roe, too, will have a nervous breakdown, though not of the same magnitude as Pye's, or, indeed, that of Charley Summers, the protagonist of Green's *Back* (1946). Newly repatriated from a prisoner of war camp, Charley is psychologically devastated by a mysterious war experience – "something in France which he knew, as he valued his reason, that he must always shut out"[10] – which the novel refuses to detail. On his return to England a delusional Charley believes, in the face of all the evidence, that a former lover whose death has coincided with his capture is still alive. Charley's unspeakable war experience only gets articulated as this fixation on a loss in which he refuses to believe.

"War, she thought, was sex," Green writes of a character in *Caught* (p. 119), and the entanglement of erotic and political feelings is central to novels produced by the war. In Mary Renault's *The Charioteer* (1953) the Dunkirk veteran Laurie Odell, gay and on the verge of coming out, has to choose between two men: the worldly veteran Ralph and the pacifist Andrew. Andrew's innocence is twofold: as a conscientious objector he is exempt from all war guilt, and, as a sheltered Christian, he is incapable of acknowledging the eroticism of his romantic friendship with Laurie. Andrew's innocence, the novel implies, is rigorously and artificially protected, and thus is not really innocence at all, and it has the potential to be far more destructive to Laurie than Ralph's "guilt" as a war veteran and avowedly gay man. As if there is no going back from the knowledge of war or sex (the two are presented here as largely the same thing), Laurie consciously chooses innocent Andrew, and yet finds himself with the more knowing, and self-knowing, Ralph. Even if Ralph is the unruly dark horse of the soul to Andrew's divinely light one – *The Charioteer* takes its overarching metaphor from Plato – it seems the dark horse is the one leading Laurie in the right direction.

War is sex, too, in Patrick Hamilton's *noir* novel *Hangover Square* (1941), which describes George Harvey Bone's infatuation with a sadistic actress whose unspoken sexual tastes supply the key to her Nazi sympathies: "she liked pictures of marching, regimented men... She liked the uniforms, the guns, the breeches, the boots, the swastikas, the shirts."[11] She torments Bone until forbearance – or "appeasement," you might say – is no longer an option, and Bone murders her to the soundtrack provided by the prime minister announcing on the wireless a state of war with Germany. Hamilton's *The Slaves of Solitude* (1947), set in a boarding house in the winter of 1943–4, revisits these themes through a less sensationalist plot: Nazi sympathies cannot be spoken aloud on wartime England's home front, but what the heroine recognizes as the bully's attraction to "Jew-exterminating, torturing, jackbooted, whip-carrying, concentration-camp Nazidom" finds covert expression in sexualized domestic malice.[12] The familiar Nazi appears, too, in

Bowen's *The Heat of the Day*, when the heroine Stella Rodney finds out that her lover is a spy who has been passing secrets to the enemy from deeply-held political convictions that Stella could never have suspected.

The Heat of the Day is preoccupied by how well it is possible to know anyone at a time when "occupied Europe...was occupying London – suspicious listening, surreptitious movement and leaden hearts," and when even home is no longer homey, but a house built of "repressions, doubts, fears, subterfuges and fibs."[13] One sees these obsessions, too, in Graham Greene's *The Ministry of Fear* (1943), which opens with the hero attending a fête that reminds him of a mythic childhood innocence "with vicarage gardens and girls in white summer frocks and the smell of herbaceous borders and security."[14] When Rowe wrongly wins a cake in the raffle, the illusion of home disintegrates and suddenly nothing is what it seems. Feeling himself "directed, controlled, moulded, by some agency with a surrealist imagination," Rowe has been drawn into the intrigues of a Nazi fifth column in which the courageous and charming Austrian refugees Willi and Anna Hilfe are somehow involved (p. 81). Their name, "aid" in German, may prove ironic: "You don't know who are your friends and who are your enemies," Anna tells Rowe (p. 181). A recurrent figure in World War I literature is the enemy who turns out to be a friend; in World War II novels, friends can turn out to be enemies.

These suspicions about the staginess and incoherence of identity refuse to go away in postwar fiction. In Denton Welch's "Brave and Cruel" (1948) a man shows up in the narrator's middle-class milieu pretending to be a Battle of Britain hero. He is no such thing: the charismatic "Micki Beaumont" is, in drab truth, Potts, the pathologically lying son of a local farm laborer. Something similar happens in Elizabeth Taylor's *A Wreath of Roses* (1949) when the middle-class Camilla Hill falls in love with a veteran who claims to be returning to his childhood home. Theatrically handsome and glamorously posh, Group-Captain Richard Elton – "so much the sort of name people don't have," Camilla muses, "The sort a woman writer might choose...for the name of her hero"[15] – is, as he seems, too good to be true. Elton is an impostor, a murderer in flight from justice.

While Camilla thinks of romantic fiction, Elton takes his cues from spy novels, describing his bogus war career as "much like the books I read as a boy – passwords, disguises, swallowing bits of paper" (p. 11). But if Elton's squalid true story – he has strangled his girlfriend – sounds as melodramatically literary as those fictions in which he and Camilla are living, it is importantly downplayed. Elton may be on the run from the police, but Taylor seems more interested in his being on the run from plebeian origins. Elton has invented a tragic family "of a higher social standing" in order to replace a "father who was proud of his son for all the things his son despised – the scholarship to the secondary school, the sergeant's stripes; the mother who fussed over his material condition and rode rough-shod over his aspirations with her cosiness" (p. 133).

So this sense that wartime upheaval has made new identities possible is seen in social terms: "people won't stay in their appointed places," Welch's narrator surmises, "they flow about like anything."[16] But something stranger than simple class anxiety drives these impostor stories: Richard Elton and especially Micki Beaumont are more sexy than sinister, as if there is something attractive and invigorating about their impostures – impostures that many around them see through at an early stage anyhow. What is more, their fake selves are only extreme realizations of a pervasive feeling that there *is* no going back to what you were: "I suppose one can't go through all the terrible experiences of modern warfare without being changed in some way" (p. 193), one of Welch's characters explains, while Taylor implies the irretrievability of prewar selves with an artist character who, in her postwar old age, has come to reject her earlier paintings: "I committed a grave sin against the suffering of the world by ignoring it"; her new work reinstates "ferocity, brutality,... violence, with flames wheeling, turmoil, pain, chaos" (pp. 118, 34).

Redeeming violence

Taylor's interest in the paradoxically creative aspects of destruction unites the poetry and fiction produced during the war. This was the era of "New Apocalypse" poets such as David Gascoyne, J. F. Hendry, and Henry Treece, whose insistently and sometimes illegibly private poetry privileged myth and dream over reason and logic. In prose fiction the redeeming power of the private imagination to make art out of catastrophe is evidenced in James Hanley's disorientating *No Directions* (1943), set in a block of flats during a single night of the Blitz. Like Taylor, Hanley uses a painter, the mad recluse Clem Stevens, to examine the convergence of public violence and the interior landscape. Clem has begun to paint again after a decade of silence, as if the Blitz has liberated his choked creativity. The novel's surrealistic final chapter sees him run, exhilarated, through the burning streets:

> All that light, a sea, an ocean of light, from what vast reservoir had it flooded up, this drenching light, blazing red, and suddenly to his left a falling green, cataracts of light, red, and yellow and green, this riot of colour shouted at you.
> "God!" he said, "it's magnificent, it's –"[17]

This is an apocalyptic scene of a particularly painterly kind: Clem's private vision has found its external corollary in the destruction of London.

One of Hanley's contemporaries, the Irish novelist Joyce Cary, also presents the artist in comparably Romantic terms: in Cary's wartime trilogy *Herself Surprised* (1941), *To Be A Pilgrim* (1942), and *The Horse's Mouth* (1944), the artist Gulley Jimson is brutally violent, coarse, erratic, and reckless, but he is also a visionary genius of religious dimensions along the lines of William Blake. (The creepiest implications of that wartime interpretation of violence as revelation would much later be exploited in William Golding's *Darkness Visible* [1979], which opens with the fanatical Matty emerging from the fires of the Blitz.)

While this neo-Romantic presentation of the war as an occasion to liberate the unconscious and proclaim the transcendent power of art borrows the language of visionary experience, other writers made the redemptive religious element a more explicit part of their work. Greene's *The End of the Affair* (1951) is the story of a relationship between the narrator Maurice Bendrix and the married Sarah Miles that begins in 1940 during the Blitz and ends with the VI rockets of 1944. Believing Bendrix dead under the rubble, Sarah vows to believe in God and renounce Bendrix so long as he is allowed to live, and when God fulfills his side of the bargain, Sarah fulfills hers. That spiritual good can come out of violence is a recurring theme in the literature of the war, prose and poetry alike. In wartime poems such as Edith Sitwell's "Still Falls the Rain" (1941) and T. S. Eliot's *Little Gidding* (1942), the bombing of London is a crucifixion and a baptism.

But another religious convert brings me to the secular efforts to rehabilitate the unsurpassed horror of World War II. Muriel Spark's retrospective *The Girls of Slender Means* (1963) is set in the summer of 1945, just as the war is ending. The girls of the title are residents of a London hostel for young ladies in straitened circumstances. But there is no shame in that, Spark ironically insists, not when "all the nice people in England were poor."[18] But "the girls of slender means" are not at all "nice," and "slender" also changes its meaning when an unexploded bomb left over from the Blitz goes off and the girls struggle to escape through a tiny window that will allow only the thinnest through. As the hostel burns, slinky Selina slips back through the window – to rescue not a resident but an expensive dress, which she carries back past her fatter friends as they stand under the narrow window awaiting their deaths. Selina's agnostic lover Nicholas converts on the spot because "a vision of evil may be as effective to conversion as a vision of good" (p. 140).

Nicholas's conversion recalls the specifically Christian effort to make the evils of war pay spiritually ennobling dividends, but what gives Spark's mordant parable its political point is Nicholas's mistaken idealization of the poverty that brings the girls together in their cheap hostel. His misconception that the May of Teck Club is "a miniature expression of a free society . . . a community held together by the graceful attributes of a common poverty" (pp. 84, 85) is proved ridiculously wrong, and Spark wants us to see that mistaking communal hardship for communal goodness is an error Nicholas shares with his compatriots. What encourages Nicholas's delusional optimism is the mythologized civilian solidarity of World War II, the camaraderie still smugly referred to in Britain as the Blitz spirit. Nicholas has to learn that enforced communality makes people no less savagely selfish.

This is why the climactic explosion takes place on the day of the general election in which the Labour Party won their famous landslide victory. Despite Churchill's celebrated conduct of the war, the dissolution of the wartime coalition government saw his replacement by Labour's Clement Attlee, almost certainly because Conservatives such as Churchill seemed unlikely to fulfill the promises of social justice that had been made since the very beginning of the conflict. All the way through, World War II was called "the people's war," and the what-are-we-fighting-for propaganda continually stressed a more equitable domestic future. The massively popular "Beveridge Report," Sir William Beveridge's *Social Insurance and Allied Services* (1942), provided the blueprint for the postwar welfare state; and if, as Spark has it, all the nice people were poor in 1945, the Labour government's commitment to the redistribution of wealth and the provision of social security would keep them "poor" a while longer. *The Girls of Slender Means* is a black moral comedy with a real political point: that social and spiritual goods – whether you attribute moral "niceness" to the genteel or pretend that temporary sharing reforms people of their poisonous self-interest – are not the same thing.

Of course many novelists felt differently about what a character in *A Wreath of Roses* calls "this evened-out England" (p. 87). J. B. Priestley's novels suggest how mid-century democratization looked to a humanist of left-liberal sympathies. The three men of his *Three Men in New Suits* (1945), written with the war ongoing, are all returning veterans: the aristocratic Alan Strete, the thriving farmer Herbert Kenford, and the laborer Eddie Mold. They are all struggling to cope with postwar life: Alan's democratic impulses put him at odds with his reactionary family; Herbert is disgusted by how well his family has done out of the war; Eddie's wife has been unfaithful in his absence. Longed-for homecomings prove privately unfulfilling, and over all these disappointments there hangs the threat of an even worse one. The broken promises of World War I haunt the novel's closing peroration from Alan Strete: "There's something in us now that will not rest nor find any lasting satisfaction while most human beings still exist in poverty, ignorance and despair . . . Either the earth must soon be the miserable grave of our species or it must be at last our home, where men can live at peace and can work for other men's happiness."[19] The reader never doubts that Priestley is speaking here, warning that unless the socialist and internationalist promises made in wartime are fulfilled, it is 1918 all over again.

All of which makes Priestley sound more pious than he is. On the contrary, some of the novel's best lines go to the crepuscular snob Uncle Rodney. "I'm sorry for you," he tells Alan, prophesying his future in an austerely bureaucratic socialist Britain:

> "To go and drudge in some hell-hole of an office or factory so that you can come home to some numbered cubbyhole at night, gobble some mess out of tins, and either go to the moving pictures to see how pins are made or sit listening to some government bully on the wireless telling you to hurry up and fill in *Form Nine-thousand-and-thirty-eight*. Once a year you and your wife, who'll be as plain as a suet pudding, and all your brats, who'll have been vaccinated against everything but stupidity and dreariness, will be given a ticket to a holiday camp, along with five thousand other clerks and mechanics and their women and kids, and there you'll have physical drill, stew and rice pudding, round games, and evening talks on tropical diseases and aeroplane engines. And I'll be dead – and delighted."   (pp. 25, 26)

Uncle Rodney's prophecy is the comic version of what George Orwell would imagine a few years later in *1984*. What Priestley is condensing into this absurd speech from an unreconstructed old Tory is a fairly widespread 1940s fear that postwar socialism promises "a paradise which will be absolutely uninhabitable for anyone of civilized taste," as one character puts it in a wartime novel by (speaking of unreconstructed old Tories) Evelyn Waugh.[20]

Priestley took seriously, without sharing, those fears about a newly socialist culture. In his *Festival at Farbridge* (1951; published in the USA as *Festival*), the aptly named Ernest Saxon is intellectually committed, politically exemplary, and totally joyless. The novel depicts a postwar Britain full of boozy Tory duffers and humorless liberals – a potentially depressing panorama, except that it is relieved by the comic, almost camp energies of the novel's misfit heroes: the bitchy but likeable Laura, the raffish Commodore Tribe, and the sumptuous Anglo-Indonesian tourist Theodore Jenks. The festival of the book's title is to be held alongside the 1951 Festival of Britain, which the Labour government had planned as a national pick-me-up after the hardships of the postwar years (the setting up of the welfare state, a massive national debt, and the loss of overseas trade placed the country in a disastrous fiscal condition). In a well-known essay, the playwright Michael Frayn described the Festival of Britain as the last hurrah of "the radical middle-classes": "the Herbivores, or gentle ruminants, who look out from the lush pastures which are their natural station in life with eyes full of sorrow for less fortunate creatures, guiltily conscious of their advantages, though not usually ceasing to eat the grass."[21] Priestley's point is not that the Herbivores' standards are wrong – not if the alternative is the carnivorous politics of self-interest – but only that real liberal humanism is potentially richer than the unreflective party-political dogma it threatens to become in the hands of an "Ernest Saxon."

The novels of Angus Wilson more aggressively ridicule the oddities of professional liberals, despite Wilson's own progressive sympathies. At least the title stories of his early short story collections, *The Wrong Set* (1949) and *Such Darling Dodos* (1950), help to explain whose side Wilson is on. In "The Wrong Set," the working-class Vi, a nightclub artiste and girlfriend of the grossly vulgar Trevor, is aghast at her nephew's new friends: "Terribly worried," she writes her sister at the end of the story, "Norman in the wrong set."[22] The joke here is that trashy Vi is a staunch Tory and Norman's "wrong set" consists of middle-class liberals. The "darling dodos" of the other collection are also middle-class liberals, this time as described by 1940s Christian conservatives – reactionary Anglo-Catholicism being, comically, more up-to-date than progressive humanism. Wilson's criticism of the Herbivores is much more astringent in his novel *Late Call* (1964). The heroine is an uneducated elderly woman who retires to the home of her son, a man of uncompromisingly progressive politics who teaches at a "secondary modern" school in one of the New Towns, the planned cities built after the war. Although the heroine eventually comes to terms with a rootless new world designed on impeccably rationalist, technocratic, and materialist principles, the novel is acutely critical of the break with the past championed with so little self-reflection by those who congratulate themselves on their progressive politics.

Barbara Pym's novels of the 1950s also describe encounters between modern professional humanists, in her case usually academic anthropologists, and the remnants of a more amateur humanism, a specifically female one dedicated to community-minded good works. Her heroines are middle-aged Anglican spinsters: they are "excellent women" – the title of one of her novels – who are altogether invisible to those who talk with pompous authority about the complex institutions of "primitive peoples" while ignoring the burden of social relations being carried at home. Pym is thoroughly sympathetic to those excellent women, even as her novels seem to poke fun at them. In *Some Tame Gazelle* (1950), for instance, Belinda Bede has secretly been in love with the married Archdeacon Hoccleve for thirty years; she seems an absurd figure until you realize that her attachment to an unattainable object saves her from the incalculably worse fate of marrying any of Pym's monstrous male narcissists. At least being in love with the appalling Archdeacon allows Belinda to elude the unromantic proposals of Bishop Grote:

> "...But a man does need a helpmeet, you remember in *Paradise Lost*..."
> Belinda interrupted him with a startled exclamation. "*Paradise Lost!*" she echoed in horror. "*Milton*...."[23]

All Pym's heroines are educated enough to recognize Milton as a misogynist, even if they consider themselves stupid next to the professional academics with whom they come into contact. Mildred Latham in *Excellent Women* (1952) ends the novel happily enough, having bridged the gap between the amateur humanism of her churchy good works and the world of professional anthropology that she encounters through her friends Helena Napier and Everard Bone. What the reader sees, though, that Mildred doesn't, is that her excellence will continue to be exploited. Indeed, her future looks like the worst of both worlds: voluntarily organizing jumble sales *and* reading page proofs. Gossip in a later novel informs us that she marries the "anthropophagist" Everard Bone – a telling malapropism since everyone cannibalizes women like Mildred.[24]

The irredeemable

In Wilson's *The Middle Age of Mrs. Eliot* (1958), an upper-class widow successfully makes the transition from private charity to paid public labor, but while Wilson's other novels are equally attentive to the changing class structure of mid-century Britain they are also concerned with more harrowing transformations ushered in by the war. The hero of his first novel, *Hemlock and After* (1952), is a successful novelist who is worried less by the legal risks he runs as a gay man in an era before the decriminalization of homosexuality than by "the growing apprehension of evil that had begun...to disrupt his comprehension of the world."[25] He has started to wonder if his long-professed liberal humanism, an E. M. Forster sort of worldview left over from the prewar era, is really adequate to the postwar condition: "peace, social justice, freedom to create, full use of material benefits in safe surroundings," he lists the classic aspirations of welfare state liberals like himself: "It sounds quite enough, I know, but it isn't" (p. 76).

His wife, meanwhile, has been in a state of nervous collapse for years. Tormented by daydreams of empty caves and barren wastes, she has a consciousness of evil that seems to signal a withdrawal from social existence and yet is also a total engagement of geopolitical reality. We learn, for instance, that her breakdown coincided with the outbreak of World War II, and the wastelands of her postwar hallucinations strongly suggest the Cold War threat of nuclear annihilation. Bernard himself will break down when he sees a young man being arrested for importuning – not because he is upset by the persecution of other gay men, but because he realizes with horror that his first response is arousal and excitement:

> But what had brought him to his senses, he asked himself, and, to his horror, the only answer he could find was that in the detective's attitude of somewhat officious but routine duty there was no response to his own hunter's thrill. Truly, he thought, he was not at one with those who exercised proper authority. A humanist, it would seem, was more at home with the wielders of the knout and the rubber truncheon. (p. 108)

Bernard's epiphany, then, is that beneath his apparent kindness, his liberal humanism, his pedagogical generosity, there lies a fascist ("the wielders of the knout and rubber truncheon"). If Ella has internalized the evil of the global situation, Bernard has found it there already in himself.

These intimations of evil that give Wilson's fiction its slightly panicky tone are important because the meticulous, and often very witty, social precision of mid-century writers can make them sound as passé as the minutiae and manners they scrutinize with such fascinated intensity. But Wilson's moral interests are in self-deceiving impulses toward tyranny and cruelty, and in a historical situation poisoned by the unleashing of those instincts by totalitarianism. The "middlebrow" epithet stalks his diminished reputation as it does those of many gifted writers of the period, but there are far more sociopaths in these novels than the middlebrow designation would lead you to expect. One transcendently brutal scene in Wilson's *Anglo-Saxon Attitudes* (1956) explicitly connects private evil and its political corollaries: the drunken sadist Yves Houdet drags his mother and another elderly woman from their beds in the middle of the night and forces them to reenact drill from the Nazi concentration camp they barely survived.

"Evil" seems an inappropriate word to use about an agnostic writer, but in his essay "Evil in the English Novel" Wilson argued that the English novel was damagingly limited by its reluctance to see morality as more than a matter of middle-class ideas of right and wrong. On the face of it, there is no obvious reason why, in the famously permissive social climate of the 1960s, evil should seem so pressingly important to a writer (and a gay writer at that) who had absolutely no interest in the reinstatement of traditional religious values; but the underlying historical imperatives become apparent when Wilson addresses modern fiction. So, for instance, he praises the late work of Woolf for letting the violent realities of totalitarianism shatter her formerly insular values: "one suddenly gets the sense of real evil – of violence coming in from outside," and goes on to suggest that the Cold War makes matters still worse: "The hydrogen bomb is not the same as Hitler; we can no longer satisfactorily and comfortably think of evil as something over the other side of the Channel, howling at the door. It is inside our house now."[26] Little in recent history could encourage humanist optimism, and Wilson was not alone in saying so. No religious writer either, Iris Murdoch remarked around the same time that contemporary fiction had proved completely inadequate to the task of representing evil: "a consequence of the facile, dramatic and, in spite of Hitler, optimistic picture of ourselves with which we work."[27] Naïve humanisms persisted, Wilson and Murdoch complained, despite everything modern totalitarianism teaches about the human capacity for instrumentalizing and brutalizing other people. A meaningful humanism would have to confront rather than avoid what people had shown themselves capable of doing to each other.

The inadequacy of humanistic values to historical reality is the theme of Wilson's most influential novel, *Anglo-Saxon Attitudes*. The historian hero, Gerald Middleton, suspects that his long-dead friend Gilbert Stokesay, a modernist writer modeled on T. E. Hulme and Wyndham Lewis, tricked his eminent historian father into the bogus discovery forty years earlier of a pagan idol in the tomb of an Anglo-Saxon bishop. The investigation seems narrowly academic – to discover whether or not this seventh-century bishop reverted to paganism – but the reader comes to see that there is more at stake in the liberal humanist Middleton's refusal to confront Gilbert Stokesay, a bestially violent proto-fascist. Thus, we learn that Gilbert's deceived historian father, the mentor whose humanism survives through Middleton, was one of the "Men of Munich" – that is, one of those people whose very high-mindedness led to appeasement in the 1930s.

Wilson's ironic point about humanists serving the vicious interests of those with whom they have least in common returns in retrospective novels about World War II. In Kazuo Ishiguro's *The Remains of the Day* (1989), the pro-appeasement Lord Darlington is thoughtful, articulate, cultured, and tolerant, entirely above divisive nationalisms and petty private interests. Disgusted by the Allies' punitive treatment of Germany after World War I, Darlington is betrayed by his own virtues: an increasingly compromising desire for reconciliation with Germany turns him from a private diplomat in the 1920s, trying to mitigate the harsh terms of the Treaty of Versailles, into an anti-Semitic Nazi sympathizer of the 1930s. *The Remains of the Day* is a novel about the liberal conscience that looks back to Wilson's novels of the 1950s (the frame story is set in 1956) and, further back, to anxieties about private motives and their public outcomes articulated in the novels of Forster. Like Forster at his least optimistic,

Ishiguro presents what he considers a very English liberal humanism – those "Anglo-Saxon Attitudes" of Wilson's novel – as infinitely superior to the political forces that oppose it and yet ineffectual and self-destructive in the face of those forces.

But the links between Wilson and another contemporary novelist, Ian McEwan, indicate the most profound postwar challenges to humanism. Along with the liberal novelist and critic Malcolm Bradbury, Wilson was one of McEwan's creative writing teachers, and McEwan's protagonists are, like Wilson's, usually of the progressive and affluent caste; as in Wilson's novels, too, an unexpected encounter with evil teaches these characters how fragile their comfortable world really is. McEwan's novels about World War II, *Black Dogs* (1992) and *Atonement* (2001), undertake a character-istically uncomfortable interrogation of liberal humanism's response to violence and cruelty.

In *Black Dogs* the narrator Jeremy is trying to write a memoir of his wife's parents: representing with diagrammatic clarity the polarization of postwar worldviews, Bernard is a left-wing social commentator and thoroughgoing rationalist, and June, a one-time Communist, is now a religious mystic. June's conversion has originated in a solitary encounter in 1946 with two vicious black mastiffs roaming the French countryside: these dogs belonged to the Gestapo and were trained to intimidate the occupied locals and per-haps also – the novel doesn't commit to this – to rape. "I didn't quite know it at the time," June explains, "these animals were the creations of debased imaginations, of perverted spirits no amount of social theory could account for. The evil I'm talking about lives in us all."[28] At first glance, she seems to be talking about "debased imaginations" of the Nazis who realized that dogs could be trained to rape women, but "debased imaginations" would also be a fair description of the village gossips who told June, perhaps untruthfully and vindictively, that Gestapo dogs raped a woman who was locally des-pised. Then you get to the end of the book to find McEwan's disclaimer that the dogs "have no basis in historical fact": the work of McEwan's "debased" imagination?

The complicity implied in this ending – June's sense that "evil . . . lives in us all" – retroactively unravels the narrator's affirmatively humanistic preface: "I would be false to my own experience," he writes, "if I did not declare my belief in the possibility of love transforming and redeeming a life" (p. xxii). The reader later learns that the narrator has his first date with his adored wife at – of all places – one of the Polish death camps. At Majdanek Jeremy walks through the heaped-up shoes of the Holocaust dead only to realize that the tourist's eye view is far closer to the perspective of the all-powerful killers than that of the people they obliterated. So much, then, for the transcendent power of love when sites of atrocity become the stimulus to erotic desire – he and Jenny leave the death camp for a hotel bedroom – and so much for the redeeming imagination when it only brings you "one step closer to the dreamers of the nightmare" (p. 88).

Atonement, too, looks back at the war with a sense of how the erotic and imaginative capacities that might have redeemed us are perverted into something death-bound and vindictive. The first part of the novel recounts the rape of a young girl at a prewar country house party, and because the naïvely moralistic thirteen-year-old Briony has witnessed her working-class neighbor Robbie (on whom she has had a childish crush) having sex with her older sister Cecilia, she punishes Robbie by blaming him for a rape she does not really believe he committed. The middle of the novel is set in 1940: Robbie, released from prison for military service, has survived the disastrous evacuation at Dunkirk and is reunited with Cecilia. At the end of this section and through the novel's final part, set in 1999, the reader learns that what she had been reading as an omnisciently narrated book in something like the period style of Elizabeth Bowen (who makes a cameo appearance in the novel) is "really" the final draft of Briony's half-century-long process of retelling what happened. Robbie did not survive Dunkirk as Briony had written, and the bereaved Cecilia was killed in the Blitz. "How could that constitute an ending?" Briony asks, explaining why she "allowed" them to live: "What sense of hope or satisfaction could a reader draw from such an account? Who would want to believe that they never met again, never ful-filled their love?"[29] So it is not simply a matter of love proving painfully unable to conquer all, but that the novel betrays a deep suspicion of cre-ativity itself – a suspicion that emerges because of Briony's comments rather than despite them. Once recognized as "fiction," Briony's atonement feels jarringly inadequate to the victimization of Robbie by Briony, and then by a social class that closes ranks around the real rapist, imprisons Robbie for a crime he did not commit, and kills him in a botched military retreat. McEwan's trick ending is so forceful because even as we concede Briony's point, however self-justifying, that the historical record is textual and thus subject to rewriting, we see in ways she seems not to that her recuperative creative act is almost cruelly incommensurate to the crime.

Notwithstanding McEwan's metafictional fascination with the textual and rewriteable, this essentially unforgiving element distinguishes his work from the more relativistic strands of postmodern thinking. It is also the aspect of his fiction that suggests continuities of anxiety about human motive that reach at least as far back as the early stages of the war, when a horrified Virginia Woolf found a secular version of original sin in the writings of Freud. At its gentlest, a questioning of the mid-century devolution of progressive beliefs into unreflective dogma appears in Priestley's friendly mockery of welfare state materialists and Pym's affectionately satirical treatment of excellent women and oblivious anthropologists; the more acidic critique comes in the work of novelists like Spark, whose malicious wit echoes, albeit in a religious idiom, wartime writers' relentless unmasking of the Nazi within. The survival of that illusion-stripping impulse through the generations represented by Wilson and McEwan is particularly interesting because their humanism can look so much like anti-humanism. It would be fair to say that the forces of sadism and cruelty in their novels that so insistently prove liberal humanism vulnerable also prove it indispensable, but the overridingly pessimistic impression these books leave is that no consoling belief in human goodness could survive a confrontation with the abysmal moral and political realities that World War II made visible.

NOTES

1 Henry Green, *Loving, Living, Party Going* (Harmondsworth: Penguin 1993), p. 53.
2 Green, *Loving*, p. 53.
3 Virginia Woolf, "Thoughts on Peace in an Air Raid," *The Death of the Moth and Other Essays* (London: Hogarth, 1942), p. 155.
4 Virginia Woolf, *Between the Acts* (San Diego, New York, and London: Harcourt, 1969), p. 99.
5 Diary entry dated December 9, 1939. Virginia Woolf, *A Moment's Liberty: The Shorter Diary of Virginia Woolf*, ed. Anne Oliver Bell (San Diego, New York, and London: Harcourt Brace Jovanovich, 1990), p. 464.
6 *Civilization and Its Discontents* was included in John Rickman, (ed.), *Civilization, War and Death: Selections from Three Works by Sigmund Freud* (London: Hogarth, 1939).
7 Sigmund Freud, *Civilization and Its Discontents*, trans. James Strachey (New York: Norton, 1989), pp. 68–9.
8 Elizabeth Bowen, *The Heat of the Day* (New York: Anchor, 2002), p. 99.
9 Henry Green, *Caught* (New York: Augustus M. Kelley, 1970), p. 188.
10 Henry Green, *Back* (New York: Viking, 1950), p. 218.
11 Patrick Hamilton, *Hangover Square* (Harmondsworth: Penguin, 1974), p. 129.
12 Patrick Hamilton, *The Slaves of Solitude* (New York: NYRB, 2007), p. 133.
13 Bowen, *The Heat of the Day*, pp. 139, 287.
14 Graham Greene, *The Ministry of Fear* (London: Penguin, 2005), p. 3.
15 Elizabeth Taylor, *A Wreath of Roses* (Harmondsworth, Penguin, 1967), p. 27.
16 Denton Welch, "Brave and Cruel," *Brave and Cruel and Other Stories* (London: Hamish Hamilton, 1948), p. 133.
17 James Hanley, *No Directions* (London: Faber, 1943), pp. 139–40.
18 Muriel Spark, *The Girls of Slender Means* (Harmondsworth: Penguin, 1966), p. 7.
19 J. B. Priestley, *Three Men in New Suits* (London: The Book Club, 1946), p. 164.
20 Evelyn Waugh, *Put Out More Flags* (Boston: Little, Brown, 1970), p. 70.

21 Michael Frayn, "Festival," *Age of Austerity, 1945–51*, eds. Michael Sissons and Philip French (Harmondsworth: Penguin, 1964), p. 331.

22 Angus Wilson, "The Wrong Set," *The Wrong Set and Other Stories* (London, Secker & Warburg, 1949), p. 106.

23 Barbara Pym, *Some Tame Gazelle* (New York: Dutton, 1983), p. 224.

24 Barbara Pym, *Jane and Prudence* (New York: Dutton, 1981), p. 126.

25 Angus Wilson, *Hemlock and After* (Harmondsworth: Penguin, 1956), p. 13.

26 Angus Wilson, "Evil in the English Novel," *Diversity and Depth in Fiction: Selected Critical Writings of Angus Wilson*, ed. Kerry McSweeney (London: Secker & Warburg, 1983), pp. 12, 22.

27 Iris Murdoch, "Against Dryness," *Encounter* 16: 1 (January 1961), 20.

28 Ian McEwan, *Black Dogs* (New York: Doubleday, 1992), p. 147.

29 Ian McEwan, *Atonement* (New York: Anchor, 2003), p. 350.

II

TIMOTHY WEISS

The *Windrush* generation

In the Anglophone world a West Indian literary renaissance came about in the 1950s because of the immigration of writers-to-be to Britain. Those writers were part of the "*Windrush* generation," a popular designation for postwar immigration to the UK that derives from the name of a converted troopship, *Empire Windrush*, which began carrying West Indians and other emigrants to England in June, 1948. The *Empire Windrush* and the immigrant surge symbolize the beginning of contemporary multiracial and multicultural Britain, and a consequent reshaping of national identity. *Windrush* generation novelists, arriving in England between 1950 and 1959, include Samuel Selvon (1950), George Lamming (1950), V. S. Naipaul (1950), Roy Heath (1951), Andrew Salkey (1952), Roger Mais (1952), Michael Anthony (1954), and Wilson Harris (1959). They introduced new subject matter into representations of English life and new ways of thinking about English literary tradition.[1]

To be sure, even before the postwar period West Indians and other British colonials with literary ambitions immigrated to England to find a forum for their work. West Indian C. L. R. James recalls in *Beyond a Boundary* a conversation in 1931 with famous cricketer Learie Constantine, who planned to emigrate, and remarks: "I too was planning to go to England as soon as I could, to write books."[2] This kind of immigration did not necessarily aim at rejection of some place or identity in exchange for a new one; but it almost always did involve surprising discovery and transformation. In 1931 Constantine and James had talked about almost nothing other than books and their shared passion for cricket; but five weeks after James's arrival in England, the friends began promoting the idea of West Indian self-government, having "unearth[ed] the politician in each other" (p. 116).

Although emigration is defined as a one-directional movement (i.e., leaving a country to settle in another), for writers from the Caribbean colonies the voyage out was predicated on the necessity of a "return trip," so to speak. They would eventually write about life in the English metropolis and about experiences of emigrants there; but to establish their identities as writers and to get their works published they had to return, imaginatively and sometimes in fact, to the ethnic communities and native landscapes that they had left. They could not be English writers *per se*; they had to be West Indian writers in England. In this sense, from the beginning, the émigré experience of West Indian writers was two-directional in its intellectual orientation, a series of *aller-retours*.

The characteristic West Indian two-directional trajectory complicates meanings of immigration and exile. For Naipaul the West Indian colonial was already in exile at home, because of his distance from the cosmopolitan and metropolitan imperial center. Emigration promised an arrival at the center: hence freedom from exile. For Lamming, in contrast, emigration to the center was a form of exile. But for both writers exile – a relationship between a person, his native place or home culture, and some other place or foreign culture – and emigration involve self-transformation and a sharply changed sense of identity in relation to place. James discusses how living in England developed hidden aspects of his personality, so that what brought him to Britain in turn carried him beyond its boundaries to other destinations: "To establish his own identity, Caliban, after three centuries, must himself pioneer into regions Caesar never knew" (p. xvii). James's allusion to Caliban in Shakespeare's *The Tempest* links James with Lamming, whose memoir *The Pleasures of Exile* (1960) elaborates the Caliban–Prospero (i.e., slave–master, colony–metropolis) analogy. Lamming equates Caliban with the migrant black Caribbean writer, descendant of slaves yet worshipper at "the same temple of endeavour" as Shakespeare's artist-ruler Prospero. Despite his worship there, however, Caliban also is colonized and excluded by his imperialist ruler's language. Accordingly, he seeks to "push [Prospero's legacy of language] further," to make it new.[3] But Lamming defines the émigré experience not only in terms of the colonial–metropolitan dichotomy. He takes a broader, existentialist perspective on voyages beyond one's native place. He says that "there is always an acre of ground in the New World which keeps growing echoes in my head"; but he also avers that "The pleasure and paradox of my own exile is that I belong wherever I am" (p. 50).

In Naipaul's semi-autobiographical *The Enigma of Arrival* (1987), a later echo of *The Pleasures of Exile*, Naipaul's narrator traces his evolution from West Indian scholarship student to international author, comparing it with the uncanny tale of a traveller who finds that the ship that brought him to his port of call departed long ago and that he has become in effect a different person. The voyage of exile divides Naipaul's self – although its decentering or fracturing of identity also makes possible a new center or identity to appear in the old one's place. Wilson Harris's novels, like those of his fellows, question all stabilities, including the idea of native home and non-native center. Harris views exile as a fundamental human condition. "Why move at all, why begin to die . . . ? To fulfil perhaps a theatre of nature that appears to be finished yet remains unfinished . . . [H]ome is always another journey."[4] Thus West Indian writers who immigrated to the UK in the 1950s did not so much exchange one home for another as initiate a process of rethinking nationality, native places and foreign places, and identity, in the context of dissolution of European empires and decolonization in the Caribbean. They arrived in London at an opportune moment for such reconsideration, inasmuch as their work could be supported by institutions such as the British Broadcasting Corporation and by members of the metropolitan literary establishment who saw in West Indian fiction both a new human interest and a reinvigorated form of modernist aesthetic experiment.

James and G. V. Desani were two writers who in the decades between the wars prepared the way for the *Windrush* generation. James, remembered for his novel *Minty Alley* (1936) and for his history of slave revolt in San Domingo *The Black Jacobins* (1938), and celebrated for his prescient writings about the black diaspora, was, in his oft-quoted phrase, "a British intellectual long before [he] was ten" (p. 18). Set apart from most black Trinidadians by his education, middle-class background, and literary passion, James found himself "intellectually . . . liv[ing] abroad, chiefly in England," his sense of exile originating in colonial society, with its reductive division of center (England) from periphery (Trinidad), and its color distinctions and barriers (p. 65). Among his important literary models James mentions Chekhov, Flaubert, and Maupassant as well as Dickens and Lawrence. The imprint of realism and naturalism – James thought of himself as a "nineteenth century" British intellectual – as well as modernism distinguish *Minty Alley*, his only novel, written five years before he immigrated to England in 1932 and published there in 1936. James describes *Minty Alley*, the first West Indian novel published in Britain, as "the West Indies . . . speaking for itself in the modern world" (p. 121). In the same decade the West Indies also spoke for itself in Constantine's *Cricket and I* (1933) and James's own *The Case for West-Indian Self-Government* (1933), which was published in England by Leonard and Virginia Woolf's Hogarth Press.

Minty Alley portrays a Port of Spain barrack-yard (boarding house) through the eyes of a middle-class young man, Haynes, who temporarily lodges there. Knowing the world primarily through books, and content at first merely to observe his neighbors from the privacy of his room, Haynes gradually sheds his innocence and enters the fray of color-conscious, ethnically complex, sexually charged, lower-class Trinidadian society. Both in its style and subject matter, *Minty Alley* mixes conventional realism with modernist features, overlaying Marxist perspectives with a Freudian sense of unconscious motives directing people's behavior. In its characterization of dominant or domineering women, such as the matron of the boarding house Mrs. Rouse, sexy yet iron-fisted Nurse Jackson, and Haynes's proto-feminist and intransigently rebellious mistress Maisie, the matriarchal aspect of lower-class West Indian society – at least in James's time – is innovatively portrayed. The novel's most memorable scenes depict domestic violence (e.g., Nurse Jackson's thrashing of her little boy, as a means of purging her own failures) and male–female power struggles (Mrs. Rouse's ejection of her unfaithful partner, and her refusal to allow him back in the household, masks her addiction to his abuse of her). All in all, the novel delineates sexually charged but ultimately economically driven hierarchies and mutual victimizations – not only between men and women in a West Indian urban milieu, but also between African-descended and East Indian-descended ethnic groups: ethnic tensions and those generated by gradations of color play a part in shaping everyone's lives.

James was a polyglot whose linguistic prowess shows itself in his innovative use of vernacular in *Minty Alley* – a reliance on "non-standard" English that links him with Desani. Although Desani was not a West Indian but a cosmopolitan son of empire, who was born in Kenya and spent his childhood in India before arriving in England, his fiction bristles with multiple languages. Its anticipation of the *Windrush* writers lies in its creolizing displacement of the metropolitan standard, in line with modernist displacements such as Joyce's in *Ulysses* and *Finnegans Wake*. T. S. Eliot and E. M. Forster championed Desani's work, as Desani did himself: "There are only two great novelists in the world today," he declared at a literary gathering in his honor; "one is James Joyce and the other is your humble servant."[5] *All about H. Hatterr* (1948), Desani's novel, hilariously, even hysterically, blends East and West. Each of the novel's seven chapters begins with a "Digest" of questions (e.g., "If Destiny should commit a feller to the wrong woman, can anything prevent it happening?" [p. 225]), with an "Instruction" wherein each "Digest" question is answered by a sage (a different one per Indian city [Calcutta, Rangoon, Madras, Bombay, Delhi, Mogalsarai-Varanasi]), and with a "Life-Encounter" that invariably exposes the inadequacy of sage "instruction" when confronted with the hard knocks of practice. The novel's spirited debunking of wise men (who often turn out to be con artists) bears a resemblance to R. K. Narayan's stories (e.g., *The Guide* [1958]) and is the precursor of Naipaul's *The Mystic Masseur* (1957).

It is above all Desani's experiments with language that stand out in his fiction, a "creative chaos," in Anthony Burgess's words,[6] that combines numerous registers of English ("rigmarole English," Hatterr calls it), tapping into its dialectal resources and its far-flung colonial–imperial variants, as in this passage celebrating Hatterr's arrival in England: "I took off my tropical-lid, the sola-*topi*, in sincere salutation, and next, without a waterproof, in my white drill shorts, I knelt on the mud-beds of the old country, the soft depths of its textilopolis County Palatine, aye, Keeper, luv, the blessed wet earth of Liverpool, Lancs., in a thousand salaams!" (36). Any given paragraph might contain smatterings of two, three, or more languages as well as minor characters drawn from the range of the dissolving Empire's people (e.g., Woog Soong, Ramfool Must, I-Tso, Bee Bee Jaan, U. Suff Ali). Modernist in his totalizing linguistic and narrative experimentation, and postcolonial in his constatation of identity that surpasses any single native locale or character, Desani is a forerunner of contemporary writers who explore multiple Englishes, inspired by multicultural environments.

Colonial writers like James and Desani needed an entry point to metropolitan institutions and literary London; for James it was cricket, political journalism, and the Woolfs; for Desani, the Ministry of Information and the BBC. The BBC's crucial role in the support and promotion of West Indian writers has already been noted. Beginning in 1946 under the direction of Henry Swanzy, the weekly radio programme *Caribbean Voices* transmitted the new literary flame to metropolitan and overseas audiences. "[A]ll the West Indian novelists . . . benefited from [Swanzy's] work and his generosity of feeling," writes Lamming, one of the writers whose career the programme helped launch (pp. 65–68).

Lamming's first novel, *In the Castle of My Skin* (1953), returns to the rural West Indian landscape of his childhood in Barbados in the 1930 and 1940s, telling the story of a boy, G., growing up in a village where people willingly give their allegiance to England and the white English landlord, and have only the vaguest sense of their own history and identity:

> [The school boys] had read about the Battle of Hastings and William the Conqueror . . . And slavery was thousands of years before that. It was too far back for anyone to worry about . . . And nobody knew where this slavery business took place. The teacher had simply said, not here, somewhere else. Probably it had never happened at all.[7]

But news about changes taking place on other Caribbean islands – black and colored players on national cricket teams, strikes and riots in Trinidad, Pan-Africanist manifestos by Marcus Garvey – filter into popular consciousness. Lamming's novel relates the political coming-to-awareness of individual and community in a colony where the advent of organized labor and the democratic influence of the United States are altering social relations between white landlords and black workers. Modernist in its radical shuttling between first- and third-person narration, the novel innovatively combines fiction, autobiography, and history – Lamming draws inspiration not only from the 1937 labor riots in Barbados but also probably from *The Black Jacobins*. Lamming's use of autobiographical elements in fiction became a leading form of storytelling for West Indian (and postcolonial) writers seeking new definitions of self and community.

Lamming's *The Emigrants* (1954) picks up where *In the Castle of My Skin* leaves off. It traces the voyage of the young man who has left his native island to take a teaching post in Trinidad and who then makes "a leap toward the sea," traveling with an array of other passengers to England.[8] Lamming's second novel is even more experimental than his first; it combines autobiographical first-person with third-person narration but also incorporates free-verse drama, as well as dreams in the form of interior monologues, and modernist-inspired multiple perspectives that decenter the dominance of any one character. Shadows, darkness, and anxiety pervade almost every scene: "[Collis, Peggy, Frederick] were eternally apart, riding the rhythm of the night that poured freely through the smoke and water of the little cage that had caught them" (pp. 223, 224). The emigrants – men and women both – go to England looking for "a better break," a phrase that recurs repeatedly (p. 33). "We had *to get out*," Lamming exclaims in *The Pleasures of Exile* (p. 41). Yet the opportunities and freedom that his characters seek are circumscribed by new barriers and restrictions that they encounter (a housing shortage, rise in unemployment, prejudice and racism, harassment by police, their ignorance of ways of life in Britain). The cabins of the passenger ship, the train that takes the emigrants from Plymouth to Paddington Station, the emigrants' hostel room, and even the nightclubs the emigrants visit convey their entrapment:

> [The room's] immediacy forced them to see that each was caught in it. There was no escape from it until the morning came with its uncertain offer of another day's work. Alone, circumscribed by the night and the neutral staring walls, each felt himself pushed to the limits of his thinking. . . . It was here in the room of garlic, onions and mist that each became aware, gradually, anxiously, of the level and scope of his private existence. (p. 192)

The Emigrants is unequalled in its formalist experimentation with place and identity. The emigrants' shared situation and circumstances (e.g., the colonial West Indies, the voyage, the hostel) provide an anchor as long as they remain within them; beyond, in England, they have to make new identities to match, and fit into, their new place – or risk "estrangement." Two of the emigrants crack, a "fate...awaiting...any man who chooses one country...in the illusion that it was only a larger extension of the home which he had left" (p. 237). To the question, what is England to these emigrants, the novel responds unequivocally that it is not theirs, although the idea of it has colonized their beliefs and desires:

> England was not only a place, but a heritage. Some of us might have expressed...hostility to that heritage, but it remained, nevertheless, a hostility to something that was already a part of us.
>
> But all that was now coming to an end. England was simply a world [in] which we had moved about at random, and on occasions encountered by chance. It was just there like nature, drifting vaguely beyond our reach.

(p. 237)

Selvon's *The Lonely Londoners* (1956) also explores historical enigmas of place and identity. A series of vignettes recounted from the first-person point of view of Moses Aloetta, a Trinidadian immigrant who has lived in London for ten years and has a habit of helping new arrivals from the West Indies and Africa get settled (and employed at jobs for unskilled workers), the novel affirms the immigrant self and the city – affirms them in spite of unfed stomachs, cold climate, bad quarters and bad jobs, and bristling racism. Moses survives the hard knocks and alienation of life in the metropole. Thanks to his insider–outsider perspective as an émigré he also discovers, and takes stoic pleasure in, aspects of London that Londoners themselves prefer not to talk about. An extended (ten-page) interior monologue, whose overall subject is Moses' compulsive attachment to the city, lays bare the underside of Londoners' lives:

> the higher the society the higher the kicks they want...everybody look like they frustrated in the big city the sex life gone wild you would meet women who beg you go with them one night a Jamaican with a woman in Chelsea in a smart flat with all sorts of surrealist painting on the walls...she only interested in one thing and in the heat of emotion she call the Jamaican a black bastard though she didn't mean it as an insult but as a compliment under the circumstances...and in the night the world turn upside down and everybody hustling that is life that is London.[9]

On the last page of the novel Moses feels "a forlorn shadow of doom fall on all the spades in the country"; and yet also senses a buoyant if nameless hope.

In its expressions of yearning metropolitan malaise, *The Lonely Londoners* exhibits similarities between its narrator, his fellow urban wanderers, and colonial Dubliners in Joyce's *Ulysses*. The novel also asserts Moses' ever curious, all-encompassing consciousness, which fuses a tragicomic mood – "the boys laughing, but they only laughing because they fraid to cry" (p. 142) – with wry acceptance – "What it is that a city have . . . that you get so much to like it you wouldn't leave it for anywhere else?" (p. 137). Lamming's existentialist angst in *The Emigrants* is missing from *The Lonely Londoners*. Selvon's London is a mythical creation as much as it is a factual portrait; he transforms the city into a legend where larger-than-life characters engage in a battle for survival with the help of wit that is worthy of the hero tricksters of Afro-Caribbean oral tradition.

The impact of London's West Indian and East Indian immigrants and their potential to rejuvenate mainstream culture made them a subject for non-Caribbean authors as well as for themselves. English-born Colin MacInnes' *City of Spades* (1957) canvasses new immigrant bars or nightclubs, such as the Candy Bowl, where African and West Indian characters with nicknames like Ronson Lighter, Tamberlaine, Jimmy Cannibal, Bumper Woodman, Karl Marx Bo, Cranium Cuthbertson and Alfy Bongo flit in and out. The novel utilizes two narrators: white Englishman Montgomery Pew, a Colonial Department welfare worker, and Nigerian Johnny Fortune, who comes to London to study meteorology and to find his Nigerian father's quondam white mistress and the half-brother his father sired twenty years before. Nothing escapes MacInnes's comic treatment: from mainstream English culture (the legal system: "It's one pack of lies fighting another"[10]) to all "minorities," whether Indian, African, West Indian, or Black American. But frustration underlies the narrative: although Johnny Fortune repeats his father's attempt at miscegenation, fathering a child, and although the novel's white and black narrators become interanimating, national, cultural and racial barriers prevail: Johnny returns to Nigeria. Yet *City of Spades* can be read as an audacious attempt by its Australian-educated author to take his 1950s English readers out of their skins – pleading with them to accommodate changes in the social landscape of London that West Indians and other emigrants had brought about.

No less than James's, Desani's, Lamming's, and Selvon's works, V. S. Naipaul's 1950s novels typify the colonial and postcolonial enigma whereby arrival at the cultural center becomes a new dispersal and a return to the periphery. *Miguel Street* (1959), Naipaul's third published novel but the one he wrote first, portrays a multicultural, inner-city neighborhood of Port of Spain through the eyes of a narrator who tells his story as if he were again a boy growing up there. But the narrator does not tell or see only from the boy's perspective; he also evaluates the boy's world from the distanced perspective that he has acquired through his émigré life in England. He writes from a double perspective of exile, viewing one culture and place through the lens of another. Neither lens is primary.

Miguel Street merits comparison with *Minty Alley* and *In the Castle of My Skin* in terms of the former novel's use of vernacular and its depiction of a West Indian urban milieu and the latter novel's autobiographical rendering of a boy's estrangement and departure from his native island. Modernist models also matter to Naipaul's formative work. Its vignettes of the neighborhood's residents dramatize colonial life's entrapment and futility in a way reminiscent of Joyce's *Dubliners* – although Naipaul's city, unlike Joyce's, is as stark and violent as it is sadly comic. The boy's friend, Bogart, admired for his imitation of Humphrey Bogart's "cool" style, is jailed for bigamy; Popo the carpenter is jailed for furniture theft; Hat, another friend, is imprisoned for murder. Domestic abuse is rampant: George, father of the boy's friend Elias, batters his wife, who dies prematurely – she "had the shabbiest and saddest and the loneliest funeral Miguel Street had ever seen" – and flogs his son and daughter with a rope soaked in the gutter of a cow-pen.[11] Several stories show the effects of the Miguel Street slum on sexual and marital relationships: Laura has eight children, seven of whom are fathered by different men; her daughter Lorna becomes pregnant in her teens. Rather than relive her mother's fate, Lorna drowns herself.

The Mystic Masseur is an exuberant contrast to *Miguel Street*, and recalls Desani. Naipaul portrays the history of Indian emigrants to the West Indies through a largely satiric yet sympathetic biography of a healer – Ganesh the masseur – who rises from his village origins to become author and intellectual, politician and – once he has emigrated to England – decorated statesman: G. Ramsay Muir, Esq., M.B.E. The novel's complexity derives from the narrator's ambiguity; his wit and comedy, and his suspended judgments, make it hard to pin down his attitude toward Ganesh. Indirection, equivocalness, and the open-endedness of utterance are the novel's narrative strategy as well as, ultimately, one of its subject matters. Both the narrator and Ganesh – for it is through books that Ganesh promotes his "vision" and achieves renown – are masseurs of words. Ganesh's travel volume, *The Guide to Trinidad*, recommends to American military personnel and other foreigners such attractions as his hut, grandiosely styled the Fuente Grove Hindu temple. To undermine a political rival, he founds a sensationalist, self-serving newspaper, *The Dharma*, which runs specious stories and carries bogus ads promising "superlative bargains in fictitious shops in unknown villages."[12] Ganesh succeeds as a politician because he has learned, through writing tracts like *What God Told Me* and *The Soul As I See It*, to give people what they want to hear. The novel is self-reflexively – in the modernist and postmodernist tradition – about the power of language and about problematically ever-shifting (perhaps one might say, ever-migrating) meanings of words.

Naipaul's *The Suffrage of Elvira* (1958) and Selvon's *Turn Again Tiger* (1958) represent democratization in rural Trinidad. In the latter, Tiger and Urmilla, a young East Indian couple from Selvon's first novel *A Brighter Sun* (1952), return from their multiracial suburb in Port of Spain to the sugarcane fields of their childhood when they receive a father's call for help. Given that *A Brighter Sun* recounts the couple's successful integration in their suburb, *Turn Again Tiger* might seem to illustrate a cultural step backward. But the novel transforms the return into a forward step in the process of West Indian identity formation. Two actions encapsulate individual and sociocultural changes: Urmilla and the other wives' banding together to demand that the village's Chinese shopkeeper refuse to grant credit to their husbands when they buy rum, an action which fails but which conveys a new spirit of gender and ethnic equality; and Tiger's sexual encounter with a white landlord's wife. Initially Tiger repels her seduction; but, after being humiliated by his timidity and sense of inferiority, he faces her and they make love. This act, standing for an end to Caliban's slavish service to imperious Prospero and for an advent of less rigid, more egalitarian relations between cultures and races in the village, liberates Tiger.

Naipaul's treatment in *The Suffrage of Elvira* of democratization in rural Trinidad is less optimistic. Caricaturing a political campaign and election in the most isolated of nine counties in Trinidad, the novel takes aim at its populace's equation of money-mindedness with enfranchisement. Naipaul's target is also a sub-world of predominantly East Indian villages character-ized by narrow loyalties, jealousies, and greed. The Elvira district – a mélange of Hindus and Muslims, Catholics, Jehovah's Witnesses, and African animists – is ethnically diverse yet, thanks to the new suffrage, increasingly defined and divided by monetary greed coupled with bigoted identity politics. Baksh the tailor speaks for Muslims; Chittaranjan the goldsmith for Hindus; the Preacher for blacks, Spanish Catholics, and ani-mists. Beliefs and traditions that serve to differentiate one group from another become convenient tags on the basis of which Elvirans can vent their private grievances with one another and politicians can trump up issues to run campaigns on. When Chittaranjan the Hindu berates his neighbour Baksh the Muslim for eating meat, Chittaranjan does so less out of reverence for Hindu principle than out of personal offence at Baksh's apparent belit-tling of Chittaranjan's daughter. The democracy of warring identities turns sour, and suffrage devolves into violence. Significantly, the backdrop of Naipaul's and Selvon's novels might be not only rural Trinidad but also 1950s Britain, where mounting ethnic and racial tensions due to West Indian immigration erupted in the Notting Hill riots of 1958, and in shameful white reprisals. The riots in some ways parallel processes of difficult democratization and postcolonial identity construction in the West Indies themselves. The unrest in England unfortunately halted the immediate forward progress of postcolonial writing there;[13] and it brought to the fore an enduring complaint against Naipaul voiced by Lamming. Lamming insisted that Naipaul's fiction was only "castrated satire," a betrayal of "the peasant sensibility" of Lamming and Selvon's West Indian roots (*Pleasures*, p. 225) at the expense of black aspiration, and for the sake of an alliance with white rule and tradition.

The post-1958 oppositions that Lamming articulated perhaps are reconciled in the visionary fiction of Wilson Harris. Mythopoeic and magical realist, Harris's fiction discloses "twinships" that underlie opposing figures: conqueror and conquered, Old and New World, the living and the dead. "I have been haunted since childhood in British Guiana . . . by vanished cultures and places and kingdoms," Harris writes.[14] Those absences are evoked by Harris's river and forest landscapes, and traces of ancient civilizations within Guyana's ethnically diverse population: Amerindian, African, Asian, and European. Harris draws on his own mixed racial and cultural background and his experience as a surveyor, which gave him opportunity to know, and imaginatively reckon with, Guyana's rural cultures and peoples. By way of "cross-cultural imagination," one of Harris's seminal concepts, an individual can bridge "chasms of time" and oppositions of race and culture to become "a vessel of composite epic, imbued with many voices." That imaginative capacity remains paradoxical and fragile, however, because the "multitude is housed . . . in the diminutive surviving entity of community and self that one is."[15] It can only be reached by a "plunge" from one's familiar self to a stranger within (*Tree*, pp. 45, 46). Exile complements the plunge, for a renovative "unborn state of the world" can be brought to birth by "the 'potential' ground of self-exile."[16]

Modernist tradition abets Harris's fiction. His novels are published by Faber and Faber, where T. S. Eliot was a guiding force until his death in the mid-1960s; epigraphs in *The Guyana Quartet* juxtapose modernist and visionary sources (Hopkins, Eliot, Yeats, Conrad, Lawrence, and Blake) with ancient, medieval, and New World ones (Amerindian legends and myths). *Palace of the Peacock* (1960), a mixture of dream and parable that is the initial volume of *The Guyana Quartet*, reinterprets and transforms the El Dorado myth. Its principal character Donne and his crew embody the conquistadores who sought out the alien American other on whom to impose their will and order. The crew's journey to the interior recalls Joseph Conrad's *Heart of Darkness*; yet unlike the latter, Harris's narrative – which Donne's twin brother tells from somewhere between life and death – ends not in illusion and emptiness but in celebration and illumination: "It was the dance of all fulfilment I now held and knew deeply, cancelling my . . . fear of strangeness and catastrophe . . . Each of us now held in his arms what he had been for ever seeking and what he had eternally possessed."[17]

Harris's novels pose more questions than they can answer because they are about endless metamorphic passage, a continuous voyage rather than arrival at a destination. One metaphor of passage and change that Harris employs refers to limbo dancing. The word "limbo" derives from Latin *limbus*, which means "edge" or "boundary"; limbo dancing is said to have its origins in cramped conditions of the slave ships that carried Africans to the Americas. Harris defines "limbo" as a sudden shift from one level of awareness to another that enables a person to translate his identity into that of another person and also thereby to cross multiple boundaries – between past and present, life and death, one racial identity and another, history as nightmare and history as possible redemption. Limbo is a "Middle passage ritual . . . a series of dancing shapes in pursuit of a universal architectonic or self." The pursuit involves the dancer with antithetical identities: "Like the sudden, perfectly normal, plunge – coincidental to shock – one takes in absent-mindedly turning a key in a door until one forgets one's skeleton hand and finds one's been locked into an antagonist's flesh" (*Tree*, pp. 48, 45–6). Fragmented and alienated though the individual may be, he still participates in "an implicit . . . dramatization of buried universal themes." In a way that a limbo dancer models when he passes like Anansi spider, a figure in West African folklore, beneath the limitary bar, the individual self can become "other" as well as all.[18] Harris's fiction is emphatically an art of cross-cultural emigration and transformation.

By introducing new subject matter and a new vernacular into English fiction, *Windrush* generation writers changed the way we think about English literature. Thanks to them it is an entity which now can be talked about only in larger terms: "literatures in English." Despite their innovations, however, these writers – as has been noted above – often reach back into modernism for their reorientations. Their works show connections with voyaging modernist émigrés and exiles such as the expatriate Irishman Joyce and the expatriate Pole Conrad who both transformed literary convention. Joyce's mark seems particularly evident in Lamming and Selvon, while Conrad's stands out in Naipaul and Harris. Naipaul elaborates his debt to Conrad in *Reading and Writing: A Personal Account* (2000); his novels *In a Free State* (1971) and *A Bend in the River* (1979) are Conradian voyages into an African interior where disorder reigns, a legacy of colonialism in post-colonial time. To the question, what is fiction, Naipaul replies with an answer, "experience totally transformed," that he borrows from another twentieth-century master, Evelyn Waugh, whose satiric brilliance shines through in Naipaul's novels from the start. Of course, *Windrush* generation writers draw upon other literary traditions: Lamming and Selvon have ties to the Negritude Movement in Africa and the Caribbean; Harris's fiction evokes Latin American writers such as Mexico's Juan Rulfo, Guatemala's Miguel Ángel Asturias, and Argentina's Jorge Luis Borges. All of which is to say that during the 1950s and after, West Indian writers who immigrated to England became more than West Indian or British. The enigma of arrival transformed them into international writers, placing them in the vanguard of globalizing linguistic and literary phenomena.

NOTES

1 In this chapter the term "West Indian writers" will mean writers from the West Indies, although today we might not think of them in this narrowly regional manner; nor do they necessarily think of themselves in that way.

2 C. L. R. James, *Beyond a Boundary* (Durham: Duke University Press, 1993), p. 110.

3 George Lamming, *The Pleasures of Exile* (Ann Arbor: University of Michigan Press, 1992), p. 15.

4 Wilson Harris, *The Tree of the Sun* (London: Faber and Faber, 1978), pp. 90–1.

5 Sheela Reddy, "G. V. Desani, le Joyce indien," *Lire*, 2001 (Avril), www.lire.fr. My translation.

6 Anthony Burgess, "Introduction," G. V. Desani, *All About H. Hatterr* (New Paltz, NY: McPherson & Company Publishers, 1970), p. 10.

7 George Lamming, *In the Castle of My Skin* (Ann Arbor: University of Michigan Press, 1991), p. 58.

8 George Lamming, *The Emigrants* (Ann Arbor: University of Michigan Press, 1994), p. 7.

9 Sam Selvon, *The Lonely Londoners* (New York: Longman Publishing Company, 1994), p. 109.

10 Colin MacInnes, *The Colin MacInnes Omnibus: His Three London Novels: City of Spades, Absolute Beginners, Mr. Love and Justice* (London: Allison & Busby, 1969), p. 203.

11 V. S. Naipaul, *Miguel Street* (New York: Penguin, 1969), p. 24.

12 V. S. Naipaul, *The Mystic Masseur* (New York: Vintage Books, 1985), p. 181.

13 Peter Kalliney, "Metropolitan Modernism and Its West Indian Interlocutors," *PMLA* 122 (2007), 89–104.

14 Wilson Harris, *Selected Essays of Wilson Harris* (London: Routledge, 1999), p. 55.

15 Wilson Harris, *Jonestown* (London: Faber and Faber, 1996), p. 5.

16 Wilson Harris, *The Eye of the Scarecrow* (London: Faber and Faber, 1965), p. 100.

17 Wilson Harris, *The Guyana Quartet* (London: Faber and Faber, 1985), pp. 116–17.

18 Wilson Harris, *Black Marsden* (London: Faber and Faber, 1972), p. 103.

12

JAMES ACHESON AND ROBERT L. CASERIO

History in fiction

The protagonist of Anthony Burgess's *A Malayan Trilogy* (1957–9) nastily formulates a relation between history and books. "'History,' said Crabbe...'The best thing to do is to put all that in books and forget about it. A book is a kind of lavatory. We've got to throw up the past, otherwise we can't live in the present. The past has got to be killed.'"[1] As soon as Crabbe makes his declaration, however, the narrator adds that "he reverted to his own past, and pronounced the very word in the Northern style...of his childhood" – a style that makes *past* sound like *pest*. Pestilent or not, emetically or not, history has been put into the twentieth-century English novel with a vengeance. It has occurred in a persistent idiosyncratic form: historical fiction by a single author about characters whose stories proliferate in multiple volumes. Burgess's trilogy is a mere mini-example of what might be called historical "series novels." Tetralogies and five- or six-unit sequences abound; some stretch to a dozen and more.

Does so much reference to the past make living in the present easier? Some novelists write about the present as a product of the past or as itself epochal. Does seeing the present as historical also have vivifying effects? Or is it just a matter of profits for writers and publishers whose readers can be captivated by characters with whom, repeatedly, they "live"? Whatever the immediate material determination of the series form, historical crises suggest a motive. A culture undergoing actual transformation from an empire into an island might want to absorb the shock by reading about it, perhaps endlessly. The American title of Burgess's trilogy is *The Long Day Wanes*, a reference to the setting sun of Empire. As if in compensation, as the day wanes, the fiction waxes.

But the traumas are not just "English." In the last century the decline of optimism about a socialist world order, intermingled with world war, is a global rather than an insular concern, and is one of the traumas the English series novel tries to assess; the development of nuclear arms is another object of anxious consideration. Enduring crisis inflates the novel form as novelists work out creditable attitudes to world-historical problems. Perhaps there is also a self-reflexive reason for expansiveness. If novelists incorporate history into fiction at such obsessive length, it might be because they want to convince themselves, and their readers, that fiction makes sense of the past and the present even more than history proper can. And novelists might go to such lengths as a way of justifying fiction in the face of the urgency of fact.

Attitudes towards history in the "series novel"

Are Olivia Manning's *The Balkan Trilogy* (1960–5) and *The Levant Trilogy* (1977–80), which follow World War II's encroachment upon Rumania, Greece, North Africa, and the Middle East, war novels; or are they studies of domesticity whose historical dimension is ever-threatening but – mere scenery? Manning's protagonists are a newly wedded couple, Guy and Harriet Pringle, whose fortunes make a reader principally wonder if their marriage can be saved. That is an odd matter for wonder, given the environment: it is as if the vicissitudes of one marriage were as important as the public fate of millions; and, inasmuch as the marriage survives, one notes that it takes six volumes as well as the war to see it through. Yet Manning's genius is located precisely where she provokes a sense of disproportion. Although Manning hews her narrative to conventional form, one might say that the bold spirit of modernist experiment motivates her insistence that the Pringles' marriage is as historically central as the armed political conflict.

And their marriage, bringing together a shyly self-possessed woman and a man whose passions are hope in a socialist future and love of literature, is indeed a political conflict. Guy's socialism instances ideological leanings that were to create the postwar British welfare state. His collectivist values model an antithesis to fascism's version of them. Harriet, especially because of her gender, represents a desire for liberation that is no less urgent than socialism's. But she also represents a perspective – at once personal and impersonal – that does not find adequate expression in ideological terms. Harriet declares to Guy, who attempts her "political education" in the service of "the answer to human fallibility: . . . a world united under left-wing socialism," that she "'cannot endure [politically] organized thought." In response he accuses her of being "lost in anarchy and a childish mysticism."[2]

Guy might be right; but even if he is, Harriet argues that truth is at stake, and that truth is "more complex than politics" (p. 718). Manning's narrative insists that Harriet's claim must be entertained, that history's warring versions of politics take account of her, even though her habit is to "relate . . . life to eternity rather than to time" (p. 392). But Harriet also relates life stubbornly to Guy, despite his frequent callous conduct towards her. His preoccupation with public good wins him popularity, and a curious incapacity for intimacy, above all in his personal relation with his wife. Guy is in flight, Harriet thinks, "from the undramatic responsibility to one person that marriage is" (p. 321); indeed, she realizes, "he did not recognize emotional responsibility" at all (p. 819).

Guy's progressivism blinds him to others besides Harriet; and also weakens his hold on historical reality. In 1939 in Bucharest (where Guy is employed by the University's English department), he shows himself out of touch with the fact of contemporary persecution of Jews by the Russians, whom he expects to save Rumania – and Jewish refugees – from the Nazis. Guy's blind side is in evidence, once Harriet and he have fled to Greece, when he rejects friendship with a decent compatriot because of the man's skepticism towards leftism. Guy prefers hanging around with an unpleasant opportunist journalist, purely on the basis of their shared Marxism. Harriet thinks of them, in their devotion to "political mysteries," as "a pair of hopeless romantics" (p. 787). In response, attempting to keep in touch with *her* realities, Harriet almost yields to an infatuation with a British officer.

The fall of Greece to the Germans sends the Pringles to Egypt, where *The Levant Trilogy* finds them, and where they part. We become privy to Guy's thoughts when he receives news that a ship Harriet is taking to Britain has been torpedoed. He acknowledges, in remorse and guilt, that he instigated her voyage because she has obstructed his public projects. Grieving, he discovers the emotional responsibility he has lacked. But when he finds that Harriet never boarded the ship and is still alive, he behaves as though his soul-searching hasn't taken place. Because of prior commitments he cuts short a celebration of reunion with her. The Pringles' marriage remains a deadlock. Curiously, because of that, it remains a victory. The couple renew at the end of the second series a recognition at the end of the first series: "They had passed both illusion and disillusion. It was no use asking for more . . . War had forced their understanding . . . and . . . for all they knew it would not end in their lifetime" (*BT*, 897). Concluding the writing of her second trilogy in 1980, Manning suggests that war still has not ended – war between socialist impulse and its enemies, and also war between history and what it treats callously or ignores.

From the Pringles' perspective the centers of political power, from which they are far removed, are history's violent engines. C. P. Snow's *Strangers and Brothers* series (eleven volumes, 1940–70) penetrates those centers, drawing its characters and conflicts from middle- and upper-class administrators who run the world from their places in Parliament, the civil service, and the national universities.

Snow's narrator Lewis Eliot, whose autobiography stretches from 1917 until 1970, rises from a bankrupt lower-middle-class family to become a barrister, a Fellow of a Cambridge University college, and a leading civil service official. Turning his back on his early circle of bohemian friends because he fears that their freedoms will compromise his future, Lewis makes no bones about his ambition. Snow's sympathy with worldly avidity merits a place in literary history's account of history in fiction, if only for the sake of the contrast it provides to novels that presume from the start the tainted historical nature of legitimate government. Distrust of power makes little sense in Snow's world, and *Strangers and Brothers* suggests that such distrust is sentimental rather than "political." Snow's terse, tense writing gives a reader practice in assessing how largely principled aims shape governmental strategies. To be sure, the series is populated with men whose "moral certainties, [and] comfortable, conforming indignation...never made them put a foot out of step." But Lewis respects those men – "they were the men who managed the world."[3] If his respect for them becomes mixed with disappointment, Snow makes clear that the disappointment needs to be earned only after thousands of pages' probation.

The New Men (1954) narrates a probationary episode. Lewis's rise in government in 1939–46 is shared with other new men, makers of the postwar welfare state who include, most significantly, nuclear scientists, of whom Lewis's brother Martin is one. The race to produce an atomic bomb gives British scientists an unprecedented voice in government. As they labor toward fission, the scientists deliberate how the bomb should be used (as a deterrent? as an activated weapon?), and to what extent information about it should be shared internationally – in the interest of science rather than nationalism. But the new men are not listened to, for governmental reasons that Lewis is shocked to find Martin exploiting. Martin allows himself to become an agent of government spy hunting. He fingers a co-worker who is collaborating with the Soviets. He does this as much out of a desire to head his nuclear research team as for any other reason – in the process virtually betraying another, perfectly loyal colleague. Lewis, instrumental in giving his brother his entry to the inner circle of scientists, is disgusted with Martin's careerism. The brothers come to feel that they are more strangers than kin. Yet it is Lewis who propels his brother in the opportunistic direction. Lewis has refused to allow Martin to publish a protest against the use of the bomb at Hiroshima – even though Lewis agrees with Martin's position. So it is Lewis who is the agent of estrangement. Martin's careerism logically follows from Lewis's quashing of his protest. As Martin says and Lewis must agree, "If you accepted the bomb, the burnings alive, the secrets, the fighting point of power, you must take the consequences...the relics of liberal humanism had no place there" (p. 476). Nevertheless, Martin decides to surrender directorship of the nuclear research he has schemed toward. Breaking with the ambition his brother has abetted, he decides that if governmental life does not lay within one's moral control, "social life lay within one's power" (p. 476). "Getting outside the machine" into "social life" might be the best hope of a better future.

Snow makes Lewis realize that his own ambitions have betrayed brotherly love to "a darkness of the heart" (p. 482). Despite that darkness (echoing Joseph Conrad), Snow and Lewis struggle to keep liberal humanism in play with power. In *Corridors of Power* (1964) Lewis compensates for the fraternal alienation he induced in the 1940s. Because he believes that "the party's nearly over . . . for dear old western man" (*SB*, p. 399), Lewis supports a defense minister's efforts to remove Britain from the nuclear arms race. Insisting that "this country . . . can't be a superpower any longer,"[4] the minister and Lewis seek to redefine national might, changing it from offensive armed force to open-handed responsibility. Because the minister is a Conservative, it is hoped that his plan will not be trashed by associations of it with radicalism. But not even middle of the roaders can tolerate a change in the meaning of power. Conservative and opposition members combine against the plan. The minister resigns, and Lewis does so along with him. His brotherhood with Martin reasserts itself; and the experiment in fraternizing with power turns into an ultimate estrangement.

But although *Corridors of Power* ends with resignations, Snow does not intend to emphasize defeat. Both Lewis and the minister plan to work onward. Lewis feels he has achieved a newly inspiring "exhiliration of freedom . . . of being bare to the world" (p. 390). On the penultimate page, one of Lewis's allies says hopefully, "We need a victory": for liberal humanism still, and for disarmament. In two more novels remaining in the series, readers can hope alongside.

As socialism's future dims and nuclear arms proliferate, the British Empire fades into history. Burgess's *A Malayan Trilogy* draws a giddy, horrible picture of empire's decline, and equally of post-colonial independence: giddy, because the series' characters, exemplifying clashing cultures, each have a lunatic streak; horrible, because the presentation is merciless. Wyndham Lewis and Evelyn Waugh gestate Burgess. Crabbe, an English teacher and education officer who supports Malay independence, appears sufficiently balanced to be a trustworthy pivot for the narrative; yet his sympathy with Malaya has a frantic edge; and his self-torturing sexual and marital guilts constitute a time bomb. Because the trilogy sees even the best colonial administrators as somewhat mad, it envisions the end of empire as urgently necessary. But what comes after colonialism is not unqualified cause for celebration.

In the trilogy's final volume, as Crabbe makes his way to a rubber-planting estate whose occupant has been murdered by insurgent Communists, the madness of empire shows in the men Crabbe meets. There is an Englishman who sells beer "all over the East," and who has no intention of departing alongside the imperialist administrators because he thinks that the English at home are "out of touch" and "crackers" (pp. 427, 429). He does not see that he is describing himself. There is an English Assistant Protector of Aborigines who has taken on his charges' beliefs, a way of going native that might be respectful, but also is bizarre. And at his journey's end Crabbe finds a newly installed planter, who, as Crabbe rightly puts it, slobbers over himself self-righteously (and alcoholically) as a white man, and continues to think Asians are fine in their place – their subordinate place. It appears as if Conrad's Kurtz has been transported to Burgess's Malaya; although reduced from heroic to quotidian size, he remains malignly crazed. In contrast, Crabbe appears sane and generous, and "just can't see any future beyond being here" (p. 429), in a postcolonial world. Nevertheless, Burgess arranges Crabbe's demise in such a way as to reveal him and the rubber-planter to be alter egos, fatally inseparable. It turns out that the planter had an affair with Crabbe's first wife: a fact Crabbe never suspected, but that is revealed by chance as the planter drones on. The first wife drowned back in England when a car in which Crabbe was driving her skidded off a bridge into icy water; now, fleeing downriver from the planter, Crabbe himself becomes a drowning victim.

Burgess's final revelation of Crabbe and the planter as two sides of the same coin throws a pall over Crabbe's politically progressive side – or what he takes to be progressive. Among his cherished hopes is a desire to "cultivate better inter-racial understanding . . . meetings, say, once a week, to try and mix up the races a bit more" (p. 375), as a prelude to Malayan independence in 1957. But Crabbe's desire faces multiple historical difficulties. A Chinese friend explains: "The fact is that the component races of this exquisite and impossible country just don't get on . . . Self-determination's a ridiculous idea in a mixed-up place like this" – and confusion is intensified, the friend and Crabbe agree, because conflicts among Buddhist, Hindu, Muslim, Christian, and other sects mean that "religion's a problem, a nasty problem" (p. 365). Moreover, ethnic differences are superimposed upon religious differences, so Muslims and ethnic Tamil Hindus, vying for places in the new nation, are at one another's throats. And Americans are coming, ready to step into the place of British imperialists (if only by way of "researching" the new nation) and to exacerbate political unrest by opposing Communism. Finally, there are generational differences within the groups, a result of the young deriving styles of dress, talk, and conduct from American music and movies. Crabbe's idea of mixing up the races is overwhelmed by his friend's picture – and Burgess's – of what is "mixed-up."

As a prime instance of chaotic diversity and conflict among Malaya's non-Western populations, Burgess creates Rosemary Michael, gorgeous offspring of a Christian Tamil family. Rosemary is a walking bundle of incoherent, contradictory desires: as foreign white government recedes, Rosemary longs for a white husband, even while she gives herself to Tamil and Chinese lovers, and toys with a Muslim one. But as Rosemary's desire clings to love of imperial subjection, the desires of her "native" lovers for her propel them into disloyalty to their ethnic and religious identities. Because of an obsession with Rosemary a Tamil lover flees into the jungle to hide from his mother and an arranged marriage. If the imperialists are "crackers," so are those they have ruled.

Burgess's picture of a burgeoning post-colonial world that is dizzyingly confused is risky, even outrageous. It perhaps respects the autonomy of satire more than the autonomy of cultures or nations. Burgess's satire is complex, however. What it licenses in one direction receives a check from another. There is a supreme flaw in Rosemary that justifies her as a target of satire: her rewriting of her history at will, so that what she wants to be true on one day she contradicts when her desires change on the next. Her rewriting of the facts of her life – her capacity for fiction – is what Burgess's narrative clearly reproves. Crabbe's demise shows that personal and collective history are inescapable: their truth will determine life's meaning. There is no getting rid of that truth in the lavatory. Satire operates upon history, but also finds a limit there.

Burgess's satire also sets a limit to itself in his narrative's final turn to a multicultural rapprochement among the young. A youthful Muslim protagonist grows sick of "race, race, race – his father's dinner-table theme" (p. 425); and he and a young Chinese composer, Robert Loo, initiate an unexpected friendship, which becomes a nucleus of a Muslim–Tamil–Chinese–English gang that has a distinctly democratic and unified feel. Crabbe's hope of "mixing" seems to get realized, after all. Crabbe had believed – despite his Chinese friend's disbelief, and despite the conflicts in which Crabbe is located – that in Malaya he was living in "the only country in the world for any man who cared about history" because Malaya's extraordinary collocation of cultures" meant that it was supremely "civilized" (pp. 432–3). The young appear to be renewing the extraordinary collocation in a happy direction. If the appearance suggests yet another instance of rewriting history, this revision is different in kind from Rosemary's, and one that Burgess's story condones.

A very different version of history in fiction emerges in Anthony Powell's *A Dance to the Music of Time* (twelve volumes, 1951–75), partly because its intelligent narrator Nicholas Jenkins is unusually impassive. Lewis Eliot or even the external narrators in Manning and Burgess can seem heatedly emotional in comparison. Jenkins is also impassive in comparison with people he lives amongst, and observes, from 1919 through the 1960s. His diffidence is a foil for the life of his schoolmate Kenneth Widmerpool, who rises out of obscurity to become an MP, a peer, and a university chancellor; and who, unfailingly self-assertive and willful, is one of fiction's most distasteful creations. It is remarkable that Powell and Jenkins give creepy Widmerpool and his wife Pamela enduring attention. Pamela's ill temper and aggression are so excessive that they strain the plausibility of Powell's realism. Widmerpool might represent a new historical openness in England to opportunism and repulsive manners; but are Widmerpool and Pamela historical at all? Are they instead stock figures of comedy or melodrama, to be invariably hissed by readers? Or do they belong, as Patrick Parrinder suggests, not to history but to an order of destructive forces that are mythical rather than empirical?

Despite mythical resonances, Powell and Jenkins keep their feet planted on historical ground, especially in regard to World War II, which catches up all the book's males, and helps shape Pamela as a kind of living death-drive. One incident of war dominates Jenkins's experience. His most enduring attachments are to two schoolmates who, after undergoing unhappy marriages, die in the conflict, one in a POW camp in Singapore, the other in Egypt. The latter death might be laid at Widmerpool's door, because Widmerpool was in charge of an intelligence operation to which the friend was sacrificed. The friend also was Pamela's uncle. If Jenkins keeps Widmerpool and Pamela in view, it is because they are displaced exponents of Jenkins's early companions, who represent the thrill of Jenkins's shared start in life (the sister of one of the friends was Jenkins's initiator into Eros). Accordingly, Jenkins registers Widmerpool and Pamela's changes from nonentity to notoriety, in order, paradoxically, to maintain Jenkins's continuity with his own past. The continuity is also instanced by a cluster of characters who have solidarity with each other and Jenkins that not even a major war disturbs. That very solidarity might produce Widmerpool and Pamela's social aggression. The villains are in revolt against a numbingly enclosed world of sameness.

But neither do Widmerpool and Pamela change. Indeed in contrast to other series novels, Powell's history shows sameness and continuity trumping transformation. Widmerpool's upward mobility is remarkable because it belies the static essence of his character. Described first and last as a long-distance runner, Widmerpool runs in place, living and dying without having been transformed. That is partly because, as Jenkins notes with a pathos that touches all Powell's figures, including Pamela and himself: it is "angry solitude of spirit that held my attention in Widmerpool."[5] Even in those who are not angry, the solitude is permanent. And the way in which Jenkins's social set switches partners in erotic dances also accents permanence. If change were more substantive, would the characters keep together as they do, even when they switch?

There is one group or class of characters, however, which appears to have a genuine capacity for innovation: the writers, artists, and musicians with whom Jenkins (himself a novelist, editor, biographer, and critic) associates. Their psychological and intellectual mobility represents for young Jenkins "a world of high adventure."[6] A talented and volatile young writer, X. Trapnel, represents such mobility to an extraordinary degree. Jenkins works with Trapnel on a new post-war literary journal, *Fission*. He notes that Trapnel clings to an identity that he prefers to perform changelessly; but Jenkins also sees Trapnel playing numerous roles: "to do justice to their number requires...an interminable catalogue of types."[7] It is significant that Powell aligns even the fixedly steady Jenkins with Trapnel's multiple personalities. He does so when Trapnel, a contributor to *Fission*, publishes a parody of Widmerpool's articles in the same journal. Jenkins marvels at Trapnel's "entirely convincing" capture of Widmerpool's style (*BDFR*, p. 185). It is what any reader of Powell's identical capture, through the medium of Jenkins, also must marvel at. The moment is not self-congratulatory as much as it is self-characterizing, for Jenkins and Powell both. It means that Jenkins identifies, albeit again indirectly, with psychological and creative mobility and change. The identification also is legible from his attachment to Robert Burton's seventeenth-century classic, *The Anatomy of Melancholy*, wherein "irresolution" and "fidgetiness," which Trapnel writes large in his changing personalities, are melancholy's symptoms (*BDFR*, p. 2).

But melancholy in Burton, despite Trapnel's frenetic instance, ultimately expresses itself as obsessive repetition, as "'chronic or continued disease, a settled humour'" (*BDFR*, p. 2), more than as change or mobility. Unwittingly confirming Burton, Pamela, also melancholic, moves from Widmerpool to Trapnel, permanently arresting Trapnel's life and his multiple personalities. Time in Powell turns out to sound the music of arrest rather than transformation. Jenkins's *Fission*, whose title announces its *au courant* nature, amounts to merely a fizzling repetition of modernism – itself perhaps only a chronic constant of creative impulse. One of Powell's most interesting artists, the composer Hugh Moreland, identifies with another seventeenth-century writer, Ben Jonson, "'who reminds one that human life always remains the same. How bored one gets with the assumption that people now are organically different from people in the past'" (*BDFR*, p. 119). That complaint in the musician's mouth says much about the meanings of Powell's series. Not the least meaning is that history is not revolutionary, despite our Trapnel-like aim of emphasizing its metamorphoses. That Powell enlists historical fiction to suggest achronic force, and that he does so in series novel mode, satirizes our emphasis upon history as change, and amounts to a comical joke on history's use in fiction.

In contrast to Powell, Nicholas Mosley's *Catastrophe Practice* (five novels, 1979–90) represents history as a matter of critical turning points whose reality cannot be evaded. Mosley also adds evolutionary biology to history. His series is founded partly on theories about "sudden jumps" in evolution, and partly on his conviction of danger "in the imposition of conventional patterns upon life: the human race had arrived at a point at which the activity of the old patterns might blow it up."[8] An old biological pattern fits us to destroy enemies; but its continuation, thanks to our invention of nuclear weaponry, now makes ourselves the object of attack. How shall we come to terms with a history of evolving self-destruction? Mosley's conflation of technological change in history with evolutionary transformation might be a stretch; nevertheless, human technology undoubtedly has rebounded upon its inventor, remaking its fabricator and influencing biology as well as culture. If capture of nuclear power amounts to a sudden jump in our evolution, can it be made to constitute a hopeful mutation?

To illustrate what his narratives want to picture, Mosley appeals to Friedrich Nietzsche's philosophy. Nietzsche "saw . . . a contemporary evolutionary gulf . . . between those . . . who remain trapped within stimulus-and-response patterns of behavior . . . and those who, by virtue of being able to distance themselves within themselves and to look upon such patterns . . . in some part of themselves become free of them – and thus become of a different kind" (*CP*, 165). "A different kind" suggests a new homo sapiens.

Each novel in the series demonstrates efforts to practice such "differences," hence to nudge catastrophe in a creative direction. The heroine of *Judith* (1986, revised 1991) belongs to a circle of actors, writers, and filmmakers whom history ensnares in erotic, religious, and political dilemmas. Judith's story begins with her performance in a new play about the Old Testament enemies, Judith and Holofernes. Mosley's account of the play suggests that violent confrontation in ancient narrative is no longer a useful pattern for engaging history's complexity. An ultimate complexity emerges when Judith, participating in a major anti-nuclear demonstration, discovers that the demonstrators want to use a dirty bomb to assert their power. The old patterns here strangle possibilities of change. It is difficult to break their hold because all change appears to be monstrous. At the end of *Judith*, the heroine searches the countryside for a friend's lost child; when she discovers him, she also finds that he has come upon a two-headed, three-eyed sheep. Is the sheep an image of history's inevitable horror; or is Judith right to associate the mutant sheep's eye with "the eye that looks inward,"[9] and that hence can distance itself from a downward spiral of violence?

In Mosley's last-written novel of the series, *Hopeful Monsters*, Mosley gathers evidence, from science and philosophy and politics, that twentieth-century history is a horror, but also a hopeful monster: "something [that is] born which things outside are not quite ready for. Or perhaps they might just about be ready; that is the hope" (*J*, p. 291). A prequel to the story of Judith and her circle, *Hopeful Monsters* traces the lives of Max and Eleanor, an English-Jewish-German pair of lovers, one a biologist, the other an anthropologist, as they range across Europe and Africa between the wars, and arrive in Spain, amidst the Civil War between fascist and republican forces. Max and Eleanor pursue a discovery of patterns that hold promise of a future, and hand their pursuit to Judith's generation. The work of the young will be to establish an environment – not necessarily a public or group-validated one – that can liberate creative mutations for which history is a germinal. One of the most interesting prospects for such an environment is one wherein "courses of action could only be said to be right if there had been a genuine interplay of conflicting moral inclinations . . . It was . . . such complexity of mind . . . that was necessary if there was to be the existence of the Bomb without the use of the Bomb."[10]

The art of fiction in historical series novels

Novelists' efforts to base fiction on history find no complement in historians' desires to base their research on novels. A divide between fiction and history's claims to truth maintains itself in cultural discourse. It is possible that series novelists aim to subvert the divide by steeping their readers in an alternative history that comes to feel like the real thing. But novelists also clearly subscribe to the discursive division between fiction and history. As they do so, or as they meditate on the division, novelists appear to use historical fiction as, paradoxically, a self-reflexive way of picturing their own art. They include such picturing, and even enlist the history of novelistic form, as part of their subject matter.

In Snow's series Lewis continually wonders if events have become too big for humankind to handle. One answer is that humankind has made itself too little for them. Lewis admires larger than life, "extravagant" persons. The pro-disarmament minister he supports is one. It is significant that the best model of extravagance Lewis can bring forward is to be found in historical fiction: he compares his minister to Tolstoy's Pierre in *War and Peace*. Snow's mediation of his narrative by reference to Pierre suggests that novels must be respected as themselves corridors of power. However extravagant the suggestion is, the transfer of historical responsibility to novelistic possibility elevates fiction to government service. How Snow and other series writers involve their attitudes towards art with their attitudes towards history is an essential part of the story of the form.

Manning's self-reflexive picturing of novelistic art in relation to history emerges in her use of fantasy and romance. At the end of *The Balkan Trilogy* Harriet realizes that she "had condemned Guy's attachment to fantasy but wondered now if fantasy were a part of life, a component without which one could not survive" (p. 919). Manning thereafter projects it as a component without which historical experience cannot survive. The vehicle of fantasy in *The Levant Trilogy* becomes romance – Shakespearian romance, as in *The Winter's Tale*, which shows a woman thought dead returning to life. In *The Sum of Things* (1980) Harriet, as a result of not boarding the fatal ship, wanders into the Holy Land before she miraculously reappears, as if resurrected, at a wedding party in Cairo that Guy is attending. Intensifying the romance structure, Manning divides this novel between Harriet and another figure who returns from the dead: a soldier who wins his way back to life from paralysis as a result of being blown up.

While the romance element is an ancient mark of fiction, it also shows Manning's reliance on modernism: on modernism's mythical method of lending historical chaos a timeless pattern in order to render history intelligible. Romance pattern provides an underlying intelligibility to *The Waste Land* and *Ulysses*. Manning relies on a modernist forebear too: D. H. Lawrence's, in whose *Women in Love* (1920) one finds a couple that struggles to define intimacy, emotional responsibility, and accountability to society, just as Manning's couple does. Both imaginary pairs – Lawrence's and Manning's – are the fictive element, along with romance, by which Manning tests her novels' wedding to history. Harriet's distrust of Guy, and her sense of timelessness and personal mystery, can be read as fiction itself, escaping from history, and returning to it; Guy is history's curious indifference to fiction – even though fiction's autonomy, personified in Harriet, might be an emblem of collective liberty, part of what Guy's politics seeks to advance.

Burgess's trilogy uses modernism as a self-reflexive vehicle in order to investigate modernism's possible complicity with the history of imperialism. Crabbe's second wife is a poet whose style is "Eliotian" (p. 427), especially in a poem that pictures Crabbe as another Prufrock. Burgess suggests that we figure Crabbe as "Eliotian" modernism, so that we might see modernism's long day, involved with empire, waning with him. There are other indications that we are to read this way. An American linguist, who represents looming American imperialism, significantly has "the rather smug voice of [Eliot's] *Four Quartets*, though much younger" (p. 449). Meanwhile, Crabbe's first wife was a pianist, whose recording of a modernist "Poulenc-like" "gay brief satire" (p. 484) on older music is the treasured property of the blimp planter, and becomes the occasion of the stinging revelation of adultery that leads to Crabbe's death by water. ("Fear death by water" is a famous line from *The Waste Land*.) Burgess appears to insist that modernist music (including modernist verse music) be associated with Crabbe and empire, and that they both merit drowning.

The appearance does not hold, however. Burgess's dramatization of another instance of modernist music suggests that aesthetic modernism, albeit equivocal in significance, is not equivalent to imperialism. Robert Loo's early compositions are modernist. Crabbe wants Loo to write a symphony for Independence Day, because Crabbe sees Loo's modernism as peculiarly fitted to express Malayan self-determination in a global context. The projected symphony would enlarge a modernist string quartet by Loo that begins with each instrument "presenting in turn a national style" – Malayan, Indian, and atonal Western – and leaving a final unity unresolved, in favor of "ironic variations on a . . .'brotherhood of man' motif" (p. 351). Loo doesn't write the symphony, however. He falls in love with Rosemary, and thereby renounces modernism, replacing it with movie score-like, pre-modernist bombast. Loo, like Rosemary, rewrites history – his own and music's – to unfortunate effect.

But here it would seem that Burgess counterbalances the nefarious historical associations he assigns to modernism. Dissonance is characteristic of modernism, and *A Malayan Trilogy* sounds a discord between the satire it deals out to every element of Malayan and Western life and the sympathy it evokes for waxing as well as waning epochs. Burgess's trilogy offers Loo's quartet as a salutary alternative to the wrong way to write art and history – and as a mirror image of Burgess's own modernist-inspired ironic variations on the brotherhood of man. The modernist impulse, Burgess's trilogy suggests, is the twentieth-century historical novelist's fate – a mode of composing and revising history and fiction that is simultaneously fatal and life-giving.

Powell is another example of modernist dissonance's enduring reverberation. Just as Trapnel parodies Widmerpool in *Fission*, Powell's fiction, inasmuch as it opposes changelessness to change, parodies history's presence in it. The parody shows itself along two self-reflexive threads, each of which has a modernist character. One thread solicits writing's place in eternity rather than time. At a Victory Day service in St. Paul's, Jenkins finds himself out of touch with any sense of historical "Great Occasion." He feels in touch instead with hymns (including Blake's *Jerusalem*) and texts that constitute the service; and the experience suggests to him a timeless dimension of verbal art. Jenkins immediately rebukes himself for being unhistorical; and in the same breath *is* unhistorical, by remarking that "freedom from one sort of humbug merely impl[ies], with human beings from any epoch, thraldom to another."[11] An unhistorical constant, in other words, overrides historical differences. Jenkins's interest in Burton's timeless relevance takes the same transhistorical path. His appeal to literary history as a way of entry into a place where literary texts speak simultaneously to each other, and to widely different historical conditions in a way that deflates the importance of their temporal origins, strikes a modernist note: its invocation of art's eternal moments is the closest Powell comes to Proust.

Abetting his appeal to timelessness, Powell adumbrates a skepticism about history that grounds his parodic thrust. Historical narrative, especially of change, depends upon an historian's ability to determine actions and events that are turning points in human experience. If those turning points cannot be adequately identified – if the rise of a Widmerpool appears to signal a vast social change, and yet turns out to be an index of stasis – then history itself becomes a perplexity. In one of Jenkins's first meetings with Moreland, the musician-composer meditates on the difficulty of defining action's key role in historical transformation: "Violence – revolt – sweep away the past. Abandon bourgeois values... I'm told on all sides that's how one should behave." But Moreland is puzzled. He intuits that "action... stem[s] from sluggish, invisible sources, [and] moves towards destinations no less indefinable... 'Is art action, an alternative to action, the enemy of action, or nothing whatever to do with action? I have no objection to action. I merely find it impossible to locate.'"[12] Like Moreland, Powell's form and his sense of history are perplexed by action, perhaps finding it impossible to locate. Modernist experiments with narrative, for example in James, Conrad, and Woolf, often made art an index of that impossibility. Although Powell does not subscribe to modernism's comprehensive spirit of revolt against the past, Powell's doubtful pictures of action and change continue what modernism initiates.

Mosley is the most experimental of the novelists in this chapter, hence the most obvious renewer of modernist aims. In line with his interest in creative possibilities of mutation, he claims (through Max) "some special verity for aesthetics" (*HM*, p. 538) because works of art, more than science and philosophy, might provide a language especially suitable to revising patterns of consciousness. Mosley experiments with narrative fiction's patterns throughout *Catastrophe Practice*. The experiment produces a constant double narration, whereby conventional form – a narrator telling about past events – occurs simultaneously with a narrator's unconventional questioning, in the present moment, of what he is telling, and of how he is telling it; and often too with a narrator's questioning of his reader. Narration thus becomes a continually probative, interactive endeavor. The aim of such narrating-questioning is to challenge the hold of deadening patterns on storytelling and history. Mosley asks his narrators and his readers to investigate the past and the present bearing of the past; and at the same time to assess how narrative – in both history and fiction – can mutate into something more prospective than retrospective. The prospective aspect evokes an environment that might support creative mutation. History in Mosley is oriented towards the future as well as towards past and present. The orientation confirms an idea that Max acquires from modern mathematics: "There is no mathematical reason why messages should not exist from the future as well as from the past; it is our structuring in accordance with time that would prevent us from recognizing these" (*HM*, p. 507).

Catastrophe Practice, the first novel Mosley wrote in his series, is the most difficult to read. Cipher-like, modernist-like, it intends to overturn all current patterns of fiction, as part of a strenuous effort to free meaning from old significances. When Mosley completed the series with *Hopeful Monsters*, he appended to that work a suggestion that the first-written novel be read after the other four. Its forward-looking obscurity, Mosley believes, is a guarantee of its escape from destructive aspects of the past. It is his best example of a hopeful monster. Perhaps all this chapter's examples of history in fiction are mutations in the novel's evolution, monster novels that complement history, or supplement it, in order to leap beyond its catastrophe-strewn course.

NOTES

1 Anthony Burgess, *The Long Day Wanes: A Malayan Trilogy* (New York: W. W. Norton & Co., 1992), p. 474.
2 Olivia Manning, *The Balkan Trilogy* (Harmondsworth: Penguin, 1981), pp. 392, 344.
3 C. P. Snow, *Strangers and Brothers*, vol. 2 (New York: Charles Scribner's Sons, 1985), p. 708.

4 C. P. Snow, *Corridors of Power* (New York: Charles Scribner's Son, 1964), pp. 380–1.
5 Anthony Powell, *A Question of Upbringing* (London: William Heinemann, 1951), p. 205.
6 Anthony Powell, *Casanova's Chinese Restaurant* (London: Heinemann, 1960), p. 15.
7 Anthony Powell, *Books Do Furnish a Room* (London: Heinemann, 1971) p. 144.
8 Nicholas Mosley, *Catastrophe Practice* (Elmwood Park, IL: The Dalkey Archive Press, 1989), p. 339.
9 Nicholas Mosley, *Judith* (Elmwood Park, IL: Dalkey Archive Press, 1991), p. 289.
10 Nicholas Mosley, *Hopeful Monsters* (Elmwood Park, IL: Dalkey Archive Press, 1990), p. 529.
11 Anthony Powell, *The Military Philosophers* (London: William Heinemann, 1968), p. 227.
12 Anthony Powell, *The Kindly Ones* (London: William Heinemann, 1962), pp. 75–6.

13

ANDRZEJ GASIOREK

Postmodernisms of English fiction

Postmodernism is hard to define. Is it a period term, a social diagnosis, a cultural dominant, an anti-aesthetic posture, a philosophical endgame, a hollowing out of time and a new substantiation of space, a sign of political defeat? Postmodernism is all of those, its vagueness as a concept matched by its voracity as a category. The all-embracing prefix is part of the problem. Does (post)modernism, coming *after* modernism in the 1950s, extend or negate the earlier movement? Or does it paradoxically *precede* modernism conceptually, bearing witness to what modernism could not represent? These unsettled questions suggest that postmodernism is both an overdetermined heir of modernist influences and an open-ended set of practices and theories whose relationship to modernism remains vexed.

An additional difficulty arises for any assessment of the nature of postmodernist fiction in Britain when one takes American popularization of the term into account. Its early formulations by critics such as Leslie Fiedler, Irving Howe, Ihab Hassan, Gerald Graff, and Fredric Jameson referred to the post-war American intellectual scene. Whether it was Fiedler describing postmodernism's blurring of a gap between "high" and "popular" culture, Howe identifying its anti-intellectualism, Hassan defining it against modernism, Graff censuring its ethical irresponsibility, or Jameson theorizing it as a cultural dominant of late capitalism, these accounts took no cognizance of postwar British society. To say so is not to criticize their exploratory work, for British literary culture after the war appeared to observers to be austere, insular, and cautious. That such a view was one-sided has become clear, but at the time it seemed as though a full-scale reversion to premodernist literary traditions was under way. In America postmodernism signaled a paradigm shift away from modernism and towards a new *episteme*; in Britain the literary culture seemed determined to go back to a time before modernism had reared its ugly head.

Until the 1970s it was thought that with few exceptions postwar British novelists had rejected modernism's literary experimentation and were bent on returning to conventional realism. Fiction, empirical in orientation, preoccupied itself with class issues, social mobility, and current sexual mores. With Fielding, Dickens, and Wells as models (not Henry James, Woolf, or Joyce) there was no place for modernism's characteristic labyrinthine syntax, subjective renderings of experience, elaborate mythical allusions, obscure symbolism, or narrative self-consciousness. Novels unfolded in an orderly manner, moral issues were handled pragmatically, and the prevailing tone was not given to metaphysics or meta-reflection. But although such characteristics were an important feature of postwar fiction, writers continued to draw upon modernist experiment. In the 1940s and 1950s Samuel Beckett, Henry Green, Ivy Compton-Burnett, Philip Toynbee, Rayner Heppenstall, Iris Murdoch, William Golding, and Muriel Spark all departed from realist conventions. *Finnegans Wake* and Samuel Beckett's fiction set a standard for a group of overtly anti-realist novelists that includes Brigid Brophy, Christine Brooke-Rose, B. S. Johnson, Ann Quin, and Alan Burns. Hostile to the empiricist tradition of the social novel, they rejected it in favor of extreme linguistic and narrative innovation. And there were others: writers who became dissatisfied with realism's limitations (John Berger, Doris Lessing, Angus Wilson); realists who, influenced by (post) modernism, both practiced realism and unmasked realism's illusions via intertextual and metafictional devices (David Lodge, Malcolm Bradbury, Anthony Burgess, John Fowles, Iris Murdoch); science fiction writers who portrayed contemporary society as an alien form of existence (J. G. Ballard, Michael Moorcock, Lessing again); women novelists who subverted cultural and literary ideologies by deconstructing and rewriting them (Angela Carter, Emma Tennant, Fay Weldon, Jeanette Winterson); satirists who dissected contemporary Britain, using techniques of comic exaggeration, gothic excess, and outrageous grotesquerie (Martin Amis, Alasdair Gray, Iain Sinclair); and metafictionists concerned with history and epistemological problems of historiography (Peter Ackroyd, Graham Swift, Julian Barnes).

The names above represent only a sample of a diverse body of work. Postmodernism, as Alan Wilde points out, is often deployed to lump together a "congeries of usually divergent impulses" informing the *oeuvre* of writers whose texts cannot be neatly categorized.[1] Postmodern fiction typically defamiliarizes, by means of parody, pastiche, fantasy, and magic realism, what we take for granted in social and literary convention; it cultivates the unconscious, the irrational, and the absurd, for comedic purposes; it focuses on technology, especially the ubiquity of communications systems; it rereads the past, concentrating on dominant narrative models by which accounts of history are constructed; it utilizes metafiction to analyze language as a signifying system and to foreground literary codes that structure fiction; and it favors textual indeterminacy as a way of indicating the complexity and opacity of contemporary society. Post-modern fiction is linked to the language of critique. It developed literary procedures to explore the phantasmagoric nature of late capitalist culture and its popular imaginaries. Jean-François Lyotard's observation that postmodern texts are "not in principle governed by pre-established rules, and they cannot be judged . . . by applying familiar categories to the text or to the work" is apposite, because in postwar British contexts we witness unfamiliar responses to contemporary life and to the challenge of representing it in fiction.[2]

Metafiction represents one possible direction for British postmodernism. Rule breaking is its *sine qua non*. Metafiction is parasitic and parodic: it battens on the novelistic genre in order to expose its inner workings, to have fun with its protocols. Because it explores how language and narrative work to make and uphold meaning it is an excellent vehicle for postmodernism's skeptical critique of fiction and historiography. Already present in Joyce and Beckett's work, metafiction is elevated to a structural principle in Flann O'Brien's *At Swim-Two-Birds* (1939) and is used in post-war novels that include Spark's *The Comforters* (1957); Johnson's *Travelling People* (1963), *Albert Angelo* (1964), and *Christie Malry's Own Double-Entry* (1973); Brophy's *In Transit* (1969); Brooke-Rose's *Between* (1968) and *Thru* (1975); and Fowles's *Mantissa* (1982).

At Swim-Two-Birds is a comic *tour-de-force*. Its premise is that its characters, once invented, will not abide by the novelist's authority. This raises the question of how much control writers have over their texts. The first-person narrator is writing a story in which a character is in turn writing a moralistic tale in which the vices of the day are condemned. The moralist is a despot, seeking to control *his* characters completely; but when he is asleep they lead independent lives. The unruly creations drug their "author" so that he is nodding off almost all of the time. Discovering their own literary bent, they write themselves into his life and torture him, thus rebelling against the narrator's claim that the novel is an exhausted genre. The text has already shown that novels can be renewed by metafiction. The narrator, announcing at the outset that he deplores limitations imposed on the genre by singular beginnings and endings, provides three openings, each written in a different style. The novel continues, proliferating styles, rhetorical devices, biographical reminiscences, and (for inattentive readers) synopses of events, all the while refusing to uphold ontological and narrative boundaries between authors, narrators, characters, and texts.

Spark's *The Comforters* is also preoccupied with narrative authority, but it takes a different tack. Spark was primarily interested in questions about the nature of reality and human identity within a context of religious belief. It becomes apparent in *The Comforters* that its characters are just that – "characters" in a narrative written by someone else. O'Brien's personages challenge their author in a way that is ontologically impossible but feasible as fiction, because novelists can make characters do whatever they please; when Trellis gets his face kicked off he is told to say he likes it, and he does so through a hole in his head. In Spark's text it is only the female protagonist who realizes that everybody inhabits a fictional world being created by someone outside it. In what is perhaps an allusion to Beckett's godlike controlling figures Moran and Mahood, she hears "voices" that appear to be scripting her life. Her fear of entrapment in a narrative not of her own making is contrasted with others' refusal to countenance her explanation of events. The question of who sees truly and who is deluded comes to the fore. A spoof detective novel, *The Comforters* unfolds an incredible plot about a septuagenarian gang of smugglers, only to demonstrate that what seems fantastic (impossible) is in fact true, since the writer made it so. The text thereby suggests an analogy between the author and a supernatural deity. The novel's characters accept the predestinate "world" of the narrative, while its protagonist rejects the "plot" and tries to take charge of her life. In a text that is ultimately about the conflict between predestination and free will, she is only granted the insight that "the narrative could never become coherent to her until she was at last outside it, and at the same time consummately inside it."[3]

Spark's characters are ciphers, her plots theorems, her novels demonstrations concerned with what lies beyond empirically knowable actuality. Her tone is that of an anatomist who dissects the cadaver of what passes for life. *The Ballad of Peckham Rye* (1960) depicts an urban-industrial world of lost souls; stupefied by an alienating environment, they are temporarily roused by a puckish interloper who is eventually banished but not before he has left a vision of "the Rye for an instant looking like a cloud of green and gold, the people seeming to ride upon it, as you might say there was another world than this."[4] *The Public Image* (1968) analyzes the fetishization of film icons. An early take on celebrity culture and a society devoted to spectacle, it discloses a chasm between an actor's real life and the mediated perception of it, and shows how public fantasy takes over the very idea of an independent private existence. *The Driver's Seat* (1970) pitilessly traces the steps by which a desperate woman plans her own death in an attempt to gain control over a life that has had no meaning. Characteristically light and spare, Spark's novels are detached, analytical experiments in narrative logic.

Another "group" of writers whose novels have affinities with postmodernism turn their fiction toward myth, fantasy, fabulation, and magic realism. Angela Carter, Emma Tennant, and later on Jeanette Winterson (for whom Carter is a precursor) rework accepted understandings of "reality" into visionary forms. They embrace lyricism, expressionism, and the carnivalesque. Taken as a whole, their work is preoccupied with identity, sex, gender, and patriarchy; their novels re-write culturally dominant narratives in order to voice ex-centric, oppositional perspectives. This writing is *dialogic*, debating other literary narratives and theoretical discourses. Carter, for example, debates feminism – and the Marquis de Sade. She and the others turn existing narrative models inside out, and subvert masculinist assumptions about gender identity and the value of individuated subjectivity. Despite their innovations, however, in this kind of writing Patricia Waugh rightly notes that "we find a postmodernism which is more an elaboration and exaggeration of already available codes than an apocalyptic break with aesthetic tradition."[5] Modernism especially is one such code.

Carter links writing to "the slow process of decolonialising our language and our basic habits of thought"; and in *The Passion of New Eve* (1977) argues that because "external symbols must always express the life within us" a "critique of these symbols is a critique of our lives."[6] She unpacks the image-store of the techno-visual landscape to articulate its representations of gender and power relations. *The Passion of New Eve* is a quest romance (perhaps an echo of Virginia Woolf's *Orlando*) in which the protagonist undergoes a sex-change as part of a search for the "truth" of gender, only to discover that although "masculine and feminine are correlatives," s/he still doesn't know "what the nature of masculine and the nature of feminine might be" (pp. 149–50). *Nights at the Circus* (1984) mocks twentieth-century history (its retrogressive patriarchal politics and its naïve utopian fantasies) by means of a Rabelaisian laughter that recodes the female "grotesque" as a shibboleth-destroying freedom fighter who is "warts and all the female paradigm."[7]

Emma Tennant, in *The Bad Sister* (1978), *Queen of Stones* (1982), and *Faustine* (1991) engaged specific precursor narratives (Hogg's *Memoirs and Confessions of a Justified Sinner*, Golding's *Lord of the Flies*, and the Faust myth) to uncover women's interpellation by patriarchy. *The Bad Sister* is of particular interest. It focuses on the power of modern imagery (photography, magazines, television, cinema) over women's ideas about their gendered identity. In a dreamlike world where the boundary between fantasy and reality is blurred, the protagonist is triply "explained": as a vampire, a victim of demonic possession by a feminist revolutionary, and a paranoid schizophrenic. The text deploys the "explanations" as images of lost identity, bodily entrapment, and sexual oppression. The protagonist becomes a specter confronted by a "terrible absence" when she looks into a mirror. She can capture no glimpse of a non-alienated female self in a consumerist and patriarchal life-world that splits women psychically in two, forcing the "woman who thinks" to "live with a demented sister" with whom she is locked in a death struggle for a right to exist as an autonomous being.[8] Like Tennant, Winterson, in open-ended and experimental novels *The Passion* (1987), *Sexing the Cherry* (1989), and *Written on the Body* (1992), weaves together fantasy, fabulation, and history, in order to present gender, sexuality, bodily being, subjectivity, and difference, as fluid processes, not as fixed entities.

The work of B. S. Johnson, Alan Burns, Christine Brooke-Rose, and Brigid Brophy is mainly motivated by a desire to investigate properties of fiction as a set of codes for fabricating meaning. The investigation attempts to renew fiction through linguistic, narrative, and typographical experiments. But there are important differences among these writers. Burns, influenced by Surrealism, sought to erase the line between poetry and fiction in order to explore links between recent history and the unconscious. In novels such as *Europe After the Rain* (1965), *Babel* (1969), and *Dreamerika! A Surrealist Fantasy* (1972) he wrote visionary fiction that was also a testament to fragmented contemporary experience – hence his experiments with typography and with American novelist William Burroughs's "cut-up" method. Brooke-Rose and Brophy, in contrast, were concerned with narratology, the mechanics of storytelling.

Johnson saw himself as an important innovator, as a hard-line anti-realist whose writing was driven by a desire for novelistic truth as opposed to fictional mendacity. His first novel, *Travelling People* (1963), was indebted to Sterne, Joyce, and O'Brien. It mimics *Ulysses* and *At Swim-Two-Birds*, utilizing a different narrative style for each of its nine chapters; uses stippled pages to indicate loss of consciousness and black pages to indicate death; and exploits earlier writers' frame-breaking devices: asides to the reader, intertextuality, glossaries of terms, random digressions. Johnson later repudiated the novel, a judgment that can be understood when we grasp how deeply he was burdened by a sense of belatedness. He operated with a progressivist view of fiction and with a modernist conviction that the writer's task is to "make it new." Realism, he insisted, "cannot be made to work for our time, and the writing of it is anachronistic, invalid, irrelevant, and perverse."[9] This led Johnson to argue that Joyce cultivated modernism's characteristic interior monologue because he recognized that social reality could be better represented by cinema, which freed novelists to explore their own imaginations rather than society. Johnson's own inward turn was motivated by his conviction that *all* narrative attempts to render the world falsify it because they impose structure on what is totally haphazard. This argument led him to distinguish between "fiction" and the "novel": the former imposed narrative form on reality and was a "lie," whereas the latter could access truth if it focused on autobiographical experience. Johnson's turn to auto-biography was then a turn *away* from the Joyce of *Ulysses* and *toward* the Beckett of *The Unnamable* (1958): "I'm speaking now of me, yes, hence-forward I shall speak of none but me, that's decided, even though I should not succeed."[10]

But Johnson's novels hardly conform to his own dicta. *Albert Angelo* shows what was at stake. It describes the life of an architect who works as a substitute teacher to make ends meet and who becomes increasingly annoyed by his inability to make a difference to the lives of his pupils. The character's frustration is paralleled by the narrator's exasperation at his inability to render experience truthfully. The novel breaks down with an infamous aposiopesis: "– OH, FUCK ALL THIS LYING!" The next section ("Disintegration") alludes again to *The Unnamable* – "I am Mahood after all and these stories of a being whose identity he usurps, and those voices he prevents from being heard, all lies from beginning to end" (p. 311) – and is a meta-commentary: "what im really trying to write about is writing not all this stuff about architecture trying to say something about writing about my writing im my hero"[11] Johnson saw this book as a breakthrough because it allowed him to speak directly to the reader. It led to the autobiographical novels *Trawl* (1967) and *The Unfortunates* (1969), the latter a box-novel consisting of loose-leaved sections that (apart from the opening and closing sections) can be read in any order in an attempt to reproduce the random nature of human experience and to resist limits imposed by the material object itself. Unable to sustain his programmatic intentions, however, Johnson in later novels, *House Mother Normal* (1971) and *Christie Malry's Own Double-Entry* (1973), moved away from autobiography, producing books in which his penchant for metafictional games was no longer hampered by a limiting poetics of fiction.

Brooke-Rose denies that Johnson's work was experimental at all. Fair or not, her criticism illuminates her own project. Influenced by Ezra Pound's *The Cantos* and by the French *nouveau roman* exemplified by Alain Robbe-Grillet's fiction, Brooke-Rose's experiments attempt "anti-novels" that self-reflexively explore the nuts and bolts of literary textuality. Robbe-Grillet took as his point of departure reality's resistance to interpretation, expunging the preterite from his work because, in Brooke-Rose's words, it "guarantees 'truth' (this happened)."[12] Robbe-Grillet experimented instead with the present tense and with an impersonal "voice" that obviated the perspective of a narrator whose account of events inevitably colors inter-pretation. His purpose was to draw attention to conventions by which fiction made sense of reality and to which readers had become so habituated that they no longer noticed them. Brooke-Rose's work pursues the same defamiliarizing aim. It explores the ways in which meanings are woven and unwoven by stories and by language's arbitrariness; utilizes the present tense to escape the ordering power of the past tense; and refuses the reality-fixing comfort of a stable narrative voice.

In Brooke-Rose's *Between* (1968) an anonymous protagonist is stuck in an airport lounge, and this womb-like textual "space" becomes a site across which play multiple national tongues and types of discourse, permeating the protagonist and destabilizing her identity. Brigid Brophy's *In Transit* (1969) is also set in an airport: its protagonist is in transit in gendered terms, unable to tell if she or he is female or male. Brophy's punning Joycean text – a tribute to *Finnegans Wake* and to the modernism of the "great Triestine compalien, the comedi-chameleon, the old pun gent himself" (p. 36) – switches from present to past tense, but also disrupts the comfort of the preterite with puns, musical notation, double columns of type, analyses of grammar, and metafictional asides. An "ALIENATING INTERLUDE" tells us that "at least one of the hero(in)es immolated throughout these pages is language" (p. 219), and then indicts realists for passing off authorial choices as fate when in fact they are trapping "villains as it arbitrarily suited them in the pincer of coincidence, ridding themselves at lordly will of unprofitable characters by contrived accidents of god" (p. 220). Brophy's novel is an extended metaphor for reading, for a reader is always "in transit" from one sentence/paragraph/ chapter to the next, as any conventional narrative moves irresistibly forward. But the text also suggests that the whole contemporary period is "in transit," so an exploration of language and narrative is combined with a historical diagnosis. Because the twentieth century "hasn't yet invented its style – only a repertory of cliché motifs" (p. 22), its "true pure feel" can be found in transitional spaces like airports. When the narrator of uncertain gender accepts transitory indeterminate existence as authentic s/he can "move into and occupy [her?] own century" (p. 28), seeing it as a time–space conjunction marked by migration and impermanence. How the transition feels is not easy to gauge: it is hysterical, exhilarating, rebellious, and suicidal by turns.

Burns, Johnson, Brooke-Rose, and Brophy have never been widely read, but their texts develop recognizably postmodernist characteristics. The typographical and linguistic "extremism" of some of their texts represents a "radical postmodernism" that needs to be contrasted with fiction by writers who have chosen to incorporate experimental techniques in their novels without jettisoning realism. Randall Stevenson usefully describes this kind of writing as "mainstream postmodernism."[13] Issues of audience, publishing practices, publicity, and marketing are of relevance; most publishers wouldn't touch the kind of work associated with extreme experimentation, and most readers are either unaware of or uninterested in it. Typically, then, whereas "radicals" have a difficult relationship with the reading public and often inveigh against what they see as its philistinism, "mainstream" postmodern novelists often write with their readers' interests in mind. Such contentions of course go back to modernism, and they have never entirely gone away. They are at the heart of questions about the nature of an assumed author/reader contract, or about the social and/or aesthetic "purpose" of fiction, or about the novelist's role in contemporary life. John Fowles dismissed much fictional experiment as "twentieth century rococo" and explained that his "own preferred contract [was] in the middle ground"; Malcolm Bradbury argued that it was "impossible" to "regard form either as a sequence of technical skills or as a pure object"; and David Lodge refused to abandon realism, arguing that because the norms governing it had been consistently held for years, any idea that it was "a completely relativistic concept" was untenable.[14] These writers were influenced by modernism and were well aware of continuing contemporary innovations in fiction, but they saw experimental extremism as a dead end.

Fowles's *The Magus* (1965) and *The French Lieutenant's Woman* (1969) explore existentialist dilemmas in stories that are as much about fictions by which people live as they are about worlds they inhabit. Although *The French Lieutenant's Woman* is set in a Victorian England that it depicts in careful detail, the novel is less concerned with historical veracity than with pursuing ontological dilemmas. Fowles's framebreaking strategies (references to literary theory, denials of authorial responsibility, multiple endings) do not destabilize the "truth" of the Victorian social milieu but question its supposedly hidebound values in order to show its characters struggling to escape the shackles of existential inauthenticity.

Fowles's early work endorsed "middle-ground" writing that was "realistic" as well as self-reflective. But he composed one thoroughly metafictional book, *Mantissa* (1982). *Mantissa* explores the nature of creativity, using sexual congress as a symbol of literary creation. The novel's male writer requires a female muse before he can produce anything. This seemingly sexist conception is undermined when the novel's muse-figure protests that male writers have misunderstood and misrepresented women, and claims that women, not men, wrote many of the recognized literary classics. But the novel persistently subverts itself. Informing readers that a "mantissa" is an "addition of comparatively small importance, especially to a literary effort or discourse," the novel's claim that "serious modern fiction has only one subject: the difficulty of writing serious modern fiction" is thus mocked as self-defeating solipsism.[15]

Angus Wilson's fiction also pursues a middle way between aesthetic conservatism and radical postmodernism. Wilson's *No Laughing Matter* (1967) offers a panoramic view of the twentieth century and does so by foregrounding the ways in which knowledge of it has been mediated by textual sources. Wilson had begun his writing career in stories that mixed historical realism with savage grotesqueries that point back to Wyndham Lewis's modernism. Wilson grew dissatisfied with the realistic component in the mixture because of what he came to see as realism's intellectual parochialism and tepid liberal assumptions. *No Laughing Matter* is a calculated riposte to his earlier work. It explores the fortunes of a single family from the Edwardian period to the 1960s, but it breaks away from expected norms for chronologically conceived historical sagas (as in John Galsworthy's Forsyte tales) by parodying the styles of twentieth-century dramatic and cinematic genres. The text ends up as a collage of multiple images, voices, techniques, and registers. They emphasize reality's dependence on discourses that shape it, deflating the pretensions of any particular narrative strand to "truth." The influence of modernist experiment in *Ulysses* returns here in Wilson.

The most prolific of novelists who steer between extremes of modernist and postmodernist experiment is Iris Murdoch, a writer whose work combines fabulation, symbolism, fantasy, magic realism, and metafiction. Murdoch's work addresses problems of representation, desire, and fantasy. *Under the Net* (1954) explores existentialist ideas about freedom and authenticity in relation to post-Wittgensteinian thinking about how language might not "fit" reality. *The Unicorn* (1963), a gothic pastiche, is structured around a doubled narrative and focuses on how the act of interpretation (the reading of the story within the story) is conditioned by the literary presuppositions imposed on the embedded text by its (fictional) readers. *The Black Prince* (1973) is a self-reflexive novel about links between fiction-making and fantasy. Its main protagonist is an aspiring writer. His search for creative power replays Marsyas' musical competition with Apollo, while his sexual affairs reprise Strauss's opera *Der Rosenkavalier*. The protagonist's first-person account offers two perspectives on events, since it oscillates between the perceptions of his younger self and his mature reflections. This doubled perspective is further complicated by competing accounts offered by other characters and by an editorial "frame" (two forewords and six postscripts) in which the tale is enclosed. The novel makes the question of narrative integral to its metafictional exploration of language, perception, and knowledge. It is, as the protagonist says of *Hamlet*, "a work endlessly reflecting upon itself, not discursively but in its very substance, a Chinese box of words as high as the tower of Babel, a meditation upon the bottomless trickery of consciousness and the redemptive role of words in the lives of those without identity, that is human beings."[16]

Alternative views or enlistments of modernism's inherited resources of experiment can be discerned in David Lodge's *The British Museum Is Falling Down* (1965) or Peter Ackroyd's *Chatterton* (1987), where the genre's putative inventiveness causes concern, out of fear that "the novel" has exhausted its possible permutations. *The British Museum Is Falling Down* borrows – again from modernist experiment's epitome *Ulysses* – the idea of structuring a novel around events of a single day, tracing a protagonist's progress (Bloom-like) through London, and imitating *Ulysses*' "Wandering Rocks" chapter by pastiching styles of other modernists. The novel also grafts Oscar Wilde's idea that nature imitates art onto Joyce's concern with migration (especially of the soul) by suggesting that life is ordered according to prearranged narrative patterns: "It partook, he thought...of metempsychosis, the way his humble life fell into moulds prepared by literature. Or was it, he wondered...the result of closely studying the sentence structure of the English novelists? One had resigned oneself to having no private language any more, but one had clung wistfully to the illusion of a personal property of events."[17] Lodge takes this undermining of selfhood a step further with a suggestion that "novelists are *using up* experience at a dangerous rate," leaving them with little to do other than to recycle existing narratives and plotlines.

Ackroyd's *Chatterton* (1987) also worries life's overreliance on fictional forms. An intellectual whodunnit, it toys with the idea that Chatterton might have faked his death, then lived into middle age while forging huge chunks of eighteenth-century literature. This conceit suggests that genius has less to do with originality than with recombining existing strands of thought. Creativity is figured as theft, pastiche, ventriloquism. When it is discovered that one character began her writing career by plagiarizing the work of an obscure novelist, another character is unable to criticize her, because his own experience of writing "had become a patchwork of other voices and other styles, and it was the overwhelming difficulty of recognising his own voice among them that had led him to abandon the project."[18] In a by now familiar postmodern move that harks back to Beckett and Spark, Ackroyd's writer realizes that he is himself a "character" in somebody else's book. The novel becomes an extended palimpsest of images and voices, until the question of who is narrating becomes irrelevant. But if Ackroyd suggests that the past survives as ghostly traces that can sustain creativity, now understood as quotation upon quotation, it also agonizes over a waning of historical consciousness in a presentist culture: "There is no history any more.

There is no memory. There are no standards to encourage permanence – only novelty, and the whole endless cycle of new objects" (p. 150). The novel responds by insisting that literature is "a dream of wholeness, and of beauty" (p. 152) and that there is "nothing more real than words" since the writer doesn't "merely recreate or describe the world" but "actually creates it" (p. 157).

Anxiety about the status of history and the viability of literature is of course a major feature of postmodern writing. (It is a major feature of modernism as well, from Conrad's *Nostromo* to Woolf's *Between the Acts*.) *Chatterton*, preoccupied with the inexplicability of reality and with apparent lack of meaning in historical process, registers its characters' puzzlement in the face of "a world in which no significant pattern could be found" and in which there is "no real *origin* for anything" (p. 232). The novel finally poses a key question: "Why should historical research not also remain incomplete, existing as a possibility and not fading into knowledge?" (p. 213). Ackroyd explores answers in *Hawksmoor* (1985), *The House of Doctor Dee* (1993), and *Dan Leno and the Limehouse Golem* (1994), in which one "possibility" is that history is more resonant and persuasive when it brings together – in an arcane *bricolage* – traces of the past that, unbeknown to most people, continue to haunt the present. A similar idea informs Iain Sinclair's *White Chappell, Scarlet Tracings* (1987), *Downriver* (1991), *Radon's Daughters* (1994), and *Lights Out for The Territory* (1997). The narrator of *White Chappell* notes that "all writing is rewriting," but what this means in these visionary novels is that the past is to be resuscitated and then cast into an entirely new form. For Sinclair the historical record is discernible in the psychogeography of lived spaces no less than in written texts, but its many meanings are hidden. For the literary explorer "what matters is what [those spaces] don't say; but what is coded there"; by unraveling their mysteries he creates an "alternative reading" of both past and present – in obscure literary texts and overlooked urban spaces – that accesses a deeper, more ramified, understanding of possible realities.[19]

Over the years a cottage industry has developed around arguing whether postmodernism fails to engage seriously with the past and trivializes historiographical questions. Ackroyd and Sinclair (as well as Barnes, Berger, Rushdie, and Swift, among others) suggest that the accusation is wide of the mark. A specific worry has been that postmodernism conflates history with fiction, treating it as a fable and thus dissolving history into a multiplicity of jostling *petits recits*, as in this view from a Julian Barnes novel: "The history of the world? Just voices echoing in the dark . . . We make up a story to cover the facts we don't know or can't accept; we keep a few true facts and spin a new story round them."[20] Linda Hutcheon argues that postmodern fiction is not skeptical about the past but asks "whether we can ever *know* that past other than through its textualized remains," an observation that is pertinent to the ways in which British novelists explore how knowledge of history is mediated by narrative.[21] Ackroyd's distinction between "possibility" and "knowledge" differentiates a hermeneutic from a positivist approach to the past, but this doesn't mean that it dissolves the historical "real" *into* the discourses by which it is accessed.

British postmodern fiction is interesting in relation to history because it manifests such divergent responses to it. In John Berger's *G* (1972), for example, the impact of Cubism creates a text that juxtaposes multiple viewpoints for the sake of making a grand refusal: "Never again will a single story be told as though it were the only one."[22] The Cubist inspiration again reminds one that *G*'s ideology is modernist as well as "post." Known only by the single letter "G," Berger's protagonist functions as a nexus of historical potentialities, of possible pasts, presents, and futures. G's mother "wants with her baby to start an alternative world, to propose from his new-born life a new way of living" (p. 24). What this might mean is left unresolved. The novel holds out a possibility that revolutionary struggle might liberate humans from oppression, but it goes no further. It refuses narrative closure in order to resist any suggestion of historical determinism. The text dramatizes the path by which an individual discovers his historical being because for Berger only thus can the possibility of political agency be opened up. G gradually becomes historically conscious, and this leads him to reject pre-scripted narratives (which imply that the future course of history has been decided in advance). Resisting George Orwell's claim that quietism is an understandable contemporary response to loss of confidence in any form of historical agency, *G* refuses to be defeatist.

G refuses consoling belief in a single overarching historical narrative. Swift's *Waterland* (1983) and Barnes's *Flaubert's Parrot* (1984) or *The History of the World in 10½ Chapters* (1989) focus on epistemological modes by which history is known. In *Waterland*, if the absence of "History itself, the Grand Narrative" is troubling, then this leads not to a disabling skepticism about a historical referent *per se* but rather to the task of establishing the truth of the overlapping mini-narratives that constitute understanding of the past.[23] The task takes the form of accepting the limitations of historiographic accounts by tracing the minutiae of daily life and the importance of natural history to human history. The novel also suggests that narratives are the main way in which people make sense of their lives, but that storytelling can also be a form of displacement. Swift's narrator has to determine "where the stories end and reality begins" (p. 179), while the text as a whole shows how the past exerts a continual pressure on the present. Although historiography is shown to be incomplete in *Waterland*, the novel concedes that "what history teaches us is to avoid illusion and make-believe...to be realistic" (p. 94). Barnes's *A History of the World* also insists on the recalcitrance of the historical record. Even if the "God-eyed version is a fake," historical veracity is still a laudable goal: to give up on it is to "fall into beguiling relativity" and to "admit that the victor has the right not just to the spoils but also to the truth" (pp. 243–4).

The status of "truth" is at stake in a different way for Ian McEwan, whose fiction displays postmodern features but steers clear of radical narrative experimentation. McEwan views literary avant-gardism as a dead end and has argued that experimentation "should have less to do with formal factors like busting up your syntax and scrambling your page order, and more to do with content – the representation of states of mind and the society that forms them."[24] This emphasis on the relationship between psychology and social forms has resulted in novels that are concerned with the impact of twentieth-century European history on contemporary life, the transformational power of science, and the political dilemmas confronted by liberal-democratic societies in a globalized world riven by conflicts over material resources and ethico-religious values. *Black Dogs* (1992) addresses the legacy of the Nazi past through a meditation on the nature of evil – "a terrible cruelty, a viciousness against life" – a malign and ever-present force that "will return to haunt us, somewhere in Europe, in another time."[25] *Saturday* (2005) is set on the day of a protest march against the imminent invasion of Iraq. It extends the theme of *Black Dogs* to life in the twenty-first century, where terrorism and violence result in uncontrollable fear and existential vertigo: "He's weak and ignorant, scared of the way consequences of an action leap away from your control and breed new events, new consequences, until you're led to a place you never dreamed of and would never choose."[26]

Saturday depicts the endgame for preoccupations that go back to the 1960s, when many writers felt they were living in a period that was becoming ever more fantastic and no longer amenable to realist modes of representation. Public life seemed to be increasingly dominated by neocolonialist wars, political assassinations, the nuclear arms race, the exacerbation of violence, and the transformation of politics into spectacle. The proliferation of communications industries presaged the advent of a world so saturated by second-order images that distinctions between appearance and reality ceased to have meaning. When J. G. Ballard claimed that life was so overladen by "fictions of every kind – mass-merchandizing, advertising, politics conducted as a branch of advertising, the pre-empting of any original response to experience by the television screen" that one should "assume that it is a complete fiction," he voiced an extreme, but by no means unrepresentative, view.[27]

It was in this context that Lessing, Ballard, and Moorcock emerged. A sense of encroaching madness and paranoia suffuses their work of the 1960s and 1970s, a fear that contemporary socio-political life is a moronic inferno whose only explanations can be conspiracy theories, hidden cultural logics, or an insane will-to-death. If rational explanations made no sense and an ever more fractured and violent world routinely exceeded the bounds of fantasy, then realist modes of representation were inadequate to the task of rendering everyday existence truthfully. In Lessing's *The Golden Notebook* (1962) breakdown and fragmentation are overriding phenomena, and the text implodes from within. The protagonist's sense of personal incoherence, political dislocation, cultural collapse, sexual confusion, and ubiquitous violence make her a symptomatic figure. The novel consists of separate diaries, each addressing a different aspect of her life. The ensuing fracture of form attests Anna Wulf's inability to order her experience into a coherent linear narrative. Violence (psychological, social, sexual, political, gendered) is the truth of the period in this text, but it constitutes an apocalyptic sublime that is unrepresentable in traditional forms. Because epistemological uncertainty saturates all modes of representation in *The Golden Notebook*, imaginative literature also is under suspicion.

The Golden Notebook registers the difficulty of evoking cultural collapse. It does so by experimenting at the level of theme and *structure* rather than of *style*. There are parallels here with Moorcock and Ballard. Those writers were associated with the avant-garde *New Worlds* science fiction magazine in which they explored compressed narrative forms that eschewed stylistic experimentation in favor of alterations to the overall shape of fictional narrative. Moorcock's Cornelius quartet – *The Final Programme* (1965), *A Cure For Cancer* (1968), *The English Assassin* (1972), and *The Condition of Muzak* (1977) – uses brief chapters, some of them single paragraphs, which function like half-page stories. The novels borrow from contemporary culture (brochure blurbs; adverts; pop songs; cartoons; captions; posters; newspaper headlines) and provide almost no contextual information, plunging the reader into Moorcock's "multiverse," in which possible alternative realms of life coexist. Ballard, in turn, had no interest in fabricating a unique style for individual sentences (Conrad's style provides a relevant contrast), because he saw Conrad's kind of avant-gardism as a distraction. Ballard's concern is with *elision* (deleting narrative cues to create greater intensity) and *juxtaposition* (arranging paragraphs so that they reflect each other imagistically, or combining repetition and difference in the manner of a filmstrip's sequence of images). Ballard strips the mechanics of writing to a minimum, producing a jagged textuality in which recycled tropes give rise to visionary revelations of the hidden truths of social life.

Ballard's *The Atrocity Exhibition* (1970) and *Crash* (1973) and Moorcock's Cornelius series evoke contemporary reality, yet attempt to resist its logics. The Cornelius books depict a dystopia wherein the population leads benumbed lives saturated by propaganda, while the protagonist desires a multiverse, where all "layers of existence [are] seen at once" so that it will be possible to destroy a "normality" that requires suppression of freedom and imagination.[28] In *A Cure For Cancer* Cornelius tries to unleash the *energeia* of randomness, what he calls the "equilibrium of anarchy" (p. 198), because he wants to "channel energy – re-direct it – re-form it" (p. 202) in order to open reality to multiple new possibilities. *The Atrocity Exhibition*, in turn, is preeminently concerned with politics, nuclear war, technology, violence, and sexuality, creating a fragmented but interlocking narrative in which scientific instrumentalism erodes subjectivity and destroys affect. *Crash* explores the erotics of the automobile, treating automobile accidents as a quintessential twentieth-century "spectacle," out of which emerges a machine-body complex whose "acts and emotions" are "ciphers searching for their meaning among the hard, chromium furniture of [their] minds" (p. 180). The search expresses a death-drive, annealing technology and commodity fetishism into a pornography of sexualized violence.

I have suggested that the catchall term "postmodernism" is of limited usefulness as a classificatory category when we are studying British fiction. That is partly because it is an imprecise term and partly because the evaluative language in which it was initially theorized continues unhelpfully to cling to it. In the British cultural context postmodernism was for a long time associated with American fiction and was treated with suspicion, if not disdain. Modernism might have threatened to dissolve a shared sense of public reality into subjective accounts of it, but postmodernism seemed to want to jettison personal vision altogether, turning the cognizing subject into a mere *effect* of linguistic systems through which he or she was spoken. Two paths opened up for novelists who saw realism as epistemologically naïve, socially narrow, and aesthetically limited. One direction led to intensely experimental novels that use a panoply of metafictional techniques to explore how language and narrative manipulate us; another direction led to a middle ground between social mimesis and linguistic self-consciousness in work that combined "realism" with "experiment." The differences between novelists *within* each of these broad categories are as important as those we might identify *across* them.

That said, explicitly antirealist postmodernist novelists rejected what might be termed a "liberal" response to life and art because they thought it failed sufficiently to address either the nature of postwar society or the consequences of modernism's rebellion against all conventions. For Brooke-Rose, Brophy, Burns, and Johnson there could be no return to realism, however self-reflexive, because they regarded it as a defunct mode, its representational purpose superseded by film, and its aesthetic viability destroyed by modernism. Notwithstanding differences among them, their novels belong to a clear modernist lineage – their links to Joyce, Dada, Surrealism, and Beckett are especially strong. Other, less radical "postmodern" novelists aimed to reinterpret contemporary reality in ways that extended the boundaries of the genre; they enlisted narrative in order to highlight problematic aspects of representation. Although few of them were political radicals, their commitment to what we might call "experimental realism" suggests an affinity with Brecht's claim that if aesthetic realism were to address altered social realities, then it had to change, had to be "wide and political, sovereign over all conventions."[29] This suggests in turn that for many British novelists postmodernist techniques represented a kind of hyperrealism that was more pertinent to their perception of the contemporary world than any earlier varieties of realism. Still other postmodern novelists embraced the imaginative resources of literary modes that bypassed the realism/antirealism issue altogether: fantasy, gothic, fabulation, myth, carnival. Discussion of British fiction needs to acknowledge the numerous fictional trajectories and aesthetic/political allegiances in play in the postwar period. To classify the novels discussed here as "postmodernist" serves a useful heuristic purpose; but their range and complexity ensures that they will always exceed such categorizations.

NOTES

1 Alan Wilde, *Horizons of Assent: Modernism, Postmodernism, and the Ironic Imagination* (Baltimore and London: Johns Hopkins University Press, 1981), p. 11.
2 Jean-François Lyotard, *The Postmodern Condition: A Report on Knowledge*, trans. Geoff Bennington and Brian Massumi (Manchester: Manchester University Press, 1984), p. 81.
3 Muriel Spark, *The Comforters* (London: Penguin, 1987), p. 181.
4 Muriel Spark, *The Ballad of Peckham Rye* (Harmondsworth: Penguin, 1974), p. 143.
5 Patricia Waugh, "The Woman Writer and the Continuities of Feminism", *A Concise Companion to Contemporary British Fiction*, ed. James F. English (Oxford: Blackwell, 2006), pp. 188–208, 206.
6 Angela Carter, "The Language of Sisterhood," *The State of the Language*, eds. Leonard Michaels and Christopher Ricks (Berkeley and Los Angeles: California University Press, 1980), p. 226; Angela Carter, *The Passion of New Eve* (London: Virago, 1977), p. 6.
7 Angela Carter, *Nights at the Circus* (London: Picador, 1985), p. 286.
8 Emma Tennant, *The Bad Sister* (London: Faber and Faber, 1989), pp. 208, 96.

9 Malcolm Bradbury, ed., *The Novel Today: Contemporary Writers on Modern Fiction* (London: Fontana, 1990), p. 153.

10 Samuel Beckett, *Three Novels* (New York: Grove Press, 1965), p. 398.

11 B. S. Johnson, *Albert Angelo* (New York: New Directions, 1987), pp. 163, 167.

12 Christine Brooke-Rose, "Introduction" to Brigid Brophy, *In Transit: An Heroi-Cyclic Novel* (Chicago: Dalkey Archive, 2002), p. iv.

13 Randall Stevenson, "Postmodernism and Contemporary Fiction in Britain," *Postmodernism and Contemporary Fiction*, ed. Edmund J. Smyth (London: B. T. Batsford, 1991), p. 31.

14 Heide Ziegler and Christopher Bigsby, eds., *The Radical Imagination and the Liberal Tradition: Interviews With Novelists* (London: Junction, 1982), pp. 121, 124; John Haffenden, *Novelists in Interview* (London: Methuen, 1985), pp. 30, 31; David Lodge, *The Modes of Modern Writing: Metaphor, Metonymy, and the Typology of Modern Literature* (Ithaca: Cornell University Press, 1977), p. 46.

15 John Fowles, *Mantissa* (London: Triad/Panther, 1984), pp. 182, 117.

16 Iris Murdoch, *The Black Prince* (Harmondsworth: Penguin, 1973), p. 199.

17 David Lodge, *The British Museum Is Falling Down* (Harmondsworth: Penguin, 1986), p. 32.

18 Peter Ackroyd, *Chatterton* (London: Abacus, 1988), p. 70.

19 Iain Sinclair, *White Chappell, Scarlet Tracings* (Harmondsworth: Penguin, 2004), p. 48; Iain Sinclair, *Lights Out for The Territory* (London: Granta, 1998), p. 1.

20 Julian Barnes, *A History of the World in 10½ Chapters* (New York: Alfred A. Knopf, 1989), p. 240.

21 Linda Hutcheon, *A Poetics of Postmodernism: History, Theory, Fiction* (London: Routledge, 1988), p. 20.

22 John Berger, *G* (London: Chatto & Windus, 1985), p. 133.

23 Graham Swift, *Waterland* (London: Pan, 1984), p. 53.

24 Ian McEwan, "The State of Fiction: A Symposium," *New Review* 5: 1 (Summer 1978) 14–76, 51.

25 Ian McEwan, *Black Dogs* (London: Vintage, 1998), pp. 172, 174.

26 Ian McEwan, *Saturday* (London: Vintage, 2006), p. 277.

27 J. G. Ballard, "Introduction" to *Crash* (London: Vintage, 1975), no pagination.

28 Michael Moorcock, *A Cure for Cancer* (Glasgow: Fontana/Collins, 1979), p. 62.

29 Bertolt Brecht, "Brecht Against Lukács," *Aesthetics and Politics: Debates Between Bloch, Lukács, Brecht, Benjamin, Adorno*, ed. Ronald Taylor (London: Verso, 1980), p. 82.

14

ALLAN HEPBURN

Detectives and spies

British detective fiction and spy fiction, descended from nineteenth-century adventure narratives, come of age in the twentieth century. Both emphasize action over character, and coincidence over probability; both qualify as thrillers. But despite their similarities, detective and spy genres have asymmetrical relations to each other. To view them as equal and merely conventional forms of mass-market entertainment obscures their differing subjects, narrative structures, and ideological values.

The subject matter of each genre is quite distinct. Detective fiction foregrounds antagonisms that inevitably concern bloodlines and inheritance within the UK. Spy fiction focuses on affairs of state between Britain and other nations. Detective narratives, unthinkable without a corpse, presume the finality of death as a meaningful event. In spy fiction violent deaths of characters are incidental to international conflict, and not mysterious in that context. Plots and plans vary widely in the two genres. A murderer in detective fiction acts according to a planned sequence of steps, but actions (including murder) in spy fiction arise from changing global circumstances. Detectives work alongside the police, drawing on their services, while showing superior ratiocinative ability. Spies, in contrast, subordinate themselves to directives from handlers in a central bureaucratic agency. Such subordination tempts spies to make renegade decisions. A spy defying orders in John le Carré's *The Perfect Spy* (1986) sums up quandaries in the genre thus: "Sometimes our actions are questions, not answers."[1]

Differences between spy and detective fiction can be stated axiomatically. A detective deduces; a spy surmises. A detective explains; a spy interprets. A detective exposes; a spy vanishes. A detective solves; a spy betrays. A detective is almost never culpable; a spy is never fully innocent. Spy fiction relies on codes; detective fiction relies on clues. Spy fiction abides by a principle that nothing is ever what it appears to be: a word might be a cipher, or a trusted employee might be a mole. In detective fiction suspicion temporarily alights on several people, but only the guilty dissimulate and are consequently unmasked. Each genre takes a stance on the nature of crime and justice. Both spy and detective fiction perpetuate ideas about guilt; but in spy fiction guilt derives from violations of national security, whereas in detective fiction guilt derives from violations of individual property and bodies.

Antecedents for twentieth-century detectives can be traced to Inspector Bucket in Charles Dickens's *Bleak House* (1853) and to Sergeant Cuff in Wilkie Collins's *The Moonstone* (1868), which T. S. Eliot called "The first, the longest, and the best of modern English detective novels."[2] More immediate precursors include Rider Haggard's *King Solomon's Mines* (1885), about a quest for diamonds in the African interior, and Robert Louis Stevenson's *Treasure Island* (1883), about high seas pirates and recovery of lost treasure. The adventure narrative, epitomized by Collins's, Haggard's, and Stevenson's novels, traces a movement from England to remote geographic locations, followed by repatriation. Maps routinely appear in adventure fiction, and subsequently in spy fiction, as a metaphor for territorialization and reconnaissance. In *Treasure Island* the adolescent protagonist sails to a remote island and recovers buried coins in multiple national currencies. Although the loot in this pirate's stash has international origins, the entire treasure is shipped to England. Colonial adventure stories prepare for the detective narrative by confirming British imperial power: treasure found abroad, irrespective of its owners, belongs to the empire.

Adventure shapes Sir Arthur Conan Doyle's Sherlock Holmes tales. Even though Holmes never leaves England in *The Hound of the Baskervilles* (1902), the narrative implies a going forth and return characteristic of imperial romance. Several generations of Baskerville men live abroad. Sir Charles Baskerville profits from South African speculation; his successor, Sir Henry, farms successfully in Canada. Yet they remain oriented toward the family estate in Devon, and return to it when they come into their inheritance. They spend their money in England either on charitable causes or on modernizing Baskerville Hall. As Sir Henry bluntly puts it, "House, land, and dollars must go together."[3] Meanwhile, Sir Charles's criminal younger brother, adventuring in Latin America where he marries a Costa Rican, has fathered a wicked son, who attempts to usurp the Baskerville inheritance by reviving a legend – to cover up his murderous designs – that a mysterious man-killing hound lives within striking distance of Baskerville Hall. The tangle of offshore interests in *The Hound of the Baskervilles* suggests that South Africa and Canada dutifully remit money to glorify Britain, whereas Central America harbors criminals who try to disrupt and sequester the remittance. The death of Sir Charles Baskerville, which instigates Sherlock Holmes's investigation, stands as a cipher for legitimate and illegitimate inheritance. By solving the mystery of the hound, Holmes consolidates the rightness and justice of one's duty to a securely bounded British national homeland.

John Buchan solders adventure narrative to problems of national security in *The Thirty-Nine Steps* (1915). Richard Hannay, the wily protagonist, makes a pile of money as a mining engineer in South Africa. Relocated to London and bored, he finds himself swept up in an international conspiracy to invade Britain. Buchan also draws on William Le Queux's popular invasion novels, such as *Spies of the Kaiser* (1909), in which Germans infiltrate bastions of British power. Buchan thought of international conflict and diplomacy as a game, albeit a game with enormous stakes. In *Kim* (1901) Rudyard Kipling refers to diplomatic maneuvering between Russia and Britain in Central Asia as "the Great Game."[4] Hannay, who outfoxes enemies in *The Thirty-Nine Steps* and its sequels, *Greenmantle* (1916), *Mr. Standfast* (1919), and *The Three Hostages* (1924), thinks of his adventures as "a crazy game."[5] If these adventures are games, they resemble hide-and-seek, for Hannay, on the run, uses disguises and borrowed identities to baffle opponents.

By calling his adventures a game, Hannay preserves his amateur status. Erskine Childers's *The Riddle of the Sands* (1903) also features two amateurs who, sailing among the Frisian Islands in the North Sea, accidentally uncover an invasion plot fostered by a former British naval officer who stockpiles armaments for an attack on the country he once served. In both *The Thirty-Nine Steps* and *The Riddle of the Sands*, amateur spies who also are spy-catchers break codes and penetrate conspiracies. In each instance, the protagonists venture outside the law to preserve the nation, for they have no help from the police or other legitimate forces. Hannay, himself pursued by the police, takes the law into his own hands. Representation of shifting relations between individuals and law is typical in spy narratives. The spy stands in opposition to law to prove that law inadequately protects national interests. He therefore embodies individual responsibility as a supralegal principle. His position outside the law isolates him, and makes cunning his sole resource.

The spy and detective use personal intelligence for different ends: the spy, to unmask state enemies; the detective, to unmask murderers. Agatha Christie's serial protagonists, professional detective Hercule Poirot and amateur detective Miss Marple, work by rational deduction based on common sense. The plot of Christie's *The Body in the Library* (1942) turns on identifying the corpse of a young woman that appears in the library of a movie producer in a coastal town. In order to gain psychological insight, Miss Marple "link[s] up trivial village happenings with graver problems in such a way as to throw light upon the latter."[6] Her deductive light reveals, in regard to the graver problem of Ruby Keene's corpse, that the dead body is really someone else's. Ragged fingernails and buckteeth confirm that one body can never replace another. A fundamental law of British detective fiction is that a body's singular identity can always be determined.

The inevitable determination of identity has implications for an inheritance plot in *The Body in the Library*. Wealthy Conway Jefferson has lost his wife and children in a plane crash. He has survived the crash, but his legs have been amputated. He cannot do much in the "active line" (p. 212), as one police superintendent puts it. Jefferson's non-sexual character impedes the conventional elements of detective story plotting: he has no blood relatives to whom he can leave his fortune because he cannot father more children. Miss Marple too remains outside an economy of reproduction; blushing over references to sex, she is a consummate spinster. But Miss Marple's childlessness enables her sleuthing, for family sentiment does not cloud her judgment. In contrast to Miss Marple, other characters in *The Body in the Library* who are without families or who renounce their families fall under suspicion: without family ties they are likely to confabulate plots to marry into money. Miss Marple's lack of family leads her to donate money to an orphanage. That she does so is charitable; but within the logic of detective fiction, orphans might be criminals in the making.

Although in detective fiction orphans are likely to become felons, crime in the genre also originates from moral turpitude inside the English family. Miss Marple condemns "some women [who] have a curious idea that crimes committed for the sake of their offspring are almost morally justified" (p. 212). Having "no blood relations in this case" (p. 155) allows Miss Marple better to perceive other people's matrimonial or family-oriented alliances (especially when they are hidden) as motives for murder. Jefferson's daughter-in-law and son-in-law remain with him in a state of indefinite mourning for their spouses. They both become suspect because of their potential for taking over the role of blood relations. And indeed, once the murder mystery is solved, Jefferson gives his daughter-in-law £10,000 and promises to leave Peter, her son by a prior marriage, the residue of his estate. Jefferson thereby authorizes a lineage that approximates biological family. In the absence of kinship ties, inheritance legitimates Peter and creates new social bonds. Like the Sherlock Holmes narratives, Agatha Christie's story works towards an affirmation of restored fortunes and a clarifying renewal of British bloodlines.

Definitions of what is properly British in terms of culture rather than family are consolidated in Dorothy Sayers's novels that feature detective Lord Peter Wimsey. At the beginning of *Whose Body?* (1923), Lord Peter, who collects incunabulae and who has authored a monograph about book collecting, is heading to a book sale. He has his heart set on a Caxton folio and a 1493 copy of *The Golden Legend*. Sayers uses Wimsey's literacy to promote cultural legacies that go along with her ideas about what constitutes being English. In *The Nine Tailors* (1934) bell-ringing exemplifies Sayers's interest in historical heritage as a defining national and parish patrimony. Lord Peter, researching bells at Fenchurch St. Paul parish, notes that they were cast to commemorate persons and events in a very long history: 1380, 1559, 1614, 1666, 1887, and other dates. Although Lord Peter has no credentials as a detective, his "hobby of criminal investigation"[7] draws on his ability to do research and to lead his investigations towards rational conclusions. Sayers draws together her cultural interests in books, book history, and architecture in *Gaudy Night* (1935). Set in Oxford at a fictitious women's college, *Gaudy Night* extols the beauty of buildings and books. Harriet Vane, a mystery writer attending her tenth class reunion, constantly notices reading material. Pursuing an investigation, she locks herself into the new college library, and admires its many bays and its 10 foot-high shelving. Harriet conjectures that an as yet empty gallery will afford space for more books in the future. To help solve the mystery in *Gaudy Night*, where crime results from anti-feminist assaults on the women's college, Harriet calls in her bibliophile lover, Lord Peter. The novel concludes with Lord Peter's proposal of marriage, which Harriet accepts. Their honeymoon, recorded in *Busman's Holiday* (1937), the last of the Wimsey and Vane novels, is taken up with solving the mystery of a blackmailer's death. The arc of Lord Peter's career inscribes him within matrimony as a proof of his British identity, already manifest in his Eton and Oxford education, his bookishness, and his military service in the Great War.

Picking up on Sayers's identification of culture as a national inheritance, Michael Innes's *Hamlet, Revenge!* (1937) begins at a live performance of Shakespeare's play. At the point in the performance when Hamlet confronts his mother Gertrude in her private chamber, a pistol shot resounds in the theatre. The prime minister explains to Appleby, the detective on the case, that "the Lord Chancellor's been shot. At Scamnum Court, playing at *Hamlet* apparently – a strange play, Mr. Appleby, a strange atmosphere about it."[8] In effect *Hamlet*, as understood by the prime minister and Appleby, is a detective fiction about a dead king. *Hamlet, Revenge!* draws upon Shakespearean drama as a common cultural legacy in which murder mystery is central to a definition of what it means to be British.

In a like manner Josephine Tey's *The Daughter of Time* (1951) reworks the inheritance plot of detective fiction in terms of Plantagenet and Tudor royal history. A family tree of English kings and queens is required to decipher usurpations of inheritance and kingship, for in this case the murder mystery is whether Richard III killed his two nephews to secure the throne. This historic crime preoccupies policeman Alan Grant while he recovers from a broken leg. Bored by bed rest, he takes to gazing at a portrait of Richard III, whose mild and wise countenance does not square with his reputation as a killer. Grant requests books about Richard III from an actress friend; and he deputes a young American historian to investigate the centuries-old case at the British Library. Grant concludes from his deliberations that history is partly police work; the historian proceeds (or should proceed, Grant thinks) along the lines of a police inquest, especially to determine who benefits from a crime.

Tey treats English history as a family drama. Although Richard III appears to proclaim his nephews illegitimate in order to secure his ascent to the English throne, Grant, weighing the evidence, determines that the first Tudor king, Henry VII, who had no legitimate claim at all, used the murder mystery to vilify Richard after his death and systematically to eliminate all rivals. Whereas Richard III had treated his enemies with respect – he restored the right of succession to the children of Hastings, his sworn foe – Henry VII faces the discontent of Englishmen who "hankered after the legitimate line again."[9] Meditating on the demise of families, including the Yorks and Plantagenets, *The Daughter of Time* presents Edward VI and Richard III as "unique in their Englishness" (p. 53) because they are implicated in plots of genealogical conflict. The disruption in royal families is a model for usurpations and continuities in the common heritage of being English.

W. H. Auden, analyzing the moral and social implications of detective fiction, claims that the genre requires "A closed society so that the possibility of an outside murderer (and hence of the society being totally innocent) is excluded; and a closely related society so that all its members are potentially suspect."[10] The perfect closed society, Auden says, is comprised of "blood relations" (pp. 149–50). The murderer works within the closed society and knows its members' foibles. Auden implies that individual deviance arises from a moral defect that is inevitable in the closed society: if society is never totally innocent, everyone becomes suspect. British detective fiction figures the closed society as a family first, a village second, and a nation third. Citizenship in those constituencies overlaps; therefore, crime inside the family is a crime against the village and the nation, on the grounds that blood relations determine nationalism and nationality.

Auden's idea that in detective fiction blood determines belonging is echoed in P. D. James's novel *Innocent Blood* (1980). Philippa Palfrey, a bright and headstrong girl about to matriculate at Cambridge, is an adopted daughter of a sociologist and his wife. Philippa insists on her legal right to know the identity of her biological father and mother. Entertaining fantasies of being the illegitimate daughter of an earl, Philippa visits the squalid house where she was born. She learns from a person who lives next door that her father was sent to Wandsworth Prison. The neighbour blurts out, " 'Where else would he be, fucking murderer? He raped that kid, and then he and his missus strangled her. What's he to do with you then?' " (p. 30). The criminal father is long since dead, but Philippa thinks that her murderous mother, about to be released from jail, can help to explain who she is. Although primary detection in *Innocent Blood* concerns revelation of identity through biological parents, a secondary and more ambiguous detection concerns a criminal taint of blood that passes from parents to children. If Philippa has inherited her parents' predispositions, she is prone to violent crime. Such genealogical obsessions in twentieth-century British detective fiction attest to a crisis of inheritance that affects orphans and blood relatives alike. Filled with an adoptee's pride, Philippa cannot live down her heritage. She embodies both legitimate and illegitimate British identity, through her upper-middle-class adoptive parents and her homicidal biological parents.

Blood is a proof of legitimacy. In the 1920s paternity was confirmed through blood tests for the first time. Karl Landsteiner, who won the Nobel Prize in 1930 for his research into blood types and agglutination, found that "blood types moved from one generation to the next by simple Mendelian inheritance, in which some genes dominate over others. In blood types the genes for groups A and B dominate over O, producing certain predictable patterns."[11] Thus blood confirms genealogical descent, for better or worse. With less scientific rigor, detective fiction insinuates that legitimacy and criminality course through characters' veins. In the first of the Holmes mysteries, *A Study in Scarlet* (1887), the letters RACHE are scrawled in blood on a wall at the site of a murder. By happenstance Holmes has been looking for an infallible test for the presence of blood, namely a "re-agent of Haemoglobin," which he thinks will be "the most practical medico-legal discovery for years."[12] Holmes deduces from footprints and the bloody writing on the wall that the killer in *A Study in Scarlet* stood "more than six feet in height, was in the prime of life, had small feet for his height, wore coarse, square-toed boots" (p. 30), was of foreign nationality, and had long fingernails. Holmes also speculates that the criminal might be a bit pale from loss of blood. Blood will out.

Ruth Rendell's *Going Wrong* (1990) revises the detective genre by associating bloodlines with a priori guilt and no murder. An Irish orphan, Guy Curran runs a protection racket and sells drugs as a teenager. As an adult he diversifies into other businesses (such as selling kitsch paintings) to make himself respectable. He flaunts his money to impress Leonora Chisholm, with whom he had a brief adolescent romance. But Leonora's family despise

Guy. They reject him as an "Irish yob" and as "a common piece of rubbish from a council house, from the worst part of London."[13] Enraged at being kept out of Leonora's life by her kin, Guy wonders, "'Did they know anyone who wasn't family?'" (p. 220). With its emphasis on the closed ranks of family, *Going Wrong* creates sympathy for Guy through allusions to Emily Brontë's *Wuthering Heights*. The adolescent Leonora, parodying Cathy's declaration in Brontë, had declared, "I *am* you. I am Guy and he's me" (p. 231). Leonora explains years later that studying *Wuthering Heights* for her O-level exams prompted her to make such a melodramatic declaration. Guy persists in believing in its authenticity. "I *am* Leonora," he says. "We were one person" (pp. 231, 242). However paranoid Guy might be, his status as an orphan with an Irish background and a petty criminal past excludes him from the elementary structures of kinship. Whereas Leonora can claim English literature as a heritage, Guy's romantic grandiosity cannot breach the defences that exclude him from marriage with Leonora. Guy's past forbids him from ever being accepted as English and properly middle class, in the same way that swarthy Heathcliff, the quondam gypsy brat, could never pass for English. *Going Wrong* represents Guy as guilty because of who he is, rather than for what he does. Although he commits only minor crimes, everyone treats him as if he were a first-degree murderer.

Tey, James, and Rendell all assume that the detective novel abides by conventions. In this regard British detective fiction in the second half of the twentieth century reflects on its legacies – generic, national, and cultural. Julian Symons's *A Three-Pipe Problem* (1975), which takes its title from a passage in *The Adventures of Sherlock Holmes*, speculates on the preservation of British heritage within a post-imperial setting. In Symons's novel, actor Sheridan Haynes plays Sherlock Holmes in a popular television series; the resemblance between their names is not a coincidence. Although the TV production team worries that a series of Holmes mysteries might appear "uproariously old-fashioned,"[14] the program, which achieves high viewer ratings, answers an essential desire to promote British heritage, even when that heritage has its origins in fiction. Haynes fancies himself a sleuth on the model of Holmes, and attempts to solve a series of murders called the "Karate Killings." In *A Three-Pipe Problem* British heritage specifically means a racial identity. One criminal articulates British identity as if it were under siege by immigrants: "This country's getting crowded out with foreigners . . . Pakis, blacks, yids. Some you can tell, but the worst are the ones you can't, the ones that look just like you and me" (p. 104). The "worst" deviance does not manifest itself in bodily markers. Other victims of "Karate Killings" include a gay man and a prostitute, whose deviance has to be detected through social behavior because it is not immediately visible or palpable. Characters in Symons's novel express rage against all forms of identity that undermine so-called racial purity. Race refracts further into urban and suburban identities. Sheridan Haynes's wife loathes central London and she wonders, "Why didn't everybody want to live comfortably in suburbs like Wimbledon?" (p. 63). *A Three-Pipe Problem* confirms conservative, middle-class, suburban, white identity as another national heritage.

Spy fiction offers a different understanding of race and nation than does detective fiction. Working with elements of both detective and spy fiction, especially in his 1930s thrillers, Graham Greene shows that individuals cannot be separated from their agonistic relations with lovers, religion, politics, race, and nationalism. To begin with, pursuit for its own sake is an existential fact in Greene. In *Brighton Rock* (1938), Ida Arnold pursues a teenage hoodlum not because she is a detective, but because she cannot relent until she satisfies her curiosity about him: "The hunt was what mattered."[15] On the lam in *A Gun for Sale* (1936), the criminal Raven tries to track down a person who double-crossed him. The police chase Raven while Raven chases the man who paid him with phoney money. Simultaneously a hunting avenger and a hunted criminal, Raven sums up the complexity of an identity that is always guilty and always justified. In all of these novels, detection begins in innate or professional curiosity, but ends in the death of the hunted person.

That law holds true when Greene's characters take it upon themselves to solve, or to intervene in, cases that are political as well as criminal. Perhaps more than any other of the novelists discussed in this chapter, Graham Greene dramatizes antagonisms that constitute political identity. In *Stamboul Train* (1932) Mabel Warren, a reporter based in Cologne, hunts down a Communist wanted on a trumped-up charge of perjury. Dr. Czinner is fleeing Europe on the Orient Express because he fears for his life, but Mabel treats him with contempt for being in hiding. Czinner wants to help the working poor in Belgrade once he arrives there; Mabel, consumed by self-righteous journalistic rage, insists on exposing him in a front-page news item. In *The Third Man* (1949) a writer named Rollo Martins turns up in postwar Vienna, which is divided into military quadrants and governed by Allied forces. Martins hopes to attend the funeral of his boyhood friend Harry Lime; he discovers that Lime is still alive and is hiding underground because he has used the black market to sell adulterated, deadly doses of penicillin to innocent victims who desperately need the drug. Turning himself into an arbiter of justice, Martins chases Lime through the sewers of Vienna and kills him. In Greene's political allegories, every individual carries within him political responsibility and its opposite, a human instinct to hide from the law.

Greene configures British identity in relation to Europe and the rest of the world. In this regard he elaborates on espionage novels by Joseph Conrad, whose work demonstrates the confluence of modernism with detective fiction and with international subject matter in novels of intrigue. In Conrad's *The Secret Agent* (1909) spies, anarchists, terrorists, foreign diplomats, police inspectors, and elected government representatives, all congregating in London, exert pressure to make themselves politically viable. A foreign embassy official instigates a plot to commit an outrage against British institutions. Adolph Verloc, a secret agent working under orders from the embassy, plans to bomb the Greenwich Observatory. His plan goes awry when Stevie, Verloc's mentally handicapped brother-in-law whom Verloc makes an unwitting accomplice, trips while carrying a pail of dynamite and blows himself up. Verloc probably obtains the explosive from a character called the Professor, who perfects a bomb-detonating device that he carries on his person at all times. Although the Professor imagines that he could annihilate any number of people were he to explode his bomb, he has ultimately no political efficacy. His death would change nothing, just as Stevie's death changes nothing. Conrad treats political action by both conservative autocratic forces and radical terrorist-anarchism as tantamount to the same thing. No catastrophe can alter British indifference to political ideals or political change; the class system remains intact and impervious to revolution. Winnie, Adolph's wife, enshrines British stolidness. She feels "profoundly that things do not stand much looking into."[16] When Winnie discovers that her husband is responsible for her brother's death, she fatally stabs Verloc. Conrad thus combines an espionage plot with a detective murder plot. Winnie's killing of Verloc parodically enacts the bloodline convention, because Winnie has married Verloc in order to secure continuity for her humble family line.

Conrad's subsequent novel, *Under Western Eyes* (1911), meditates on political allegiance as a mode of recruitment. If detectives feel compelled to solve murders because of a primal curiosity, spies more often than not are recruited to clandestine activity by being in the wrong place at the wrong time. In *Under Western Eyes* the terrorist Victor Haldin, after assassinating the head of the Russian Repressive Commission, arbitrarily takes refuge in the room of a fellow university student, Razumov. Outraged by this presumptuousness, Razumov betrays Haldin to the police. The police in turn recruit Razumov, who voices his hatred of revolution to them, as a counterterrorist spy. Once recruited, Razumov, who only wants to be left alone, is sent to Geneva to infiltrate a terrorist revolutionary cell. He compromises his revolutionary credentials, however, when he meets Haldin's sister in Switzerland and falls in love with her. Looking like her brother, she constantly reminds Razumov of his own treachery. His guilty conscience leads him to denounce himself to the revolutionaries, who brutally assault him and burst his eardrums. In *Under Western Eyes* the spy represents an inevitable politicization of individual lives and an impossibility of making extreme political positions compatible.

Razumov had aimed to win a gold medal at the university for his cleverness and assiduity. His transition from student to spy evokes the role of intelligence in political life. A surprising number of spies in fiction are professors or, at a minimum, have bookish tendencies. Charles Latimer in Eric Ambler's *The Mask of Dimitrios* (1939; US title, *A Coffin for Dimitrios*), a thriller about Balkan politics, teaches "political economy at a minor English university."[17] Smiley, the master of a spy ring in John le Carré's novels, has a comprehensive knowledge of seventeenth-century German literature and can quote it with ease. Jim, a spy lying low in *Tinker Tailor Soldier Spy* (1974), takes a job teaching at a boys' school; at night, he reads stories by John Buchan to help the students fall asleep.

Learned spies work out complex problems abstractly. Hence spy fiction often resorts to metaphors of mathematics as an analogue to deciphering codes. In *Tinker Tailor Soldier Spy* one spy is a "better performer" than another because he is "better at the arithmetic."[18] Smiley, debriefing an unreliable agent, hears her commentary with doubt: "to Smiley's tidy mind her speculations, in terms of the acceptable arithmetic of intelligence, seemed even wilder than before." Documents in the archives at the spy headquarters in *Tinker Tailor Soldier Spy* rationalize defence and brinkmanship, which Smiley thinks of as "the higher mathematics of the balance of terror" (pp. 109, 139). Whereas reason in detective fiction applies to a probability of guilt, in espionage fiction arithmetic eliminates improbability and counteracts terror.

In Ian Fleming's *Casino Royale* (1953) James Bond plays with probability at the casino. His opponent, whose name means "number" in French, enacts a mathematical function within Cold War antagonism. As do most spy novels, *Casino Royale* traffics in codes. The title of Buchan's *The Thirty-Nine Steps* is a code that, once broken, allows Hannay to grasp the specifics of the international "Black Stone" conspiracy. Not only is James Bond coded as 007, but he works for M and Q, encrypted names for members of an espionage hierarchy. Bond is embedded in alphabetical and numerical sequences. Because 007 has a replaceable position within the spy network – he could be superseded by 008 or 009 – he signifies iterability; he designates a function rather than a character. He has a job to do, and if he does not fulfil it, another agent will take over. Someone tells Bond in *Casino Royale*, "'don't let me down and become human yourself. We would lose such a wonderful machine.'"[19]

In le Carré's *The Spy Who Came in from the Cold* (1963), a tough-guy spy, Leamas, is also known on his national identity card as "PRT stroke L 580003 stroke one."[20] Like Bond, Leamas protects national security in the Cold War by subordinating his identity to Her Majesty's service. He is a number as much as he is a human being. Despite his existence as a cipher, nothing about Leamas or the spy agency for which he works can be taken as straightforward or self-identical. The "cold" in *The Spy Who Came in from the Cold* refers to Soviet bloc territory that a mole penetrates without having contact with his handlers. The unmonitored Leamas works according to intuition and probability. He operates under pseudonyms, "Herr Thomas," "Amies," and "Robert Lang." To earn the trust of Soviet agents, Leamas pretends to be disaffected with British intelligence; he takes to drinking, starts rows, goes to prison, and defects to East Germany. He fakes this entire sequence of actions. On rare occasions, when alone in bed at night, Leamas "allow[s] himself the dangerous luxury of admitting the great lie he lived" (p. 127). Even the title of the novel falsifies truth: neither Leamas nor another double agent comes in from the cold. Leamas dies trying to scale the Berlin Wall as he crosses from the East German sector to West Berlin. Leamas's double agency is instructive about the differences between spy and detective fiction. The spy hides his true nature and develops a talent for disappearing into new identities and foreign countries in order to preserve national security. Whereas spies are experts at disguising political convictions and identities, detectives are experts at unmasking false alibis and impersonations.

In novels published since *The Spy Who Came in from the Cold*, le Carré has turned to Israeli politics, globalization, African revolution, and post-Cold War subjects. Other novelists have turned their attention to the past as a resource for espionage plots. Spy fiction is not exempt from the postmodern turn to historical and "heritage" settings. World War II provides a backdrop for plots of betrayal, traffic in secrets, and infiltration of enemy strongholds. Robert Harris's *Enigma* (1995) is set at Bletchley Park, where codebreakers worked on cracking the German "Enigma" code during the war. Alan Furst's *Blood of Victory* (2002) revisits British struggles to cut off oil supplies from Romania to Germany. Michael Frayn's novel *Spies* (2002) concerns a German spy hiding in a London suburb despite hostilities. These novels owe a debt of imagination to Elizabeth Bowen's *The Heat of the Day* (1949), which tracks the emotional consequences of Stella Rodney's love affair with Nazi sympathizer Robert Kelway, denounced as a spy by a counter-espionage agent.

The persistence of detective and spy fiction across the last century speaks to changing political conditions in Britain. Detective fiction registers a shift in domestic politics from centralized imperialism to post-imperial decentralization, especially under the impact of changing attitudes towards race and class. Against the grain of the shift, a conservative bias in detective fiction is apparent in its championing of legitimacy in terms of cultural and familial inheritance. Spy fiction, on the other hand, registers the changing role of Britain in the world. The figure of the spy particularly illustrates the complexity of political identity that disregards national allegiances. From a nationalist point of view the spy is always treacherous because he crosses boundaries jauntily. From an international perspective the spy challenges the parochialism and protectionism that nationalism breeds. As a writer in Graham Greene's *Stamboul Train* says, " 'the world is a fine adventurous place.' "[21] Different though they be, however, both spy and detective fiction represent continuing attempts to define cultural and political phenomena that go by the name "British."

NOTES

1 John le Carré, *The Perfect Spy* (Harmondsworth: Penguin, 1986), p. 37.
2 T. S. Eliot, "Wilkie Collins and Dickens," *Selected Essays* (New York: Harcourt, 1950), p. 413.
3 Sir Arthur Conan Doyle, *The Complete Novels and Stories*, vol. II (New York: Bantam Books, 1986), p. 47.
4 Rudyard Kipling, *Kim* (Oxford: Oxford University Press, 1987), p. 129.
5 John Buchan, *The Thirty-Nine Steps* (Oxford: Oxford University Press, 1993), p. 57.
6 Agatha Christie, *The Body in the Library* (New York: Signet, 2000), p. 15.
7 Dorothy Sayers, *Whose Body?* (London: Hodder and Stoughton, 2003), p. 3.
8 Michael Innes, *Hamlet, Revenge!* (London: Penguin, 1961), p. 80.
9 Josephine Tey, *The Daughter of Time* (London: Penguin, 1954), p. 43.
10 W. H. Auden, "The Bloody Vicarage," *The Dyer's Hand and Other Essays*, ed. Edward Mendelsohn (New York: Vintage, 1989), p. 149.
11 Douglas P. Starr, *Blood: An Epic History of Medicine and Commerce* (New York: Knopf, 1998), p. 61.
12 Arthur Conan Doyle, *A Study in Scarlet* (London: Penguin, 2001), p. 18.
13 Ruth Rendell, *Going Wrong* (London: Hutchinson, 1990), p. 144.
14 Julian Symons, *A Three-Pipe Problem* (London: Penguin, 1988), p. 38.
15 Graham Greene, *Brighton Rock* (London: Penguin, 1970), p. 151.
16 Joseph Conrad, *The Secret Agent* (Oxford: Oxford University Press, 1988), p. 177.
17 Eric Ambler, *A Coffin for Dimitrios* (New York: Knopf, 1945), p. 4.
18 John le Carré, *Tinker Tailor Soldier Spy* (New York: Penguin, 1989), p. 149.
19 Ian Fleming, *Casino Royale* (London: Hodder and Stoughton, 1988), p. 164.
20 John le Carré, *The Spy Who Came in from the Cold* (London: Penguin, 1989), p. 79.
21 Graham Greene, *Stamboul Train* (London: Penguin, 1975), p. 62.

15

REBECCA L. WALKOWITZ

The post-consensus novel: Minority culture, multiculturalism, and transnational comparison

A Conservative Party election victory in 1979 inaugurated a post-consensus era in British politics and culture. Decisively opposed to a lingering sense of national collectivity, prime minister Margaret Thatcher's new government promised to liberate all of its constituents from unwanted, outdated social solidarities. But the Thatcher ascendancy redefined liberty by identifying it with divisiveness, and paradoxically by stimulating new constraints. The new government encouraged a resurgence of English nativism, xenophobia, and nostalgia for the British Empire's centrality in international affairs. And it tried to contain the impact of immigrant communities on the languages, literatures, and traditions of Britain. While political and economic conservatism flourished, however, the project of cultural containment was largely unsuccessful. In the age of Thatcher, immigrant novelists such as Kazuo Ishiguro, Timothy Mo, Salman Rushdie, and V. S. Naipaul were transforming the Anglophone literary landscape. Their fiction brought international attention to contemporary British writing, consolidated the *Windrush* generation's contribution to the English novel, and ensured that geographies, vernaculars, and political histories of India, China, Japan, and the West Indies would have a lasting prominence in English letters. In 1981 Rushdie's *Midnight's Children* won the Booker Prize, a major international award for English fiction. Since then, the prize (renamed the Man Booker Prize in 2002) has gone to Anglophone novelists who hail from Australia, Ireland, Canada, Nigeria, Sri Lanka, India, South Africa, and Scotland more than it has to writers born in England.

Immigrant novelists established three microgenres that remain dominant: the novel of minority culture; the novel of multiculturalism; and the novel of transnational comparison. Those genres now extend beyond the work of immigrants. In the past two decades a broad range of novelists have focused their attention on Britain's neo-imperial ambitions; on the English legacy of Britain's colonial ventures in Asia, Africa, and South

America; on longstanding tensions between England and national territories of Ireland, Scotland, and Wales; and on vernacular communities organized around sexual, ethnic, or social marginality. The English novel today is the product of many Anglophone cultures. While this chapter is limited to writers who have lived in Britain, it is surely true that fiction's turn to minority culture, multiculturalism, and transnational comparison has been encouraged by global migrations of English-language books, which are translated and circulated faster than ever before, and by the address of those books to multiple niches and networks of readers around the world.

The novel of minority culture

The novel of minority culture includes both Kazuo Ishiguro's *A Pale View of Hills* (1982), about a Japanese woman who migrates from the ruins of Nagasaki to the English countryside, and William McIlvanney's *Strange Loyalties* (1991), about a Scottish detective who tracks the economic and emotional hopelessness of Glasgow while investigating his brother's mysterious death. Ishiguro's novel, his first, takes aim at British stereotypes about Japanese character, at assumptions about the tranquility and desirability of English rural life for Asian immigrants, and at immigrant and native fantasies of pastoral "Englishness" rooted in soil and blood. *Pale View* associates postwar ethnic antagonisms with imperialist attitudes of superiority and self-righteousness. McIlvanney's novel, his third featuring detective Laidlaw, shares *Pale View*'s implied criticism of British imperialism but does so from the perspective of "devolution." Proponents of devolution in the United Kingdom, like those who called for the independence of Britain's colonial territories abroad, argue that centuries of English rule have thwarted the economic growth and cultural autonomy of Scotland, Ireland, and Wales. Devolution's advocates seek decentralization and elected national assemblies, an aim partially achieved in 1998 by the creation of the National Assembly for Wales and by the revival of Scotland's Parliament. While *Strange Loyalties* does not refer to political aspects of devolution, it understands Glasgow's economic and social depression in the context of English domination; and it replaces timeless, pastoral images of Scotland with scrupulously mean portraits of violence and urban poverty. By opening English literary history to British-Japanese memories and perspectives, and by focusing on Glasgow's regional population, Ishiguro and McIlvanny's novels illustrate a new thematic emphasis on the historical fate of political minorities.

Ishiguro, who came to England from Japan at the age of five, criticizes in *Pale View* both postwar English journalists, whose newspapers turn out clichés about Japanese suicide, and interwar Japanese politicians, who promote militarism and suppress political dissent. Ishiguro's double vision is also present in his next novel, *An Artist of the Floating World* (1986), in which American neo-imperialism of the postwar occupation is compared to Japanese expansionism of the 1930s. In *Pale View*, *Artist*, and *The Remains of the Day* (1989), Ishiguro shows powerfully that Cold War rhetoric about nationalist loyalty, regularly animated by Tory politicians in the 1980s, echoes the interwar language of imperialist drumbeating. Ishiguro's novels are sly: while seeming to focus on the aggressive nationalism of interwar Japan (*Pale View* and *Artist*) and Germany (*Remains*), they draw attention to British anti-Semitism of the 1930s, to US expansionism, and to English imperialist nostalgia in the 1950s – represented in *The Remains of the Day* by a villager who laments "all kinds of little countries going independent."[1] By "little countries," the villager does not mean Wales or Scotland; he means British colonial possessions such as Burma, Ceylon, Malaya, Ghana, Nigeria, and India, some of which were geographically small, and some of which were only small from the economic and political perspective of England.

Because of Ishiguro's subject matter and Japanese-sounding name, he has been understood as a writer of "Black British literature," a catchall that was used in the 1980s to register the emergence of new writing by Britons of Asian, West Indian, and African origin.[2] Rushdie's *Midnight's Children*, Mo's *Sour Sweet* (1982), Caryl Phillips's *The Final Passage* (1985), Naipaul's *The Enigma of Arrival* (1987), Ben Okri's *The Famished Road* (1989), and Hanif Kureishi's *The Buddha of Suburbia* (1990) are regularly considered under this heading. Ishiguro's early novels are not about his own immigrant experience in any autobiographical way: the narratives take place before or during the decade in which he was born. Yet they reflect on the history of immigration and on two divisive questions related to it. First, what constitutes a Japanese, American, or English community? Second, can the ethnic or cultural qualities of such community change? "Black British literature" continues to raise those questions about identity and transformation.

The novel of minority culture shows how novels by "Black British" writers intersect with works focused on other subcultural or micronational communities. One point of intersection is tone: novels of minority culture tend to emphasize difficult experiences of separateness, prejudice, and "making do" rather than "conviviality," a term Paul Gilroy employs to describe the fluid, heterogeneous sociability we find in the novel of multiculturalism.[3] In contrast minority culture novels often represent cultural separateness by incorporating vernacular idioms, local anecdotes whose referents are imperfectly explained, and neighborhood street names, housing blocks, and landmarks. *A Pale View of Hills* fits the genre in two principal ways. It registers the alienation and racism that Japanese-British immigrants experience in England. And it presents a Japanese-speaking narrator whose words appear in English and whose memories, like her language, are distant, translated, and halting. The translated voice, because it strives for the customary sound of English novels, suggests that national characteristics are themselves fictions. We see this when Etsuko, the protagonist of *Pale View*, says of the countryside that "it's so truly like England out here"[4] and when Ono, the protagonist of *Artist*, finds that the most "Japanese" songs of the 1930s – songs calling for military sacrifice – are pronounced divisive and contrary and not so Japanese in the late 1940s. Ishiguro's novels engage minority culture by suggesting that national characteristics have an arbitrary nature, an ever-changing historical contingency. Such a perspective suggests, in turn, that the separate character of minority culture may also be somewhat illusory.

Ishiguro proposes that minorities, like majorities, are not prima facie either ethical or unethical. As we can see in his antagonism to both English provincials and Japanese nationalists, Ishiguro draws attention to the demonization of minority communities; but he is reluctant simply to replace bad images with good ones. Nor will he offer a more precise account of Japanese culture to counter narrow stereotypes. His reluctance is shared by several other writers of the period. Hanif Kureishi, in an essay responding to criticism of his screenplay for the film *My Beautiful Laundrette* (1985), complains about pressure on writers from immigrant communities to offer idealized portraits at the expense of complex realism: the film made some British-Asian viewers uncomfortable because it presents a love affair between a young British-Pakistani man of the middle class and a white, working-class man. Channeling James Joyce, Kureishi argues that "a serious attempt to understand present day Britain . . . can't attempt to represent any one group as having a monopoly on virtue."[5] Accordingly Kureishi suggests that young minority writers should favor naturalism (showing things as they are) and complexity (resisting appeals to idealization or apology), and should avoid sanitizing "types, clichés and simplicities."

McIlvanney makes sanitization the subject of *Strange Loyalties*. He aligns the cover up of a hit-and-run accident in the distant past with present-day obscuring of Glasgow's slums by tourist images of Scotland. The protagonist's brother is damaged by a legacy of the first cover up, but all of Glasgow, McIlvanney suggests, is damaged by the second. The brother's desire to confront brutal reality is conveyed by one of his paintings, which Laidlaw remembers when he notices:

> lighter patches on the walls where Scott's paintings had been hanging. My memory rehung one of them. It was a big canvas dominated by a kitchen window. In the foreground on the draining board there were dishes, pans, cooking utensils. Through the window was a fantastic cityscape of bleak

places and deprived people and cranes and furnaces. The people were part of the objects, seemed somehow enslaved by them. I remember a face looking out of a closed window as if through bars. It was meant, Scott had told me, to be an echo of the face that was looking at his painting... The whole thing was rendered in great naturalistic detail, down to recognizably working-class faces below the bonnets, but the total effect was a nightmare vision. On the left side of the kitchen window, like an inaccurate inset scale on some mad map, was a small, square picture. It was painted in sugary colors in vivid contrast to the scene outside. It showed an idealized highland glen with heather and a cottage pluming smoke from the chimney and a shepherd and his dog heading towards it. Scott had called his painting "Scotland."[6]

The style of the painting resembles the style of McIlvanney's novel: in both, human agency is ineffective, working-class characters are given greater attention and greater value than upper-class characters, and routine domestic existence is in its banality more sane than cliched highland fantasy. Laidlaw's critical gaze and poetic humanism ("My memory rehung one of them") tempers naturalistic detail with an ethics of friendship. In contrast, the novel's title invokes not only collective loyalty to false national images but also loyalty to personal convenience and self-protection at the expense of collective honesty and kindness. McIlvanney's three Laidlaw novels, *Laidlaw* (1977), *The Papers of Tony Veitch* (1983), and *Strange Loyalties* mourn the ways that socialization, the effort to "fit in to society," can stifle care (p. 278). Laidlaw, for all his failings as a father, lover, husband, and colleague, seems more willing than his police colleagues to sympathize with working-class communities they patrol, and to understand crime in the context of poverty and economic disparity.

Devolution and globalization

Other devolution novels focused on Scotland appeared in the 1990s, perhaps most famously James Kelman's *How Late It Was, How Late* (1994), and Irvine Welsh's *Trainspotting* (1993), which attracted a wide international readership with the release of a film adaptation. Both novels use Scottish vernacular as the principal language of narration, an innovation that Cairns Craig calls "the devolution of the word": the use of Scottish idiom, Craig argues, asserts "at the level of culture an independence as yet unachieved at the level of politics."[7] Like McIlvanney's Glaswegians, the protagonists of Kelman and Welsh's novels are unable to alter or even to fully acknowledge the paralysis of their lives. Craig's barbed comment comprehends authors as well as characters: the new Scottish novelists have achieved a place of influence within English letters, he suggests, but that prominence does not match, and has done little to improve, the Scottish nation's political influence within the United Kingdom.

While *Trainspotting*'s interest in Scots idiom is undeniable, the novel's emphasis on globalization might be even more significant. Its narrator speaks in an Edinburgh slang punctuated by references to violent Hollywood action films. The novel begins, in fact, with a scene of movie-watching that self-consciously imitates visual priorities and "dramatic openings" in American fight-movies:

> The sweat wis lashing oafay Sick Boy; he wis trembling. Ah wis just sitting thair, focusing oan the telly, tryin no tae notice the cunt. He wis bringing me doon. Ah tried tae keep ma attention oan the Jean-Claude Van Damme video.
>
> As happens in such movies, they started oaf wi an obligatory dramatic opening. Then the next phase ay the picture involved building up the tension through introducing the dastardly villain and sticking the weak plot together. Any minute now though, auld Jean-Claude's ready tae git doon tae some serious swedgin.[8]

In its physical description of Sick Boy suffering from heroin withdrawal, in its careless oscillation between the trembling friend and the narrator's desire to watch Jean-Claude, and in its casual use of obscenity, Welsh's initial scene is legible – for all its Scots idiom – to a broad range of younger Anglophone readers, who are well-versed in the global language of cinematic violence. We expect Welsh's devolution novel to emphasize the accents and social mores of working-class Edinburgh, as it does; but we might be surprised by its suggestion that Edinburgh is saturated by American popular culture. But the novel's Americanized Scottishness cannot be generalized into a national or even cross-generational phenomenon: Welsh's text reminds us that the characters' sarcasm about psychology, the state, and liberalism needs to be understood in the context of Edinburgh's history as a source of Enlightenment reason. Like McIlvanney, then, Welsh describes a local way of life. And yet he associates that experience with new urban and even transnational customs linked with youth and the rejection of adult socialization. His characters rail against the legacy of British imperialism, but one notes with irony that they are critical, too, of those who would deny or seek to retract the nascent globalization of immaturity.

Difficult arrivals

From the perspective of youth culture, *Trainspotting* appears less like Kelman and McIlvanney's novels and more like other novels about social marginality and newly constructed minority communities. Take, for

example, two books about very different minority cultures: Anita Brookner's
The Latecomers (1988), about German-Jewish emigrants in London, and
Colm Tóibín's *The Story of the Night* (1996), about an Anglo-Argentine
community during the Falklands War and the AIDS crisis. *The Latecomers*
appears to be a modest story of friendship, but it is also a moving account of
survival and adaptation. The novel's protagonists, Thomas Hartmann and
Thomas Fibich, were among many German-Jewish children who were sent
alone to England in the 1930s. They are "latecomers" in a broad sense,
because they arrived long after Eastern European Jews who came to Britain in
the late nineteenth century. But they are also "latecomers" in a narrower
sense, because their unhappy experience of childhood delays their experience
of adult equanimity.

Not Jewishness *per se* but a specific experience of thwarted childhood is
central to Brookner's account of minority culture in Britain. Because they
lost their own families, Fibich and Hartmann are attracted to people whose
parents are in some way missing: Fibich marries Christine, whose mother
died prematurely and whose father and stepmother ignored her; Hartmann
marries Yvette, whose father was a Nazi collaborator and whose French
mother married an English businessman after the war. Neither Hartmann
nor Fibich believe in God, nor do they participate in London's Jewish
institutions, but at the end of the novel their experiences as Jewish refugees
remain determinative: Fibich leaves his son a notebook with an account of
"your history and as much of mine as I can remember," and with a prayer-
like reminder that "Your grandfather's name was Manfred. Your grandmother's name was Rosa."[9]

Set in England and focused on a specific community of recent immigrants
of limited resources, Brookner's novel can be grouped with Naipaul's fictions, which for decades have returned to the theme of difficult arrival. Caryl
Phillips's novels also relate the difficult experience of arrival, not only for
those leaving the Caribbean, his place of birth, but also for those fleeing
racial discrimination in Germany, Ethiopia, and Rwanda. Phillips often
compares anti-immigrant racism to other systems of discrimination. *A
Distant Shore* (2003), whose title encompasses several stories of arrival, asks
us to notice that English villagers reject strangers of several kinds: a man
from an unspecified African country whose family has been murdered; a
British doctor with a conspicuously Jewish surname and children named
Rachel and Jacob; and a retired urban woman who has been left by her
husband and seems to be psychologically unmoored. Although Britain's
increased openness to emigrants since World War II is an historical fact,
Phillips's novel implies that the post-consensus emphasis on liberated differences and diversity has gone hand in hand with a renewal of self-centered

individualism and a diminished concern for social welfare and collective political responsibilities in global as well as national terms.

Sexual minorities

A Distant Shore picks up on a theme that has been explored even more vigorously in minority culture novels by Colm Tóibín and Alan Hollinghurst: intersections among racism, imperialism, and histories of sexual discrimination. Tóibín's *The Story of the Night* gives us Richard Garay, a young gay son of an English mother and an Argentine father who was brought up in a British expatriate community in Buenos Aires. This community is not lacking in economic comfort, but it is isolated, provincial, and unprepared for military violence and economic downturn in the early 1980s. The novel begins with the first election of Thatcher and her response to Argentine invasion of the British Falkland Islands in 1982. Richard is an Anglophone narrator, but he feels Argentine, and he is disappointed when the British retake the islands at the end of the Falklands/Malvinas conflict. Still, Richard's command of English endears him to US spies and businessmen who arrive in Argentina to exploit oil resources and support right-wing governments in the region. These connections, in turn, allow Richard to meet other gay men in situations that are, at least temporarily, exempted from the more traditional, homophobic society of Buenos Aires. From a visiting American diplomat, he first learns about AIDS, and from an Argentine lover who has lived in California, he learns about gay communities that have responded collectively to the AIDS crisis. While globalization brings American neo-imperialism to Argentina, it also brings, at least for Richard, greater access to anti-retroviral drugs, solidarity with other gay men, and financial independence.

In its concern with gay minority culture and the history of imperialism, Tóibín's novel should be considered with Kureishi's *The Buddha of Suburbia*, which recounts the upwardly mobile adventures of bisexual British-Asian Karim, whose acting career succeeds the more he loans himself to commercialized representations of "minority culture"; and Hollinghurst's *The Swimming Pool Library* (1988), which presents young Will Beckwith, a narrator who thinks he is rejecting Britain's imperial past and resisting sexual persecution but is in many ways reproducing both. Central to the effectiveness of *The Swimming Pool Library* is its glamorous, witty protagonist: Hollinghurst uses Beckwith's charm to make the reader participate in his character's naïveté. Hollinghurst's *The Line of Beauty* (2004) also presents a young charmer, Nick Guest, who admires Henry James, prefers sex with black men, allows himself to be patronized and manipulated by Tory families and prejudices, and seems oblivious – perhaps fatally – to his complicity in the divisive side of post-consensus sexual and racial politics in the 1980s. Another meditation on complicity is Tóibín's *The Master* (2004), which finds occasion in a narrative about Henry James's emotional intimacies with men to relate the earlier novelist's experience of anti-Irish prejudice and British imperial arrogance during a visit to Dublin. Tóibín suggests in *The Master*, as he did in *Story of the Night*, that a character's ability to move between public and private selves, as Richard Garay does with some success and as James does with less, may be aided by his experience of belonging to multiple national communities. By contrast, Hollinghurst is wary of characters who overestimate any commutability of sexual and racial politics. Both novelists are ultimately skeptical about the long-term political efficacy of intimate liaisons – even minority homosexual ones.

The novel of multiculturalism

The novel of multiculturalism shares with the novel of minority culture a concern with antiracist politics in the post-consensus era, but it tends to focus on collaborations and clashes among characters of different national and ethnic origins. If the minority culture novel emphasizes separation, which it attributes to national divisiveness and the assertion of traditional ethnic communities or sexual orientations, the multicultural novel privileges mixing, which it presents both as a spur to divisiveness and as an occasion for new collectivities. The novelists whose careers are most closely tethered to these concerns are Nobel laureate Naipaul and two-time Booker prize recipient Rushdie. Naipaul's interest in mixed-up communities extends from *The Mimic Men* (1967), his early novel about Caribbean emigrants in London, to *The Enigma of Arrival*, based on Naipaul's own emigration to rural England, to the later *Half a Life* (2001) and *Magic Seeds* (2004). The last two novels tell the story of a mixed-caste Indian man, Willie Chandran, who is a serial emigrant, as it were, to London, to an unnamed Portuguese African colony, to Berlin, and to guerrilla communities in rural India. Naipaul's books generously mock both the willful ignorance of colonial rulers and the apparent naïveté of anticolonial idealists. In Naipaul's fiction cross-class and crosscultural solidarities are false, empty of real understanding, or simply embarrassing. To be Portuguese living in Africa, to be a Caribbean man in London, to be an Indian woman married to a German man, to be a Brahmin married to a "backward" – all of these mixed-up conditions, Naipaul suggests, lead to "half a life." At the same time a whole life appears impossible, an enigma whose realization never arrives.

Multiculturalism refers to the belief that individuals as well as societies benefit from contact with different cultural, ethnic, and linguistic traditions, and from allowing themselves to be transformed by contact. It would be fair to understand Naipaul's books, therefore, as novels of anti-multiculturalism, even though they offer some of the most compelling, moving accounts of postcolonial consciousness. Rushdie's novels, by contrast, celebrate the "mixed tradition" that imperialism has left behind and that new forms of globalization continue to produce. Born in India but educated in England and now resident in New York, Rushdie embraces "eclecticism," which he defines as "the ability to take from the world what seems fitting and to leave the rest."[10] The mix-up has important resonances in Rushdie: it points to the mixing up of culture generated by colonialism and migration; it refers to misunderstandings that immigrants have about the culture they enter, and that colonial communities have about native cultures they are exploiting; it signals, too, the purposeful ruses used by Rushdie and some of his characters to unsettle exclusive conceptions of community.

In *Midnight's Children*, Rushdie's celebrated novel about Indian independence, the narrator is exchanged at birth with another infant and then raised by his non-biological parents. The novel takes up one of the English novel's central concerns – inheritance – and suggests that colonialism forever disrupted India's narrative, personal, political, and cultural beginnings. Rhetorically, the novel is full of what the narrator calls "chutnification," a preservation of the past that is also an alteration – like the integration of an Indian condiment into the history of English fiction (p. 548). But whereas *Midnight's Children* presents cultural mix-ups as the unintentional result of colonialism, Rushdie's later novels and narrative fictions present immigrant characters who mix things up on purpose.

Linking Rushdie's tactics in *The Satanic Verses* (1988) to South London antiracist riots in the early 1980s, which the novel describes, Ian Baucom has argued that the novel serves to "re-create England through an act of disorderly conduct."[11] Like devolution writers Welsh and Kelman who use Scots vernacular to decentralize the tradition of English letters, Rushdie uses references to Indian foods, popular culture, mythology, and idioms to make an English novel in the image of British multiculturalism. But unlike Welsh and Kelman, who tend to pit Scottish culture against English, Rushdie suggests that British culture has been mixed up from the start. One of the characters in *Satanic Verses* asserts, in a widely quoted stuttering sentence, "The trouble with Engenglish is that their hiss hiss history happened overseas, so they dodo don't know what it means."[12] This jibe is meant to reverse the usual anti-immigrant litany directed against British Indians and other minorities by repeating – and interrupting – a rhetoric of impersonal generalization. By "hissing" at history and comparing the English to a "dodo," proverbially foolish and extinct, Rushdie's character uses the insulting rhetoric of racist discourse for antiracist critique. He asserts that postcolonial immigrants know more about England's history than the English do.

An epitome of Rushdie's exuberant multiculturalism is "The Courter," in a story collection *East, West* (1994), in which flirtatious mix-ups of a group of recent immigrants from "the East" offer a sharp contrast to the unfulfilling camaraderie in Naipaul's novels. "The Courter" features more of the mixed-up English – what other critics have called "rotten English" or "weird English" – that we have come to associate with the literary idiom of Rushdie and other minority writers.[13] The story's title refers to an apartment house porter from Eastern Europe whose name is mispronounced by an Indian ayah. In her speech, "porter" becomes "courter." The ayah's mistake creates an accidental invitation: the porter, used to his employers' angry epithets, decides to adopt his new identity: " 'Courter courter caught.' Okay. People called him many things, he did not mind. But this name, this courter, this he would try to be."[14] The porter becomes the ayah's courtier, and they create together a temporary "wonderland" of private languages. Yet this community is permanently disrupted by violence: thugs pull a knife on the ayah and her employer, whom they misidentify as the family of another Indian man; when the porter runs out to save his beloved, he is attacked and badly injured. While Rushdie seems to acknowledge that mix-ups of language are no match for the rhetorical and physical thuggery that is racism, the story is not simply about the porter's flirtation but about the narrator's memory, which survives and flourishes as the literature, and the innovative novels, of mixed-up Britain.

Although "The Courter" looks back at the 1960s, it comments on 1990s Britain. As Rushdie knows well, it is not only in fiction that mixing up can provoke threats of violence. Many readers of *The Satanic Verses* were offended by its impious references to the Koran and the history of Islam. The novel was burned in some places and banned in others, and Rushdie was condemned to death for blasphemy by the Ayatollah Khomeini of Iran; the sentence was upheld by the Iranian government until 1998. The burning of *The Satanic Verses* by Muslims in Bradford makes an appearance in Zadie Smith's *White Teeth* (2000), which signals its homage to Rushdie's style, tone, and subject matter. Smith's novel holds together overlapping stories of North London characters from English, Bengali, and Jamaican backgrounds. Like *Midnight's Children* it moves back and forth among time periods, using well-known events from world history as well as private events from characters' pasts to historicize present-day London.

If we follow a line of recent historical novels that also embrace Britain's new diversity, we find our way, perhaps surprisingly, to Ian McEwan's *Atonement* (2001), which begins in rural England of 1935 and ends in multicultural London of 1999. *Atonement* is focused on a child's terrible lie and its relation to horrors of World War II, but in the final section we meet the now-grown child's extended family. While class and ethnicity seemed to be transparent in the country-house world of the novel's beginning, the grown narrator reflects at the end, while talking to her "cheerful West Indian" taxi driver,

> It is quite impossible these days to assume anything about people's educational level from the way they talk or dress or from their taste in music. Safest to treat everyone you meet as a distinguished intellectual.[15]

The novel's embrace of multiculturalism is even more pointed. In its coda a homemade play about a tragedy of "extrinsic" marriages is performed by great-grandchildren of mixed national and social backgrounds (p. 346). There is no violent incident to interrupt this final scene, as there is in Rushdie's story. Instead, *Atonement* celebrates a new public culture that James Proctor has tartly associated with "New Labour's hegemonic vision."[16] Proctor argues that ethnic difference can only "make a difference" when we "historicize and challenge the forms of exoticist multiculturalism that prevail in the present" (p. 113). He refers here to the eager marketing of immigration that helped to make a bestseller of Monica Ali's *Brick Lane* (2003), which celebrates London's Bangladeshi immigrants; but Proctor is criticizing more generally a tone of multicultural triumph, which we find in *Atonement*, and which Proctor associates with the New Labour optimism of Tony Blair.

The novel of transnational comparison

The project of historicizing multiculturalism has been taken up forcefully by novels of transnational comparison. When we consider how many important British writers now live outside of the British Isles, or divide their time between Britain and other places, it becomes less surprising to find a wave of English novels that approach British history comparatively. Caryl Phillips and Peter Ho Davies have been recognized among the journal *Granta*'s "Best of Young British Novelists," Phillips in 1993 and Ho Davies in 2003.[17] But Phillips, who was born in St. Kitts and educated in England, resides in both New York and London. Ho Davies, who is of Welsh and Chinese parentage and was raised in England, lives in the United States. Kiran Desai, who won a Man Booker Prize in 2006 for *The Inheritance of Loss*, was educated in

India, England, and the United States, and divides her time between the United States and India. Desai's novel and Ho Davies's *The Welsh Girl* (2007) are two of the most interesting recent examples of the transnational comparison genre.

Earlier examples include Ishiguro's *The Remains of the Day* (1989), which asks us to consider the interwar activities of an English country house within several larger contexts – private, national, and international; Phillips's *Crossing the River* (1993), *The Nature of Blood* (1997), and *A Distant Shore* (2003), which collate experiences of arrival that are separated by geography and sometimes by hundreds of years; and the novels of W. G. Sebald, a German-language writer who lived most of his adult life in England before his death in 2001 and whose novels have been recognized as significant contributions to British fiction. While the linked narratives of *The Emigrants* (English version, 1996) ask us to compare four Germans (three of them Jewish or part-Jewish) who emigrated to the US, France, or Britain, Sebald's *The Rings of Saturn* (English version, 1998) uses its narrator's walking tour through Suffolk to sew together the history of British imperialism with other histories of violence, including the German massacre of Jews in concentration camps and the Allied fire-bombing of German cities. Sebald suggests that thinking about the Allied air war and European imperialism alongside the Holocaust can serve to correct, among British and US readers, an uncritical self-righteousness about German violence and Anglo-American liberalism. At the same time Sebald understands that, for German readers, comparing the Holocaust to other events can seem like denial or apology. Sebald's novels of transnational comparison explore those contextual differences.

Phillips's *The Nature of Blood* also compares histories of European racism, showing where discrimination against people of African descent has intersected with anti-Semitism. Unlike *The Rings of Saturn*, which is framed by a single narrator whose interviews, conversations, and readings allow him to incorporate other voices, *The Nature of Blood* weaves among several narrators, each of whom lives in a different time and place. There is Stephan, a German Jew who has joined the Zionist cause in Cyprus in the 1940s; Eva, Stephan's niece and a concentration camp survivor in postwar Germany and then in London; a third-person narrative about Jews accused of murdering a Christian child in Italy in the 1480s; a character called Othello, who visits a Jewish ghetto in Venice in the late sixteenth century; and Malka, an Ethiopian Jew who experiences racism in post-independence Israel, where she spends a night with Stephan. Phillips's interwoven stories argue that racism in present-day Britain needs to be understood in the context of a much longer European history. To represent the connections between events separated by time and place, Sebald and Phillips expand the scale of their novels well beyond the geography of any single nation.

In a truly comparative novel, expansion of scale means multiplication rather than simply enlargement of geographies. Sometimes this means that a single novel takes place in Israel, Cyprus, Italy, and England, as in *The Nature of Blood*. But sometimes, as in *The Rings of Saturn*, a novel will hew to a single county of England while the narrator's memories, anecdotes, and commentaries range from the Congo and South America to Ireland and West Germany. Desai's *The Inheritance of Loss* and Ho Davies's *Welsh Girl* adopt a combination of those models, shuttling between multiple narratives set in disparate spaces and representing spaces that gather together characters of different origins. Desai's narrative follows Biju, a young man from the Himalayas trying to survive as an illegal immigrant kitchen helper in New York, and Sai, a teenaged girl whose Indian parents have died while working in the Soviet Union and who comes to live in the Himalayas with her crusty Anglophile grandfather and his cook, Biju's father. *The Inheritance of Loss* is not set in Britain, but it analyzes the consequences of British colonialism and global networks of migration that send young men like Biju into an underworld of New York restaurants. The novel ends not with a celebration of migration and the multicultural West but with Biju's happy return to the Himalayas and Sai's realization that "Never again could she think there was but one narrative and that narrative belonged only to herself, that she might create her own mean little happiness and live safely within it."[18]

The Welsh Girl is filtered through the perspectives of Rotheram, a German-Jewish interrogator who fled Nazi Germany and later enlisted in the British Army; Karsten, a German prisoner of war who is imprisoned in Wales; and Esther, a Welsh girl who works in a nearby village and befriends Karsten. Their perspectives add up to one narrative, but their differences expose tensions between anti-British Welsh nationalism and anti-German British patriotism. *The Welsh Girl* is in some ways a devolution novel, because it represents the costs of British consensus: although anti-German sentiment helps to generate a fragile peace among Welsh locals and British soldiers, the unity suggests a likeness to the process that forged an anti-Semitic consensus as a basis for German nationalism in the 1930s. In line with its devolutionary mode, the novel embraces *cynefin*, a Welsh term for "the sense of place" that allows even a flock of sheep to recognize its territory as a specific locality. But *The Welsh Girl* also presents unexpected alliances that appear to move towards hitherto unrecognized transnational affiliations: the escaped German prisoner, Karsten, helps Esther, who has been raped by an English soldier, to maintain her sheep farm through the end of the war; meanwhile, Karsten, despite feeling intensely ashamed of having surrendered to the British, extends friendship to Rotheram, who laments having fled Germany, where he was ashamed to think of himself as Jewish. *The Welsh Girl* admires transnational cooperation because nationalist solidarities, in comparison, seem everywhere compromised by internal histories of English colonialism in Wales and anti-Jewish sentiment in Germany. The novel's transnational sensibility accommodates an ethics of hospitality, exemplified by Welsh farmers who offer to house German ex-prisoners after the war. At the beginning of the twenty-first century, then, the English novel looks back on the solidarity of wartime in order to find a model of collectivity that transcends national consensus by amalgamating a respect for localized cultural and historical differences with an understanding of transnational interdependence and affiliation.

NOTES

1 Kazuo Ishiguro, *The Remains of the Day* (New York: Vintage, 1996), p. 192.
2 Mark Stein, *Black British Literature: Novels of Transformation* (Columbus: The Ohio State University Press, 2004).
3 Paul Gilroy, *After Empire: Melancholia or Convivial Culture?* (London: Routledge, 2004), p. xi.
4 Kazuo Ishiguro, *A Pale View of Hills* (New York: Vintage, 1990), p. 182.
5 Hanif Kureishi, "Dirty Washing" in *Time Out*, November 14–20, 1985, p. 26.
6 William McIlvanney, *Strange Loyalties* (New York: William Morrow, 1991), p. 26.
7 Cairns Craig, "Devolving the Scottish Novel," *A Concise Companion to Contemporary British Fiction*, ed. James F. English (Oxford: Blackwell, 2006), p. 135.
8 Irvine Welsh, *Trainspotting* (New York: Norton, 1996), p. 3.
9 Anita Brookner, *The Latecomers* (New York: Vintage, 1990), pp. 247–8.
10 Salman Rushdie, "'Commonwealth Writers' Do Not Exist," *Imaginary Homelands: Essays and Criticism, 1981–1991* (New York: Penguin, 1991), p. 67.
11 Ian Baucom, *Out of Place: Englishness, Empire, and the Locations of Identity* (Princeton: Princeton University Press, 1999), p. 200.
12 Salman Rushdie, *The Satanic Verses* (New York: Picador, 2000), p. 353.
13 Dohra Ahmad, ed., *Rotten English: A Literary Anthology* (New York: Norton, 2007); Evelyn Nien-Ming Ch'ien, *Weird English* (Cambridge: Harvard University Press, 2004).
14 Salman Rushdie, *East, West* (New York: Random House, 1994), p. 177.
15 Ian McEwan, *Atonement* (New York: Anchor, 2003), pp. 341–2.
16 James Proctor, "New Ethnicities, the Novel, and the Burdens of Representation," *A Concise Companion*, ed. English, p. 213.
17 www.granta.com
18 Kiran Desai, *The Inheritance of Loss* (New York: Grove, 2006), p. 355.

16

REED WAY DASENBROCK

An absurd century: Varieties of satire

The nineteenth century's dominant narrative of the history of painting described a progress in accuracy of representation, from a two-dimensional world of medieval art to a three-dimensional modern realism. A similar view of prose fiction held sway: the novel, supposedly beginning in caricatures characteristic of satire, was said to have moved steadily toward committed realism as its primary mode. E. M. Forster's famous distinction in *Aspects of the Novel* (1927) between flat and round characters is one point of overlap between this view of fiction and theories of representation in the visual arts. Although Forster assigned a role to "flat" characters, the role was secondary. The primary function of the novel, like painting, was to be "round," to give thereby a more real representation of life. In this context, narrative tending to rely on the less realistic style of satire was eclipsed, and assigned to an earlier era. The "great tradition" of fiction – as critic F. R. Leavis identified it – was not the satiric tradition of Smollett or Peacock but the realism of Austen, George Eliot, James, and Conrad. Writers with a strong satiric bent such as Dickens either were presented as "early" realists; or were misread so as to fit into this progressive narrative.

As the nineteenth century gave way to the twentieth, realism gave way to new forms of artistic representation that include modernism. The revolutionary impact of modernism on visual representation was immediate, and the narrative of progress towards accuracy of representation lost its hegemony. In fact, the dominant narrative became inverted: a narrative of progress away from representation toward abstraction. Neither narrative holds much water now. But modernism in literature, though often seen as in league with modernist painting in overthrowing conventions, did not replace the narrative of increasingly accurate representation. It complicated it. Perhaps the major innovation of modernist fiction – whether one calls it stream of consciousness or interior monologue – was to move inside characters' minds in unparalleled ways. This represented a stylistic break, but it was considered a more thoroughgoing realism. Other aspects of modernist fiction support a view of it as a more comprehensive mode: Joyce's *Ulysses* (1922), in addition to using interior monologue, represents outward aspects of Dublin on June 16, 1904, to an extent never before attempted in fiction. *Ulysses* instances a continuing realistic inspiration, even if Joyce's fiction doesn't represent the real as much as intersect with it in dizzying ways.

This continuing realism is not the whole story; but it remains a dominant story even though it does not do justice to literary history, particularly English literary history. Anglo-American modernism is, after all, London-based more than it is truly English, because modernism was primarily a product of Irish and foreign-born writers (Yeats, Pound, and T. S. Eliot in poetry; Conrad and Joyce in fiction). A key figure amidst the complex directional movements of English fiction in the twentieth century is another outsider: Wyndham Lewis, born on his American father's sailboat off the coast of Nova Scotia, but raised in England by his English mother after the collapse of her marriage. Lewis trained as a painter at the Slade School of Art. In an autobiographical essay, "Beginnings," he paradoxically assigns the start of his career as a writer to his painting: he began to write in order to capture things his painting couldn't express. A key modernist innovator, founder of the art movement Vorticism, friend of Pound, Eliot, and Joyce, Lewis carved out a satiric and comic approach to fiction that was sui generis yet deeply influential.

Lewis's first novel *Tarr* (1918) represents an international cast of artists living bohemian lives in Paris. The novel's protagonist is an Englishman, Frederick Tarr, and what his consciousness observes constitutes the real center of the book. The focal point of his observation is a penniless German painter, Kreisler, whose collapse into financial ruin, prison, and suicide takes over the narrative. Kreisler is a spectacular and compelling grotesque (and not the only one in the novel). *Tarr* does not attempt to render the grotesqueries in terms of a referential realism. Lewis innovatively rejects a use of words to mirror the world and instead highlights the character of language as a machine for artificial invention. Moreover, the book's interest derives from a split between observers and the observed: the presence of the disinterested observers Tarr and the narrator allows for a continuous cerebral commentary on Kreisler. The disinterested reflections hark back to the novel of ideas, and Kreisler instances a tragicomic bodily being that echoes English fiction of the eighteenth century (Smollett especially) as well as Rabelais and ancient satire. The satiric antecedents are not worn on the novel's sleeve, however, because the contemporary setting in the art circles of Paris makes the novel very much about the absurdities of the present. Accordingly, Lewis, in an author's preface, ties Kreisler's character to the Great War. The attempt is implausible, because Lewis finished *Tarr* just before the war began; nevertheless, the Preface's references to Nietzsche and Futurism do reinforce the action–reflection split between Kreisler and Tarr in the narrative, and further connect Lewis to Tarr in his role as observer and commentator.

Another of Lewis's prefaces (actually a postface), attached to prewar fiction collected in his *The Wild Body* (1927), gives us Lewis's most extended theory of what he calls the comic. "The root of the Comic," writes Lewis, "is to be sought in the sensations resulting from the observations of a *thing* behaving like a person."[1] "All men are necessarily comic" because we are all things. It is not just that we all have bodies, though this is an important part of the comic. As things, we are absurd because we can be observed to fall into patterns, groupings, totalities. It is also comic that any grouping or category we are outside of is "ludicrous" when seen from the outside. Nationality is Lewis's preferred example of absurdity: it is absurd for Lewis that Frenchmen act like Frenchmen and Germans act like Germans. But this must also extend to ourselves as well, because we too fall into categories and patterns of identity of all kinds, and we enact those identities. (Lewis refers to group identifications as "insect communism" [p. 246]). The root of the comic for Lewis is the absurdity of the difference between observer and observed, or more precisely since we are all both observer and observed at times, between our role as one and our role as the other. The task of the artist is to be the observer, and here Lewis's metier as a painter comes out, which means that the work of fiction is to portray the world as a comic creation because observed from the artist's point of view.

Lewis's later work grows in complexity. He spent the 1920s composing interrelated works of philosophy, political and cultural reflection, and fiction. The most important are *The Art of Being Ruled* (1926) and *Time and Western Man* (1927), sweeping critiques of the modern world and of modernist literature and philosophy; and their fictional counterparts, *The Childermass* (1928) and *The Apes of God* (1930). In those works, Lewis's comic style deepens into a more purely satiric fiction, as the comic techniques of the early work are complemented by social criticism.

The Apes of God, a blistering satire of contemporary London intellectual life, attacks what Lewis saw as the malign influence of Virginia Woolf's Bloomsbury, which he identified with people aping the life of the artist without creating any real art. Art is those apes' religion, hence the artist is their god; but rather than drawing a firm line between the space of the profane (ordinary life) and the space of the sacred (art in its detachment from ordinary life), they blur the line. Lewis retains the fundamental distinctions in *Tarr* and "The Meaning of the Wild Body": both Tarr and

Kreisler were artists or thought they were, but Lewis identifies the true artist with the observer-intellect, Tarr, not with the actor-body, Kreisler. However, in the landscape of *The Apes of God*, the world is so crowded with would-be artists that there is not a genuine observer-intellect – a genuine artist – to be found.

The plot of *The Apes of God* is about the introduction of a nineteen-year-old "genius," Daniel Boleyn, into the world of Bloomsbury. His introduction is handled by Horace Zagreus, who is an emissary of a mysterious artist and thinker, Pierpoint. Pierpoint has written an Encyclical on the fate of the artist in the modern world that is incorporated in Lewis's text. It sounds remarkably like Lewis's reflections in his non-fiction; and Zagreus claims Pierpoint as his "master." But it is clear from the start that Boleyn is no genius, and it is clear by the end that Zagreus is completely part of the fake-artist world of Bloomsbury, not at all removed from it. So how then can Pierpoint be connected to Zagreus and still not be part of the fake-world he is dissecting? Lewis's contention that all contemporary claims to art are inauthentic puts him in an impossible position: if there is no room for the artist in the modern world, where can we find the artist (or the detached and observing intellect) in the world being depicted? To be consistent, Lewis leaves Pierpoint off stage; the locus of reflection in the novel is therefore not inside the action but rather outside it, primarily in the external mind of the author. But Lewis's resort to a *deus ex machina* means that the narrative itself remains entirely in the world of the apes, and it loses the dramatized dynamic tension between external observer and insider-observed that gives *Tarr* its spark. Meanwhile, the potential interplay and conflict between reflection and action tips strongly in the *Apes* against action, as nothing really happens in this work of over 600 pages.

The Apes of God represents a high water mark of abstraction and anti-narrativity in Lewis's work. Thereafter, Lewis moves away from abstraction towards a renewal of representational and realist aims. *The Revenge for Love* (1937), Lewis's most powerful fiction, is set in Spain just before the Spanish Civil War and is imbued with the tug of war between communism and fascism. Lewis's political analysis of the 1920s led him to complicate the actor-observer dichotomy that structured his earlier fiction. From the perspective of a disinterested observer, action is comic because it falls into organized regularities that are absurd. But Lewis begins to ask why we fall into those organized regularities, particularly in the modern world when other cultures and ways of being are available alternatives. His answer is that in addition to artist-observers, there are also concealed actors, whose role it is to organize us. We are "ruled" by others in that we are led to act in ways that we believe to be inwardly spontaneous but are in fact outwardly manipulated. Politics is the most obvious manifestation of this; but we also are ruled in culture and social life.

In this context the role of the artist grows more complex: it is not just a matter of his observing life's surfaces, it is now also a matter of his understanding how they are being created and manipulated. Those who practice the organized regularities that Lewis earlier found comic are not aware that their practice is created for them. We act as if we are free, but we are not; moreover, we are not truly equal in our lack of freedom. For there are the ruled, there are the rulers, and there is the occasional artist who can see what is going on. The artist is also one of the ruled, yet like the rulers, the artist can penetrate the surfaces and illusions that trap others. Moreover, it is not just the artist who sees our lack of freedom: those who are creating and manipulating the scene of our lives are in a curious way parallel to the artist in terms of their insight, if not in terms of what they do with that insight.

Although our self-deceiving and deceived lack of awareness remains comic for Lewis, he also recognizes its tragic dimension. *The Revenge for Love* is the work where Lewis's theory of comedy gives way to deeper strains of tragicomedy that permeate the remainder of his career. The novel's protagonist is Percy Hardcaster, a Communist agent, someone committed to the world of action. Hardcaster understands the distinction between ruled and ruler that is central to Lewis's thinking about politics, and he believes strongly that he is one of the rulers, inasmuch as he is one of the manipulators of appearances that others take for the truth, and of habits that others mechanically adopt. *The Revenge for Love* begins and ends in Spain, but the middle sections in London could also be called "The Apes of God," except that adulation of artists in the 1920s has been replaced in the 1930s by worship of political action. Percy is feted in London, particularly as an amputee shot by Spanish prison guards in a botched prison break. Lewis's point is that those who fete Percy are no closer to being actual Communists than they are to being actual artists. But the worlds of politics and art are closely intertwined in *The Revenge for Love*: the other important character in the novel is a penniless Australian artist, Victor Stamp, who is forced to find work counterfeiting Van Gogh paintings in a workshop run by collaborators in Hardcaster's political schemes. The political and art plots fuse when Percy, Victor, and Victor's wife Margot get involved on the border between Spain and France in gun-running for the Spanish Republicans. It turns out that the protagonists are simply manipulated decoys, running bricks across the border in a setup for their exposure to the police while the real gun-running takes place elsewhere. Victor and Margot lose their lives in this "adventure," while Percy is returned to a Spanish jail.

The superficial resemblance of the end of *The Revenge for Love* to the denouement of *Tarr*, where the artist Kreisler dies because he is caught up in the world of non-art and action, belies important differences. Percy's fate shows that those who seek to manipulate can be, and will be, manipulated by others. Lewis's working title for the novel was "False Bottoms," a pointer to layers of illusion manufactured within the novel by the political activists as well as by the art forgers. The more important difference from *Tarr* is that *The Revenge for Love* exhibits an awareness that life is not simply made up of comic externalities offering themselves to others as a source of amusement. We are made to care about Victor and Margot's death in a way that is not the case with Kreisler's, and we care at least partly because Hardcaster cares. There is an inner life to Lewis's characters that had not been present before.

Lewis's major accomplishment in his final years was to supplement *The Childermass* with *Monstre Gai* and *Malign Fiesta* (both 1955), novels set in the afterlife that conclude a trilogy Lewis called *The Human Age*. *The Human Age*, a meditation on a cosmic struggle between God and Lucifer, represents a shift away from Lewis's satiric attacks on human and political absurdity; but it is relevant to this chapter. A number of satiric writers in the 1930s and 1940s, preeminently Aldous Huxley and George Orwell, move to create other worlds, less utopian than dystopian. *The Childermass* has not been seen as an influence in this development, and the line of indebtedness is not immediately obvious; but the parallel development does show how satiric impulse is closely wedded to a desire to create other worlds. We can get a more analytic perspective on the world we live in by creating a version of reality in a wildly different form, and so the relation between the satiric and the utopian tradition is a complexly linked one.

It is hard to characterize *Monstre Gai* and *Malign Fiesta* as either utopian or dystopian. The protagonist James Pullman, a famous writer who is loosely based on James Joyce, and his quondam schoolmate Satters, are pretty sure they are not in hell when they enter the afterlife, but they keep asking whether they have arrived in heaven. It turns out that life after death, and cosmic politics and morality, are at least as hard to read as this world is. Both volumes are set in something called Third City, a place that resembles postwar London. Divine and maleficent forces are contending there; and Pullman will be called to choose which side he is on. This turn to a form of spiritual struggle is not without similarity to the more explicit spiritual turn Aldous Huxley's fiction undergoes. In *The Human Age* Lewis definitively identifies the false bottoms of the cosmos as malign. But the malignity does not constitute the totality of what is: there are forces for good. Although Lewis was content for most of his life to analyze and unmask fakery, he felt in his latter years that the artist needed to choose the good rather than simply to satirize, castigate, or laugh at the bad.

If there is a tradition of satire in English fiction in the twentieth century it descends from Lewis. Lewis's satire comes in two forms: satiric representation of actual English society, focusing on artistic and political London society; and utopian or visionary literature, enlisting an imagined world as a way to represent English society at a remove. Both traditions are strongly influential, with the social satire more important in the 1920s and 1930s, and the visionary work taking center stage thereafter.

The key figures of the social satire of the 1920s and 1930s are Huxley and Evelyn Waugh. Huxley burst on the scene with *Crome Yellow* (1921). And though I have presented Huxley in the context of Wyndham Lewis, anyone reading *Crome Yellow* will see another forebear, the country house novels of Thomas Love Peacock a century earlier. Peacock developed the device of bringing characters together in a country house in order to compose a satiric novel of ideas in which little can happen (everyone is immured in the house) but a great deal can be said. Huxley gave Peacock's conventions a modern setting. *Crome Yellow* tells the story of a young poet, Denis Stone, and his stay at Crome, where a cross section of English literary and artistic society has gathered. Crome is a send-up of Lady Ottoline Morrell's famous salon at Garsington Hall, near Oxford, where Huxley lived during the war doing labor as an alternative to military service. (Lewis also always made fun of his former patrons in his fiction; ingratitude seems essential to the character of a satirist.) The conversation is brilliant, the characters delightful and absurd, and what gives the whole its coherence is that Denis is gradually maturing, both through disappointments in love and exposure to absurdity. Although the sophistication of the narrator's tone contrasts sharply with Denis's immaturity, particularly concerning sex, in effect the book is narrated by the artist that Denis is about to become. And since the tone adopted towards the society being depicted is always verging on satire's aggression, it is clear that Denis will move away from a cosy relationship with his host and fellow guests: he soon will see their shortcomings as sharply as the narrator does.

Huxley's evolution follows Denis's. His most ambitious satire of modern London, *Point Counter Point* (1928), fuses the inspiration of Lewis and Peacock with formal experimentation characteristic of fiction by Joyce and Woolf. Another aspect of Huxley's development especially converges with Lewis. In *Time and Western Man* Lewis attacks modernism because of its reliance on what he calls a time-space continuum that reduces experience, thought, and art to a temporal flux of indeterminacies and relativisms. Authentic art (and authentic intellect too), Lewis believes, discloses absolutes that are decided alternatives to the time-space flux. Huxley's later novels, starting with *Eyeless in Gaza* (1936), argue an urgent need to resist time, and to redefine human being in terms of transcendent absolutes of mind and spirit. Huxley's affinity with Lewis – inasmuch as both writers share the rebelliousness of modernism but are at the same time critical of modernism's relativist orthodoxies – has gone unremarked.

Like Lewis and Huxley, Evelyn Waugh initiated his career by taking aim at London society. But the differences are significant: Waugh's subject is not intellectuals but the "Bright Young People" of London who go at a dizzying speed from party to party, restaurant to restaurant, and cocktail to cocktail that lead them nowhere. *Vile Bodies* (1930) focuses on the attempts of a young writer, Adam Fenwick-Symes, to garner enough income to marry his fiancé, Nina, after British Customs at Dover burns the manuscript Adam intends to publish (his autobiography) because they consider it pornographic. He becomes a gossip columnist for the *Daily Excess*, and a repetitive round of party, column, party, column begins. Huxley's densely intellectual conversations are replaced in Waugh by rapid-fire patter more characteristic of drawing-room comedy. Although Adam pursues a Major who owes him money, and keeps trying to get Nina's dotty father to agree to their engagement, the failure of his devices to lead to anything is symptomatic of a larger stasis. Even the advent of war doesn't change the empty partying: Adam goes to war, loses Nina to his rival, but in the midst of battle encounters both the Major – now a General – and one of the novel's party girls. At the novel's close they sit in the General's car drinking champagne while battle rages around them.

Waugh's *A Handful of Dust* (1934) again dramatizes the frenetic, pointless existence of Bright Young People with little sense and less money. Waugh is explicit about his indebtedness to modernism: his title comes from Eliot's *The Waste Land*, and sections of the novel – "Du côté de chez Beaver" – allude comically to Proust. Toward the end the novel takes a turn to the absurd with a resonance deeper than that of *Vile Bodies*. Tony Last leaves his adulterous wife and goes off on an expedition to Guyana. The expedition is a disaster. Last finds a refuge in the jungle, but it turns out to be a kind of prison in which his host requires him daily to read aloud the complete works of Dickens for hours at a time. Everyone in England thinks Last has died, but he lives on, in the jungle, reading Dickens. Dickens works perfectly as an image of the kind of English culture Tony emphatically does not represent: no Victorian earnestness or sentimentality in this Bright Young Person. His living entombment is made all the worse by his subjection to a monument of English heritage. We are of course invited to laugh at the image of someone compelled to read Dickens for the rest of his life, though theorists of influence might read these references in a more complex manner – as a species of modernist anxiety about its ties to the past – than readers did at the time. In *Brideshead Revisited* (1945), however, Waugh equates modernism with the Bright Young People, and aggressively rejects both as already things of the past.

As the Great Depression arrived, as fascism and communism grew in power, and World War II approached, the satiric tradition in English literature took a different turn, towards the visionary or utopian, in which the moral stance of the author and the basis for his condemnation of what he depicted was crystal clear. The first to make this turn (aside from Lewis in *The Childermass*) was Huxley, in his *Brave New World* (1932). *Brave New World* was a remarkable leap for the novelist to take, away from the realism of his sociological observations hitherto. It is dystopian science fiction, set in a future when science and rationality have conquered the world, so that all breeding of children occurs in controlled laboratory environments, and life is happy due to its control by drugs. The only people who maintain a traditional family life are primitives restricted to reservations. One primitive, the Savage, opposes society, keeps some sense of the nuclear family (and therefore some sense of love as opposed to sex), and maintains the cultural heritage of the past, represented by Shakespeare. The satiric nature of the work shows itself in Huxley's effort to ask us if we are en route to the brave new world, and how close we are to arrival.

Before he began his writing career, Huxley taught French at Eton, where one of his students was Eric Blair, later to become world famous under the pen name George Orwell. Orwell was a committed socialist until his experiences in the Spanish Civil War turned him decisively against what communism appeared to be doing to collectivist ideals. This led him to write *Animal Farm* (1945) and *1984* (1949). Both works belong to the visionary satiric tradition I am describing. *Animal Farm* is a short fable about what happens when a group of farm animals rid themselves of their human overlords. After a brief period of revolutionary bliss and equality, old patterns reassert themselves; and the pigs take up the overlord position. By the end of the story, though "all animals are equal," "some animals are more equal than others," in the famous phrase from the novel; and the new ruling class, the pigs, are working in harmony with humans on other farms. The point of the satire is clear: the farm is the Communist Soviet Union, by the end of the war one of the victorious allies rubbing shoulders with its former capitalist enemies, Britain and the United States. The other point of the satire concerns the official lie that the farm is a revolutionary state in which all animals are equal.

The employment of official lies as a substitute for truth is, of course, a key theme of *1984*. *1984* is a more traditional utopian fiction than *Animal*

Farm, set 35 years ahead of its publication in a world divided into three warring powers, Oceania, Eurasia, and Eastasia. So much of *1984* has passed into ordinary parlance ("Big Brother is Watching You," "doublespeak") that reading it today can be like the experience of the person who doesn't like *Hamlet* because it is full of clichés. Huxley praised *1984* but he argued that *Brave New World*, with its soft epicurean totalitarianism, was more prescient than Orwell's landscape of torture and mind control – a landscape we still call Orwellian. One's stance on this issue depends on one's location in space and time: life in Western Europe or the United States today feels more like *Brave New World*, while residents of dictatorships might consider *1984* closer to home. But both novelists point to exactly the same potential counterforces: the plot of *1984* focuses on resistance to the new order by isolated individuals, and in particular on Winston Smith as a kind of everyman in opposition. He is in love, and he desperately tries to hold onto what historical memory he retains; and so again, it is love, family, and history that resist the crushing force of the new order. The fact that so much of the novel still has currency is testimony to the power of Orwell's satiric vision: far more than Tarr or any of Lewis's other characters or meditations, Orwell's analysis has captured how we undergo attachment to those group identities that Lewis laments. His dystopian satire has given us a powerful antidote to such undergoing.

One final example of visionary satire has to suffice, William Golding's *Lord of the Flies* (1954). More a fable than a satire, more like *Animal Farm* than *1984*, *Lord of the Flies* presents itself as a realistic story of what happens to British boys stranded on an island after their plane crashes, killing all adults on board. A Hobbesian war of all against all quickly establishes itself. Some boys are murdered by others, while some are terrorized; only the arrival of a British navy vessel prevents a bloodbath. Golding is commenting on how thin the veneer of social order is; and the comment's inspiration is the war that Golding had fought in and that had just ended, in which many more civilians than soldiers were killed, and on a colossal scale.

Brave New World, *Animal Farm*, *1984*, and *Lord of the Flies* have had a broader readership and more influence than almost any work of literature from the past century. They are not, I should be quick to point out, works often taught in university literature classes, any more than *Tarr* or *The Revenge for Love* or *Crome Yellow* or *A Handful of Dust*. But these experiments in visionary satiric tradition have had a widespread public resonance, mostly because they have responded immediately and memorably to major historical anxieties. In the way Lewis expects of satire, each gives its readers critical distance from social and political norms or practices that are absurd, and thereby exhibits ways in which those norms have been constructed and packaged. The visionary satiric tradition also instances a powerful moral criticism of the established order. It roots itself less in the language and perspective of the avant-garde artist above the fray than in the perspective and values of common men and women. But the power of visionary satire in these broadly influential works is unthinkable without the social satire that came before it. No *Crome Yellow*, no *Brave New World*; and in fact Huxley after *Brave New World* oscillates between writing that continues his earlier vein and writing that creates counterfactual realities. His final novel, *Island* (1962), is an answer to *Brave New World*, depicting a utopia within reach based on eastern religious principles that were important to Huxley from early on.

After the work of Huxley, Orwell, and Golding, the tradition I have delineated essentially comes to a halt, as new forms of fiction gain attention and power. In subsequent decades there is a strong comic bias in English fiction, in writers such as Kingsley Amis, David Lodge, Malcolm Bradbury, and Kingsley Amis's son Martin Amis. In my judgment, their work is not satiric because their comic moments do not add up to a thorough opposition to the society they describe. No sustained alternative to what they depict is being explicitly advanced or even implicitly adumbrated.

Satire's inability to justify its attacks on society on the basis of an authoritative alternative perspective is a problem that pervades the Amises' novels. Kingsley Amis's *Stanley and the Women* (1984) tells a story of compromised satiric aggression. Stanley's first and second wives, unable to stay in touch with truth of any kind, are somewhat deranged. Is Stanley in contrast a touchstone of sanity? When Stanley's son becomes clinically insane, the course of his therapy impresses Stanley with the idea that psychiatric medicine is another madness. After all, the son's female psychiatrist turns treatment of her patient into a tool of crazy aggression against his father. There appears to be no exit – certainly not a trustworthy one – from insanity, either in medicine or social order. And the cause of confinement appears to be "the women," whom Stanley identifies with the root of all madness, and towards whom he expresses a virulent misogyny, as if it encapsulated an absolute assessment of gendered reality. Yet at the height of his misogynistic declaration Stanley is drunk, and about to welcome back with open arms his temporarily estranged second wife, despite his knowledge of her pathological deceitfulness. It appears that Stanley is thrown back into the arms of his own inescapable irrationality. Thirty years earlier Amis's famous first novel *Lucky Jim* (1954) showed its eponymous hero's unmasking of middle-class university intellectuals as the latest apes of god. But it also showed its hero's complicity in what he attacks. Amis's fiction apparently means that there is no possibility of a satirist's maintaining an uncompromised satirical stance in regard to his objects of derision.

Martin Amis's *Money* (1984) reiterates the compromise. The novel's narrator, Anglo-American John Self, is an advertising executive who confesses that, as "a product of the Sixties," all his hobbies "are pornographic in tendency."[2] So are Self's other activities, above all, making money: money is "the great addiction . . . You just cannot beat the money conspiracy. You can only join it" (pp. 354, 267). Self participates in the conspiracy by becoming a film director. His film, *Bad Money*, looks like an allegory of the hoggish and maniacal absurdity of Western capitalist social order: "It's the twentieth century feeling. We're the joke. You . . . got to live the joke" (p. 270). But as Self lives the joke, his film production is foundering, so he calls in a writer, a character named Martin Amis, to revise the film's grittily realistic script. Amis produces a revision remarkable for its "sinister adaptability": transforming grit into "treacle" and "cuddling," the new script shows that Amis is in tune with the "next growth area" in the "addiction industries": "generating warmth and safety" (pp. 316, 262, 91). But when the film production resumes, it turns out to have no backing. The film's producer is a confidence man; and Amis is revealed to be identical with a sinister figure who has stalked Self ominously throughout the narrative. Lewis's Pierpoint is echoed here. Yet Amis's Self-stalking appears to admit his inculpation in the addictive century that Self exemplifies. *Money* suggests that in a sinister way fiction is hopelessly adaptable to everything that it might aim to satirize. Fiction too is an addiction industry, exhibiting compromises that make it – perhaps especially its satiric impulse – another of the century's jokes. The narrative shows Self reading, for the first time, Orwell's *Animal Farm* and *1984*. Significantly, he finds it difficult to understand Orwell, except that "Airstrip One seemed like my kind of town . . . In addition, there was the welcome sex-interest and all those rat tortures to look forward to" (p. 207).

The Amises, Bradbury and Lodge make fun of what they see, but they do not in any profound sense try to move us in a new direction. One conspicuous exception presents itself, however. It is an exception that makes my case. The best writers in the English-language world over the past half-century come from once colonized lands, especially from former British colonies. Although those writers were educated in a British system and their work stands in dialogue with English literary history, nonetheless they do not engage closely with English social order. The one living British writer who has a powerful satiric bent – i.e., someone who wants to remake society, not just make fun of it – is Salman Rushdie, whose sequence of novels about India, Pakistan, and Islam, *Midnight's Children* (1980), *Shame* (1983), and *The Satanic Verses* (1988), have a satiric force directed against the social causes of lawsuits, book bannings, and the *fatwa* issued against Rushdie by the Ayatollah Khomeini. Rushdie's work subsequent to the *fatwa* has less resonance because it turns away from powerfully satiric impulses to gently comic ones. When Rushdie in *Midnight's Children* says that Indira Gandhi's hair – part white and part black – represents the Indian economy in which there is more "black money" (black-market money) than "white" or legitimate money, he captures a total social reality in an indelible passage. As a result of aiming satire at whole cultures with no self-inculpating irony, Rushdie has earned a notoriety and danger that few English writers have had. But the contextual understanding needed to grasp the full force of Rushdie's satiric onslaughts does not come from reading Lewis, Huxley, or Orwell. The presence of Rushdie as the leading exception to my generalization about the decline of English satire marks a point at which conventional literary history must make room for a more globalized narrative of literature in English.

NOTES

1 Wyndham Lewis, *The Wild Body* (London: Chatto & Windus, 1927), p. 246.
2 Martin Amis, *Money* (Harmondsworth: Penguin, 1984), p. 67.

17

M. KEITH BOOKER

The other side of history: Fantasy, romance, horror, and science fiction

Is fantasy the dominant mode of English twentieth-century fiction? The vast popularity of J. R. R. Tolkien suggests an affirmative answer.[1] And numerous writers can support a vision of the importance of a genre that comprehends science fiction, horror, and romance. H. G. Wells's scientific romances ushered in the twentieth century; the so-called British Boom, a blend of science fiction, horror, romance, and fantasy, ushered it out. Although fantasy and its companions certainly have escapist aspects, in a way that seems a departure from "the novel's" investments in realism and history, they powerfully address contemporary life; by opening the door to unlimited imaginative possibilities, by contemplating the other side of history – the fantastic side – they can lead to action in the real world.

The ascendency of fantasy forms would seem to be at odds with capitalist modernity, which the German sociologist Max Weber saw as havng stripped experience of all magic and wonder by the beginning of the twentieth century. However, as Fredric Jameson argues, it is the very thoroughness of capitalist rationalization of life that gives fantasy forms their staying power, fulfilling as they do longings for meaning beyond the workaday world of commodification and consumerism. Such genres "offer the possibility of sensing other historical rhythms, and of demonic or Utopian transformations of a real now unshakably set in place."[2] "The great expressions of the modern fantastic, the last recognizable avatars of romance as a mode, draw their magical power from an unsentimental loyalty to those henceforth abandoned clearings across which higher and lower worlds once passed" (p. 135).

This notion of certain subgenres as sites for the concentration of utopian impulses and energies is most obviously applicable to science fiction, which writers and critics (especially those on the Left) often identify with political aims. Darko Suvin has famously declared the political potential that inheres in science fiction's ability to produce "cognitive estrangement," causing readers to see their worlds from fresh perspectives that alienate them from

251

the status quo.[3] Although realistic fiction builds fictional worlds no less than other kinds of fiction do, close resemblance between a novel and our own historical world simplifies the process of world building, and limits potential for creative estrangement.

Subgenres of the kind this chapter considers result from contrastive ways in which they construct fictive worlds. The worlds of science fiction generally operate according to the same physical principles as our own, but they subordinate those principles to changes caused by rationally explicable developments, primarily scientific or technological. Horror fiction is also set in a world similar to our own, but involves monstrous intrusions of super-natural (or at least extraordinary) beings or events. Romance, which usually is a story of a purposeful quest, projects a world in which magical or supernatural powers also intrude – but those powers are more intelligible, and some are more beneficent, than those in horror fiction. Fantasy operates entirely according to principles of its own, differing from our world in ways that are not limited by the laws of physics, and responding to whatever variations (usually magical or supernatural) the author chooses to invent. Because worlds of horror and fantasy differ from our own in ways that are not scientifically or rationally explicable, Suvin declares that such modes have very limited potential for creating the utopian energy derived from cognitive estrangement. But much of the last century of English speculative fiction (as it was denominated briefly in the 1960s) suggests that Suvin's derogation of fantasy needs reexamination, if only because fantasy pervades the other modes. And the theoretically separable modes are themselves mutually porous.

Wells's "scientific romances" (as he called them) make science fiction, political progressivism, and utopian speculation indissociable. *The Time Machine* (1895) warningly projects consequences of class inequality: eons in the future the division between working and rentier classes endures; but the workers, who have been driven underground, are farming the upper class, who have become imbeciles on whom the workers literally feed. *The War of the Worlds* (1898) amounts to a defamiliarizing critique of colonialism. *A Modern Utopia* (1905) presents an alternate world that is radically different from past utopias. Unlike them, Wells's is not a sequestered, islanded place, but is global; it does not subordinate individual life to collective values, but combines rational world order with cultivation of unique individuals, some of whom voluntarily administer the globalized state. Wells's utopia develops technology in order to free humanity from labor; it supersedes representative democracy, liberalism, and imperialism; permits alternatives to monogam-ous marriage; honors religious impulse; and, promoting miscegenation, bans racial and ethnic division.

Wells makes himself the narrator of *A Modern Utopia*, and successfully quests to encounter his double in the alternative world, as a strategy for persuading readers that we all carry within us utopian alter egos, and can bring them to life. To be sure, cosmic evolution, if we are to judge by the entropic universe of *The Time Machine*, shows that the cards are stacked against humanity's future. As a counter to *The Time Machine*, yet as a corroboration of Wells's utopian hopes, the English socialist Olaf Stapledon's *Star Maker* (1937) pictures cooperation rather than entropy as an evolving cosmic force. Symbiosis, including amalgamations of widely different species to each other, vitalizes intergalactic life. Such vitality makes human egos and internecine conflicts look sorry and stupid in the light of the grand aims of Stapledon's eponymous Creator. But Stapledon's narrative hopes that a finer conjunction with Star Maker awaits us.

The same hope informs novels by Katharine Burdekin and Arthur C. Clarke. Burdekin's *Proud Man* (1934) is narrated by a time traveler who returns from the future to the present, to report on what, from the perspective of the future, is a subhuman stage of life. Male existence, especially because of its misogyny, is unusually subhuman. It is good to learn that it will be a thing of the past. Clarke's work, two decades and a world war after Stapledon and Burdekin, represents humanity's upward evolution, typically propelled by the intervention of nonterrestrials who have been overseeing humanity's progress from its beginnings. In *Childhood's End* (1953) alien Overlords, partly through advanced technology and partly through trickery, establish dominion on earth, imposing rules that will prevent the human race from destroying itself. The Overlords undo nationalism and establish a single World State, which brings about unprecedented peace and prosperity. To be sure, Clarke displays some skepticism toward this utopian condition, noting that many find it boring, given that humanity now has no challenges to face. Artistic and other forms of creativity are also greatly curtailed, partly because human culture comes to be dominated by television. Finally, however, it is revealed that the Overlords have arrived on earth in service to their master, an "Overmind" consisting of the fusion of a variety of species with vastly advanced psychic abilities. The Overlords are not so advanced, and human beings have a greater potential to realize those abilities; so the Overlords join with humanity in order to merge with Overmind, and abandon earth.

Clarke was a major figure in postwar science fiction, at a time when Americans dominated the genre. Roger Luckhurst argues that the association of science fiction with "Americanized modernity ... is ... part of the reason that the most notable form of writing in England in the wake of the war was the more indigenous form of fantasy."[4] Luckhurst argues that the work of C. S. Lewis and Tolkien "responds directly to the condition of modernity in England, and to what [those writers] perceived as a disastrous defeat of tradition" (p. 124). But the indigenous tradition in English fiction is too deeply rooted to have justified such fear. And even before World War I, as Wells's case shows, fantasy was already responding directly to a transnational, rather than merely American, phenomenon of capitalist modernization.

It was doing so even in novels for children. In fiction by the Fabian Socialist Edith Nesbit, young protagonists regret that the world, as Weber was pointing out, is disenchanted. To their delight, however, they come to experience time travel and learn to practice magic, thereby revealing "weak spots in the curtain that . . . hangs . . . between the world of magic and the world that seems . . . to be real."[5] One result of those weak spots in Nesbit's *The Enchanted Castle* (1907) is a wedding that breaks down class barriers, and hence brings about progressive change in "reality." That an involvement of fantasy and science fiction can lead in a progressive direction is surprisingly, strikingly apparent in Kipling's career. Kipling's volumes about English history, *Puck of Pook's Hill* (1906) and *Rewards and Fairies* (1910), appoint Shakespeare's Puck as a guide to the island past. Puck's chronicles, mixing magic and fact, suggest an undermining of imperialist ideology. Meanwhile, Kipling competed with Wells in inventing English science fiction: he wrote affirmative fantasies about human symbiosis with technology – including engineering, bridge-building, and nuclear-powered airships – that influenced subsequent developments in the genre.

Wells, Nesbit, and Kipling enlist fantasy as an optimistic way to confront capitalist modernization. Another optimistic enlistment is James Stephens's *The Crock of Gold* (1912), a Blakeian quest romance in which a philosopher and his family, wrongly accused of stealing gold from leprechauns, traverse both bourgeois reality (represented by the police) and the divine world (represented, to begin with, by Pan) to prove their innocence. Along the path of their quest they undergo ontological revelations. Despite such upbeat visions, however, given the anxiety-ridden period leading to the Great War, it is not surprising that fiction often drifted into horror, and produced Bram Stoker's *Dracula* (1897). Stoker's vampire, tapping into turn-of-the-century fears concerning sexuality, colonialism, and class conflict, and establishing the genre's potential for constating social commentary alongside sensation, remains the best-known celebrity of the mode.

Other early works of modern British horror crossed the generic boundary into the realm of fantasy, or even science fiction, setting precedents for hybrid compounds. Lord Dunsany's tales, *Time and the Gods* (1906) and *The Book of Wonder* (1912), blend romance with grim satire of intellectual and spiritual aspirations: quests in Dunsany are endless and abyssal, and the gods themselves undergo extinction. M. R. James's stories, focusing on a traditional scientific technology – bibliographical and textual study – reveal the technology's embroilment in ghostly or vampiric worlds. William Hope Hodgson's *The House on the Borderland* (1908) is especially dark. The novel reproduces the diary of an owner of an isolated Irish mansion attacked by horrifying swine-creatures that seem to emerge from hell into the building's basement. The attack is a preliminary to the diarist's time travel, beyond the death of the earth and sun, to the collapse of the universe. Offering the swine creatures as emblems of animality in general, Hodgson suggests a fundamental opposition between human and other biological life; he also suggests the bestiality of the psyche, and the cosmic insignificance and isolation of humanity. *The House on the Border Land* chillingly refutes the optimistic side of *The Time Machine*.

A less shadowy quest romance, but one that is lined with menace, is David Lindsay's *A Voyage to Arcturus* (1920). Its protagonist, another time-traveler, journeys to far-flung temporal domains and multiple worlds. Every person and world he encounters is illusory, the mask of yet another self or another cosmic agent. The multiplicity of selves, times, and worlds, it is at last revealed, are all emanations of Crystalman, a cosmic demon masquerading as pleasure and as God. The protagonist learns that he must die, be reborn as an alternative self, and voyage on in solitude and pain if he is to gain any advantage over the adversary. Lindsay's universe is better than Hodgson's only inasmuch as it inspires its victims to endure and oppose it, in the name of a Gnostic-like god who is antithetical to Crystalman, and who suffers as much as he creates.

Can "demonic transformations" of reality such as those just surveyed really tap utopian longings? Arthur Machen's work, which also exemplifies fantasy's multimodal character, provides a test case. His *The Great God Pan* (1894) starts out as science fiction, with a focus on experimental brain surgery; it then veers into horror, disclosing Satan as the demiurge. Machen's *The Hill of Dreams* (1907), another modal hybrid, combines an artist's *Bildungsroman* with fantasy. Aspiring writer Lucian Taylor, growing up in rural Wales, takes his inspiration from an otherworldly experience in the ruins of an old Roman fort. Machen focuses on Lucian's sense of alienation, and his disgust at the banal strivings of bourgeois society, from which his visions of Roman days, however disturbingly apparitional, provide escape. The book's contrast between Lucian's fantasy world and the real world mirrors its more mainstream opposition between the ideality of artistic creation and the reality of day-to-day life, both art and fantasy serving as alternatives to capitalist routinization. That these alternatives ultimately fail does not diminish the power of the utopian longing that informs them, under the sign of the occult. According to Jameson, in the context of modern capitalism, perhaps the best that utopian desire can achieve is to make us aware of limits imposed on our imagination of alternatives to history. "The best Utopias are those that fail the most comprehensively."[6]

It should be noted that writers usually identified with modernism (inexplicably, Wells tends to be left out) showed willingness to veer into the territory of the fantastic or the supernatural, even though modernist fiction, however experimental, was relatively realistic. One thinks of Woolf's *Orlando* (1928), whose protagonist lives for hundreds of years, changing gender along the way; of Rebecca West's *Harriet Hume: A London Fantasy* (1929); of Sylvia Townsend Warner's animal fables in *The Cat's Cradle Book* (1940) and her revisions of Kipling and Tolkien in *Kingdoms of Elfin* (1977); of Flann O'Brien's hopping from one level of reality or myth to another in *At Swim-Two-Birds* (1939) and *The Third Policeman* (1967); of *Finnegans Wake* (1939), in which not only imagery and themes but language itself becomes fantastic; and of Wyndham Lewis's trilogy, *The Human Age* (1928–55), about cosmic war between God and fallen angels. But, perhaps unfortunately, the popularity of Tolkien (and C. S. Lewis) may have tended to identify their work with fantasy in a way that wrongly separates fantasy from the history of the novel.

In the context of secularist or religiously heterodox components in modernist writing, Lewis and Tolkien's dependence on Christian tradition made them appear to occupy a place set apart. Certainly Lewis's adult fiction – a "Space Trilogy" that concludes with *That Hideous Strength* (1945) – is a dissent from modernism and even modernity, both of which are represented in *That Hideous Strength* by an all-embracing intellectual and moral relativism enshrined in the novel's N.I.C.E. Institute. Lewis's protagonists, the Ransoms, coming to learn that N.I.C.E.'s relativism is a front for evil interplanetary spirits, engage in a tug of war with N.I.C.E. for possession of King Arthur's magician Merlin, who has come back to life, and who represents Logres, an eternal unfallen England, one that has perennial power to recover Britain from hostile invasions by enemies without or within.

Among the enemies within for Lewis, one gathers, are theological speculations that suggest ambiguous divinities, gods who figure a merely relative difference between good and evil. Stapledon's Star Maker worried Lewis on this score. Lindsay's divinity is similarly uncertain; so, it might be argued, are more direct predecessors of Lewis's theological science fiction: G. K. Chesterton and Charles Williams. Chesterton's *The Man Who Was Thursday* (1907) suggests that the Judaeo-Christian God is a supreme anarchist-terrorist, and that a terrorist God is not fearful, because He inspires human courage to break free of law's rigidity – a freedom that is a cosmic principle. Chesterton insisted that his suggestion be understood as a nightmare vision, not as a theodicy; but the nightmare has persuasive force, especially thanks to Chesterton's paradox-saturated aphoristic style. Charles Williams's theological science fictions are, unlike Chesterton's, not at all playful; but, in hinting at a Gnostic god as well as an orthodox one, Williams involve struggles between good and evil with gothic dimensions on both sides. In *All-Hallows Eve* (1947) the ordinary world is enclosed in a penumbra inhabited by beings who are neither living nor dead. The dead-alive sphere is a horror; yet those who enter its uncertain realm find it to be a crucial medium of cosmic change, for better as well as for worse.

Lewis and Tolkien write fantasy in order to disambiguate differences between divinities and demons, between good and bad. It is not only theology that is at stake. Both writers dramatize ambiguities that afflict worldly power and lead to power's abuse in world-destroying ways. *That Hideous Strength* opposes power more even than spiritual doubt: N.I.C.E. technology and science are not bad in themselves, but bad inasmuch as necromancers acquire them as instrumental means to world domination. Herein lies the secular utopian aspect of Lewis and Tolkien. *The Lord of the Rings* (1954–5) is a trilogy of novels about a quest to divest dangerous worldly power, rather than to gain it. Abusive exploitation of the rings is inevitable for their possessors. That is why Frodo must set out on a hair-raising adventure to rid Middle Earth of his magic property. Tom Shippey emphasizes the importance of Tolkien's revision of the romance formula: Tolkien constructs an anti-quest; his protagonist must lose a treasure, not gain it. And as Donald Davie writes, "the driving force of [Tolkien's] book is unheroic, even anti-heroic."[7] A measure of that driving force can result from comparing Tolkien's romance with an immediate predecessor, E. R. Eddison's *The Worm Ouroboros* (1922). Eddison inspires Tolkien's fantastical ethnographies, his minute attention to imaginary geography, his spooky cross-country treks, and his mimicry of antiquated English. But whereas Eddison gives us heroes and villains who are all supermen, Tolkien's story gives us hobbits, creatures that are not heroic, and not even human. The density of Tolkien's description of the hobbits and Middle Earth might be said to naturalize his fantasy to the point where cognitive estrangement does not operate; but the narrative makes clear that it is hobbits, not men, who find it possible to renounce power. There is a decided alienation effect in the fact that "hobbits, who are less than human, are the only beings in Tolkien's world that a human reader can . . . 'identify with' " (*Thomas Hardy*, p. 95).

While Lewis and Tolkien were forging trilogies of redemption and salvation, their contemporaries produced extended gothic and romance-inspired novels that showed both spiritual and secular salvation as being hard to come by. Mervyn Peake's "Gormenghast" trilogy, *Titus Groan* (1946), *Gormenghast* (1950), and *Titus Alone* (1956), demonstrates a surprising compatibility between oppressive social convention and upstart class mobility. The former is exemplified by the ancient Gormenghast dynasty and its claustrophobic nightmare castle; the latter by the castle's social climber and opportunist Steerpike. Titus, the dynastic heir, wanting neither his strangulating heritage nor the snaky mobility that operates within established confines, renounces both alternatives. But it takes Titus three volumes to extricate himself from the land of Groan, which is populated by figures who recall Wyndham Lewis's human "contraptions" in *The Wild Body* (1927), and whom Peake renders in an anti-realist verbal style derived from Lewis the modernist. The upshot of Titus's exit is a hopeful liberty but an isolated one; moreover, no story is available to express his saved state. If Jameson is correct about the best utopias being those that fail, the liberation of Peake's Titus would support his point.

T. H. White's Arthurian tetralogy, *The Once and Future King* (1939–58), also exemplifies the paradoxical effect of failed utopian desire. White's book has rivalled the popularity of Tolkien, and amounts to a bleak but tonic alternative to C. S. Lewis's pious imagination of Merlin and Logres as salvific spiritual centers. In White the saving agents are not transcendental. Instead, they are animal nature and human homosexual eros. White's Merlin is a time-traveler (he lives in the future, like Burdekin's protagonist, so he sees present events retrospectively) and also is an eco-traveler: he can metamorphose himself into animal forms, and he teaches young Arthur to do so, as a way of training the future king in pacificism. For in non-human nature, Merlin points out, there are scarcely any species that engage in internecine warfare. Arthur holds onto the lesson, and it inspires him to oppose race-based antagonisms in his kingdom. Unfortunately his pacificism does not succeed, thanks to the perversity of heterosexual eros in the person of Lancelot. White imagines Lancelot as unconsciously in love with Arthur, and as using adultery with Guinevere as a repressed mode of making love to the king. Without the Guinevere–Lancelot adultery, which is one of the sources of the realm-destroying quest for the Holy Grail, Camelot would have been saved. White's moral, his Arthurian fantasy suggests, is that if homosexual love had been permitted in Camelot, its utopia would have endured. The fantasy thereby also suggests that the return of the king depends upon the future of pacifism and a further sexual liberation.[8]

In the later twentieth century, post-Tolkien British fantasy seems increasingly antagonistic to Lewis and Tolkien, in effect refuting their visions. Philip Pullman's trilogy, *His Dark Materials* (1995–2000), directly opposes the Christian tradition (especially of Lewis), albeit echoing some of Chesterton's paradoxes. Michael de Larrabeiti's *The Borribles* (1976), *The Borribles Go for Broke* (1981), and *The Borribles: Across the Dark Metropolis* (1986) feature streetwise wild children in London who gain supernatural abilities, apparently through their anarchistic rejection of traditional authority. The children are antithetical to gentle hobbits (and to Nesbit's well-bred youngsters). DeLarrabeiti's sequence is unusual for its slum-world setting, refusing to gloss over the crime, violence, refuse, and profanity that are an integral part of urban reality. Nevertheless, its notion of an unknown London coexisting with the one we think we know, and the solidarity and cooperation that the Borribles figure, lessening any need for authoritarian power to check their aggressive impulses, reminds us again of utopian non-competitive social order. It remains for the current century to assess the relation of J. K. Rowling's Harry Potter narratives (1997–2007), and their staggering popularity and importance to the culture industry, in regard to the adult and children's fantasy traditions that preceded them.

In the heyday of Tolkien and White's fantasy, science fiction was dominated by American writers. But that dominance was mitigated in the 1960s due to the prominence of British authors and editors in the so-called "New Wave," a movement that sought greater sophistication for science fiction, in terms of its literary properties and its engagement with real-world problems. The British journal *New Worlds*, edited by Michael Moorcock, was the force behind the New Wave, itself driven by the utopian strivings of the 1960s.

Moorcock's prolific work, combining fantasy and science fiction in a mode that seemed distinctively postmodern, also looks back to Edwardian fantasists and modernist classics. In *The Warlord of the Air: A Scientific Romance* (1971) Moorcock borrows his protagonist, Edwardian soldier Oswald Bastable, from Nesbit's invented children; and he has Bastable meet up with Joseph Conrad, who appears under his Polish surname, Korzeniowski. The meeting occurs as a result of Bastable's time travel into what has come to be known, thanks to inventions like Moorcock's, as alternative history. Bastable is fast forwarded from 1903 to 1973, where life has continued on a side of history other than the one we know: there have been no world wars; nineteenth-century empires have settled down peaceably to rule the globe; technology has advanced, but without, as yet, developing jet planes or nuclear weaponry. Old-style racism also is unchanged; and Bastable gets into trouble in 1974 by protesting against a racist named Ronald Reagan. As a result of this trouble Bastable falls, unwillingly, into the company of a gang of utopist-terrorists who include Joseph Conrad and Lenin. They and their Chinese leader have founded an anticolonialist socialist utopia in the middle of China that initially horrifies Bastable; but it wins him over when he realizes that utopian social relations are preferable to the competition and coercion he has encountered in capitalist societies. But the novel, the first of a trilogy, ends ominously. The utopists have developed an atomic bomb; hoping to end imperialism, in 1974 they drop it on Hiroshima. Bastable at this point is blown back into 1903.

Among the political and cultural concerns of Moorcock's work (and of the New Wave as a whole) was staunch opposition both to the American war effort in Vietnam and to American cultural hegemony in science fiction. One of the most unusual of the British New Wave writers who took on America as a subject was J. G. Ballard, whose practice of mixed modes, in which science fiction, surrealism, and the historical novel merge, makes classification difficult. Ballard's *The Drowned World* (1962), *The Burning World* (1964), and *The Crystal World* (1966) involve vaguely science-fictional visions of future catastrophic transformations of the landscape, and thus can be considered – along with John Christopher's *The Death of Grass* (1957) – forerunners of environmentalist science fiction. In *Crash* (1973) and *The Atrocity Exhibition* (1969, revised 1990), Ballard pushes a characteristic New Wave interest in frank representation of sexuality to an extreme, though (especially in the latter) the formal experimentation that marks such works is even more daring than the content.

Constructed of fragments designed to be read in no particular order, *The Atrocity Exhibition* features protagonists who attempt to make sense of the Vietnam War, American celebrity culture, the Kennedy assassination, pornography, and nuclear arms. Are those phenomena symptoms of cultural insanity; or are attempts to make sense of them, in a totalizing and scientifically rational way, insane? Chapters such as "Why I Want to Fuck Ronald Reagan" (which caused Doubleday to destroy the first American edition of the novel) include mock-scientific studies that detail experimental subjects' sexual fascination, often involving violence, with parts of Reagan's body; and draw conclusions about the anality of Reagan, who was then governor of California, and who emerges in Ballard as a sinister Presidential contender, with similarities to Hitler or Nixon. It should be noted, however, that *The Atrocity Exhibition* is not dystopian in its treatment of sex and violence. They are for Ballard two parts of the same phenomenon; they inform drives that are crucial to human happiness, even if we have yet to find adequate social and political forms within which to express them. *The Atrocity Exhibition* thus has a certain utopian potential both in its content as well as in the sheer postmodern hubris of its form.

Also riding the New Wave to prominence was John Brunner. His fantasy satires construct future societies in which trends of Brunner's own day have developed to horrifying extremes. *Stand on Zanzibar* (1968) explores overpopulation and its ramifying geopolitical complications. International strife is a permanent fact of life in this near-future world, with the United States and China engaged in a conflict driven by competition for dwindling resources. *The Sheep Look Up* (1972) projects future environmental degradation that is made worse by the actions of the US government, led by a swaggering President who bears an uncanny resemblance in political style, three decades in advance, to George W. Bush. *The Jagged Orbit* (1969) focuses on the racism and criminalistic tendencies of the military-industrial complex; and *The Shockwave Rider* (1975) outlines a nefarious worldwide communications explosion, in many ways anticipating the later (largely American) phenomenon of "cyberpunk" science fiction, a movement that has shown considerable dystopian leanings.

Despite Brunner's dystopian content, however, his novels convey utopian energy and hope by virtue of the exuberance and inventiveness of their style and form, which partly is influenced by American writer John Dos Passos's *U.S.A.* (1931–7). Brief narrative segments advance Brunner's plot, while the world depicted gains substance from a narrative embedding of segments of contemporary journalism, advertising, and popular culture. Brunner's dedication to intricate artistry may suggest one reason why he believed that the intensively crafted fantasies of Kipling "influenced my work more than anybody, more even than Wells."[9]

An intensively aesthetic character pervades the fantasy fiction of M. John Harrison, a collaborator with Moorcock, and the literary editor of *New Worlds* from 1968 to 1975. Harrison rose to prominence as an author in his own right because of a sequence of fantasy stories and novellas (1971–85) that comprise his history of "Viriconium," a capital city of an empire that has become a decadent "Evening Culture." Life there combines a violent archaic order – hand-to-hand combat between members of long-drawn rival historical and political factions – with devotion to artists who have achieved extraordinary accomplishments in theater, dance, and painting. The city's strange blend of trashed grandeur and aesthetic nostalgia figures its indeterminate, intermediate character: it exists in and out of history, in and out of art. One citizen, speaking of the world in general, appears to sum up Viriconium in particular: it is

> "so old that the substance of reality no longer knows quite what it ought to be. The original template is hopelessly blurred. History repeats over and over again this one city and a few frightful events – not rigidly, but in a shadowy, tentative, fashion, as if it understands nothing else, but would like to learn."[10]

Does Harrison reflect metafictionally here about the general character of fantasy fiction? It might be construed as a mode especially attuned to a hopelessly blurred historical condition, one that, for all its uncertainty, would yet like to learn about itself from Harrison's kind of art form.

British science fiction and fantasy have experienced a remarkable rebirth from the early 1990s to the present in the phenomenon known as the British Boom. Following in the footsteps of the New Wave, the works of Boom writers tend to be more literary than those of their predecessors. They are often fiercely political as well. Luckhurst implies that the Boom has been made possible by just the right balance between repression and freedom of expression in contemporary Britain; and partly by the fact that the low value accorded science fiction, fantasy, and horror has allowed those genres to "flourish largely below the radar" of the British cultural establishment.[11] Whether it is below the radar or not, however, the British Boom has restored some of the prestige that British science fiction enjoyed in the first half of the twentieth century, when Wells towered over the genre. The reemergence of British science fiction has been particularly strong in subgenres once almost entirely the province of American writers – space opera (the science fiction equivalent of the Western, i.e., "horse opera") and cyberpunk, which emphasizes interaction for better or worse between human and artificial intelligence. Boom writers characteristically merge those subgenres.

Worthy of special note among Boom space operas are the "Culture" novels of Iain M. Banks. They elaborate the political, social, and cultural practices of "the Culture," a vast (and vastly advanced) intergalactic federation governed by hyper-intelligent artificial intelligences (Banks harks back to Stapledon and Clarke). The Culture manages human and other species' affairs better than their constituents can hope to. Consequently, human beings in Banks's affluent machine-ruled society have rich and active lives, with potentially limitless longevity. A principal problem for them and other species, however, is a potential for feeling impatient with "self-satisfied Culture: its imperialism of smugness."[12] The imperialism shows itself in the Culture's tendency to meddle in the affairs of other civilizations it encounters in space, by trying to nudge them toward the Culture's egalitarian kind of society. Although the meddling sounds menacing, Banks clearly presents the interventionism of the Culture as a very different phenomenon from the imperialism of earth's past. While Europeans felt justified in colonizing most of the globe because of their confidence in the superiority of their way of life, the Culture is not interested in colonization; it is only generously trying to share with others. Moreover, because the Culture's controlling intellects are so vast (and so objective), cultural relativism might not apply here: the Culture might really *be* the best possible society. But even the Culture can make mistakes, just as those who live within it can make mistakes – adventurous ones to be sure – by traveling outside its bounds. The reader's opportunity to watch such mistakes unfold provides a measure of how, in comparison with even especially exciting alternatives, the Culture is more desirable, and more utopian than otherwise.

Just as Wells in *A Modern Utopia* exists as both himself and a double, Banks exists under two names and two writing personalities. As Iain Banks he is a mainstream novelist, or almost that, if one can count novels such as his gothic-tinged *The Wasp Factory* (1984) in such a category. But Banks and Banks's differing modes of production demonstrate the increasing difficulty of making distinctions between conventional "literary fiction" and fantasy fiction – though we should recall that even Wells, a century earlier, had a dual career as a writer of scientific romances and realist social satires. In any case, Boom writers frequently mix science fiction with fantasy, though their tendency has been to add science fictional elements to a matrix that is primarily fantasy, rather than the other way around.

Perhaps the most omnipresent Boom writer associated with fantasy is Neil Gaiman, best known for his work in the medium of comics, especially his highly successful "Sandman" sequence of 75 graphic novels (1988–96). But no discussion of the Boom would be complete without mention of China Miéville, who, as Andrew Butler notes, comes as close as anyone to being the signature figure of the movement.[13] To describe his own complex work, Miéville prefers the term "weird fiction"; he leads a group of mostly British writers, denominated the "new weird," who want to move beyond the clichés and superficiality of many instances of the fantasy genre, especially those bearing marks of Tolkien. In pursuit of their aim, "new weird" writers (including Harrison, Ian R. MacLeod, Mary Gentle, and Justina Robson) tend to challenge genre boundaries even more than other Boom writers.

Miéville's first novel *King Rat* (1998) is a horror tale that evokes an alternative, multicultural London, in which a half-rat protagonist leads a political revolution of London's rats against King Rat and the Pied Piper of Hamelin. The book also evokes political dimensions that suggest an imaginative range seldom realized in horror writing, and that attest to its author's Marxism. (Miéville recently published his London School of Economics doctoral thesis, which is a Marxist theory of international law.) In *Perdido Street Station* (2000) Miéville introduces a full-blown alternative world, Bas-Lag, and one of its cities, New Crobuzon. Miéville's spaces are as detailed and dense with history as Tolkien's Middle Earth, but far more grounded in a palpable material reality, albeit one that is of peculiarly mixed character. New Crobuzon echoes Viriconium, inasmuch as it is a city that is at once advanced and archaic, sophisticated and decadent. Remarkable technological and magical powers thread it; but simultaneously it is ruinous and polluted, a foul wasteland. Repressive political agents administer the city; and they have an uneasy alliance with New Crobuzon crime bosses, and can hire denizens of Hell if they need help. The populace seethes with tensions among its multicultural, indeed multi-species groups, principal among which are a frog-like order, the vodyanoi, who can sculpt water; and an insect population, the khepri, one of whom, Lin, a talented artist, is the lover of Isaac, a human scientist. Their inter-species love is an object of shame and public censure. The city's conglomerated variety also comprehends a nascent network of self-starting computers that has evolved autonomous consciousness; and a vast spider-like creature, the Weaver, who inhabits multiple dimensions of reality and whose language sounds like a debased dialect of Joycespeak in *Finnegans Wake*. These are just some of the components with which Miéville remakes the historical and literary worlds that we know into a new template for fantasy.

Because utopian imaginations are a way of remaking the real world into a speculative alternative, it is worth noting how Miéville shapes *Perdido Street Station* as a self-conscious narrative about metamorphic processes. The story pits varieties of remaking against each other: Lin's mimetic art is one variety; another variety is Isaac's science, enlisted in the cause of rehabilitating flight capacity for a garuda whose wings have been cut off as punishment for a crime he has committed; New Crobuzon law also is a remaking agent, because it punishes criminals by submitting them to grotesque bodily reconstruction; yet another variety of remaking is represented by the computer constructs that have started to program themselves. New Crobuzon is a world entirely devoted to transformative fabrications. But how are the constituents of such a world, and how are Miéville's readers, to sort out what processes of remaking or fabrication, in a life saturated by them, are better than others? The question becomes critical when, thanks to a chance convergence between Isaac's experiments (on behalf of the garuda) and secret business-government experiments (on behalf of prospective drug profits), horror is let loose in the city. The subjects of the experiments are vampiric moths. When the moths escape from laboratories, they make New Crobuzon a nightmare landscape.

Isaac saves the day, thanks to an engine of "crisis energy" that he has invented as a way of enabling the garuda to fly again and as an alternative to remaking his wings. The engine destroys the moths. But then Isaac realizes that he cannot use "crisis energy" to help the garuda. For he learns that the garuda's crime was a rape, which is considered in the garuda's home territory in Bas-Lag as a theft of another being's life-choices. That theft is a wrong sort of remaking, just as the city's experiments on the moths is a wrong sort. Isaac cannot bring himself to erase – in other words, to remake – a law that has justly punished the garuda for his injury of another. But the garuda himself no longer wants to be remade. His aspirations change as a consequence of his helping Isaac and a ragtag multi-species handful of heroes to defeat the vampires; he is content, without resentment any longer, to bear the guilt of his past. The ending of *Perdido Street Station* is almost a happy one, were it not for the fact that Lin has been raped and permanently disabled by a crime boss who is one of the most horrifically re-made of Miéville's figures.

Given that fantasy and science fiction re-make the historical world as we know it, it is startling to note numerous aspects of *Perdido Street Station* whereby Miéville expresses opposition to modes of remaking history and fabricating it anew. It is as if the very production of fantasy contains a dystopian element. Yet, once again, the other side of dystopic fabrication is a utopian prospect. *Perdido Street Station*'s sequels, *The Scar* (2002) and *Iron Council* (2004), dramatize the remaking process in terms of violent rebellion against New Crobuzon's anti-egalitarian economic order. As Carl Freedman observes, the violence allegorizes the violence and coercion that are inherent in capitalist systems. Utopian possibilities remain, however, possibilities that Freedman sees as "rigorously and precisely Marxist,"[14] no matter what defeats are suffered by progressive forces as the plots play out.

Miéville is unusually self-conscious about his relationship with political and literary predecessors, openly declaring his work as a rejoinder to conservative forebears like Tolkien, while celebrating his relationship with progressive predecessors like Wells and aesthetic influences like Harrison. "New weird fiction," and the future of British nonrealist fiction as a whole, takes a long, vital twentieth-century tradition of fantasy with it as it moves into the future.

NOTES

1 Tom Shippey answers affirmatively in *J. R. R. Tolkien: Author of the Century* (Boston: Houghton Mifflin, 2001), p. vii.
2 Fredric Jameson, *The Political Unconscious: Narrative as a Socially Symbolic Act* (Ithaca: Cornell University Press, 1981), p. 104.
3 Darko Suvin, *Metamorphoses of Science Fiction: On the Poetics and History of a Literary Genre* (New Haven: Yale University Press, 1979).
4 Roger Luckhurst, *Science Fiction* (Cambridge: Polity Press, 2005), p. 123.
5 Edith Nesbit, *The Enchanted Castle* and *Five Children and It* (New York: Barnes & Noble, 2005), p. 345.
6 Fredric Jameson, *Archaeologies of the Future* (London: Verso, 2005), p. xiii.
7 Donald Davie, *Thomas Hardy and British Poetry* (New York: Oxford University Press, 1972), p. 94.
8 For this reading of White, see Robert L. Caserio, *The Novel in England 1900–1950: History and Theory* (New York: Twayne, 1999), pp. 308–9.

9 John Brunner, "Introduction," *John Brunner Presents Kipling's Fantasy Stories* (New York: TOR, 1992).

10 M. John Harrison, *Viriconium* (London: Millennium, 2000), p. 15.

11 Roger Luckhurst, "Cultural Governance, New Labor, and the British SF Boom," *Science Fiction Studies* 30.3 (November 2003): 417–35, 423.

12 Iain M. Banks, *The State of the Art* (San Francisco: Night Shade Books, 2007), p. 13.

13 Andrew M. Butler, "Thirteen Ways of Looking at the British Boom," *Science Fiction Studies* 30 (2003): 374–93, 376.

14 Carl Freedman, "Speculative Fiction and International Law: The Marxism of China Miéville," *Socialism and Democracy* 20.3 (2006): 25–40, 25.

FURTHER READING

Introduction

English, James F. *The Economy of Prestige*, Cambridge: Harvard University Press, 2005.

Gibson, Andrew, and Robert Hampson. *Conrad and Theory*, Amsterdam: Rodopi, 1998.

Marcus, Jane. *Hearts of Darkness: White Women Write Race*, New Brunswick: Rutgers University Press, 2004.

The art of English fiction in the twentieth century

Bradbury, Malcolm. *The Modern British Novel*, New York: Penguin, 1993.

Connor, Steven. *The English Novel in History, 1950–1995*, New York: Routledge, 1996.

Eysteinsson, Astradur. *The Concept of Modernism*, Ithaca: Cornell University Press, 1990.

Hale, Dorothy J. *Social Formalism: The Novel in Theory from Henry James to the Present*, Stanford: Stanford University Press, 1998.

Nussbaum, Martha C. *Love's Knowledge: Essays on Philosophy and Literature*, New York: Oxford University Press, 1990.

The British Empire and the English modernist novel

Baucom, Ian. *Out of Place: Englishness, Empire, and the Locations of Identity*, Princeton: Princeton University Press, 1999.

Begam, Richard and Michael Valdez Moses (eds.), *Modernism and Colonialism: British and Irish Literature, 1900–1939*, Durham: Duke University Press, 2007.

Booth, Howard J. and Nigel Rigby, eds. *Modernism and Empire: Writing and British Coloniality 1890–1940*, Manchester: Manchester University Press, 2000.

Fogel, Aaron. *Coercion to Speak: Conrad's Poetics of Dialogue*, Cambridge: Harvard University Press, 1985.

Gikandi, Simon. *Maps of Englishness: Writing Identity in the Culture of Colonialism*, New York: Columbia University Press, 1996.

Gorra, Michael. *After Empire: Scott, Naipaul, Rushdie*, Chicago: University of Chicago Press, 1997.

Suleri, Sara. *The Rhetoric of English India*, Chicago: University of Chicago Press, 1992.

Realism and rebellion in Edwardian and Georgian fiction

Batchelor, John. *The Edwardian Novelists*, New York: St. Martin's Press, 1982.

Caserio, Robert L. "Edwardians to Georgians," *The Cambridge History of Twentieth Century English Literature*, Cambridge: Cambridge University Press, 2004, pp. 83–99.

Bloom, Harold, ed. *Edwardian and Georgian Fiction, 1880–1915*, New York: Chelsea House, 1990.

Di Battista, Maria. *First Love: the Affections of Modern Fiction*, Chicago: University of Chicago Press, 1991.

Di Battista, Maria, and Lucy McDiarmid. *High and Low Moderns: Literature and Culture, 1889–1939*, New York: Oxford University Press, 1996.

Hynes, Samuel. *The Edwardian Turn of Mind*, Princeton: Princeton University Press, 1968.

Priestley, J. B. *The Edwardians*, New York: Harper and Row, 1970.

The Great War in English fiction

Ayers, David. "Richard Aldington's *Death of a Hero*: A Proto-fascist Novel," *English*, 47: 188, 89–98.

Cecil, Hugh. "Henry Williamson: Witness of the Great War," *Henry Williamson: The Man, the Writings*, ed. Brocard Sewell, Padstow: Tabb House, 1980, pp. 69–82.

Cohen, Debra Rae. *Remapping the Home Front: Locating Citizenship in British Women's Great War Fiction*, Boston: Northeastern University Press, 2002.

Edwards, Paul. *Wyndham Lewis: Painter and Writer*, New Haven: Yale University Press, 2000.

Haslam, Sara. *Fragmenting Modernism: Ford Madox Ford, the Novel and the First World War*, Manchester: Manchester University Press, 2002.

Willis, Jr., J. H. "The Censored Language of War: Richard Aldington's *Death of a Hero* and Three Other War Novels of 1929," *Twentieth Century Literature*, 45: 4 (Winter 1999), 467–88.

Post-war modernism in the 1920s and 1930s

Bluemel, Kristin. *George Orwell and the Radical Eccentrics: Intermodernism in Literary London*, New York: Palgrave Macmillan, 2004.

Kermode, Frank. *History and Value*, Oxford: Clarendon Press, 1988.

Mengham, Rod. *The Idiom of the Time: the Writings of Henry Green*, Cambridge: Cambridge University Press, 1982.

Trotter, David. *Paranoid Modernism: Literary Experiment, Psychosis and the Professionalization of English Society*, Oxford: Oxford University Press, 2001.

Wright, Patrick. *On Living in an Old Country*, London: Verso, 1985.

Regionalism between the wars

Lane, Denis, ed. *In the Spirit of Powys: New Essays*, London and Toronto: Associated University Presses, 1990.

MacPhee, Graham and Prem Poddar, eds. *Empire and After: Englishness in Postcolonial Perspective*, New York: Berghahn Books, 2007.

McGann, Jerome J. "The Grand Heretics of Modern Fiction: Laura Riding, John Cowper Powys, and the Subjective Correlative," *Modernism/Modernity* 13: 2 (2006), 309–23.

Ireland and English fiction

Backus, Margot. *The Gothic Family Romance: Heterosexuality, Child Sacrifice and the Anglo-Irish Colonial Order*, Durham: Duke University Press, 1999.

Cleary, Joe. *Outrageous Fortune: Capital and Culture in Modern Ireland*, Dublin: Field Day Publications, 2006.

Fogarty, Anne, and Timothy Martin. *Joyce on the Threshold*, University of Florida Press, 2005.

Gibson, Andrew. *Joyce's Revenge: History, Politics, and Aesthetics in Ulysses*, Oxford: Oxford University Press, 2002.

Ingman, Heather. *Twentieth-Century Fiction by Irish Women: Nation and Gender*, Aldershot: Ashgate, 2007.

St. Peter, Christine. *Changing Ireland: Strategies in Contemporary Women's Fiction*, London: Macmillan, 2000.

Feminist fiction

Bluemel, Kristin. *Experimenting on the Borders of Modernism: Dorothy Richardson's Pilgrimage*, Athens: University of Georgia Press, 1997.

Brooks, Ann. *Postfeminisms: Feminism, Cultural Theory and Cultural Forms*, New York: Routledge, 1997.

DuPlessis, Rachel Blau. *Writing beyond the Ending: Narrative Strategies of Twentieth-Century Women Writers*, Bloomington: Indiana University Press, 1985.

Ellmann, Mary. *Thinking about Women*, New York: Harcourt, 1984.

Garrity, Jane. *Step-Daughters of England: British Women Modernists and the National Imaginary*, Manchester: Manchester University Press, 2003.

Lassner, Phyllis. *Colonial Strangers: Women Writing at the End of the British Empire*, New Brunswick: Rutgers University Press, 2004.

Showalter, Elaine. *A Literature of Their Own: British Women Novelists from Brontë to Lessing*, Princeton: Princeton University Press, 1977.

Wachman, Gay. *Lesbian Empire*, New Brunswick: Rutgers University Press, 2001.

Wiesenfarth, Joseph. *Ford Madox Ford and the Regiment of Women*, Madison: University of Wisconsin Press, 2005.

Working-class fiction across the century

Klaus, H. Gustav, ed. *The Socialist Novel in Britain: Towards a Recovery of a Tradition*, Brighton: Harvester, 1982.

Fordham, John. *James Hanley: Modernism and the Working Class*, Cardiff: University of Wales Press, 2002.

Hoggart, Richard. *The Uses of Literacy*, Harmondsworth: Penguin, 1992.

Williams, Raymond. *The English Novel from Dickens to Lawrence*, London: Hogarth Press, 1987.

Williams, Raymond. *Problems in Materialism and Culture*, London: Verso, 1980.

World War II, the welfare state, and postwar "humanism"

Drabble, Margaret. *Angus Wilson: A Biography*, New York: St. Martin's Press, 1995.

Lassner, Phyllis. *British Women Writers of World War II*, New York: St. Martin's Press, 1998.

Gorra, Michael. *The English Novel at Mid-Century: From the Leaning Tower*, New York: St. Martin's, 1990.

MacKay, Marina. *Modernism and World War II*, Cambridge: Cambridge University Press, 2007.

Munton, Alan. *English Fiction of the Second World War*, London: Faber, 1989.

Sinfield, Alan. *Literature, Politics, and Culture in Postwar Britain*, 2nd edition, London: Athlone Press, 1997.

Treglown, Jeremy. *Romancing: The Life and Work of Henry Green*, London: Faber, 2000.

The Windrush *generation*

Forbes, Curdella. *From Nation to Diaspora: Samuel Selvon, George Lamming, and the Cultural Performance of Gender*, Jamaica: The University of the West Indies Press, 2005.

Hart, Matthew. "Tradition and the Postcolonial Talent," *The International Reception of T. S. Eliot*, eds. G. MacPhee and P. Poddar (New York: Continuum, 2007), pp. 5–24.

Kalliney, Peter. *Cities of Affluence and Anger: A Literary Geography of Modern Englishness*, Charlottesville: University of Virginia Press, 2006.

King, Bruce. *V. S. Naipaul*, 2nd edition, Houndmills, Basingstoke and New York: Palgrave Macmillan, 2003.

Weiss, Timothy. *On the Margins: The Art of Exile in V. S. Naipaul*, Amherst: University of Massachusetts Press, 1992.

History in fiction

Birns, Nicholas. *Understanding Anthony Powell*, Columbia: University of South Carolina Press, 2004.

Felber, Lynette. *Gender and Genre without End: The British Roman-Fleuve*, Gainesville: University Press of Florida, 1995.

Karl, F. R. *C. P. Snow: The Politics of Conscience*, Carbondale: Southern Illinois University Press, 1963.

Keen, Suzanne. *Romances of the Archive in Contemporary British Fiction*, Toronto: University of Toronto Press, 2001.

Parrinder, Patrick. *Nation and Novel*, Oxford: Oxford University Press, 2006.

Postmodernisms of English fiction

Acheson, James. *Samuel Beckett's Artistic Theory and Practice*, London: Macmillan, 1997.

Bradbury, Malcolm. *The History Man*, London: Martin Secker & Warburg, 1975.

Gasiorek, Andrzej. *Post-War British Fiction: Realism and After*, London: Edward Arnold, 1995.

Gray, Alasdair. *Lanark*, Edinburgh: Canongate, 1981.

Hoban, Russell. *Riddley Walker*, London: Jonathan Cape, 1980.

MacKay, Marina, and Lyndsey Stonebridge, eds. *British Fiction after Modernism*, Houndmills: Palgrave Macmillan, 2007.

Detectives and spies

Cawelti, John, and Bruce Rosenberg. *The Spy Story*, Chicago: University of Chicago Press, 1987.

Hepburn, Allan. *Intrigue: Espionage and Culture*, New Haven: Yale University Press, 2005.

Reitz, Caroline. *Detecting the Nation: Fictions of Detection and the Imperial Venture*, Columbus: Ohio State University Press, 2004.

Rowland, Susan. *From Agatha Christie to Ruth Rendell: British Women Writers in Detective and Crime Fiction*, Houndmills: Palgrave, 2001.

Symons, Julian. *The Detective Story in Britain*, London: Longmans, 1962.

Post-consensus fiction

Ball, John Clement. *Imagining London: Postcolonial Fiction and the Transnational Metropolis*, Toronto: University of Toronto Press, 2004.

Crawford, Robert. *Devolving English Literature*, 2nd edition, Edinburgh: Edinburgh University Press, 2001.

Friedman, Susan Stanford. *Mappings: Feminism and the Cultural Geographies of Encounter*, Princeton: Princeton University Press, 1998.

Kavanagh, Dennis. *Thatcherism and British Politics: The End of Consensus?*, 3rd edition, Oxford: Oxford University Press, 1990.

King, Bruce. *The Internationalization of the English Novel*, The Oxford Literary History, vol. XIII, Oxford: Oxford University Press, 2004.

Walkowitz, Rebecca L. *Cosmopolitan Style: Modernism beyond the Nation*, New York: Columbia University Press, 2006.

Walkowitz, Rebecca L., ed. *Immigrant Fictions: Contemporary Literature in an Age of Globalization*, Madison: The University of Wisconsin Press, 2007.

An absurd century: varieties of satire

Appignanesi, Lisa, and Sara Maitland, eds. *The Rushdie File*, Syracuse: Syracuse University Press and Institute of Contemporary Arts, 1990.

Dasenbrock, Reed Way. *The Literary Vorticism of Ezra Pound and Wyndham Lewis*, Baltimore: Johns Hopkins University Press, 1985.

Dasenbrock, Reed Way. "Wyndham Lewis's Fascist Imagination and the Fiction of Paranoia," *Fascism, Aesthetics and Culture*, ed. Richard J. Golsan, Lebanon, NH: University Press of New England, 1992.

Elliott, Robert C. *The Power of Satire*, Princeton: Princeton University Press, 1968.

English, James F. *Comic Transactions: Literature, Humor, and the Politics of Community in Twentieth-Century Britain*, Ithaca: Cornell University Press, 1994.

Green, Martin. *Children of the Sun: A Narrative of 'Decadence' in England after 1918*, New York: Wideview, 1980.

Jameson, Fredric. *Fables of Aggression*, Berkeley: University of California Press, 1979.

Paulson, Ronald. *The Fictions of Satire*, Baltimore: Johns Hopkins University Press, 1967.

The other side of history: fantasy, romance,
horror, and science fiction

Amis, Kingsley. *New Maps of Hell*, New York: Harcourt Brace, 1960.

Booker, M. Keith. *The Dystopian Impulse in Modern Literature*, Westport: Greenwood Press, 1994.

Bould, Mark, Andrew M. Butler, and Istvan Csicsery-Ronay, Jr., eds. Special issue on the British SF Boom, *Science Fiction Studies* 30.3 (November 2003).

Brooke-Rose, Christine. *A Rhetoric of the Unreal*, Cambridge: Cambridge University Press, 1981.

Delany, Samuel R. *Shorter Views*, Hanover and London: Wesleyan University Press, 1999.

Fiedler, Leslie A. *Olaf Stapledon: A Man Divided*, Oxford: Oxford University Press, 1983.

Mathews, Richard. *Fantasy: The Liberation of Imagination*, London: Routledge, 2002.

Oser, Lee. *The Return of Christian Humanism: Chesterton, Eliot, Tolkien and the Romance of History*, Columbia: University of Missouri Press, 2007.

Roberts, Adam. *The History of Science Fiction*, New York: Palgrave Macmillan, 2005.

Saunders, Corinne. *A Companion to Romance*, Malden: Blackwell, 2004.

Smith, Andrew, and William Hughes, eds. *Empire and the Gothic*, New York: Palgrave Macmillan, 2003.

Weiss, Timothy. *Translating Orients: Between Ideology and Utopia*, Toronto: University of Toronto Press, 2004.

INDEX

Cambridge Companions to...

AUTHORS

Edward Albee edited by Stephen J. Bottoms
Margaret Atwood edited by Coral Ann Howells
W. H. Auden edited by Stan Smith
Jane Austen edited by Edward Copeland and
    Juliet McMaster
Beckett edited by John Pilling
Aphra Behn edited by Derek Hughes and
    Janet Todd
Walter Benjamin edited by David S. Ferris
William Blake edited by Morris Eaves
Brecht edited by Peter Thomson and
    Glendyr Sacks (second edition)
The Brontës edited by Heather Glen
Frances Burney edited by Peter Sabor
Byron edited by Drummond Bone
Albert Camus edited by Edward J. Hughes
Willa Cather edited by Marilee Lindemann
Cervantes edited by Anthony J. Cascardi
Chaucer, edited by Piero Boitani and Jill Mann
    (second edition)
Chekhov edited by Vera Gottlieb and
    Paul Allain
Kate Chopin edited by Janet Beer
Coleridge edited by Lucy Newlyn
Wilkie Collins edited by Jenny Bourne Taylor
Joseph Conrad edited by J. H. Stape
Dante edited by Rachel Jacoff (second edition)
Daniel Defoe edited by John Richetti
Don DeLillo edited by John N. Duvall
Charles Dickens edited by John O. Jordan
Emily Dickinson edited by Wendy Martin
John Donne edited by Achsah Guibbory
Dostoevskii edited by W. J. Leatherbarrow
Theodore Dreiser edited by Leonard Cassuto
    and Claire Virginia Eby
John Dryden edited by Steven N. Zwicker
W. E. B. Du Bois edited by Shamoon Zamir
George Eliot edited by George Levine
T. S. Eliot edited by A. David Moody
Ralph Ellison edited by Ross Posnock
Ralph Waldo Emerson edited by Joel Porte and
    Saundra Morris
William Faulkner edited by Philip M. Weinstein
Henry Fielding edited by Claude Rawson
F. Scott Fitzgerald edited by Ruth Prigozy
Flaubert edited by Timothy Unwin
E. M. Forster edited by David Bradshaw
Benjamin Franklin edited by Carla Mulford
Brian Friel edited by Anthony Roche
Robert Frost edited by Robert Faggen
Elizabeth Gaskell edited by Jill L. Matus
Goethe edited by Lesley Sharpe
Thomas Hardy edited by Dale Kramer
David Hare edited by Richard Boon

Nathaniel Hawthorne edited by
    Richard Millington
Seamus Heaney edited by Bernard O'Donoghue
Ernest Hemingway edited by Scott Donaldson
Homer edited by Robert Fowler
Ibsen edited by James McFarlane
Henry James edited by Jonathan Freedman
Samuel Johnson edited by Greg Clingham
Ben Jonson edited by Richard Harp and
    Stanley Stewart
James Joyce edited by Derek Attridge
    (second edition)
Kafka edited by Julian Preece
Keats edited by Susan J. Wolfson
Lacan edited by Jean-Michel Rabaté
D. H. Lawrence edited by Anne Fernihough
Primo Levi edited by Robert Gordon
Lucretius edited by Stuart Gillespie and
    Philip Hardie
David Mamet edited by Christopher Bigsby
Thomas Mann edited by Ritchie Robertson
Christopher Marlowe edited by Patrick Cheney
Herman Melville edited by Robert S. Levine
Arthur Miller edited by Christopher Bigsby
Milton edited by Dennis Danielson
    (second edition)
Molière edited by David Bradby and
    Andrew Calder
Toni Morrison edited by Justine Tally
Nabokov edited by Julian W. Connolly
Eugene O'Neill edited by Michael Manheim
George Orwell edited by John Rodden
Ovid edited by Philip Hardie
Harold Pinter edited by Peter Raby
Sylvia Plath edited by Jo Gill
Edgar Allan Poe edited by Kevin J. Hayes
Alexander Pope edited by Pat Rogers
Ezra Pound edited by Ira B. Nadel
Proust edited by Richard Bales
Pushkin edited by Andrew Kahn
Philip Roth edited by Timothy Parrish
Salman Rushdie edited by Abdulrazak Gurnah
Shakespeare edited by Margareta de Grazia and
    Stanley Wells
Shakespeare on Film edited by Russell Jackson
    (second edition)
Shakespearean Comedy edited by
    Alexander Leggatt
Shakespeare on Stage edited by Stanley Wells
    and Sarah Stanton
Shakespeare's History Plays edited by
    Michael Hattaway
Shakespearean Tragedy edited by
    Claire McEachern

TOPICS